ART AGAINST CENSORSHIP

Manchester University Press

Art against censorship

Honoré Daumier, comedy, and resistance in nineteenth-century France

ERIN DUNCAN-O'NEILL

MANCHESTER UNIVERSITY PRESS

Published by Manchester University Press
Oxford Road, Manchester, M13 9PL
www.manchesteruniversitypress.co.uk

British Library Cataloguing-in-Publication Data
A catalogue record for this book is available from the British Library

ISBN 978 1 5261 6839 9 hardback
ISBN 978 1 5261 7601 1 paperback

First published 2024

Typeset by Newgen Publishing UK
Printed in Great Britain by Bell and Bain Ltd, Glasgow

For Connor

Contents

Illustrations

Acknowledgements

I have immense gratitude to those who have contributed to the completion of this book. First, I would like to extend my deepest and most sincere thanks to my graduate adviser, Bridget Alsdorf. Bridget sparked my initial interest in Daumier and has been an unflagging advocate at every stage in my research. She is an inspiring model of teaching and scholarship who extends herself with uncommon generosity. I cannot imagine having a better mentor.

Research for this book was generously supported by an Arts and Humanities Faculty Fellowship at the University of Oklahoma in addition to a Junior Faculty Fellowship, co-funded by the Arts and Humanities Forum, the Office of the Vice President for Research and Partnerships, the College of Fine Arts, and the College of Arts & Sciences. An Arts and Humanities Forum Manuscript Development Workshop provided support to bring in Patricia Mainardi, Lynne Ambrosini, Jennifer Davis Cline, and Julia Abramson, to whom I am greatly indebted. Pete Froslie, Bette Talavacchia, and Dean Mary Margaret Holt have advocated on my behalf for institutional support at critical moments in the research and writing of this project.

I have been very lucky to benefit from the knowledge and advice of Anne McCauley, Rachael DeLue, Betsy Rosasco, Anna Arabindan-Kesson, and the support of the Art & Archaeology faculty at Princeton University in this project's earliest stages. I also wish to extend my thanks to the librarians and staff at Marquand Library for all of their assistance. I found great help from archivists and librarians at the Musée d'Orsay, the Bibliothèque nationale de France, the Bibliothèque de l'INHA, the département des Arts graphiques at the Musée du Louvre, and particularly the Bibliothèque nationale de France's département des Estampes et de photographie.

I am grateful to my colleagues for their insights and friendship. Scholars and artists at OU have offered writing companionship, childcare, and community. Sarah Hines, Traci Voyles, Leslie Kraus, Tess Elliot, Jamie Bates, Elyse Singer, and Zeynep Aydogdu – thank you. I carry a deep appreciation for Jane Dacey, Amanda Cooke, Rio Battliana,

Haneen Rabie, Megan Goldman-Petri, Ellen Macfarlane, Stephanie O'Rourke, and Madeleine Haddon for their friendship and support. I am especially thankful for Nancy Demerdash, with whom I am lucky to have navigated French museums and libraries during important stages of research.

My family, to whom I owe everything, has been unwavering in their encouragement. Mary Jo O'Neill, Bud Duncan, Bill Ryan, Beverly O'Neill, Lena, Sean, Charlotte, and Ella have held me up and cheered me on. Nancy O'Neill enrolled in art history classes so she could make sense of my drafts and has, along with my dear friend Emily Caesar, been a kind and enthusiastic reader. Robert Craig has been an insightful listener and a loving support. All this noise is dedicated to them.

This publication is made possible in part by the Barr Ferree Foundation Fund for Publications, Department of Art and Archaeology, Princeton University.

Introduction

On the first day of the Russian invasion of Ukraine, 24 February 2022, Yulia Zhivtsova was arrested in Pushkin Square. She sat with two books from the Harry Potter series: one violet-blue, one canary yellow. Instead of marching, she was reading a ubiquitous young adult series, not an obvious sign of protest, and so she was not immediately detained. However, the book covers demonstrated sympathy with Ukraine by showing the colours of the nation's flag, and the rebellious content of the stories offered enough signals of resistance that the police eventually hauled her into the station.[1]

Yulia's act of creative defiance is a recent example of a historic and powerful strategy of political resistance. Making an analogy between literary narrative and current political repression offered a form of meaningful critique: 'I was just reading about the Dark Lord ascending. And I think it's quite, well, funny. If we may call anything funny these days.'[2] The subject of this book mines a longer history of the revival of literary motifs to make contemporary political commentary. It was the very strategy used by the nineteenth-century French artist Honoré Daumier during moments of intense censorship of political material. Like Yulia sitting in Pushkin Square, he deployed familiar literary figures to make subtle, subversive allusions to political resistance.

Celebrated as a political cartoonist, Daumier developed a deep and abiding engagement with literary satire in a period when explicitly political subjects were censored in the illustrated press. Forced to think beyond caricature, Daumier tested motifs from literary and theatrical satire in painting, sculpture, and watercolour. For an artist so attuned to the contemporary world, Daumier's decision to look back to seventeenth-century satire must be seen as deliberate, emerging from the same driving commitment to political dissent and intervening in contested spaces of expression. The artworks examined in this book functioned as critiques of the repressive authority of the government in large part because their publics understood Daumier's appropriation of Jean de La Fontaine (1621–85), Molière (Jean-Baptiste Poquelin, 1622–73), and Cervantes (Miguel de Cervantes Saavedra, 1547–1616) as coded forms of subversive dissent. This book will examine how Daumier drew on theatre and literature at moments of intense repression of explicitly political critique, contextualizing his citations within the broader popular revivals of seventeenth-century authors who were masters of dissimulation and critique in their own time. La Fontaine, Molière, and Cervantes offered Daumier vital representational strategies in the face of stifling censorship, and their famous characters, narratives, and motifs allowed him to filter his political statements through a newly glorified literary past. Literature, theatre, and politics converge in Daumier's oeuvre in a way that is unique in art history, demonstrating the importance of artistic appropriation and media shape-shifting to political expression in nineteenth-century France.

Honoré Daumier's first paintings appeared on the walls of his prison cell. In 1832 he received a six-month sentence and a 500-franc fine for exciting hatred against the king and offending the person of the king through the caricature *Gargantua* (1831, Figure 0.1), a brutal condemnation of the king's corruption. In this print, the newly enthroned king, Louis-Philippe (1773–1850), appears as the loutish, lazy hero of François Rabelais's epic farce *Gargantua et Pantagruel* (1532–35).[3] Following a trial, Daumier was sent to the prison at Sainte-Pélagie, a private hospital for political prisoners and the mentally ill. It was on the walls of cell 102 that he defiantly painted *Gargantua* again, emphasizing his monstrous mouth and including figures that resembled high-level government ministers.[4] Daumier also produced a series of watercolours and drawings in prison, some of which would appear as lithographs in the illustrated journals *La Caricature* and *Le Charivari* (Figure 0.2).[5] Daumier's political imprisonment would earn him early recognition as an incendiary artist, and in his long career Daumier would become the most

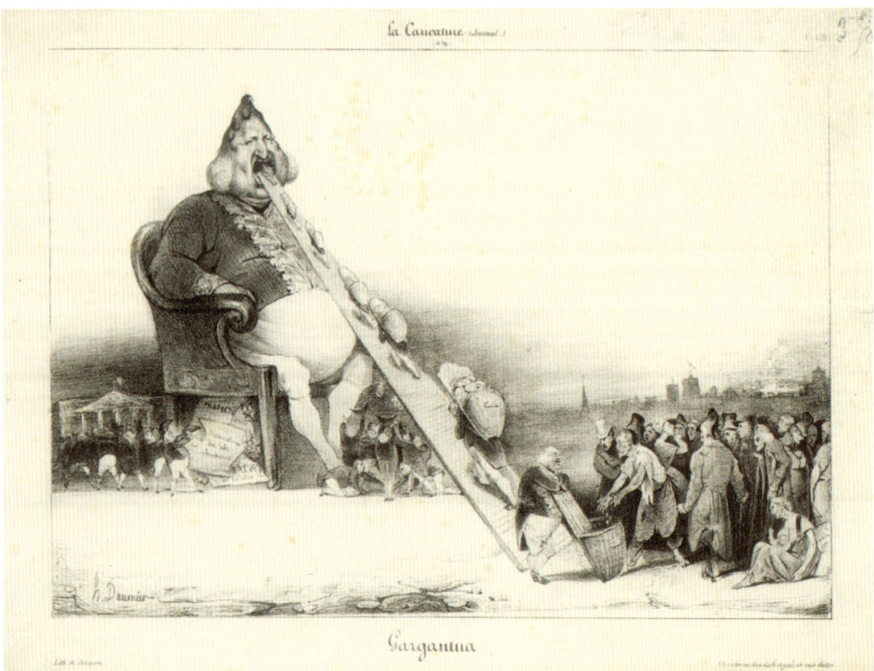

Figure 0.1 Honoré Daumier, *Gargantua*, submitted to Dépot légal on 16 December 1831

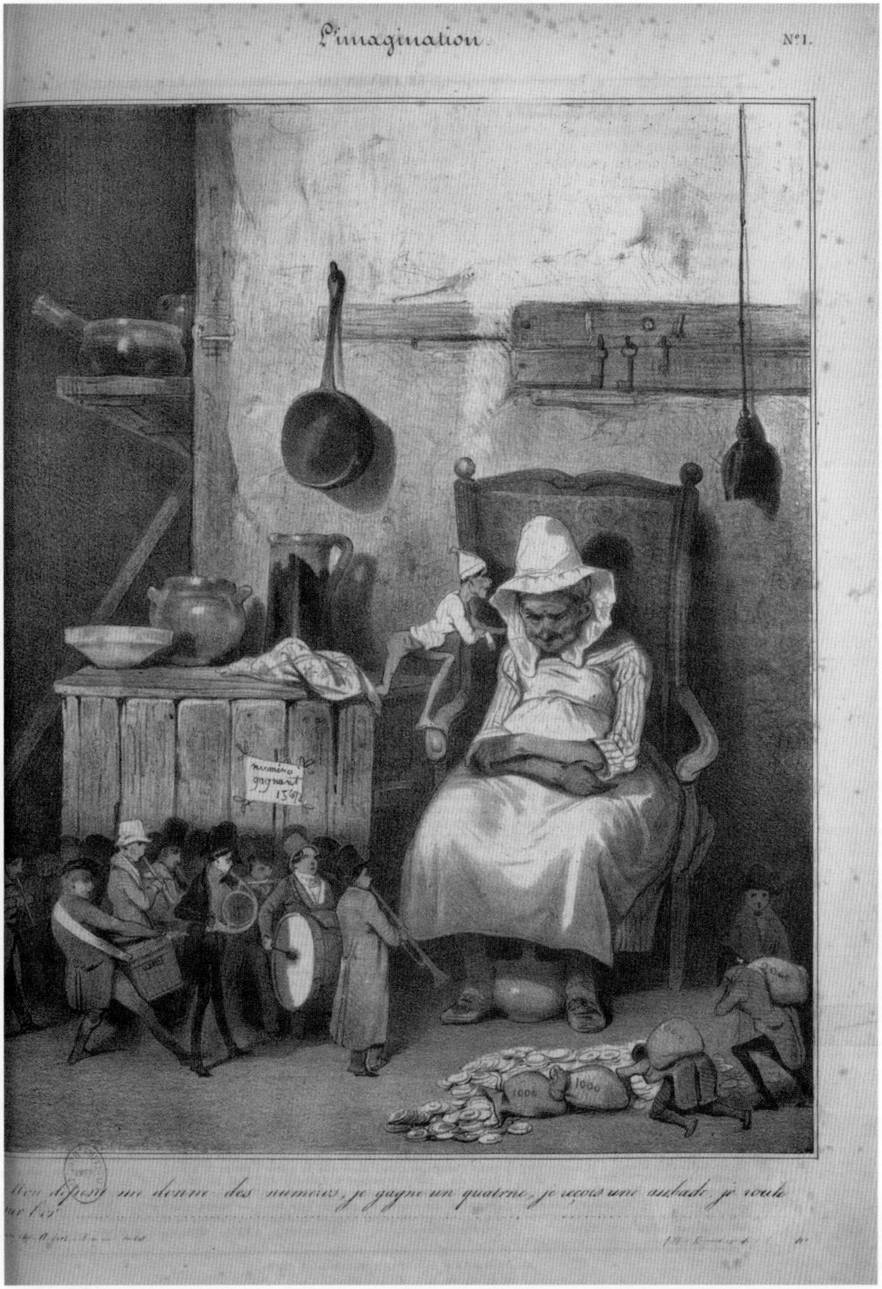

Figure 0.2 Honoré Daumier, 'Chimera of the imagination' ('Chimère de l'imagination'), *Le Charivari*, 14 January 1833

famous caricaturist of the time – perhaps of all time. This first act of painting was a feat of cutting contemporary political speech made through the force of a well-known literary motif, and it was a translation of a subject first produced in print. Daumier would continue to draw on theatre and literature at moments of intense repression of political speech in the press, and his citations should be contextualized within the broader popular revivals of these authors to show that they offered important representational strategies to the visual arts in the face of stifling censorship. Taking brush to canvas to paint figures from La Fontaine, Molière, and Cervantes, Daumier originated his painting practice with the yawning mouth of Gargantua, and it is important to see this commitment as a critical piece of his political project.

Daumier's early imprisonment was just one episode in a career shaped by entanglement with government censors. Working primarily for the illustrated newspapers founded by republican caricaturist and publisher Charles Philipon (1806–62), including *La Silhouette* (1829–31), *La Caricature* (1830–43), and *Le Charivari* (1832–1937), Daumier developed a reputation as a fierce combatant in a war over free expression.[6] When popular disenfranchisement gave way to revolution in July 1830, Charles X was forced to abdicate. Instead of passing the crown to Charles's heir, the Orléanist and liberal-leaning Louis-Philippe was selected to rule and was handed a constitutional charter revised from a version attempted in 1814. The liberal press was a major organizing force for the 1830 revolution, and press freedoms became one of the first policies of the new administration. Article seven of the constitutional charter abolished censorship and declared it could 'never be re-established'.[7] Suffrage was only moderately expanded, but the public gained a new capacity for political influence, and France experienced a dramatic shift towards popular political expression.[8] Because Louis-Philippe, the so-called 'Roi populaire', had emerged from the barricades of the July Revolution, the extent to which his continued legitimacy relied on public opinion was an open question. For this reason, he met unprecedented criticism not just from staunch republicans like Philipon but also from legitimists and every shade in between. Tolerating a certain amount of speech and participation in the early 1830s, Louis-Philippe's anxiety about the importance of his popular appeal nevertheless quickly led to intense scrutiny of the newspapers. Already by 1833 there were over 300 instances of prosecutions against newspapers in Paris.[9] This periodic repression is evidenced by Daumier's imprisonment and the frequent trials of Philipon. However, when Louis-Philippe instituted the official and devastating reversal to the liberalizations of 1830 with the September Laws of 1835, citizens had already gained a taste and talent for political activity, and the illustrated press was booming.[10]

Censorship of the written word, epitomized by the trials of Gustave Flaubert and Charles Baudelaire (both in 1857), was central to government repression in nineteenth-century France. In part, it was writers' negotiations with repressive legal standards that produced the aesthetic strategies that have defined literary modernism; for example, indirect expression and multiple authorial voices.[11] The censorship of illustrations and theatrical performances was consistently more severe than the censorship of texts, and while scholars have traced the ways in which censorship laws periodically drove the illustrated press to politically inoffensive social satire, the literature has yet to contend with the extent to which these laws provoked experimental approaches to authorship, media, and humour in the visual arts.

Honoré Daumier was born in Marseilles in 1808. He had a working-class background and lacked a formal education. He rarely wrote letters, in part because he lived and worked in constant close collaboration with others, surrounded by friends who were often painters, sculptors, and illustrators, and he was not often responsible for the texts for his caricatures.[12] We do know that the artist formed strong attachments to literature and the theatre early in life. Until Honoré was seven years old, his father, Jean-Baptiste Daumier (c. 1775–1851), worked as a glazier in Marseilles. He was a craftsman whose skills in framing doors and windows likely included some retouching of framed paintings and engravings.[13] Daumier senior was an avid reader, encouraged by a family friend and second-hand bookseller Chaix, who provided books to the young man from authors like Jean-Jacques Rousseau, André Chénier, and Jacques (Abbé) Delille, who published well-known translations of Virgil's *Georgics* and *Aeneid* as well as poetry.[14] Young Honoré would have seen his father writing poetry at night, drawing inspiration from Sunday trips to the countryside around Marseilles.[15] Jean-Baptiste wrote poetry in the style of Delille and gave a reading at the Academy of Marseilles to warm acclaim, leading to his publication of *Un matin de printemps* (Paris: Imprimerie royale, 1815). He moved to Paris in April of 1815 to pursue his literary ambitions, bringing his family with him soon after.[16] Honoré's home was steeped in classical texts, poetry, and plays, and the course of his life – its geography and professional horizons – hinged on a move driven by his father's literary ambitions.

In Paris, Jean-Baptiste secured an audience with Alexandre Lenoir (1761–1839), Director of the Musée des monuments français. Lenoir, a painter and archaeologist who wrote histories of the arts and monuments of France, remained a friend and advocate for Jean-Baptiste, and was impressed with young Honoré's promise as a draughtsman, offering him an early apprenticeship. Drawing was one way for a young man from the provinces to earn a living, and Daumier would soon find work in caricature and illustration right at the moment when the new technology of lithography burst onto the scene in France.[17] Lenoir also famously preserved the remains of Molière and La Fontaine at the Couvent des Petits-Augustins, which became the Musée des monuments français in 1795.[18]

Daumier's career roughly spanned the years 1822 to the mid-1870s, and in these important decades France saw an explosion in the number and sophistication of books and newspapers and a voracious new reading public. The number of books published in France quintupled during the eighteenth century and there was another quintupling again as the number of published titles jumped from 3,357 issues in 1815 to 14,195 in 1875.[19] Literacy and education rates increased, but book prices remained quite high until mid-century. In Paris, many readers had access to both classical texts and popular political journals at *cabinets de lecture*, or commercial rental or circulating libraries, where modest rental fees would provide access to all quarters of society. They became spaces for informal literary circles and liberal political gatherings, in part because these commercial circulating libraries carried political journals and newspapers not available at the large research libraries.[20]

Beginning in the 1830s, illustrations were increasingly woven into books and journals through a variety of new reproductive technologies, and the line between periodicals and books began to blur. Texts included more reproduced artworks, narrative illustrations, and cartoons capturing political events and social mores. Graphic satire both parodied and advanced new formats of illustrated publications, and in addition to being at the cutting edge of lithography in France, Daumier was involved in novel forms of illustrated book production, including albums of images reissued in collections, 'physiologies', and comic almanacs.[21] Journals published serial stories that were later compiled into novels, and the kind of imagery that colonized the illustrated daily press also appeared more frequently in books of all kinds, from inexpensive popular books to rare editions.[22] In this world of increasingly close image–text relationships, Daumier's paintings of literary motifs should be set in closer dialogue with his prints for illustrated journals and the satiric texts circulating in the nineteenth century.

Daumier's father also introduced his son to the theatre. Jean-Baptiste's play *Philippe II* was performed in Paris in 1818–19. He first submitted the tragedy unsuccessfully to the Comédie-Française, and it was eventually staged at a small amateur theatre, the Salle Chantereine, where young Honoré (then ten or eleven) would almost certainly have helped his father at rehearsals. At his father's heels, he would have seen the contortions of the actors' faces and bodies as they rehearsed the tragedy and been mesmerized by this world of expressive drama and costume. This intimate and exciting first encounter with performance and spectatorship inspired a lifelong fascination with the theatre's audiences and performers, and the construction of spectacle.[23]

His father's engagement with classical literature and theatre engendered Honoré Daumier's longstanding exploration of these themes in his lithographs, and we know that Daumier remained engaged with the theatre. His lithographs of theatrical scenes show an acute sensitivity to the melodrama of the stage, boredom during intermission, the baroque systems of finance behind the scenes, and the class structures of audiences and actors alike. In the scant correspondence that exists, we find Daumier writing to Bocage (Pierre-Martinien Touzé, 1799–1862), the politically-oriented actor and director of the théâtre de l'Odéon, for theatre tickets to pay back a debt.[24] Daumier collaborated with Ernest Jamie, a playwright and journalist, on captions for his prints, including the 1844 series 'Les carottes' based on Jamie's vaudevilles.[25] Arsène Houssaye (1814–96), director of the Comédie-Française from 1849 to 1856, who began his tenure with a dedication to reviving Molière's plays on the famous stage, recounted that Daumier was often in attendance.[26]

An early print, 'Nero murdering his mother', published in *Le Charivari* on 9 April 1834, shows the artist making contemporary political commentary through a scene of classical theatre (Figure 0.3). Nero, whose raised, knife-wielding hand covers the face of a recognizable proxy for King Louis-Philippe, grabs the throat of Liberty, whom he is about to annihilate. Jean Cherpin, who traces Daumier's interest in theatre and melodrama to the artist's father, sees this as an unusually early work exploring the confluence between politics and classical drama in print, but it is useful to see it as one experiment in a practice that was already beginning to shift political critique to literary and theatrical subjects.[27] In the same year, 1834, Daumier found form for political speech in La Fontaine's fables, driven to referential and indirect modes of expression by new and urgent threats of censorship.

Indeed, in the early 1830s, Daumier and his colleagues frequently excavated familiar figures from the literary world, especially to illustrate the monstrous qualities of political leaders.[28] Daumier's incendiary *Gargantua* had, of course, already pictured Louis-Philippe as the hero of François Rabelais's *Gargantua et Pantagruel* (1532–35), a behemoth from comic literature who drew derision for his voracious appetite and excessive spending. In what would become an iconic image of official corruption, Gargantua sits on a monumental throne, consuming money extracted by his ministers from a miserable mob at right and defecates awards and favours in return. Kings had appeared as Gargantua before in vicious political caricatures in the 1790s, mocking Louis XVI's gluttonous appetites and infantile impulses.[29] Revolutionaries lauded Rabelais as a

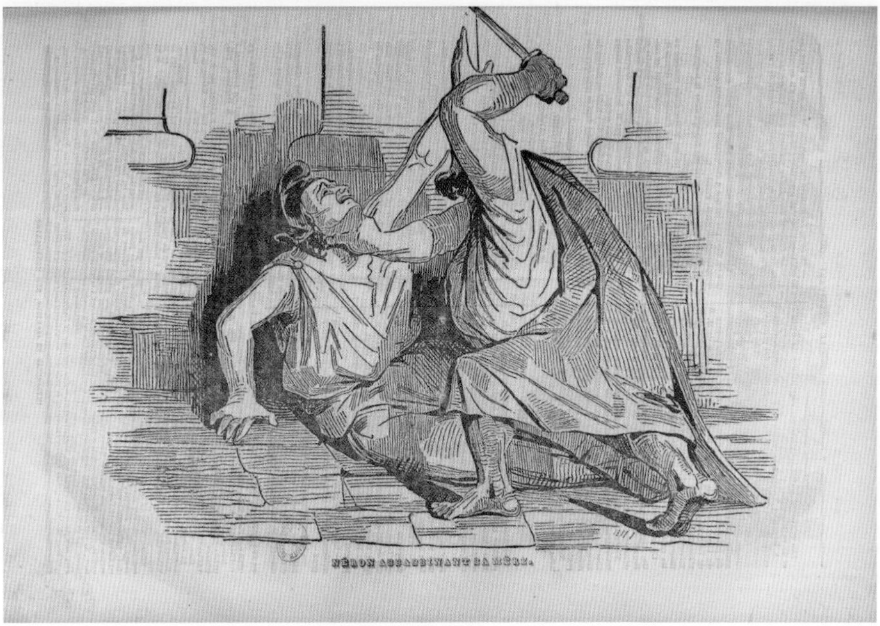

Figure 0.3 Honoré Daumier, 'Nero murdering his mother' ('Néron assassinant sa mère'), *Le Charivari*, 9 April 1834

fellow progressive, renaming his hometown from Chinon to Chinon-Rabelais. In 1791, Pierre-Louis Ginguené published 'On the Influence of Rabelais on the revolution of our time and on the decree concerning the clergy', framing Rabelais as a model of resistance to monarchical power.[30] New editions and illustrations of Rabelais's *Gargantua* were in wide circulation in the early decades of the nineteenth century, and images of excessive consumption and problematic digestion derived from the text were especially popular.[31] Just a year after he began working consistently for Charles Philipon's illustrated journals, Daumier seized on this figure from literary satire for a powerful political metaphor. He also gives visual form to one device of satire invoked in *Gargantua*, the juxtaposition of opposites.[32] Gargantua's corpulence and wealth are emphasized by the smallness and physical distress of the poor in the lower foreground. This is an early moment of the artist finding visual form for not just the motifs but also the procedures or modes of satire. It also demonstrates Daumier's interest in drawing from the literary canon to find a form for contemporary political dissent.

In the period in which Daumier would have read *Gargantua*, criticism in the introduction to various volumes of the work held that Rabelais had intended it as a political satire. Gargantua was understood to stand in for François I greedily consolidating monarchical power and Pantagruel as Henri II, François's successor. The book had been banned in 1533, so Daumier might also have seen a productive parallel between an author who navigated an authoritarian regime and the pressures of censored expression in his career as a visual artist.[33] Nineteenth-century reprints of Ginguené's revolutionary-era interpretation of *Gargantua* suggest that Rabelais's books contained an important allegory for the criticism of monarchical regimes.[34] His remarks were also included in an 1823 edition published by Dalibon in Paris, especially in citations describing Rabelais's ridicule of the clergy, using Rabelais as a cipher for growing anticlerical sentiment in the 1820s.[35] In a moment that was critical in his formulation of professional identity, Daumier would establish a pattern of drawing on literary sources for political critique, especially from authors who had themselves navigated censorial regimes.

This was also the case for his colleagues at Philipon's illustrated journals. In the early 1830s, when hard-won press freedoms promised by the July Revolution in 1830 were under steady threat by Louis-Philippe's government, Daumier, J. J. Grandville, and Bernard-Romain Julien adapted fables by Jean de La Fontaine to express anxieties about the king's overreach and especially the suppression of the opposition press. La Fontaine faced hostility from the court of Louis XIV, which suspected him of advocating for rebellion through the moral messages of his writing and took exception to his defence of the king's adversary, Nicolas Fouquet.[36] Images like Grandville and Julien's 'Nothing is as dangerous as an ignorant friend. Better to want a wise enemy' (*La Caricature*, 16 August 1832, Figure 0.4), the anonymous 'The vipers of April and the press. – Free imitation of the Serpent and the File' (*Le Charivari*, 2 June 1834, Figure 0.5), and Daumier's 'The

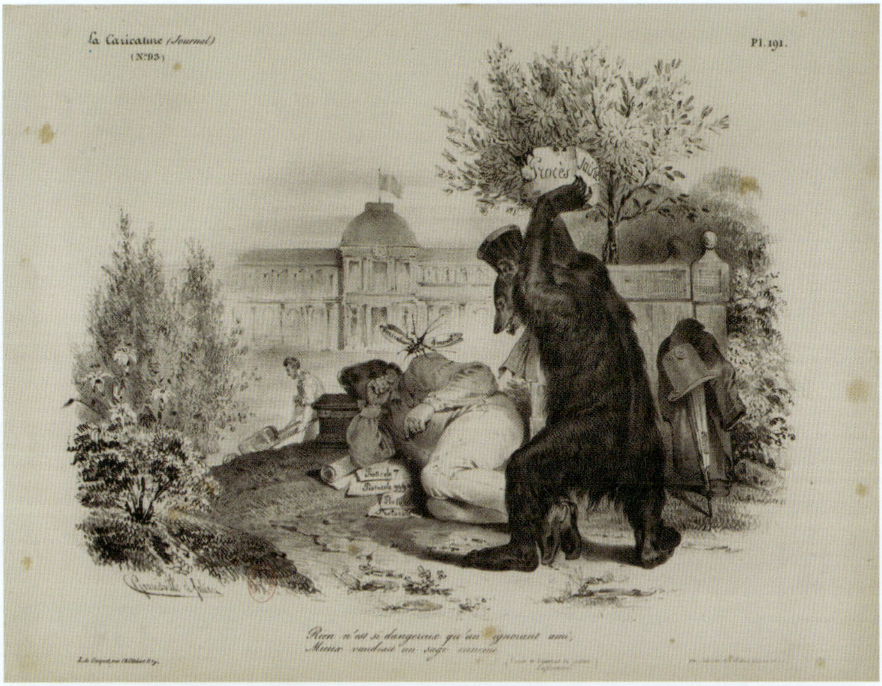

Figure 0.4 J. J. Grandville and Bernard-Romain Julien, 'Nothing is as dangerous as an ignorant friend. Better to want a wise enemy', *La Caricature*, 16 August 1832

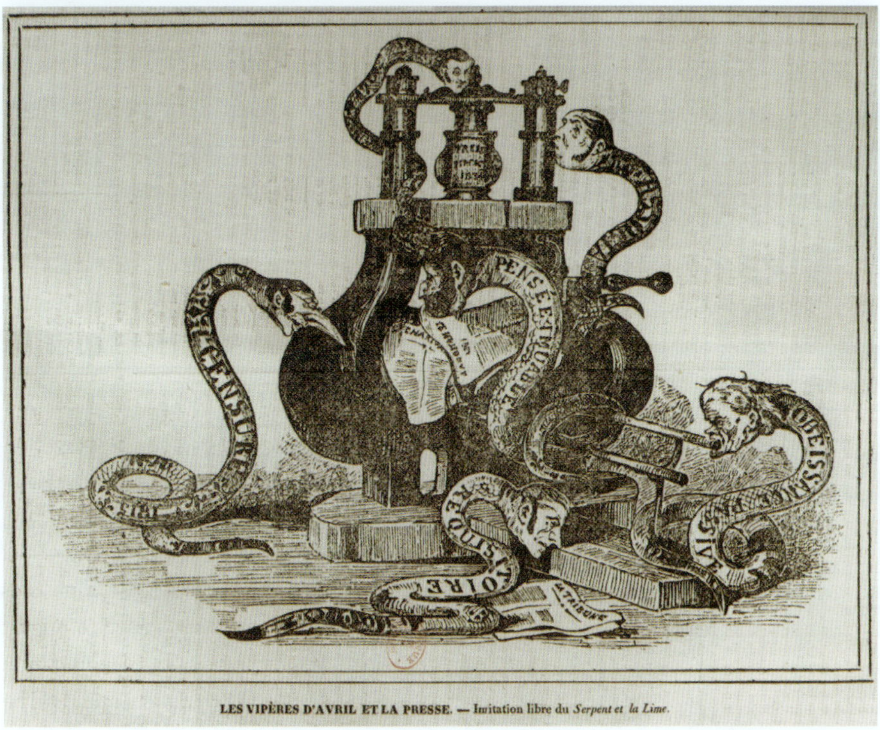

Figure 0.5 Anonymous, 'The vipers of April and the press. – Free imitation of the Serpent and the File', *Le Charivari*, 2 June 1834

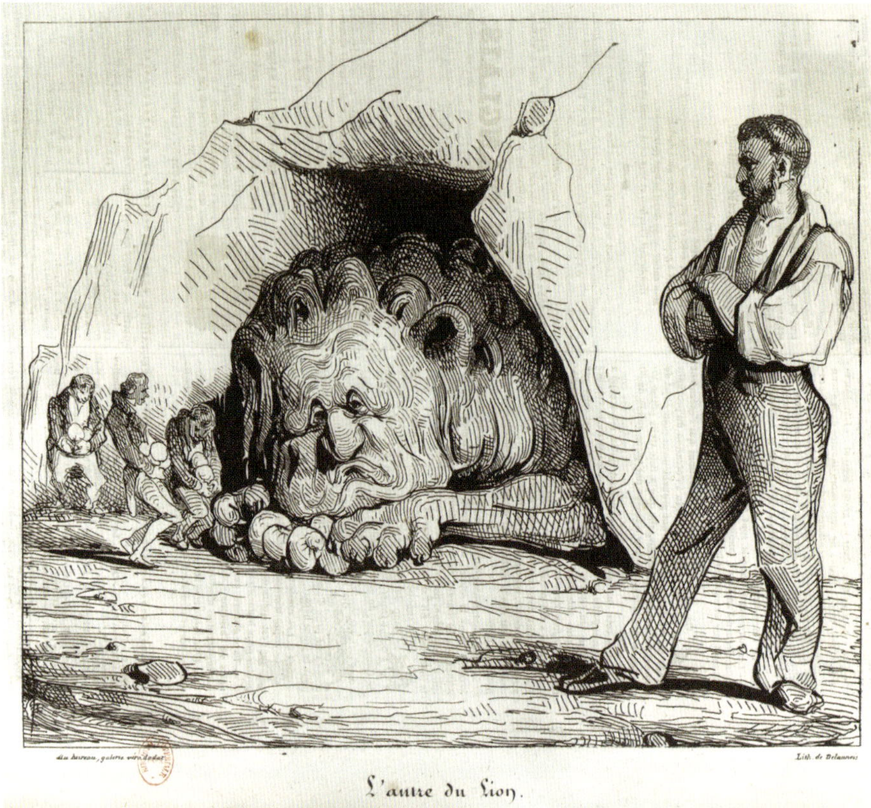

Figure 0.6 Honoré Daumier, 'The lion's lair' ('L'antre du Lion'), *Le Charivari*, 21 September 1834

lion's lair' (*La Caricature*, 21 September 1834, Figure 0.6) draw on the didactic strategies of fables to warn Louis-Philippe's regime about the immorality of censorship and the persistent strength of the press.[37]

Additionally, in a volume of parodies of La Fontaine fables published by the bureau of *Le Charivari* in 1839, *Fables démocratiques*, F.T. [François-Théodore] Claudon (1802–82) writes about the ability of literature to speak both to timeless truths and contemporary events:

> Every work is composed of two necessary but quite distinct elements: one generally and eternally true, the other true but in a relative and consequently transitory way. To take up a work after a lapse of time has removed all the relative truth and to show, with the first faithfully preserved, some truth or some satire that is more current, without changing any or almost any of the original framework, is the rightful way to make a parody.[38]

The writers and artists at *Le Charivari* and *La Caricature* revived canonical works from literature or the theatre to smuggle subversive content to readers in visual form, using the characters and methods of fable, satire, and plays to comment on contemporary politics when direct speech was impossible. In this light, Daumier's first submission to the Salon (1849), a painting that found novel visual form for La Fontaine's fable *The miller, his son, and the ass*, was a continuation of a longer investigation into the productive exchange between enduring truth and contemporary speech in La Fontaine's *Fables*.

After a brief (but not total) reprieve during the Second Republic, the Second Empire reinstated strong censorship restrictions, especially on the graphic arts and performance. From 1852 to 1866 the government required caricaturists to seek authorization for their work, not only from the censors at the Ministry of the Interior or the appropriate prefect but also from the persons being caricatured, an impossible task that resulted in the near total disappearance of cartoons with a political theme during these years.[39] Ostensibly as a result of this intensified pressure on the illustrated press, in March 1860 Daumier was fired from the journal *Le Charivari*.[40] Having lost his primary source of income after thirty years of working as a caricaturist, Daumier turned to painting, a pursuit that until then had been a largely secret, nocturnal labour. Between his 1848 submission of *Competition of 1848, sketch of the Republic* and 1860, Daumier submitted only three paintings and one drawing to the Salon, including one based on the work of La Fontaine and one from Cervantes. He also produced a number of unfinished and unexhibited canvases and found some modest commercial success selling watercolours of subjects his buyers recognized from his most popular lithographic series, including lawyers and domestic life.[41] After he was fired, Daumier continued to sell watercolours to some loyal patrons and began working more seriously and ambitiously in oil. This break from daily work for the illustrated press was the beginning of an almost obsessive representation of scenes from Molière, La Fontaine, and Cervantes in paint, paintings that must be understood to exist in dialogue with the artist's more explicitly political prints.

Molière was a particularly rich source for the artist. In 1820s France, revivals of Molière's plays became sites of vocal – and sometimes violent – public commentary about censorship and government overreach.[42] Daumier began representing characters and scenes by the playwright, who himself had faced repeated censorship restrictions from his royal patron, as early as 1831, returning in earnest in the 1860s. Like La Fontaine and Rabelais, Daumier's representation of works by Molière functioned as a critique of the repressive authority of the government in large part because of broader nineteenth-century associations between Molière and subversive artistic practice. He used the comic mask – a motif found throughout Molière's plays – as a means to incorporate subversive content and evade the censor's shears. In this way, Daumier used theatrical satire to activate powerful strategies of artistic collusion with his audience during times of oppressive censorship and contested speech.

The character of Daumier's satire is fundamentally theatrical and literary. We see Daumier excavating the humour that emerges in Molière's comic exaggerations, for example. The psychological and moral truths revealed in the difference between inner self and outward appearance in Molière's plays become a generative model for Daumier's visual satire.[43] This same productive tension characterizes Daumier's interest in La Fontaine's *Miller*, Molière's doctors, and Cervantes's *Don Quixote* in paint. These are figures wrestling with perception and deception. They are stories that explore the fragility of the masks one wears in the world – masks of expertise or chivalry – and the humiliation of being truly seen. This gives some stakes to Daumier's representation of literary satire in print and paint. Trickery and truth are tested against what we can see, and Daumier interrogates the distance from the real and the potential for special insight offered in the *visual* revival of these stories.

Daumier's version of satire has also been described as Macairist, characterized by a pitiless, sharp derision grounded in anti-bourgeois, anti-capitalist sentiment.[44] Robert Macaire was a character first developed in the theatre. The actor Frédérick Lemaître (1800–76) appeared as Macaire initially in 1823, and then took on what would become his most famous role in the comedy *Robert Macaire, 'ce cynique scapin du crime'* (1834). The play was produced by and starred Lemaître and was quickly banned in 1835 because censors believed it insulted the July Monarchy. Ever fascinated by the theatre, Daumier gave visual form to this character throughout the 1830s, most conspicuously in a series published just after the September Laws of 1835.[45] Evading censorship restrictions prohibiting the mockery of specific political figures, in Daumier's hands Macaire was a recurring reference and avatar for Louis-Philippe. Writing in 1850, Karl Marx called Louis-Philippe 'Robert Macaire on the throne'.[46] Macaire gave form to critiques about the speculation, swindling, and bourgeois political power of the July Monarchy, and so we see that Daumier's approach to satire is rooted in an act of subversive substitution, expressing criticism of government and sympathies to working-class and lower-middle-class protest.[47] His version of satire therefore is theatrical, cynical, political, and shaped by its opposition to censorship.

Satire is not a genre; it is, in Charles Knight's description, parasitic and pre-generic.[48] It relies upon the distance between appearance and idea, on familiarity with an image or discourse and also its subversion. Imitating forms of expression, genres, or artistic movements, the mimetic nature of satire lends itself particularly well to visual formats, especially caricature and the grotesque. And while his graphic satire is almost universally beloved, Daumier also demonstrates the subversive potential of the visual arts, probing the different ways in which art can mimic, mutate, and deceive, thereby adding to our understanding of the politics of his paintings.

In order to understand the development of a form of satire that was so deeply tied to substitution and censorship evasion, as well as Daumier's turn to theatrical interpolations for contemporary political speech, it is necessary to begin this book with an examination of Daumier's early sculptural series, *Celebrities of the juste milieu* (1832–35), a group of unbaked painted clay sculptures that acted as reference points for lithographic portraits in the illustrated press. The series is a vital first case study to understand one of the artist's first negotiations with fragile expansions to political freedom and the abolition of censorship, a fragility that is underscored by his decision to sculpt plaster statuettes that both memorialized and preserved access to the newly-opened legislative chamber. Responding to a broader pull towards popular expression and anti-government sentiment, the series made a claim to the democratic reach of the new medium of lithography and demonstrated an interest in a productive dialogue between fine arts and mass media that would be formative to his later explorations in paint.

Celebrities of the juste milieu parodied contemporary efforts to memorialize 'great men' and elevate the reputation of the July Monarchy. Daumier's *portraits-charge* of contemporary cultural figures and politicians exaggerated physiognomies and frequently invoked masking traditions, presaging later explorations of performance and deception. Masking was a part of popular protest and political *charivaris* in the early 1830s. On 11 March 1832, on the last day of carnival, a masked parade journeyed through the streets of Grenoble. The organizers wore masks and costumes referencing prominent politicians from the July Monarchy, and two carried attributes (a candlestick and a syringe) based on lithographs published by Philipon in *La Caricature* from November 1831, which placed July Monarchy politicians in a procession parodying parliamentary procedure and feckless diplomacy. The prefect in Grenoble treated this display as seditious, and tried to arrest the masked participants, setting off a riot that first took the form of a *charivari*, a popular protest expressed through a noisy racket of banging pots and pans through the streets. After the violent suppression of this second parade, there was an insurrection that made waves throughout the country as a politically important moment of mockery and its suppression.[49] Likeness, mask, portrait, parade, caricature, performance, and violent revolt are interlaced too in Daumier's *Celebrities* series beginning in 1832. When *portraits-charge* of contemporary politicians were censored definitively in 1835, the artist would turn back to another strategy developed in the early 1830s: instead of building a grotesque *grand homme* museum, he would exploit the worship of literary heroes to create paintings that smuggled in stories and authors that challenged the powerful, slandered the head of the house, and dramatized the encounters between imagination and the brutal constraints of the state.

In the pantheon of nineteenth-century European artists, Daumier remains one of the most frequently cited and least understood. Though he was championed by the likes of Charles Baudelaire, Henry James, Edgar Degas, and Paul Cézanne – writers and artists acutely attentive to matters of aesthetics and form – analyses of his work tend to neglect questions of form and restrict their interest to the content of the caricatures for which he became famous.[50] Moreover, discussion of his work remains divided into camps unwilling to think across media or outside the categories of Realism or Romanticism.[51] Writers' tendencies to restrict their focus either to his work for the illustrated press or to work that better fits into the traditional beaux-arts categories of painting, drawing, and sculpture are both practical and ideological. Daumier produced nearly 6,000 works, approximately 4,000 prints alone, in a career spanning many decades and several changes in France's political regime, so any account of his work requires a radically selective approach. Rather than examine the representational strategies of Daumier's oeuvre as a whole, his advocates have either lamented the fact that he was financially compelled to squander his time and skill on the 'passing quarrels' of caricature or dismissed his paintings as an unfortunate side project which lacked the technical facility and historical resonance of his graphic work.[52] In a contemporary review of *The miller, his son, and the ass*, for instance, a critic for *L'Union* newspaper said that he could hardly recognize the familiar fable in Daumier's hands: 'My God! What a strange mistake our excellent cartoonist M. Daumier has just fallen into! ... Now dear Monsieur Daumier, no more bad jokes like this. Make caricatures! Make caricatures! Make caricatures!'[53]

Those who laud his paintings tend to interpret them in isolation from the lithographs with the inadequate justification that their social realism diverges from the humour of his cartoons.[54] Daumier's first retrospective exhibition, organized by Victor Hugo, Karl Daubigny, and others, sought to shift attention to Daumier's fine arts practice in order to add his cultural power to the republican pantheon, asserting his status as a fine artist whose political commitments happened to align with the republican cause. It did not, however, emphasize the subversive threads throughout his practice.[55] One representative response written by Viollet-le-Duc for *Le dix-neuvième siècle* on 18 May 1878, observed:

> I made several visits, yet, despite Daumier's widespread reputation as a caricaturist, I heard nobody laugh. This is because, taken as a whole, his work in many respects belongs to art – if not to what is habitually called high art, then certainly to great art, which remains in the memory, stirs emotion and never falls from fashion.[56]

This divide is predicated on a belief that painting cannot or should not engage with humour. Daumier's reputation as a fine artist was, in other words, established by the absence of laughter. In such a construction, humour – being base and contingent – is antithetical to art of lasting significance. In 1851, M. Méry of *La Mode* also separated laughter from fine arts, writing: 'Comic painting does not exist. The crayon provokes laughter, the paintbrush never; the palette is serious.'[57] He goes on to use Daumier as an example of comic genius, but in print, unaware or simply ignoring the fact that the artist had four paintings on display at the Salon he was reviewing.

Some of Daumier's paintings and sculptures are funny – I believe *Miller* is, and the *Celebrities of the juste milieu* certainly are – but satire does not always cause one to laugh.[58] Daumier's late paintings of subjects from Molière and Cervantes help us see that his model of satire developed into one that could be cynical and biting, critically oriented to point out the tragic realities of the human condition. The physiognomic abbreviations of the early caricature of the Carracci brothers and Bernini showed the skill of capturing human expression in a few lines and the humour in the difference between a grotesque and a likeness, but Daumier's exploration of the procedures and modes of satire in literature helped him create a form of satire that was more tragic, more violent, and more profound.

This book seeks to resolve the divide between Daumier's sensational political work for the illustrated press and his more private paintings, sculptures, and drawings by illuminating the ways in which literary and theatrical satire shaped his approach to politics and the problems of representation across his oeuvre. Daumier's artwork would influence nineteenth-century artists such as Paul Gauguin, Edgar Degas, and Jean-Léon Gérôme, and yet no one has confronted his serious and sustained investigations into satire as a subject of his paintings and sculptures, in part because 'great art' has been seen as being entirely separate from laughter. This book is a novel investigation into the nearly identical legal restrictions on caricature and the theatre in nineteenth-century France and shows the ways in which artists responded to shifting censorship laws. It demonstrates how an artist, who was imprisoned early on for a politically offensive cartoon drawn from literary satire, continued to find a form for dangerous political dissent in literary subjects.

In recent years, the creep of authoritarianism has forced new threats and pressures over the arts. Members of the Russian punk rock and performance art collective Pussy Riot have been censored and imprisoned.[59] America's former president threatened a sketch comedy show with federal investigation.[60] William Shakespeare's seventeenth-century plays *King Lear* and *Julius Caesar* have been cited and performed by critics of that same president.[61] Dissidents in countries such as China and Turkey have been forced to creatively evade censorship restrictions imposed by governments closing themselves to critical speech.[62] Increasing numbers of American school districts have instituted book bans.[63] In 2015, twelve members of the staff of *Charlie Hebdo*, a satirical illustrated newspaper in France, were murdered, and eleven of their colleagues were injured, a particularly pointed example of the real consequences facing critical voices in the arts and graphic satire.[64] It is my hope that readers of this book can learn from this case study about creative strategies for the evasion of censorial regimes, links between satire and political speech, and the subversive language of literary revival. The story of Daumier's persistent, subversive engagement with social and political issues provides historical context and a set of strategies for these questions. *Art against censorship* excavates revivals of seventeenth-century satire in nineteenth-century France, showing the force of Daumier's role in the broader stories of image–text relationships and political expression, and sheds new light on the complex interplay between visual art, literature, and theatre in the formation of modern art. And like Daumier's work itself, the book reaches back through satire to express universal themes of humour, violence, and dissent.

Notes

1 Mary Louise Kelly, Ashish Valentine, and Patrick Jarenwattananon, 'An anti-war protester in Moscow says the risk of arrest is worth it', All Things Considered, NPR, last updated 5 March 2022, www.npr.org/2022/03/04/1084627201/one-russian-anti-war-protester-on-why-shes-risking-arrest-to-speak-out (accessed 26 January 2024).

2 Kelly, et al., 'An anti-war protester'.

3 Darmaing, 'Chronique', *Gazette des tribunaux* (23 February 1832): 4. Delaporte and Aubert were also charged for printing and selling the caricature. See: Elizabeth C. Childs, 'Big trouble: Daumier, Gargantua, and the censorship of political caricature', *Art Journal* 51, no. 1 (1992): 26–37 for the most comprehensive study of this print.

4 '… pour le numéro 102; on y voit un *Gargantua* ayant des favoris très connus, sa bouche monstrueuse engloutit des hottes d'écus qui lui sont versés par des personnages dont j'ai vu la ressemblance aux ministères de la justice, de l'intérieur, des finances et de la guerre. – Ami Daumier, vous êtes passé par-là!' *Gazette de Sainte-Pélagie et de toutes les maisons de détention* 3 (17 January 1833): 1–4.

5 See for instance 'Dessin' in *Le Charivari* (14 January 1833): 3. This briefly explains that the artist composed the images for the series 'Scènes de l'imagination' in prison, which were then lithographed by Ramelet.

6 David S. Kerr, *Caricature and French Political Culture 1830–1848: Charles Philipon and the Illustrated Press* (Oxford: Clarendon Press, 2000), 9.

7 Robert Justin Goldstein, *Censorship of Political Caricature in Nineteenth-Century France* (Kent, OH: Kent State University Press, 1989), 119–21.

8 Kerr, *Caricature and French Political Culture*, 146–7. See also: Maurice Agulhon, '1830 dans l'histoire du XIXe siècle', in *Histoire vagabonde II. Idéologies et politique dans la France du XIXe siècle* (Paris: Gallimard, 1988).

9 Goldstein, *Censorship of Political Caricature*, 119. Prosecutions from 1830–33 proffered more than 100 convictions, totaling something like 50 years in prison and 300,000 francs in fines.

10 Kerr, *Caricature and French Political Culture*, 146–7.

11 William Olmstead, *The Censorship Effect: Baudelaire, Flaubert, and the Formation of French Modernism* (New York: Oxford University Press, 2016), 1–6. See also: Roland Barthes, *Le degré zero de l'ecriture* (Paris: Seuil, 1953), 30–7 on Flaubert; and Matei Calinescu, *Rereading* (New Haven: Yale University Press, 1993), 247–57 regarding textual concealment through citation as a means of evading censorship.

12 In 1846 Daumier moved to 9 Quai d'Anjou on the Île Saint-Louis in Paris, extremely close to Charles Daubigny at number 19 and Camille Corot at 15 Quai Voltaire. Bruce Laughton, *Honoré Daumier* (New Haven: Yale University Press, 1996), 176. The captions in Philipon's papers would have been the result of the close collaboration of a handful of individuals, requiring negotiations between the editor, artist, director, printer, and at times government censors. The conception of a caricature typically emerged from the artist or Philipon, which was followed by a preliminary drawing made on the lithographic stone (except for those by Grandville, with a background in illustration, which another artist would transfer to the stone for him). Captions would come from Philipon, who would also typically write longer commentaries included in the newspapers, though Cler or Altaroche also contributed. Kerr, *Caricature and French Political Culture 1830–1848*, 43.

13 Jean Adhémar, *Honoré Daumier* (Paris: Tisné, 1954), 7–8.

14 Roger Passeron, *Daumier* (New York: Rizzoli, 1979), 13–16.

15 Adhémar, *Honoré Daumier*, 8.

16 Adhémar, *Honoré Daumier*, 9–10; and Passeron, *Daumier*, 14–17.

17 Charles de Lasteyrie, for instance, opened the first commercial lithographic shop in Paris in 1816. A Mellerio & Louis de Nussac, 'La lithographie en France, Charles de Lasteyrie', *Gazette des Beaux-Arts* 14 (1935): 106–19.

18 Passeron, *Daumier*, 17–18.

19 Roger Chartier, Henri-Jean Martin, and Jean-Pierre Vivet, *Histoire de l'édition française. Du Romantisme à la Belle Époque* 3 (Paris: Promodis, 1985), 31.

20 Claude Pichois, 'Les cabinets de lecture à Paris, durant la première moitié du XIX siècle', *Annales. Economies, sociétés, civilisations* 3 (1959): 521–34; and Harry Earl Whitmore, 'The "cabinet de lecture" in France, 1800–1850', *The Library Quarterly: Information, Community, Policy* 48, no. 1 (January 1978): 20–35.

21 Chartier et al., *Histoire de l'édition française*, 325–34.

22 Chartier et al., *Histoire de l'édition française*, 326.

23 Passeron, *Daumier*, 26–7.

24 Daumier to Bocage (Pierre-Martinien Bocage-Tousez), April 1850, private collection, reproduced by The Daumier Register at www.daumier.org/biography/signatures-letters/ (accessed 20 September 2021). For more on Bocage, see Eugène de Mirencourt, *Bocage* (Paris: Gustave Havard, 1856); and Paul Ginisty, *Bocage* (Paris: Librairie Félix Alcan, 1926).

25 Daumier Register notes on Carotte dramatique – (Couplet au public) 'DR number 1265' at www.daumier-register.org/hintergrundlist_popup.php?key_m=1265 (accessed 26 January 2024).

26 Rouben Cholakian, 'Arsène Houssaye and the "Comédie-Française"', *Romance Notes* 5, no. 2 (1964): 147; and Oliver Larkin, *Daumier: Man of His Time* (New York: McGraw-Hill, 1966), 190.

27 Jean Cherpin, *Daumier et le théatre* (Aix-en-Provence: Edisud, 1978), 15–17.

28 Childs, 'Big trouble', 26–7; and Kirsten Powell, 'The press repressed: Themes of suppression of censorship of the press in caricatures of La Fontaine's fables', in *Proceedings of the Western Society for French History* 17 (Auburn, AL: Auburn University, 1990): 347–59.

29 James Cuno, 'Obscene humor in French revolutionary caricature', in *Representing the French Revolution: Literature, Historiography, and Art*, ed. James A. W. Heffernan (Hanover, NH: University Press of New England, 1992), 200–1. These include *The Gargantua of the century, or The oracle of the divine bottle* of 1790 and *The ci-devant great family feast of the modern Gargantua* (1791). Bourgeois hedonism takes the form of Gargantua too in the anonymous French prints *Gargantua at his table* and *Gargantua after dinner*, both c. 1805, referenced in Grunwald Center for the Graphic Arts, University of California Los Angeles, Bibliothèque nationale (France), *French Caricature and the French Revolution, 1789–1799* (Los Angeles, Chicago: Grunwald Center for the Graphic Arts Wight Art Gallery, University of California, Los Angeles: Distributed by the University of Chicago Press, 1988), 266–8.

30 Mikhail Bakhtin, *Rabelais and His World*, trans. Hélène Iswolsky (Bloomington: Indiana University Press, 1965), 199.

31 Childs, 'Big trouble', 27–9.

32 Edwin M. Duval, 'Rabelais and French Renaissance satire', in *A Companion to Satire*, ed. Ruben Quintero (Malden, MA: Blackwell Publishing, 2007), 73.

33 Childs, 'Big trouble', 29.

34 'Qu'il ait voulu désigner dans le personnage de Grand-Gousier notre on roi Louis XII, ou qu'on lui ait prêté depuis cette intention, toujours est-il vrai qu'il a représenté dans cette famille royale une famille de mangeurs, et, sous cette allégorie, ce qu'est pour un état monarchique l'entretien de la maison d'un roi.' Pierre-Louis Ginguené, *De l'autorité de Rabelais dans la révolution présente et dans la constitution civile du clergé* (Paris: Librairie des bibliophiles, 1879), 17.

35 François Rabelais and Pierre-Louis Ginguené, *Œuvres de Rabelais. Edition variorum augmentée de pièces inédites ... avec des remarques de ... Ginguené* (Paris: Dalibon, 1823).

36 René Bray, *Les Fables de La Fontaine* (Paris: Edgar Malgère, 1929), 110–11.

37 Powell, 'The press repressed', 347–59. Powell does not mention Daumier's print, which is one of several prints drawing from La Fontaine's fables during this period and criticizes the king's high taxes. The figure at right seems to reference 'Liberty of the press: Do not meddle with it' from April 1834.

38 'Tout l'œuvre se compose de deux élémens [sic] nécessaires, mais bien distincts: l'un généralement et éternellement vrai, l'autre vrai aussi, mais d'une manière relative et par conséquent transitoire. Or, reprendre l'œuvre après un laps de temps qui a enlevé à la seconde partie toute sa vérité, et montrer sur la première, fidèlement conservée, quelque vérité ou quelque satire plus actuelles, sans changer rien ou presque rien au cadre original, c'est faire proprement une parodie.' Louis Bergeron and François Théodore Claudon, *Fables démocratiques* (Paris: Aux bureaux du Charivari, 1839), 8.

39 Robert Justin Goldstein, *Censorship of Political Caricature in Nineteenth-Century France* (Kent, OH: The Kent State University Press, 1989), 179–80.

40 Charles Philipon, 'L'abdication de Daumier 1er', *Le Journal amusant: journal illustré, journal d'images, journal comique, critique, satirique, etc.*, no. 297 (7 September 1861): 7. Daumier was rehired at *Le Charivari* in 1863.

41 Laughton, *Honoré Daumier*, 49.

42 Sheryl Kroen, *Politics and Theater: The Crisis of Legitimacy in Restoration France, 1815–1830* (Berkeley, CA: University of California Press, 2000). This will be the subject of greater discussion in the chapter 'Molière's whisper / Daumier's clamour'.

43 Erich Auerbach, *Mimesis: The Representation of Reality in Western Literature*, trans. Willard Trask (Garden City, NY: Doubleday Anchor Books, 1957), 317–26.

44 Stanislav Osiakovski, 'History of Robert Macaire and Daumier's place in it', *The Burlington Magazine* 100, no. 668 (November 1958): 388–93.

45 Osiakovski, 'History of Robert Macaire and Daumier's place in it', 389.

46 Karl Marx, *The Class Struggles in France (1848–50)*, ed. C. P. (Clemens Palme) Dutt (London: Martin Lawrence, 1895), 36.

47 Osiakovski, 'History of Robert Macaire and Daumier's place in it', 388–93. See too: Richard Terdiman, *Discourse/Counter-Discourse: The Theory and Practice of Symbolic Resistance in Nineteenth-Century France* (Ithaca, NY: Cornell University Press, 1985).

48 Charles A. Knight, *The Literature of Satire* (Cambridge: Cambridge University Press, 2004), 1–3. Not all scholars agree that satire is outside genre. Leon Guilhamet, for one, argues the opposite, that satire is itself a genre, although the 'appropriation of other forms is unique to satire and is one of its chief identifying characteristics'. *Satire and the Transformation of Genre* (Philadelphia: University of Pennsylvania Press, 1987), 13.

49 Kerr, *Caricature and French Political Culture*, 197–203. This insurrection was later cited on 7 December 1832 in *Le Charivari*.

50 For Daumier's influence on Cézanne see: Roger Fry, *Cézanne: A Study of His Development* (New York: Noonday Press, 1960), 13–26. See also: Charles Baudelaire, 'Quelques caracturistes français', in *Curiosités esthétiques* (Paris: Michael Levy Brothers, 1868); Henry James, *Daumier, Caricaturist* (Emmaus, PA: Rodale Press, 1954); and Carol M. Armstrong, *Odd Man Out: Readings of the Work and Reputation of Edgar Degas* (Chicago: University of Chicago Press, 1991).

51 The divide in the reception of Daumier's work began as early as the first retrospective of his art with a review by Louis Edmond Duranty: 'Daumier launched into politics with a kind of fury, but I believe nonetheless that the instinct of his artistic accent and intense expression was leading him more and more to colours and a hatred of political parties.' 'Daumier: Suite et fin', *Gazette des beaux-arts* (June 1878): 553. A notable exception that explores the translation of

motifs across media is the excellent exhibition catalogue *Daumier: 1808–1879* (Ottawa: Musée des Beaux-Arts du Canada, Ottawa, 1999).

52 '[W]e approach these lithographs purely from an artistic perspective and can only regret that such fine genius was squandered on passing quarrels … Yes, Honoré Daumier will certainly remain one of the most outstanding artistic personalities of the age, but he will owe nothing to the bastardized and formulaic genre of caricature … If he is great, he is so because of his draughtsmanship's inherent qualities, because of his gifts as a colourist and his powers of observation, by everything which makes a painter great.' ('Aujourd'hui que les passions politiques que l'artiste subissait sont disparues avec les personnages mis en cause, on n'étudie ces lithographies qu'au point de vue purement artistique et on en arrive à regretter qu'un si beau génie se soit dépensé dans des querelles d'un jour … Oui, certes, Honoré Daumier restera comme l'une des figures artistiques les plus saillantes de ce temps, mais il n'en devra rien à la caricature, genre bâtard et conventionnel, obligé d'employer deux langages pour se faire entendre, et qui ne correspond qu'à des passions fugitives et stériles … S'il est grand, c'est par la qualité extrinsèque de son dessin, par son don de coloriste, par sa force d'observation, par tout ce qui fait qu'un peintre est grand.') Emile Bergerat, *Journal officiel* 114 (26 April 1878): 4454–55. For thematic treatments of Daumier's oeuvre, see: Julien Cain, *Honoré Daumier: Lawyers and Justice* (Boston: Boston Book and Art, 1971); *Law and Justice: Twenty-Four Lithographs* (New York: Pantheon Books, c. 1944); Jacqueline Armingeat, *Lib Women: Bluestockings and Socialist Women*, trans. Howard Brabyn (Paris: L. Amiel, 1974); and *Hunting and Fishing: Twenty-Four Lithographs* (New York: Pantheon Books, 1945).

53 Ch. de. B., 'Exposition des ouvrages d'art aux Tuileries en 1849', *L'Union* 205 (24 July 1849): [n.p. (1)].

54 K. E. Maison, who wrote Daumier's massive catalogue raisonné, claimed that the artist's lithography and painting were 'not only separate entities in his life; they were opposed to each other. The dominant comic element, essential to his lithographic oeuvre, is totally absent in the artist's paintings.' K. E. Maison, *Honoré Daumier: Catalogue Raisoneé of the Paintings, Watercolors, and Drawings*, vol. 2 (Greenwich, CT: New York Graphic Society, 1968), 29.

55 Michel Melot and Neil McWilliam, 'Daumier and art history: Aesthetic judgement/political judgement', *Oxford Art Journal* 11, no. 1 (1988): 5–6.

56 Quoted in Melot and McWilliam, 'Daumier and art history', 6.

57 M. Méry, 'Salon de 1850', *La Mode* (29 March 1851): 713.

58 'For in and with Daumier the tradition of physiognomic experiment began to be emancipated from that of humor. Very early in his career Baudelaire had noticed that his lawyers, judges, or fauns are far from humorous. They are creations of his own right, often terrifying in their intensity, masks of human passions which probe deeply into the secret of expression.' E. H. Gombrich, *Art and Illusion: A Study in the Psychology of Pictorial Representation: The A.W. Mellon Lectures in the Fine Arts* (Washington: The National Gallery of Art, 1956), 355.

59 Sophie Mayer, 'The size of a song: Pussy Riot and the (people) power of poetry', *Soundings* 54 (Summer 2013): 147–58.

60 Jamilah King, 'Trump threatens to sue "Saturday Night Live" over "It's a wonderful life" parody', *Mother Jones* (16 December 2018), www.motherjones.com/politics/2018/12/trump-saturday-night-live-lawsuit-wonderful-life/ (accessed 4 July 2023).

61 These associations included an infamous performance of *Julius Caesar* by the Public Theater in Central Park in 2017 that dressed the emperor as Donald Trump, prompting sponsors to withdraw because of the scene of assassination. Michael Paulson and Sopan Deb, 'How outrage built over a Shakespearean depiction of Trump', *The New York Times* (12 June 2017),

www.nytimes.com/2017/06/12/theater/donald-trump-julius-caesar-public-theater-oskar-eustis.html (accessed 3 July 2023). See also: Jeffrey R. Wilson, *Shakespeare and Trump* (Philadelphia, PA: Temple University Press, 2020); Chris Thurman, 'Burying Caesar.. or praising him? Shakespeare and the populist right in the United States', *English Studies in Africa* 63 (2020): 22–44, last modified 9 October 2020, https://doi.org/10.1080/00138398.2020.1780749 (accessed 26 January 2024); numerous opinion pieces comparing President Trump to King Lear including W. Edward Blain, 'Opinion: Trump calls to mind a modern, farcical King Lear', *The Washington Post* (14 November 2022), www.washingtonpost.com/opinions/2022/11/14/trump-king-lear/ (accessed 3 July 2023); Paul Thornton, 'Opinion: Trump, King Lear, and the Jan. 6 hearings: Why Trump was so much worse', *Los Angeles Times* (18 June 2022), www.latimes.com/opinion/newsletter/2022-06-18/opinion-newsletter-trump-jan6-hearings-delusion-opinion (accessed 3 July 2023); Anna North, 'Opinion: President Trump's King Lear moment', *The New York Times* (17 May 2017), www.nytimes.com/2017/05/17/opinion/president-trumps-king-lear-moment.html (accessed 3 July 2023); James Shapiro 'The Shakespeare play that presaged the Trump administration's response to the Coronavirus pandemic', *The New Yorker* (8 April 2020), www.newyorker.com/culture/culture-desk/the-shakespeare-play-that-presaged-the-trump-administrations-response-to-the-coronavirus-pandemic (accessed 3 July 2023), which makes the case that the better comparison is with Shakespeare's *Coriolanus* (1608).

62 For example, Q. Tai, 'China's media censorship: A dynamic and diversified regime', *Journal of East Asian Studies* 14, no. 2 (2014): 185–210; Li Shao, 'The dilemma of criticism: Disentangling the determinants of media censorship in China', *Journal of East Asian Studies* 18, no. 3 (2018): 279–97; Karrie J. Koesel and Valerie Bunce, *Citizens and the State in Authoritarian Regimes: Comparing China and Russia*, edited by Jessica Chen Weiss (New York, NY: Oxford University Press, 2020); R. Deibert and R. Rohozinski, 'Control and subversion in Russian cyberspace', in R. Deibert, J. Palfrey, R. Rohozinski, and J. Zittrain, eds. *Access Controlled. The Shaping of Power, Rights, and Rule in Cyberspace* (Cambridge, MA: MIT Press, 2010); Yauheni Kryzhanouski, 'Managing dissent in post-Soviet authoritarianism. New censorship of protest music in Belarus and Russia, 2000–2018', *Europe-Asia Studies* 74, no. 5 (2022): 760–88; Murat Akser, 'News media consolidation and censorship in Turkey: From liberal ideals to corporatist realities', *Mediterranean Quarterly* 29, no. 3 (Sept. 2018): 78–97; Esra Arsan, 'Killing me softly with his words: Censorship and self-censorship from the perspective of Turkish journalists', *Turkish Studies* 14, no. 3 (2013): 447–62.

63 'American Library Association Releases Preliminary Data on 2022 Book Bans', American Library Association, 16 September 2022, www.ala.org/news/press-releases/2022/09/ala-releases-preliminary-data-2022-book-bans (accessed 27 December 2022).

64 'Comment s'est déroulée l'attaque contre "Charlie Hebdo"', *Le Monde* (7 January 2015), last modified 8 January 2015, www.lemonde.fr/attaque-contre-charlie-hebdo/article/2015/01/07/comment-s-est-deroulee-l-attaque-contre-charlie-hebdo_4550930_4550668.html (accessed 26 January 2024).

1

The comic mask

> Censorship
> alone is a sure
> means of governing, I guarantee it;
> Censorship
> painlessly
> cures the disease
> of liberalism.
>
> (Biffard the censor, *Cagotisme et liberté*)[1]

On 8 March 1832, less than a month after Daumier, his publisher, and their printer were brought to trial for *Gargantua*, the illustrated journal *La Caricature* published his large-plate lithograph, *Masks of 1831* (Masques de 1831) (Figure 1.1).[2] It depicts fourteen parliamentary delegates from the Chamber of Deputies arranged in three rows and surrounding King Louis-Philippe, who appears symbolically as a pear at the centre.[3] Their likenesses reproduce essential characteristics of the deputies' appearances, including the hooked nose of d'Argout, Lameth's sunken cheeks, and Dupin's long whiskers. But they were also distorted portraits that were stretched and bloated to exaggerate the physical flaws of the politicians' faces. Below each *portrait-charge* is an abbreviated title in cursive, shorthand for each subject's identity. The abbreviated inscriptions below each visage offer thin deniability under censorship restrictions and follow a similar procedure to satire: they signal deputies' names and then distort them, prompting the reader to form a judgement in the ellipses. Like their titles, the exaggerated portraits mediate between imitation and malformation, negotiating the tension between offering readers humorous portraits and creating some deniability of direct offence to avoid the censors' shears.

The fourteen deputies are caricatured as masks, a joke that implies deception and creates a pretence for their grotesque expressions. Masking is a typical device in satirical plays because it points beyond the stage to the performance of social roles more broadly. In theatre, the mask draws the viewer's attention to the mechanisms of theatrical illusion

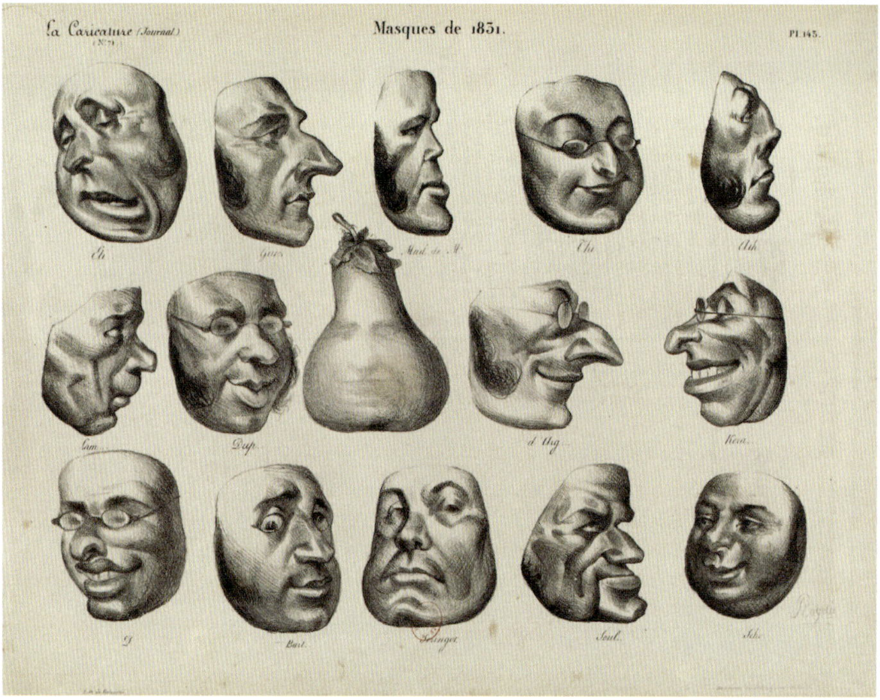

Figure 1.1 Honoré Daumier, *Masks of 1831*, *La Caricature*, 8 March 1832

and prompts her to think about the costumes and disguises required in life.[4] To achieve the effect of a mask, Daumier shaded three-quarters of the disembodied faces, setting deep modelling against the thin boundaries that define flat edges against the surrounding negative space, typically around the forehead or temples. The masks translate the sculptural qualities of a three-dimensional referent into the two-dimensional medium of print, creating a hollow object that mocks the politicians' artificiality, tendencies towards impersonation, and lack of substance.

This chapter will examine the series of sculptures and lithographs that emerged out of the experiment of *Masks of 1831*, the *Celebrities of the juste milieu* (c. 1832–35), a critical moment of negotiation with censorship at the beginning of Daumier's career. The series will be situated within the context of a broader push for popular expression in 1830, showing how Daumier worked to find a form for a newly-empowered group of political representatives under the promise of new levels of democratic scrutiny of government. This new representational project is connected to the cult of great men and celebrity culture, a case study that will be instructive for the rest of the chapters in this book, which show the artist continuing to reinterpret and politicize the reputations of great men. Establishing Molière as a source for comic masking practices and theories of masking, this chapter traces the close relationship between Daumier's political critiques, mechanisms of theatrical illusion, and the performance of social roles.

The *Celebrities of the juste milieu* series appeared at a moment of a profound representational shift in France, politically and technologically. On 26 July 1830 Charles X made an extremist and illiberal move that critics had long feared. The king enacted the so-called 'Four ordinances', decrees which dissolved the elected assembly, changed elections to create a chamber more favourable to the regime, restricted the suffrage of many in the bourgeoisie, and intensified already harsh press censorship laws, sparking demonstrations and barricades throughout Paris in July of 1830.[5] The government emphasized the important role of the press in mass unrest: 'It would be denying the obvious not to see in the newspapers the main site of a corruption whose progress is more noticeable every day and the first source of the calamities which threaten the kingdom.'[6] On 27 July, only four newspapers defied the ordinance and published their opposition to the new laws, and they were read widely in cafés, reading rooms, and shops. The prefect of police sent officers to seize the presses, ordering a use of force that drew crowds and protests, one of the sparks of the broader conflagration, and crowds soon turned to mobs.[7]

By August, a new king was crowned, the duc d'Orléans, now Louis-Philippe I, a new constitution was hastily written, and a new ministry installed.[8] The constitutional Charter of 1830 ended hereditary succession for the throne and seats in the Chamber of Deputies. It expanded suffrage, required the king to share lawmaking power with parliament, opened the upper chamber of parliament to public view, and abolished censorship.[9] Because the charter was organized around the idea that power emerged from the consent of the people, albeit a limited number, popular opinion became important in the construction of government in unprecedented ways, and the press seized upon new freedoms of expression.

At the same time, technologies of representation became more responsive to current events. Aloys Senefelder invented the lithographic process in 1798, and it came to thrive in France in the 1820s. The first lithographic newsprint, *View from the Isar bridge after the flood* by Domenico Quaglio, was published on 17 September 1813, just four days after the flood in question.[10] Unlike other contemporary reproductive procedures such as engraving or woodblock printing, lithographic technology captures the loose strokes of the artist's crayon or chalk directly on stone, obviating the intermediary step of painstaking incising. Romantic artists like Eugène Delacroix and Antoine-Jean Gros enthusiastically experimented with lithography's expressive capabilities. Charles Philipon came to lithography as early as 1821, perhaps inspired by another Romantic artist, Théodore Géricault.[11] However, in Philipon's own telling it was Nicolas Toussaint Charlet who, having also studied under Baron Gros, taught Philipon how to use the reproductive technology.[12] Lithography emerged as an essential tool for the burgeoning press in France, and the speed of the news accelerated dramatically. In the five decades of Daumier's career (c. 1829–79), newspaper circulation increased by 4,000 per cent.[13]

Having gained a hold in publishing in the months before the July Revolution, Charles Philipon was poised to capitalize on the expansion to the freedoms of the press in 1830 and seize a place at the forefront of political satire and the illustrated press. Philipon came to edit and organize the most important political caricature in its golden age. As a young man, he staged his first act of political satire in Lyon, a parade enacting a 'burial of commerce' in order to lampoon an ongoing recession. He and his fellow organizers were arrested and accused of trying to start an insurrection. Around 1819, after the charges were dismissed, Philipon moved back to Paris to study in Baron Gros's atelier. On 31 October 1829, with a small financial stake, he became one of the founders of the newspaper *La Silhouette* (1829–31), the first French paper to publish regular lithographic illustrations.[14] Philipon maintained his commitment to satire, in spite of obvious legal threats, translating his interest in public satire critical of the government from performance and the parade to the pages of the illustrated press.

La Silhouette collected and trained some of the most promising young artists of the day and marshalled their skills to satirize contemporary literature and political events. The comic newspaper was revolutionary in terms of its frequent use of lithography and its tendency to relate text to image. Its artists included Honoré Daumier, J. J. Grandville (Jean Ignace Isidore Gérard, 1803–47), and Charles-Joseph Traviès de Villers (1804–59).[15] The new journal appeared weekly and featured two large-format lithographs, typically with political or social themes. Philipon's success was predicated on his ability to supply political cartoons at or near the pace of current events. For instance, Daumier's 'Les bons gendarmes' is dated 28 August 1830, just thirteen days after Charles X went into exile (Figure 1.2). The print shows three ministers hiding in a garret. One bars the door, another is disguised in women's clothing, and the third crouches in abject fear. The former prime minister, the Comte de Polignac, is likely the central figure peering out of the window, dressed as a woman.[16] Daumier's early style in 'Les bons gendarmes' is strikingly different from his later work. He tended towards drawing elongated, knobbly figures and shallow forms that failed to offer a convincing sense of dimensionality. The ministers' legs are flattened to paper-doll delicacy, but the knees of the leftmost figure hint at the potential for a looser, abbreviated caricatural style to come. Under Philipon's direction, Daumier worked directly on the lithographic stone, erasing dry chalks before finalizing his image in greasy crayon, accelerating the speed of production and – like those Romantic artists Philipon admired early on – encouraging tendencies towards loose expression.[17]

The young artist seems not to have yet found his confidence, adhering to strict profile and three-quarter views of faces, often to the point of absurdity, such as spinning Polignac's nose to land on the top of his spine. Despite the interesting interplay of light and shadow dramatizing the emotional distance between the men in this tight space, the garret is an architectural impossibility, as Daumier fails to draw a corner where its two walls should meet. In 'Encore un petit moment', we also observe some trouble with proportions and anatomy. See in particular the mad, double-jointed knee of the figure in the striped pants. The grotesque swollen head and neck of the figure in the boat reveal that Daumier has not yet learned how to incorporate caricatural distortions and

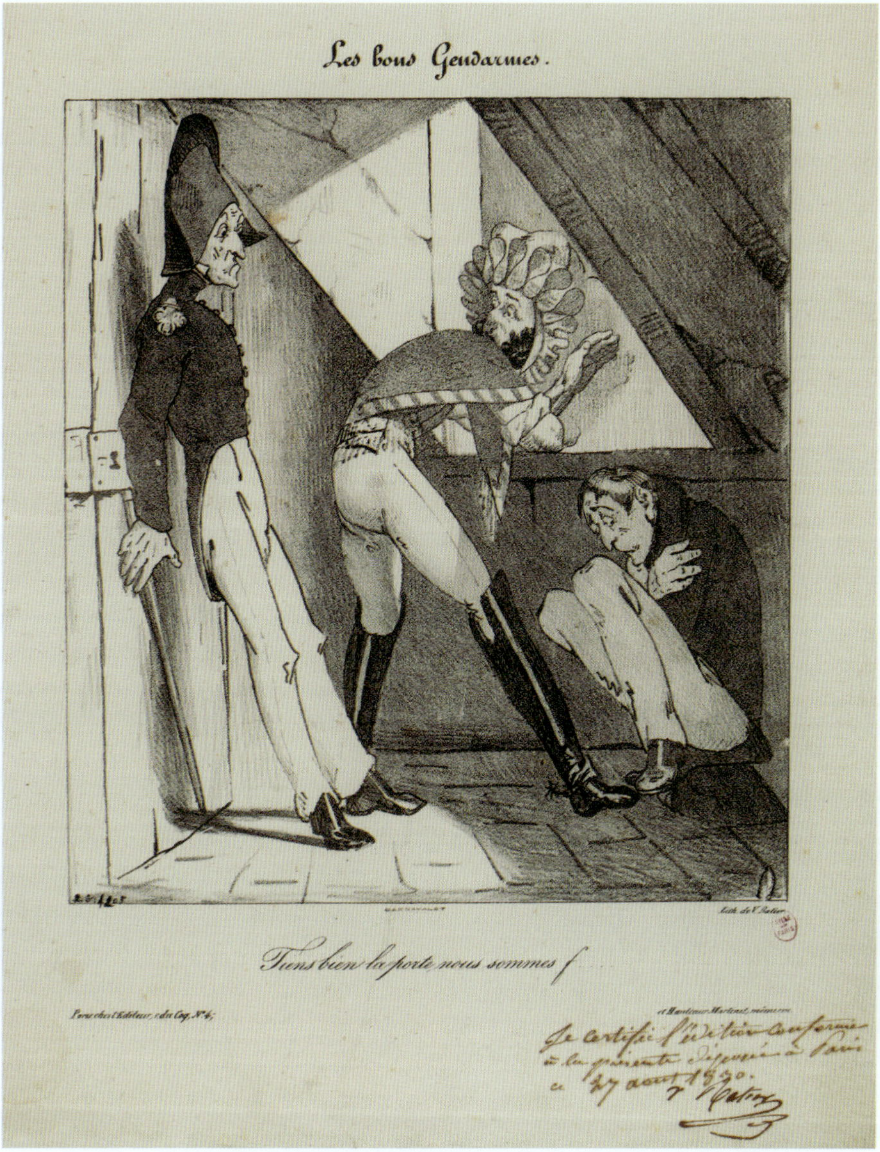

Figure 1.2 Honoré Daumier, 'The good gendarmes. Make sure the door is locked' ('Les bons gendarmes: Tiens bien la porte, nous sommes f…'), 28 August 1830

exaggerations within the normal proportions of a body. In his earliest work, Daumier had not distinguished himself from the routinized commercial work of the other young artists in the early illustrated press and mimicked the style of Nicolas Toussaint Charlet (1792–1845), Edmé Jean Pigal (1798–1872), Grandville, and Traviès.[18] In this print, Daumier stages a moment of suspense, dramatizing the fall of Charles X's government and the flight or arrest of his ministers. Costume reemerges as a source of humour here.

Philipon used the notoriety generated by trial and scandal at *La Silhouette* to establish his own magazine, *La Caricature*, in November 1830.[19] A weekly paper, *La Caricature* followed in the tradition of *La Silhouette*'s comic illustrations, but with a decidedly partisan republican bent.[20] In 1830, Honoré de Balzac was the text editor for *La Caricature*. Grandville was the most illustrious cartoonist, and Daumier would join a few months after the journal began and once it started shifting to increasingly political caricature and representing the opposition with greater force.[21] In 1832, Philipon established another journal, *Le Charivari* (1832–1937), in response to censorship difficulties. *Le Charivari* was a daily paper printed on four pages, with one large-plate lithograph taking up the third page along with some smaller vignettes embedded into the text.[22] In *La Caricature*, lithographic prints were included as inserts and could be framed separately democratizing access to art. This was one of his most savvy marketing tools, particularly because the cartoons were drawn by artists from his distinguished stable of talent, many of whom, like Daumier, were recruited from *La Silhouette*. In spite of its small print run (initially only 850 copies), *La Caricature* gained widespread recognition because the prints were exhibited by the publisher Aubert and could be viewed without purchase.[23]

While censorship was officially abolished at the dawn of the July Monarchy, the government still demanded security from publishers in the form of bonds and stamp taxes, and the press and the state engaged in a series of legal battles over the contours of speech and over how freedom was balanced against direct offences against the king.[24] In August 1830, just after Louis-Philippe's ascension to the throne, the Chamber of Deputies declared: 'The French have the right to publish and print their opinions, in accordance with the laws. Censorship can never be reestablished.'[25] Despite the freedoms and duration promised, the clause 'in accordance with the laws' turned out to be an important caveat. Between October 1830 and April 1831 five laws had already been enacted which set vexing conditions on press freedoms. On 8 October 1830, a new law stated that insults against the parliamentary chambers could be punished by the Court of Assizes as criminal matters or by the chambers themselves. A 29 November law outlined the punishments for attacks from the press on the king's dignity, the order of succession, or the authority of the chambers. Newspapers with a pattern of offences could be shuttered.[26]

In April 1832, the first of Daumier's *Celebrities of the juste milieu* appeared in print in *La Caricature* (Figure 1.3), initiating a series that would feature many of the same deputies as the *Masks of 1831* lithograph. Lithography swept through France, allowing the illustrated press to respond to current events at the urgent pace of historical change and consumer demand, and the medium became an important means for citizens to engage with the political sphere. As politicians were restructuring ideas about power, reputation, and legitimacy, Daumier's work posed the question: what does it mean to represent the present moment and to be represented by politicians?

Before taking his waxy crayon to stone for the now famous lithographic series, Daumier created at least thirty-six clay sculptures of parliamentarians and political personalities. Ranging from approximately twelve to twenty-three centimetres in height,

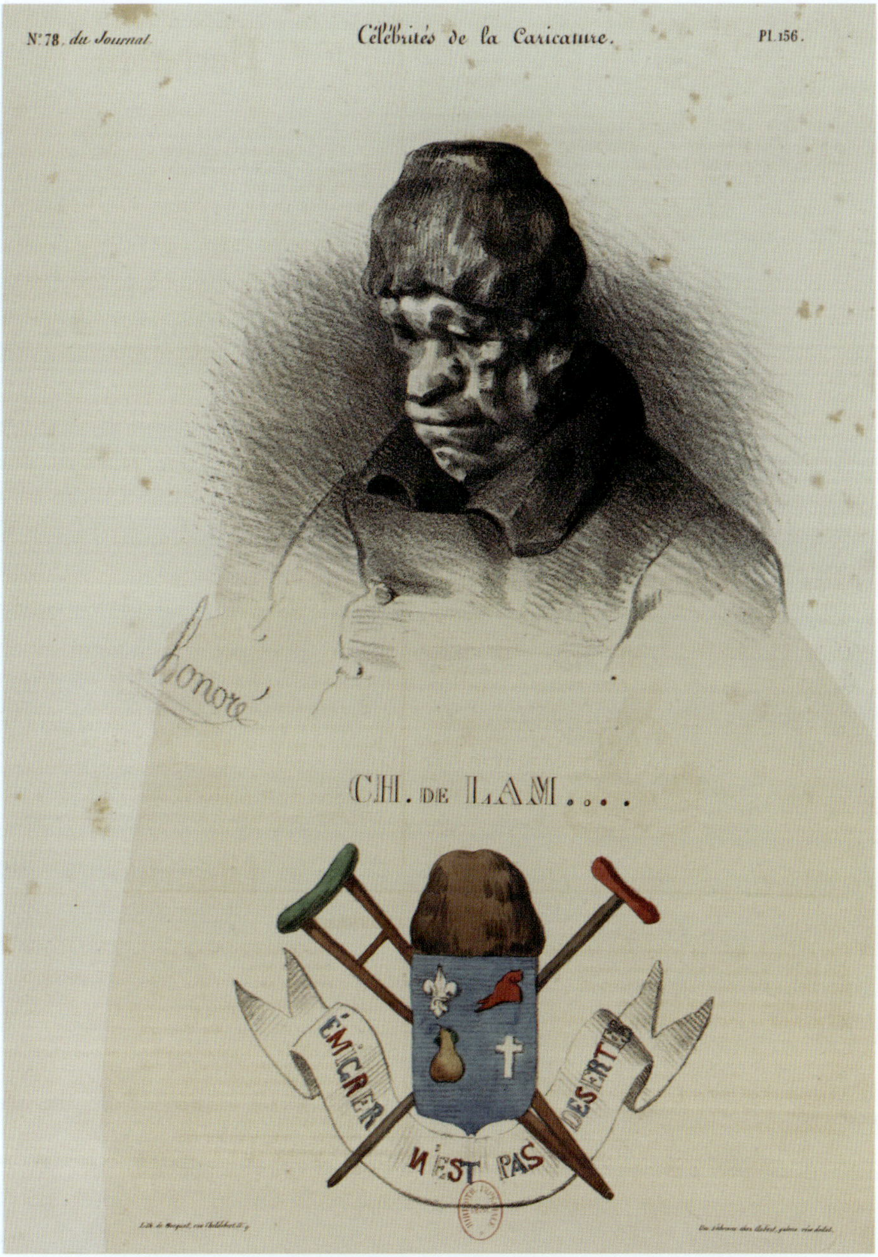

Figure 1.3 Honoré Daumier, 'Ch. de Lam…', *La Caricature*, 26 April 1832

the unbaked clay *charges* would serve as the basis for twenty-three busts and over eighteen full-length portraits published as lithographs in Charles Philipon's illustrated journals from April 1832 through September 1835, when the government imposed sweeping censorship restrictions, essentially ending this kind of explicit political caricature for over a decade. Daumier began to sculpt the small clay busts of members of the *juste milieu* around 1831, likely at the behest of Philipon.[27] The group was mostly politicians; of the thirty-six extant sculptures, twenty-six had a parliamentary or peer mandate. Career politicians, ministers, magistrates, Orléanist personalities, bankers, and enemies of Romantic art were caricatured mercilessly by Daumier's hand.

In order to understand the decision to initiate a series of portraits based on sculptural referents and what that series was trying to say about political and artistic representation, it is important to trace how the *Celebrities of the juste milieu* series emerged from two engagements with the mask. The development of the prints through 'Oh! the dreadful mask!!!' and *Masks of 1831* offers insights into the ways in which Daumier and Philipon seized upon this moment of popular expression, moving from images of a singular king to a larger political class, all while navigating new liberties and encroaching restrictions. The mask represents an early strategy for Daumier, creating plausible deniability for violating censorship laws by creating a scrim of distance between representative and representation.

On 1 April 1830, before the July Revolution, Philipon published a small woodcut of King Charles X dressed in the costume of a Jesuit in *La Silhouette*, titling it simply 'A Jesuit' (Figure 1.4).[28] Philipon was able to slip it past the strict censors of Charles X's regime because they typically focused their attention on larger lithographs for offensive content. Philipon did not sign this small subversive work, and after its publication the journal's editors Victor Ratier and Benjamin-Louis Bellet were prosecuted for offending the person of the king. Bellet was given six months in prison and a 1,000-franc fine. The defence attorney, Wollis, succeeded in arguing that Philipon's woodcut fell under the category of 'printers' ornaments', small decorative arabesques or vignettes usually inserted as a design element next to long passages of text, as defined by the government's circular of 14 June 1830, and thus did not violate censorship laws.[29] The content of images is notoriously slippery to the police, so size, structural support, and access became parameters for both the government's repressive authority and the artist's subversion of the censorship restrictions.

The subject of this woodcut, King Charles X, formerly Charles-Philippe, the comte d'Artois (1757–1836), was both intransigent and deeply devout. Sparking particular concern to republicans in France, he allowed Jesuits to rekindle their domestic missionary activity.[30] He even went so far as to make sacrilege a crime punishable by death.[31] By picturing him as a Jesuit, Philipon made a dangerous allusion to potential clerical influence on the king.

Philipon's woodcut of Charles X in the costume of a Jesuit was likely modelled on a small caricatural sculpture bust. The events of 1830 briefly drew Jean-Pierre Dantan (1800–69), better known as Dantan jeune, into the realm of political *portraits-charge*. He had achieved commercial success as a sculptor, participated in the Paris Salon between 1827 and 1869, and gained a reputation among the cultured elite for his small sculptural portraits and caricatures of celebrities. Buyers in-the-know could see his work in the

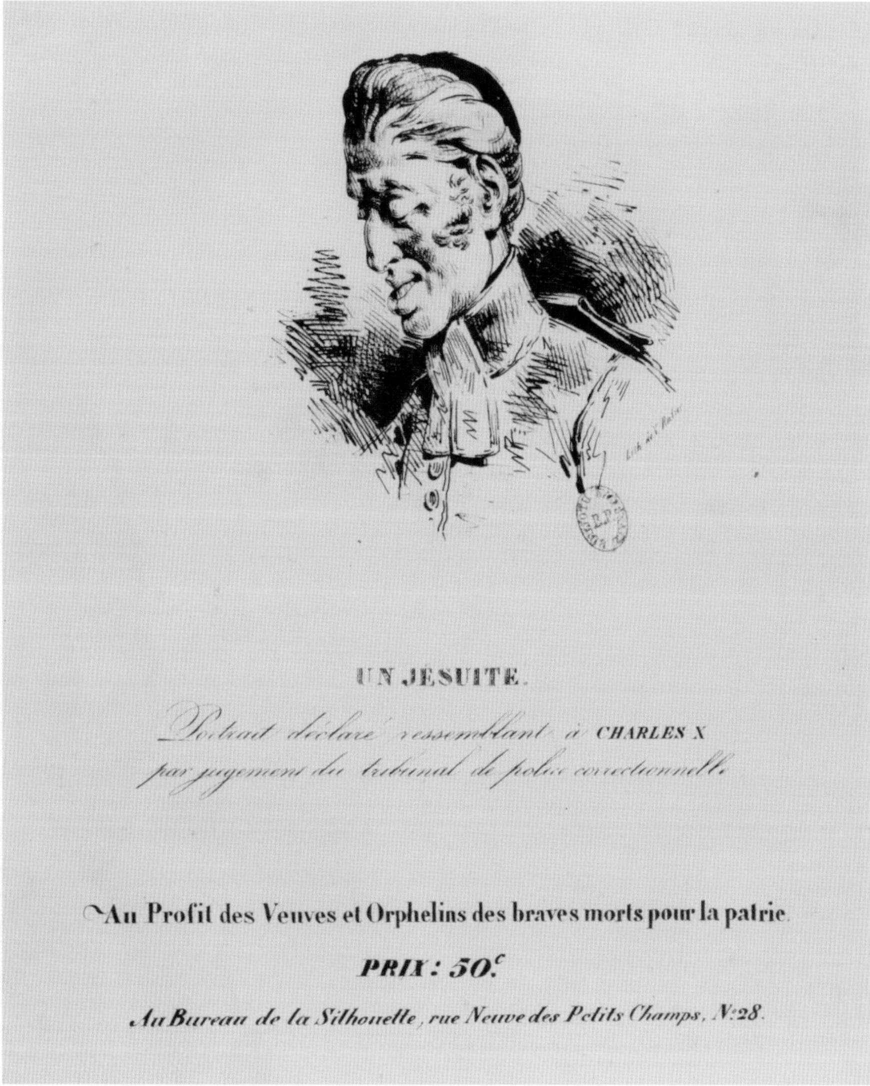

Figure 1.4 Charles Philipon, 'A Jesuit' ('Un Jésuite'), *Au Bureau de la Silhouette, rue Neuve des Petits Champs* 28, 1830

salon in the back of the Susse frères shop in the passage des Panoramas and also a visitors' space in Dantan's atelier, the so-called Musée secret or Musée Dantan that the artist maintained through multiple decades and apartments (Figure 1.5).[32] In certain circles, the sculptor's name even became a verb: when celebrities became the subject of one of his comic busts, they were said to be 'Dantanisés' or Dantanized.[33]

Dantan made political caricatures only from around 1831–33 and largely because of contact with Philipon, Louis Huart, and Grandville, among others.[34] Typically satirizing

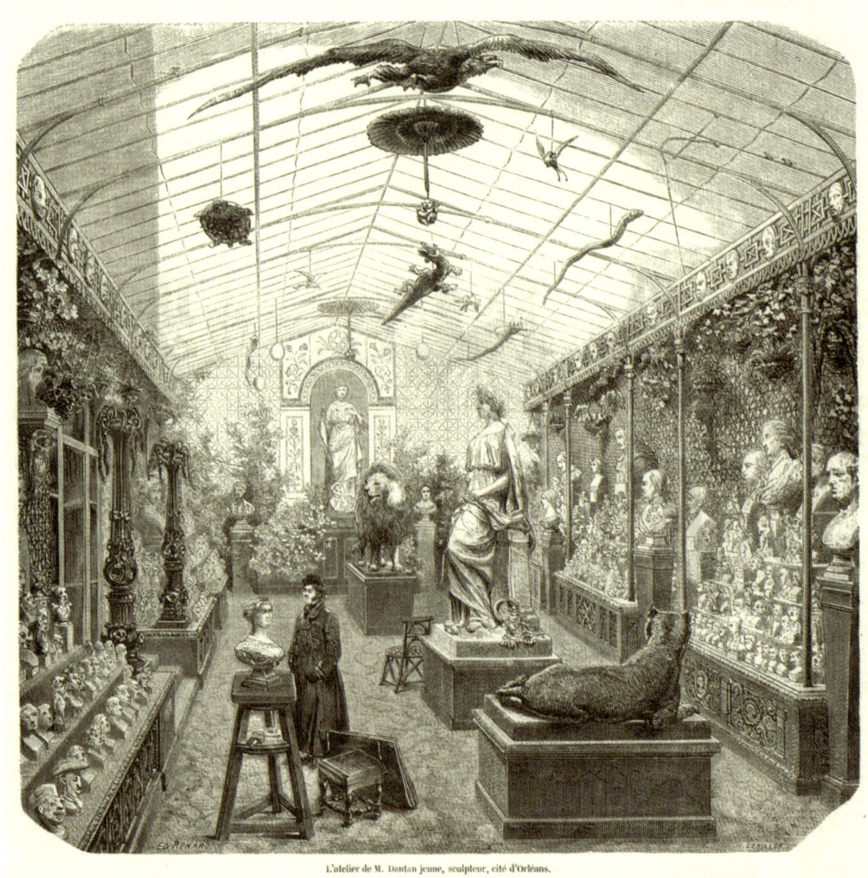

Figure 1.5 'The Studio of Dantan jeune' ('L'atelier de M. Dantan jeune'), *L'Illustration* 29 (January–June 1857: 30 May 1857)

celebrities and musicians, one of the rare exceptions to Dantan jeune's political detachment is a caricatural bust of Charles X in the costume of a Jesuit, a sculpture that can be linked directly to Philipon's woodcut in *La Silhouette* and Daumier's *Juste milieu* series (Figure 1.6).[35] His *Portrait-charge of Charles X* exaggerates the narrowness of the king's countenance, his lumpy nose, and his sagging chin. In Dantan jeune's sculpture, the monarch is costumed in a cap and collar, bowing his head in reverence to an authority above his own. Dantan did not sign the sculptures, but dated them March 1830.[36] They initiated a series of media translations that would be repeated, and then reversed, by Philipon and Daumier.

Philipon's woodcut in *La Silhouette* is a clear repetition of Dantan jeune's satirical *charge*: it has the same long face, the same slack underbite, pointed coif, and heavy lids. It even mimics the clerical coat and collar in Dantan's sculpture and preserves the sculptural quality of a model in the round. In August of the same year, Philipon looked again

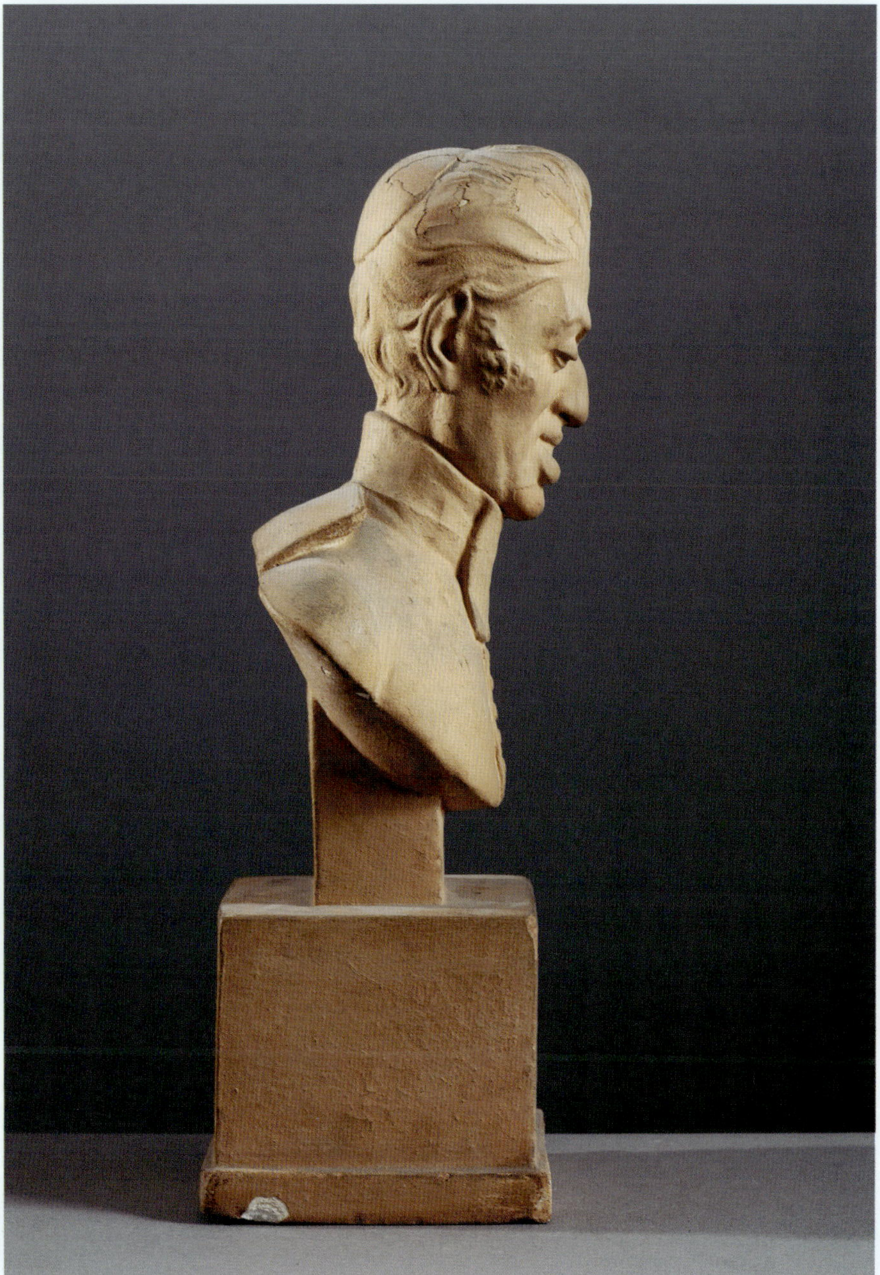

Figure 1.6 Dantan jeune, *Portrait-charge of Charles X (1757–1836), King of France*, 1830

to the sculpture to create a lithograph of Charles as a broken and hollow pitcher, drawing 'Pitcher that the Jesuits used for their provisions' (Figure 1.7).[37] Here, Philipon emptied the sculptural vessel in order to mock the king's intelligence and to pictorialize the allegation that he was merely a tool in the service of the Jesuit order.[38]

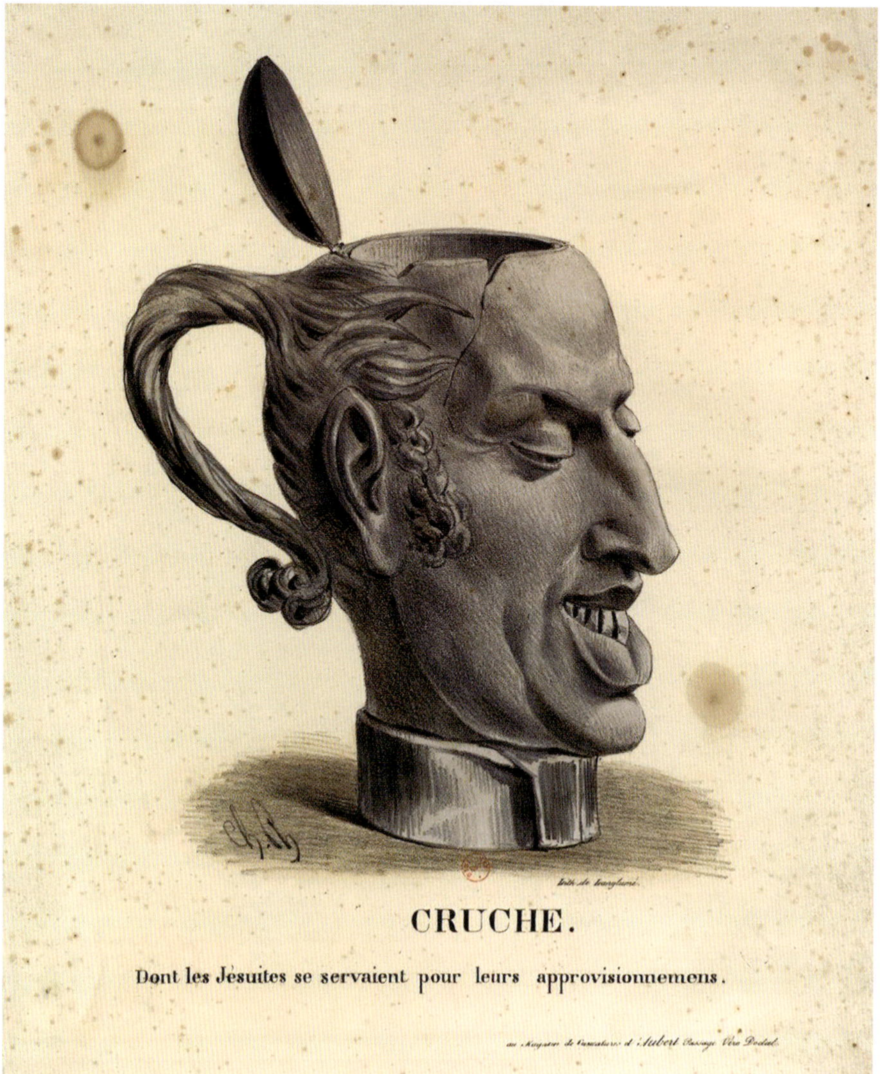

Figure 1.7 Charles Philipon, 'Pitcher that the Jesuits used for their provisions.' ('Cruche. Dont les Jésuites se servaient pour leurs approvisionnemens.'), Au Magasin de Caricatures d'Aubert Passage Véro Dodat, submitted Langlumé, 1830

The 'Pitcher' print was deposited at the censor's office on 9 August and then another print satirizing the king, titled 'Oh! The dreadful mask!!!', followed just two days later on 11 August (Figure 1.8).[39] Like Philipon's other caricatures of Charles X, 'Oh! The dreadful mask!!!' was sketched after Dantan jeune's sculpture, this time however with greater exaggeration of the king's bottom lip, chin, and teeth, which seem to spill perilously forward. His representation of the king as a mask reinforced his earlier accusation that Charles X would willing adopt whatever costume would further his ambitions. Associated with deception, disguise, and superficiality, the mask suggests a pathological

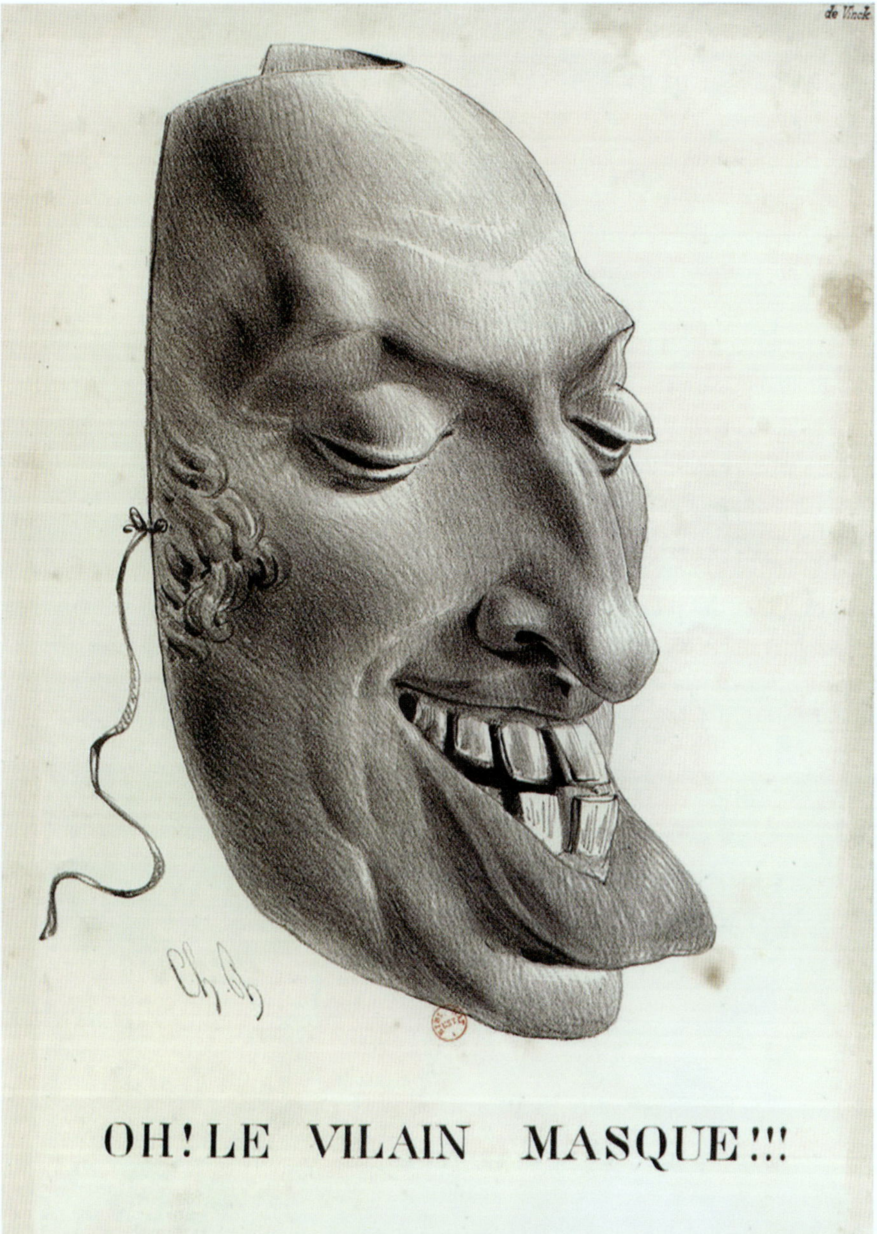

Figure 1.8 Charles Philipon, 'Oh! The dreadful mask!!!', *La Caricature*, 11 August 1830

artificiality. The mask, for Philipon, is a useful tool for making portraits of the king when direct insults were prohibited, not only because its referent was removed from direct likeness but also because a mask is itself an object which plays with the line between illusion and distortion, recognition and disguise.

Replacing a sitter with a sculpture was a radical move by Philipon, and his translation of Dantan's plaster bust to print helps us both understand Daumier's unusual sculptures as well as some of his formal strategies. Daumier would soon use the same procedures to create the *Celebrities* lithographs, alluding to the planarity and immobility of Philipon's mask through heavy modelling, suggestive cuts, and hollowed eyes.

In Philipon's prints of Charles X as a Jesuit, the king's costume prompts the viewer to think about whom he truly represents. In August of 1830, after demonstrations calling for his removal, Charles X escaped France at Cherbourg, fleeing to Portsmouth. Daumier's print 'Just a little bit longer, please' depicts the king begging for a few more moments of power before being dragged away to exile (Figure 1.9).[40] His face resembles Philipon's caricatures of Charles so closely that Daumier must have been emulating Philipon, a repetition that would signal their artistic collaboration and remove the representation one step away from a direct likeness, which might serve as a legal defence.

Daumier's *portraits-charges in the Celebrities* series emerged out of two engagements with the mask. The first, 'Oh! The dreadful mask!!!' may be the most important stylistic model for the *Celebrities* prints. But unlike 'Oh! The dreadful mask!!!', *Masks of 1831* aims to caricature a *group* of politicians, not just the king.[41] *Masks of 1831* was published on 8 March 1832 in *La Caricature*, a month before *Celebrities* appeared and features many of the same parliamentary deputies as the *Celebrities* lithographs. Like Philipon's mask of King Charles, the side of each likeness is flat and gathers more volume under the chin.

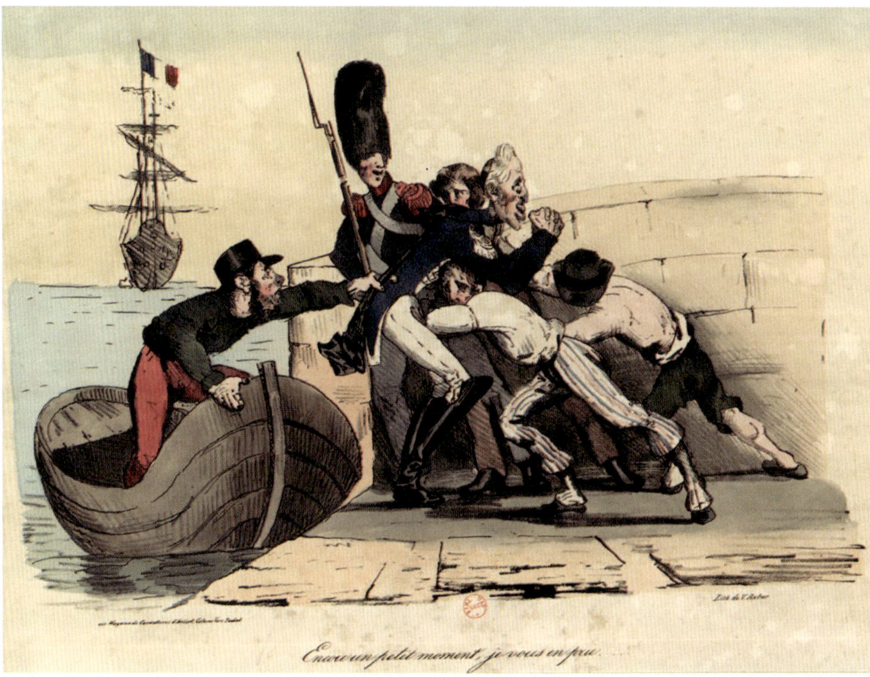

Figure 1.9 Honoré Daumier, 'Just a little bit longer, please' ('Encore un petit moment, je vous en prie ...'), 1830

Daumier carefully shaded the stony surfaces of cheeks and beaks, slicing a horizontal boundary at the top of each forehead and just in front of the ears. Below each mask is an abbreviated title in cursive, shorthand for each subject's identity. For instance, 'd'Arg…' is shorthand for Antoine-Maurice-Apollinaire d'Argout (1782–1858), Minister of the Fine Arts and later Governor of the Bank of France.[42] This system of display calls to mind taxonomies from natural history, as if Louis-Léopold Boilly's *Grimaces* were uncluttered and mounted with pins. The popularity of this group print likely encouraged Philipon's interest in commissioning more images of the *juste milieu* in his papers.[43] It also prefigured the titles on the *Celebrities* prints, which include puns and similar abbreviations, including d'Argout (*d'Arg*) and Charles-Malo-François, comte de Lameth (1757–1832) (*Lam…*). These titles reduce and disfigure the names of the deputies in an analogous operation to caricature, invoking the typological and even the taxonomic. Abbreviations also likely helped avoid libel suits. A standard legal defence involved the claim that the government could not establish a clear identification for the person being caricatured.[44]

While Daumier initially took up the same trope Philipon had used to ridicule the king in *Masks of 1831*, the act of mocking middle-class deputies was a fairly new ambition in French caricature. It also shares the same joke as Philipon's 'Oh! The dreadful mask!!!', namely that the politicians rising to power were trying to deceive the public. The public critique of a politically-empowered middle class or their representatives was a new phenomenon in the illustrated press. Before 1830, political caricatures were mainly reserved for the king.[45] And caricatures of the king could not serve as a direct model for images of deputies. In the realm of representation, the king's body had long occupied the strange position of being at once both absolutely physical and also a symbol of state, and it was the same reliance on symbols that caricature subversively exploited in order to continue its critique as it faced increasingly repressive restrictions. This duality of the king as both a material body and the body politic was one that monarchies had long established and promoted, but it made the body of the king vulnerable to symbolic hyperbole in representational spaces. The corpulence of the king, for example, was a popular trope, as it was understood to betray not only gluttony, but also self-serving impulses and ambitions, inequity, and corruption of the state.[46]

Daumier adopted this trope in a print mocking the parliament in 1834, 'The legislative belly' ('Le ventre législatif', Figure 1.10). Set in the legislative chamber, Daumier rhymes the curved architecture of the amphitheatre with the round bodies of the deputies. Clément François Victor Gabrielle Prunelle, recognizable from Daumier's earlier clay bust (Figure 1.11), stands in the heart of the chamber, bridging the space between viewer and legislature, his corpulence suggesting that the deputies were driven by a hunger for self-satisfaction. 'The legislative belly' would not have been quite as effective as a group portrait without the caricatural likenesses appearing in *La Caricature* and *Le Charivari* for two years in the *Celebrities of the juste milieu* series by the time of its publication. Without the caricatural sculptures preceding them, *Masks of 1831* did not offer these layers of reference or ease of identification, but it did succeed in making the general claim that the group of politicians were deceptive.

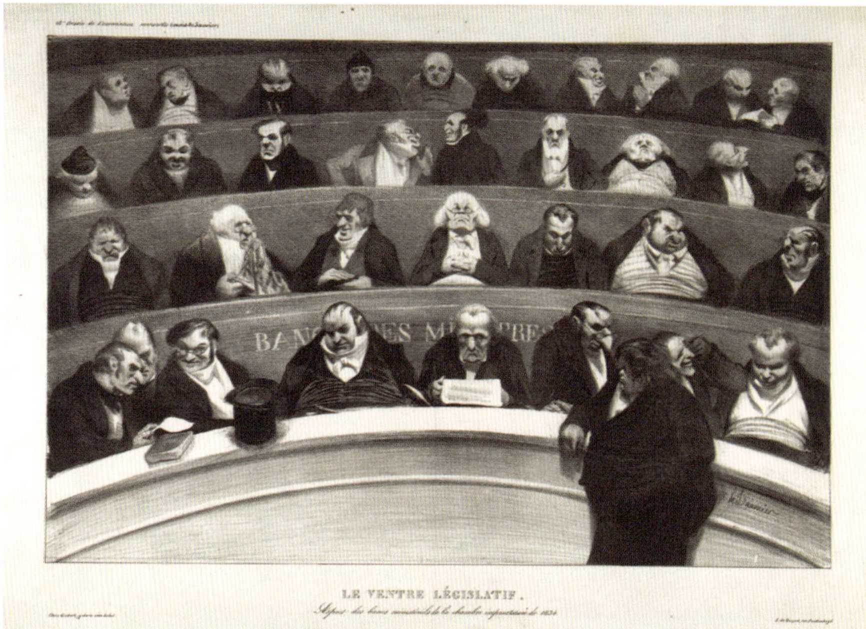

Figure 1.10 Honoré Daumier, 'The legislative belly' ('Le ventre legislative: Aspect des bancs ministériels de la chambre improstituée de 1834'), published by Association Mensuelle, January 1834

The revolutionary Charter of 1830 strengthened liberal principles and improved the representative character of government, prompting Daumier to deepen his investigations into representation and giving him a new cast of politicians to mock in his caricatures. Under the July Monarchy, the Chamber of Deputies became an organization dominated by the business interests of an ambitious middle class.[47] Louis-Philippe expressed the hope that this new group of bourgeois legislators would act as a cooperative middle ground, negotiating a middle way between the interests of the king and France's populace.[48] Pierre-Paul Royer-Collard and François Pierre Guillaume Guizot, credited as the group's major theorists, sought to represent the middle class, spurning both legitimist and liberal extremism and seeking a golden mean, or *juste milieu*, between them.[49] As Alexis de Tocqueville (1805–59) described in his memoirs,

> In 1830 the triumph of the middle class had been definite and so thorough that all political power, every franchise, every prerogative, and the whole government was confined and, as it were, heaped up within the narrow limits of this one class, to the exclusion of all above. Not only did it thus rule society, but it may be said to have formed it … The particular spirit of the middle class became the general spirit of the government … an active, industrious spirit, often dishonorable, generally orderly, occasionally reckless through vanity or egoism, but timid by temperament, moderate in all things except in its love of ease and comfort, and last but not least mediocre.[50]

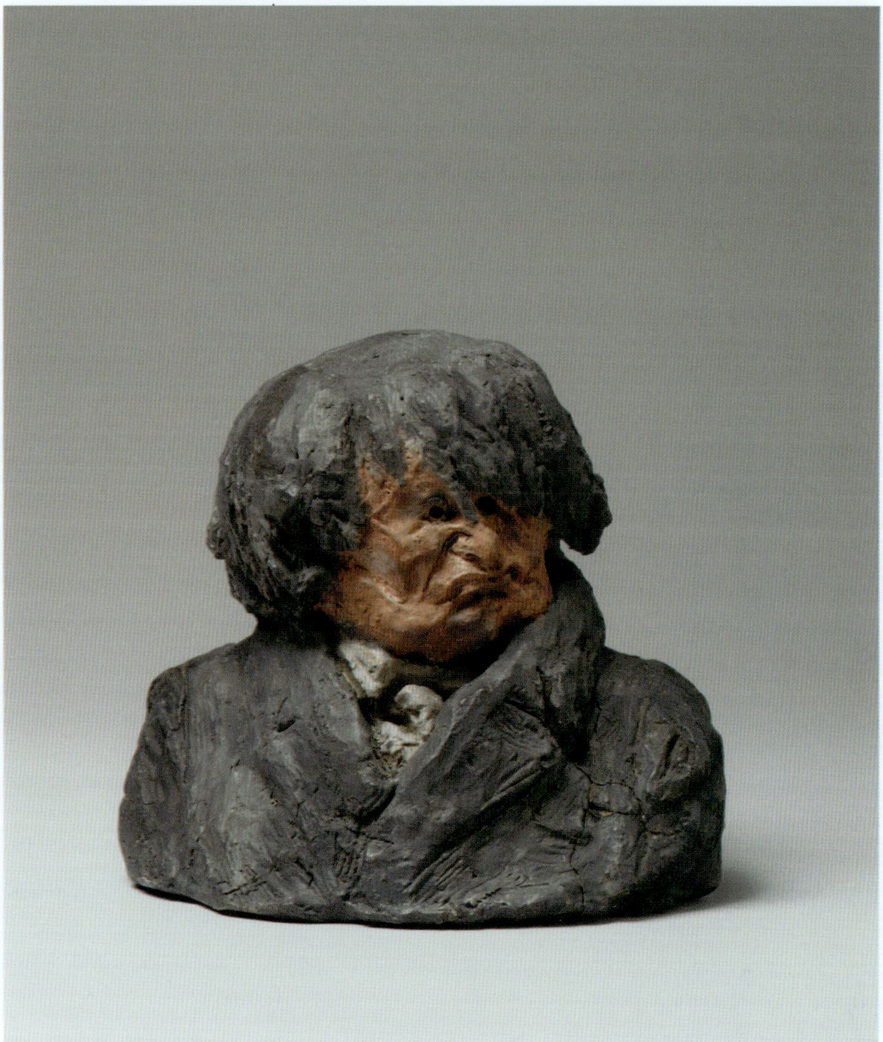

Figure 1.11 Honoré Daumier, *Clément François Victor Gabrielle Prunelle*, c. 1832

The *juste milieu* became a new rising power class that supported the interests of the monarchy and the middle class, one which increasingly silenced the voice of the opposition in the name of social order. As it emerged as a political force, its members came under increased public scrutiny. They quickly became targets of the illustrated press, which criticized their moderation and tried to make them recognizable.

Daumier's sculptural work was broken up by his six-month stint in prison, a break which accounts for some of the discrepancies in the size and style of his busts. They offer an enormous variety of faces and expressions. One can identify significant differences in size, pigmentation, and exaggerated features. The sculptural busts double in size and then shrink again.[51] The sides of some of the busts are cut just after the lapel, while others have fully-defined shoulders. While together the sculptures seem to share the black dress of the rising bourgeoisie, the artist varied the colour of cravats and waist-coats, and even painted the dark coats of each sculpture in idiosyncratic shades of dark blue and black.

Daumier refused to give a systematic description of parliamentary deputies or to provide stylistic cohesion. The caricatural busts' eyes are most convincing as shadows and are at their most effective when they are pinched shut, as on Count Auguste-Hilarion de Kératry (c. 1833, Figure 1.12), deputy and peer of France. Rather than betray a psychological interiority in their eyes, Daumier focused on mouths to enliven the

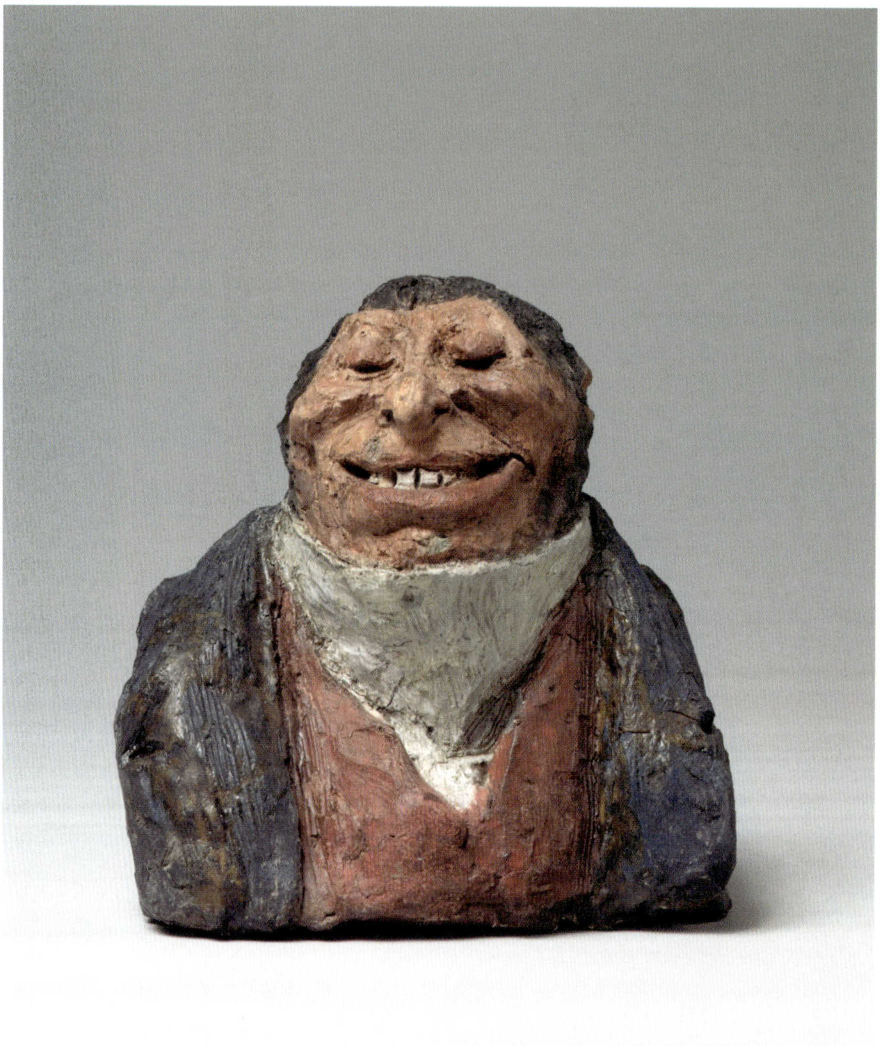

Figure 1.12 Honoré Daumier, *Comte Auguste-Hilarion de Kératry*, c. 1833

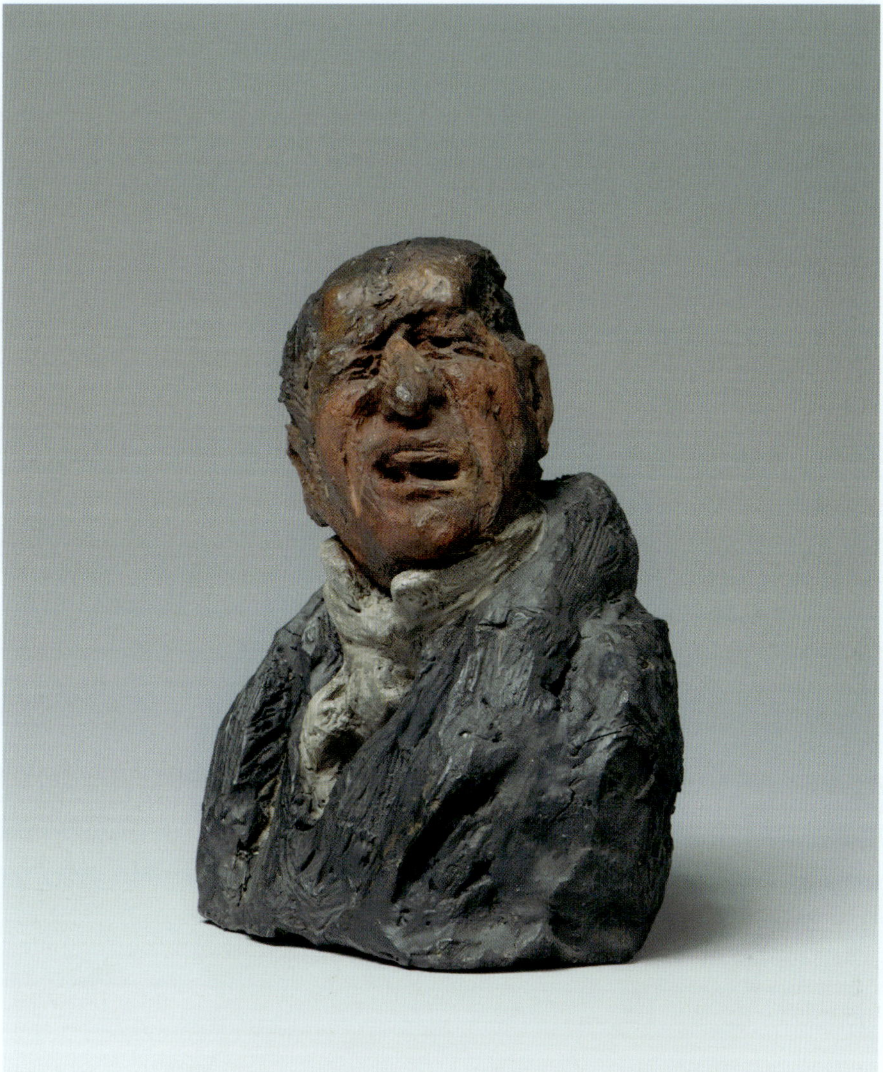

Figure 1.13 Honoré Daumier, *Unknown, Charles-Louis Huguet, marquis de Sémonville?* c.1834–35

sculptures: Kératry and Charles-Louis Huguet (Figure 1.13) grin in blind avarice or stupidity; there is a sense of wheezing breath in Fruchard, Harlé, and Fulchiron; a hint at an impending speech with Gady, Dupin, and Philipon; and a ruffled harrumph from Cunin, Odier, the massive Etienne, and Barthes. Even with Chevandier de Valdrome, who is muzzled into silence by his black cravat, the dramatic impact centres on his mouth (Figure 1.14). This fixation on mouths gives the sense of a group of legislators either all talking at once, pausing before speech, or refusing to speak. There is little sense that members of the *juste milieu* are listening or absorbing. They are all output or

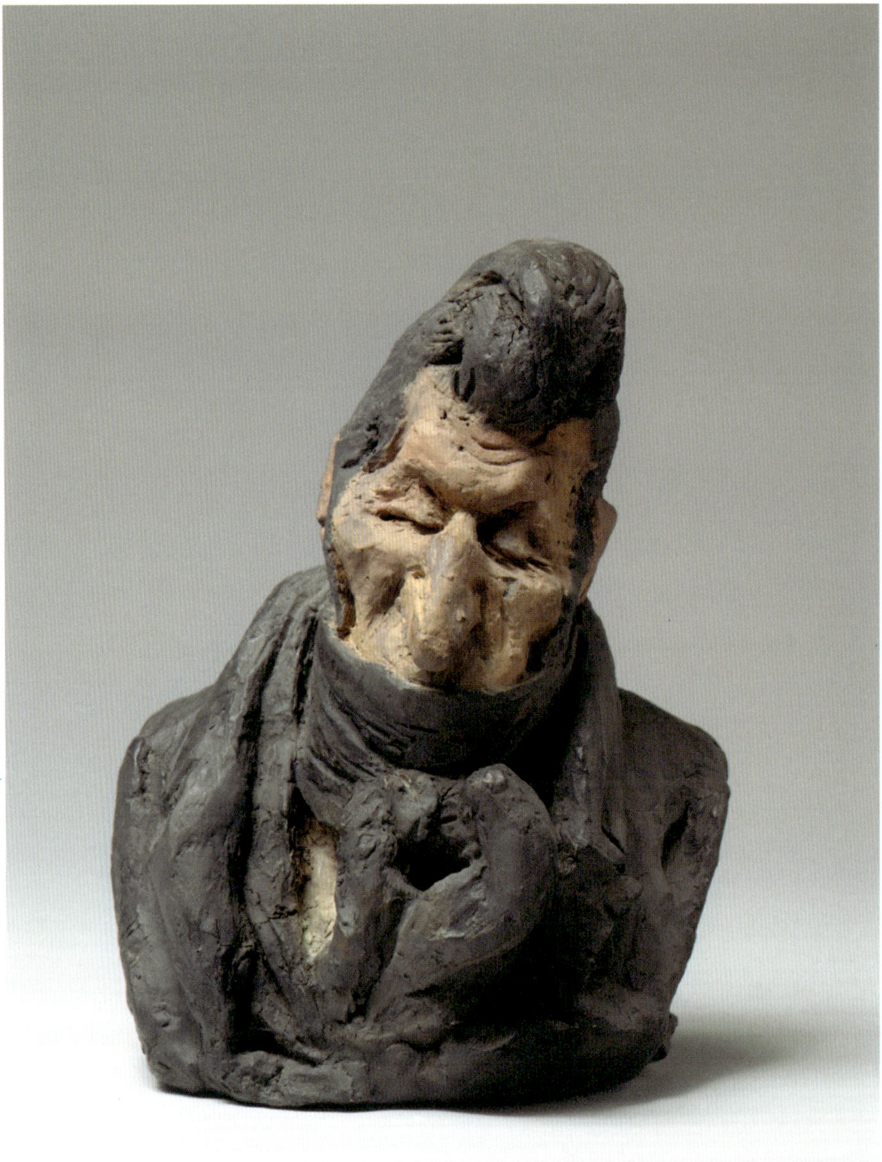

Figure 1.14 Honoré Daumier, *Jean-Auguste Chevandier de Valdrome*, 1833

self-containment. It is not a group that can effectively communicate, much less agree. Tocqueville again:

> I doubt whether any parliament (not excepting the Constituent Assembly, I mean the true one, that of 1789) ever contained more varied and brilliant talents than did ours during the closing years of the Monarchy of July.

> Nevertheless, I am able to declare that these great orators were bored to death listening to one another, and, what was worse, the whole country was bored with listening to them.[52]

The *Celebrities of the juste milieu* series is materially dispersed and stylistically diverse, being refused the kind of uniformity that would suggest effective political cohesion. This would also be an early and telling exploration of Daumier signalling sound, broadcast or withheld, as a proxy for political speech.

Masks of 1831 aimed to hold together a new tension between representing individual politicians and indicting the traits of a group. One of Daumier's fundamental issues with the *juste milieu* was their individualism. The increasing influence of business on middle-class legislators was at odds with liberal ideas, and their entrepreneurial self-interest, given enough power, could be tempted into corruption:

> Posterity, which sees none but the more dazzling crimes, and which in general loses sight of mere vices will perhaps never know to what extent the government of that day, towards its close, assumed the ways of an industrial enterprise, which conducts all its transactions with a view to the profits accruing to its shareholders. These vices were due to the natural instincts of the dominant class, to its absolute power, and also to the character of the time. King Louis-Philippe had contributed much to their growth. [he was the accident which made the malady mortal].[53]

Alexis de Tocqueville outlines the ways in which a synthesis of the *juste milieu* would gloss over the specificity of individual misconduct. It was important for him and Daumier to make specific crimes and flaws vivid for the historical record while also commenting on collective sins. In *Masks of 1831*, Daumier individualized his *charges* through small differences in expression and physiognomy which were constrained by the mask. His *Celebrities* lithographs, on the other hand, created a whole iconographic system to detail the vices of the deputies. The shackles and saw in the crest under Jean-Charles Persil's *portrait-charge*, for example, were specific to his overreach as a censor (Figure 1.15). Taken together, the *Celebrities of the juste milieu* illuminated the broader tendencies of the dominant class while creating enough space to show the individualism and specific attacks on liberalism that lay at the heart of their corrupt dealings.

At Daumier's first retrospective exhibition, writer and critic Champfleury (Jules Husson, 1821–89) wrote that the artist's lithograph of Persil, Minister of Justice and deputy of Condom, was one of the most important portraits in the artist's oeuvre. Daumier's caricatural portrait appeared on 11 April 1833 with this accompanying text: 'We offer the portrait of the cruellest enemy of liberty and principally of the press.'[54] In translating sculpture (Figure 1.16) to print, Daumier's lithograph retains the clay bust's colouration in the vinous, bruised-red pigmentation of Persil's nose, but carves his cheeks to near blackness in crayon and renders his eyes as impenetrable caverns rather than as blank,

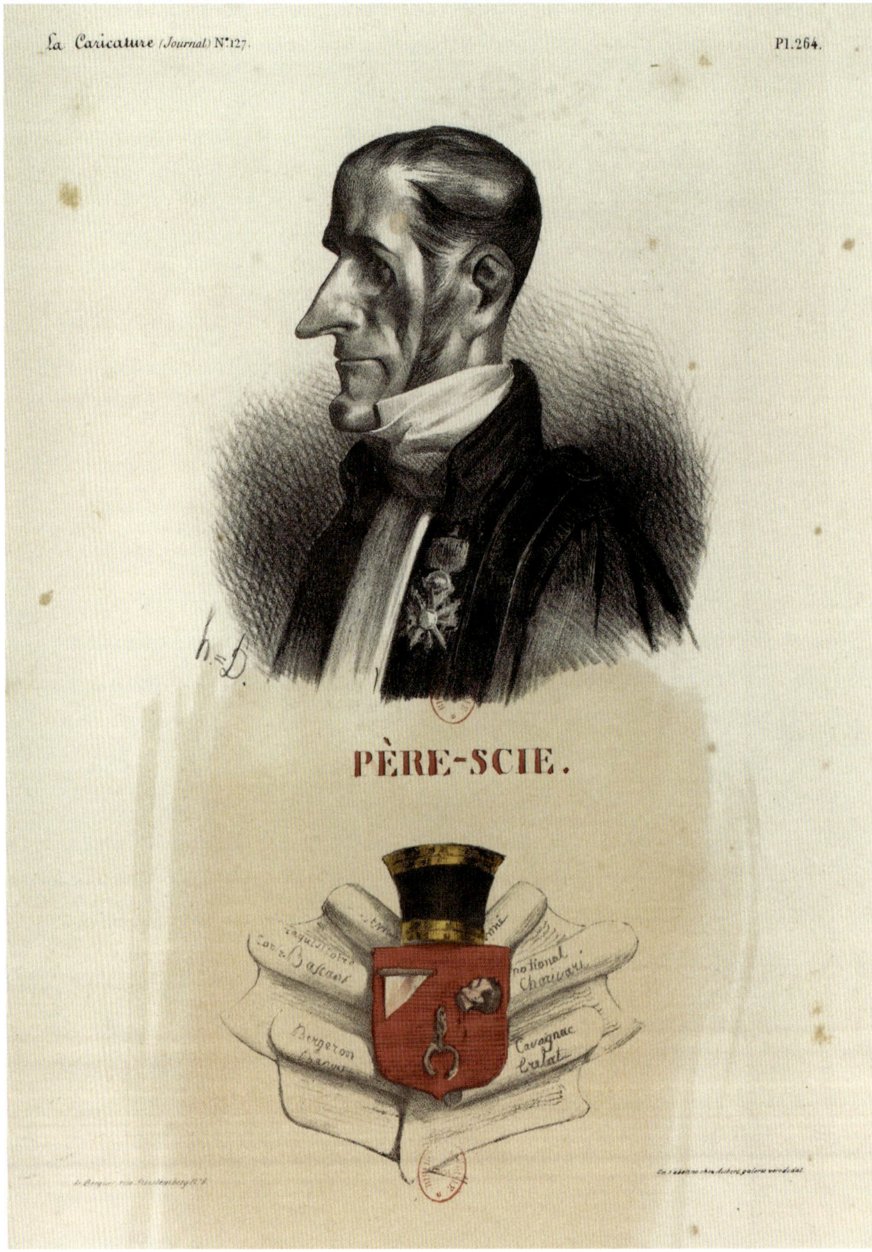

Figure 1.15 Honoré Daumier, 'Père-sci', [pun for Persil] *La Caricature,* 11 April 1833

furrowed cavities. In a lithograph unusual for its intensive modelling and dimensionality, a sideburn cuts from Persil's hairline to below his collar, creating a strange incision dividing the front part of the face from the rest of his rounded head. This effect is even more dramatic because his punctured eye sockets disappear into deep shadow, and his high, starched collar sharply severs his face from any connection to a body below. Where

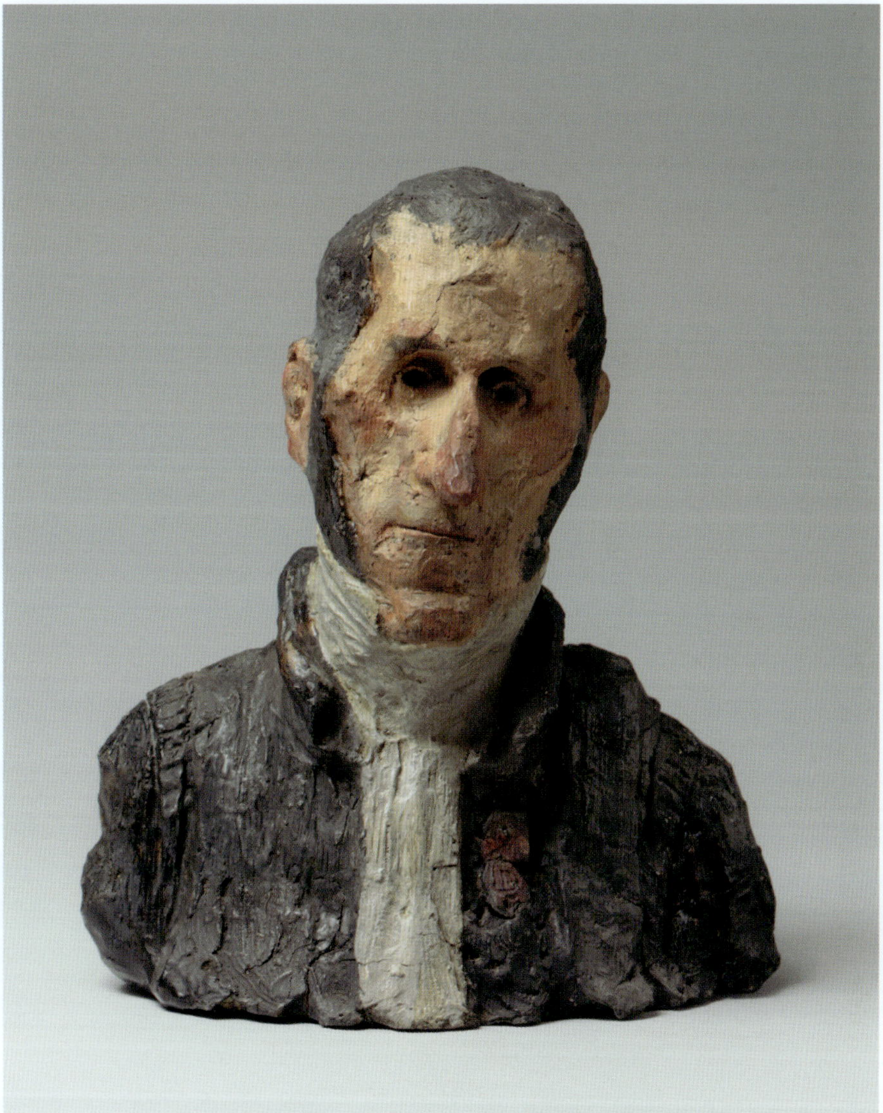

Figure 1.16 Honoré Daumier, *Jean-Charles Persil*, 1833

is his neck? Do we believe one exists? All of these severings give Daumier's lithograph the analytical remove and gelid lifelessness of an inanimate object, like a two-dimensional rendering of a rounded mask.

Persil was one of the most zealous advocates of stricter censorship laws.[55] The title of Daumier's lithograph, 'Père-Scie' or Father (Hand)saw, is a pun on the deputy's name. This verbal play indicts his suppression of the press and his love of slicing words from the page. It is also a means to evade the very censorship restrictions Persil was trying to enact. Similar puns are included in the *Celebrities* prints of Messieurs Tu-Bois (Dubois),

Bataille (Pataille), and De l'or (Delort). Even those deputies whose names did not lend themselves so easily to puns took on emblematic titles, for example, Jean-Claude Fulchiron, also called 'La Tartuffe', or 'The Imposter', a reference to Molière. Below the portrait, Daumier invents an elaborate crest in order to mock the aristocratic pretensions of the upper-middle-class legislators. Persil's crest is topped with a magistrate's hat and includes a shackle, a severed head, and a small, guillotine-like saw. The association between censorship and violence is echoed in Auguste Bouquet's lithograph of the same name, where, dressed in magisterial robes, Persil tries to decapitate Daumier's editor Charles Philipon with a nose that has grown into a lethal saw (Figure 1.17).

Édouard Papet called Daumier's *Persil* 'a moral portrait' in contrast to a caricature.[56] For Champfleury, writing at the distance of many decades and several regime changes, Daumier's power went beyond exaggerating the specific features of the deputies. In Daumier's lithograph, Persil stood in for an office – the censor, the magistrate – and ultimately became an emblem for power more broadly.

> M. Persil had power that was nothing more than a mask. A young artist with his pencil arrived at a medal relief and nothing could efface it. The politics of the time are forgotten, royalty disappeared, the man dead; what remains is a piece of paper with a mask of a procurer general. Still, in the moments of trouble, the crowd can see in their public accuser a figure that resembles this portrait. The individual is effaced in order to make room for a type.[57]

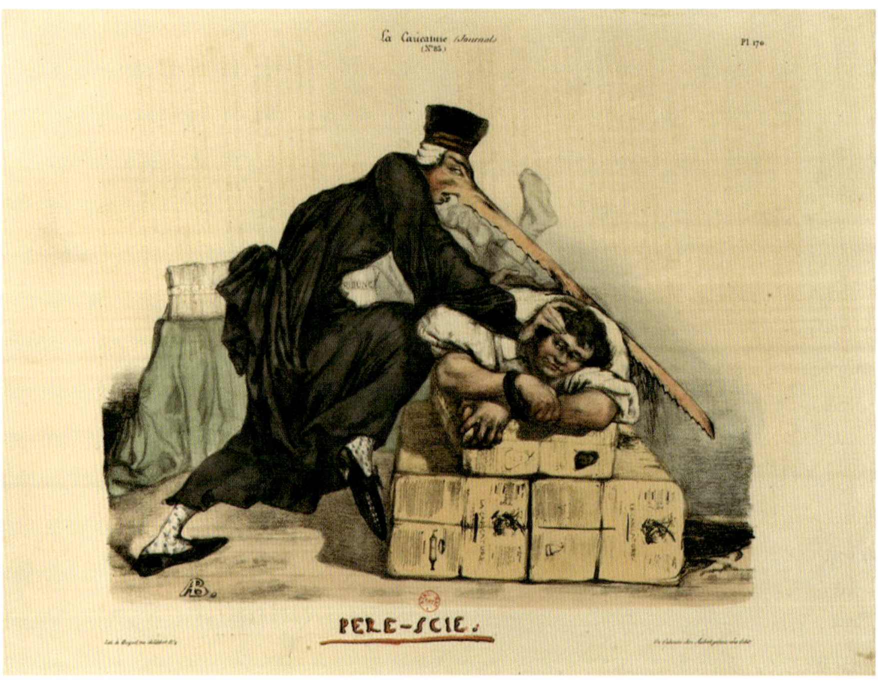

Figure 1.17 Auguste Bouquet, 'Père-Scie' [pun for Persil], 1832

Over time, the particularities of Daumier's grievances or the politicians' protruding noses mattered less than the symbolic authority offered by the lithograph 'Père-Scie', a typological abstraction that Daumier suggests through the shadowed ambiguity of the deputy's face, the medal on his chest, and the insignia the artist invents below. The mask, for Champfleury, is both a deception and a metaphor for the transformation into an archetype, of a portrait transformed into an enduring idea.

In his first attempt at this group, Daumier's faces are primarily studies in expression, not likenesses. In other words, they were pathognomic, not physiognomic. These masks are, therefore, different from the later portraits, which carried the ambition of not only exaggerating the appearance of these same legislators, but also of revealing overstated physiognomic traits and persistent historical *types*.

As we see with the print of Persil, the mask still underlies this series. The themes of costuming and masking would recur in Philipon and Daumier's practice, underscoring how a critical facet of satire explores identity and the performance of social roles. This is especially true in theatrical satire. Georges Buraud has theorized that the masking impulse initially emerged from the desire to steal the face of another. In order to live in a community, man must separate his essential self from the social roles required of him, a demand that leads to a doubling (*se dédoubler / un dédoublement*) of interior and surface.[58]

The tension between normal social performance of self and outright deception is thematized in many of Molière's plays. Molière played with the relationship between dressing up for the stage and for the world, revealing that the act of costuming is both theatrical and essentially social. Plots that pivot on concealment, on the recognition and misrecognition of disguise, appear over and over again in Molière's plays. Clitandre in *L'Amour médecin* and Adraste in *Le Sicilien* use 'substitution-disguises' in their respective plots.[59] Clitandre dresses himself as a doctor in order to marry Lucinde, and Adraste poses as a painter to access Isidore because fathers jealously guarded both women. Similarly, in *The imaginary invalid*, Cléante, suitor of the protagonist Argan's daughter Angélique, poses as the music teacher's replacement in order to see the young woman at home. Cléante's true feelings are only revealed within a performance for the family, when the couple sing an improvised opera costumed as shepherd and shepherdess. While Molière was likely not the only source of masking for Daumier, many literary critics in nineteenth-century France took note of this practice, and Daumier incorporated the mask in many paintings of Molière's plays, as the third chapter will describe.[60]

Molière also made use of actual masks in his performances. He incorporated typological characters and masks from the *commedia dell'arte*, a theatrical tradition that emerged in fifteenth-century Italy and became quite popular at the turn of the seventeenth century in France as the *comédie italienne*. In Daumier's lifetime it was commonly evoked in revivals of Molière, marionettes, and pantomimes.[61] Typically, in performances drawn from the *commedia dell'arte* tradition, a mask was used in farce or satire to link a character to an archetypal role.[62] The use of the mask by Daumier and Philipon suggests simultaneously an evasion of legal prohibitions on insulting against the chambers and an awareness of Molière's theatrical satires and their political activation during the troubles of the theatre in the years immediately preceding 'Jesuit', 'Oh! The dreadful mask!!!', and *Celebrities of the juste milieu*. The mask was a useful device to suggest the deception of politicians both as collective and historical types. As Daumier negotiated with censors representing politicians early in his career, masks helped to distance those representations by one step of removal. The motif of the mask made evident the playful performance of identity and the absurdity of political theatre.

Smuggled clay and democratic scrutiny

The pinched beaks and ruddy cheeks of the painted clay busts of the *Celebrities of the juste milieu* were not meant for exhibition, but rather they stayed in Philipon's office as referents for lithographs. On 26 April 1832, Philipon announced the *Celebrities* as the product of a transposition of likenesses from life to clay to lithography:

> *La Caricature* promised a gallery of portraits of the Celebrities of the juste milieu on schedule, from which the consciously studied resemblances should have possessed in addition to an energetic character, this burlesque trait known as a *charge*. Accustomed to carrying in its publications all the possible conditions for success, *La Caricature* deferred the realization of this project for some time because we had to create a model for each figure. It is then after these clay moulds that the sketches were executed.[63]

The Charter of 1830 opened the upper chamber of parliament to public view, a move towards openness echoing the end of hereditary succession and small expansions to suffrage.[64] In his presentation of the series, Philipon set the caricatures apart from other illustrative work in the journal by publicizing the project's genesis in the observation of contemporary figures, expanding access to the parliamentary body for his readership.

Since Philipon's early fame originated in the scandal generated by his 'Jesuit' print, based on Dantan jeune's caricatural sculpture, it makes sense that he would commission Daumier to create a set of sculptural models for celebrity lithographs to be published in his new illustrated journal. The lithograph, 'Ch. De Lam...', accompanied the *Celebrities* series announcement on 26 April 1832 (Figure 1.3). Daumier closely emulates his clay bust of Lameth (Figure 1.18), reproducing his downturned face, brimless hat, and side-buttoned coat in three-quarter view in the lithograph. Daumier's colleague Charles-Joseph Traviès also looked to the sculpture for his print, 'Musicien de la Chapelle ...', published in *Le Charivari* on 25 December 1832 (Figure 1.19). The sculpture's sullen face is replicated almost exactly in the two resultant prints. In the lithographs, Lameth's skin looks like roughly hewn rock, drawn after a bluntly chiselled three-dimensional model rather than a human face. Additionally, Traviès' print is a reverse image of Daumier's. Traviès' description of

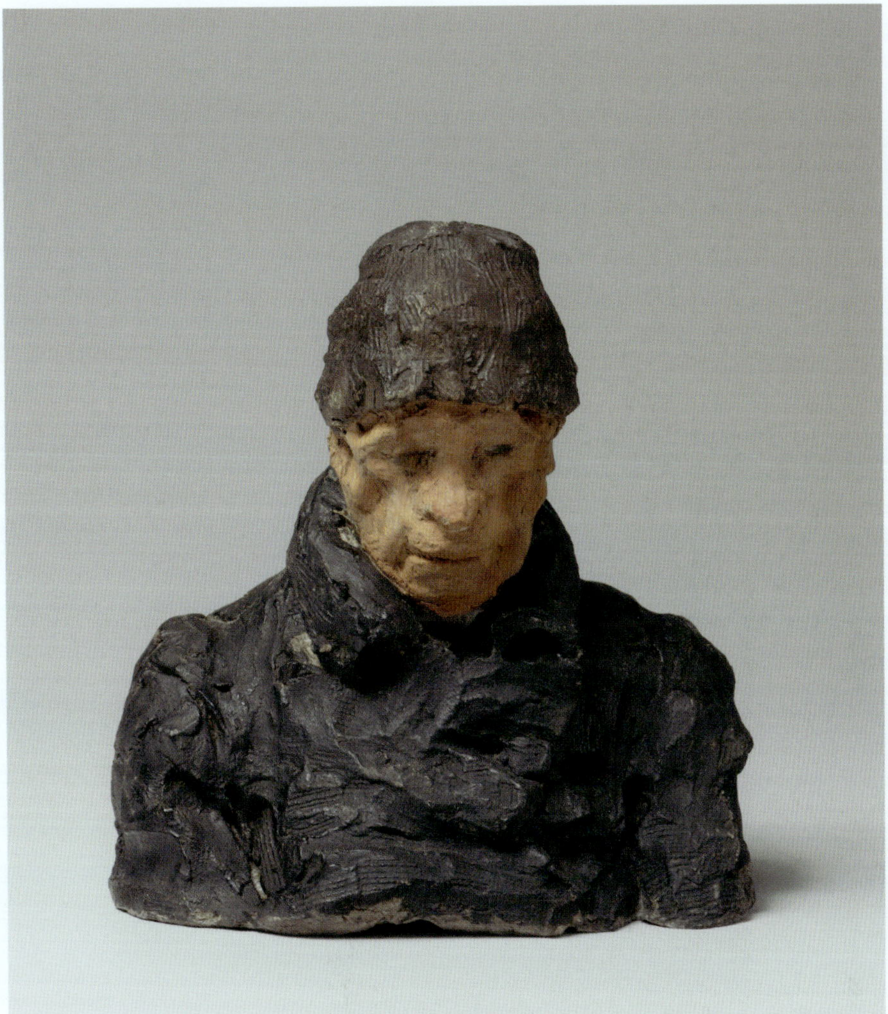

Figure 1.18 Honoré Daumier, *Comte Charles-François-Malo de Lameth*, 1832

Lameth's coat becomes less sure as Daumier's model fades, and he clumsily inserts a flute, played by disproportionately large hands.

Many artists working for Philipon would use Daumier's three-dimensional models, and these *portraits-charge* made individual parliamentarians recognizable in the illustrated press. Daumier, Traviès, and Grandville were able to extrapolate the original busts into a variety of angles and full-length views, and so the sculptures allowed for greater formal variety over many years. Like Dantan's sculpture of Charles X, Daumier's clay maquettes became a stable from which a world of lithographic images could emerge, images that announced their filial ties and sculptural origins and offered at least potential deniability to censors.

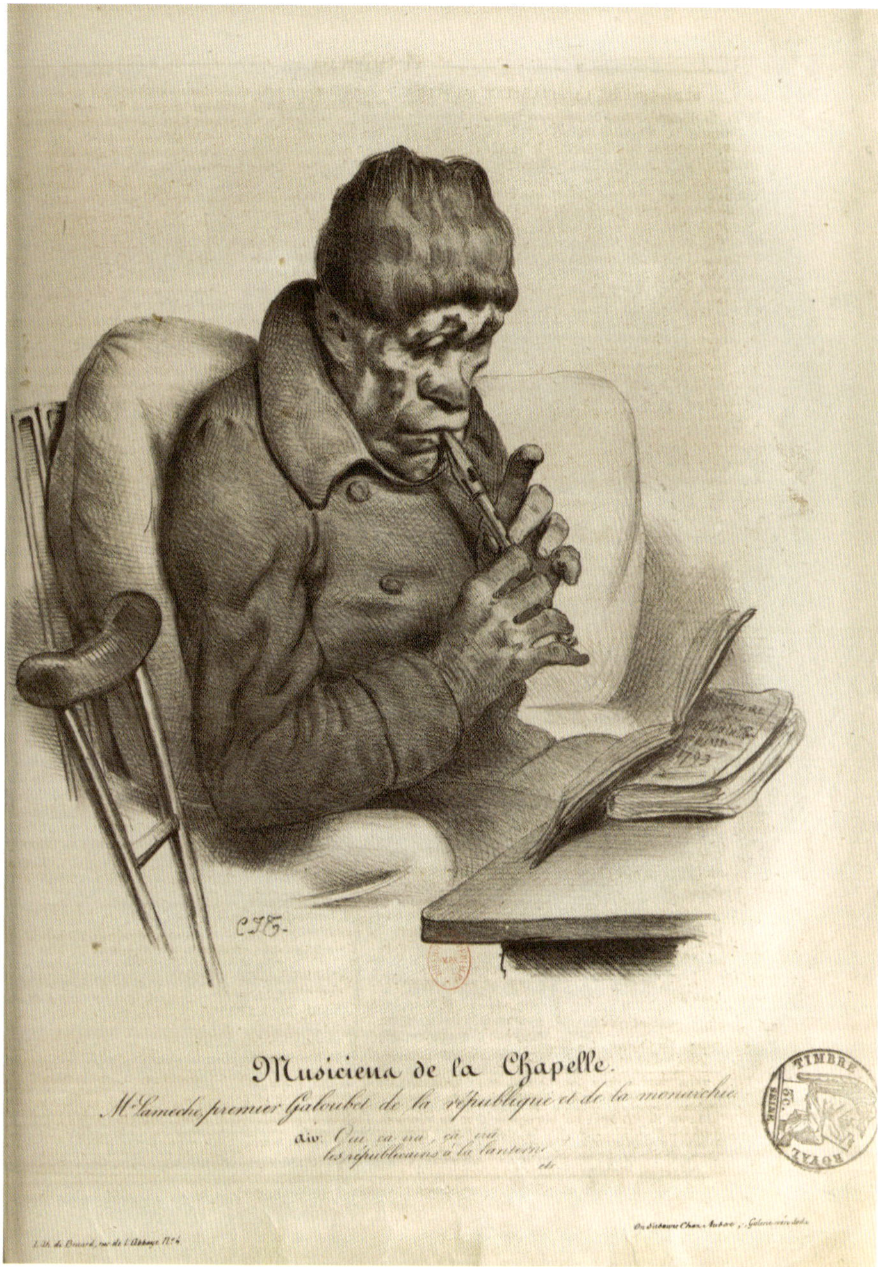

Figure 1.19 Charles-Joseph Traviès, 'Musicien de la Chapelle ...' *Le Charivari*, 25 December 1832

Accustomed to the responsive pace of lithographic technology, the illustrated journal was slowed down by Daumier's labour in an intermediary medium. In Philipon's announcement, a narrative of his thoughtful, tactile modelling in clay is set into tension with the paper's drive to deliver the news. Yet Daumier's particularized scrutiny of each of the figures of the *juste milieu* also lends authority to the images. The *portraits-charges*, however exaggerated or mocking, are rooted in realism and reportage. *La Caricature* did not always have the time for such projects – this delay was an exception, Philipon tells us – but Daumier had given the journal a set of clay sculptures from which many other sketches could be drawn. This is how the intermediary step in clay becomes subversive. Daumier shifted access to, and authority over, the physical model of politicians' likenesses to *La Caricature*. Solidified in hard matter and styled as sculptures from popular or celebrity culture, Daumier's caricatural distortions became the new referents for Lameth, Kératry, Falloux, and their political cohort. As the new source for subsequent portraits of the *Celebrities*, Daumier's sculptures emerged as a defiant act of artistic intervention into political representation and celebrity satire.

Daumier's *Celebrities of the juste milieu* sculptures included both François Guillaume Guizot and Pierre-Paul Royer-Collard. Guizot, a historian and minister in Louis-Philippe's regime, drew Daumier's ire by advocating for qualified suffrage, increased censorship, and the repression of republican leaders.[65] Daumier's clay portrait of Guizot features small, penetrating eyes, deeply incised frown lines, and rough-hewn cheekbones (Figure 1.20). A bump towards the top of Guizot's nose, subtly described in an oil portrait painted by George Healy about a decade after Daumier's bust (Figure 1.21), becomes magnified and increasingly hooked in Daumier's hand. Guizot seems to be balding by the 1830s or 1840s, but Daumier exaggerates the sloping forehead of the minister, carving in wrinkles and making his ocular bones more rugged and pronounced. While Daumier's *portrait-charge* amplifies physiognomic flaws, it also enlivens Guizot, lending the intellectual orator a thoughtful tilt to his head absent in the sculptures of some of his duller colleagues.

Daumier's sculpture bust of Royer-Collard is more caricatural and more humorous than Guizot's (Figure 1.22). A deputy and philosophy instructor, Royer-Collard was so frightened by the potential of Eugène Delacroix's painting *Liberty leading the people, 28 July 1830* (1830) to incite audiences to further rebellion that as Director of Fine Arts he took it off exhibition and put it into storage after only four months on display.[66] In the sculptural portrait, Royer-Collard's black hair crests implausibly above his forehead and ears. His nose, depicted quite handsomely in an engraved portrait from 1844 (Figure 1.23), slides precipitously down towards his lower lip in Daumier's sculpture. Eyebrows that seem to give up towards the outside of the eye, narrow downcast eyes, and a smallish head that sinks into an oversized coat make Daumier's sculptural portrait of Royer-Collard appear shrinking and pitiable in ways not characterized in Giroux's engraving. It is evident that Daumier created especially unflattering physiognomic exaggerations of advocates of censorship.

As Judith Wechsler has suggested, Daumier may have been satirizing the field of phrenology with these *portraits-charge*, sculpting meaningful ridges and reducing a person or personality to absolute externalities.[67] The exaggerated physical defects in Daumier's *charges* take on a moral dimension. Their beak-like noses, ruddy pallor, and corpulence

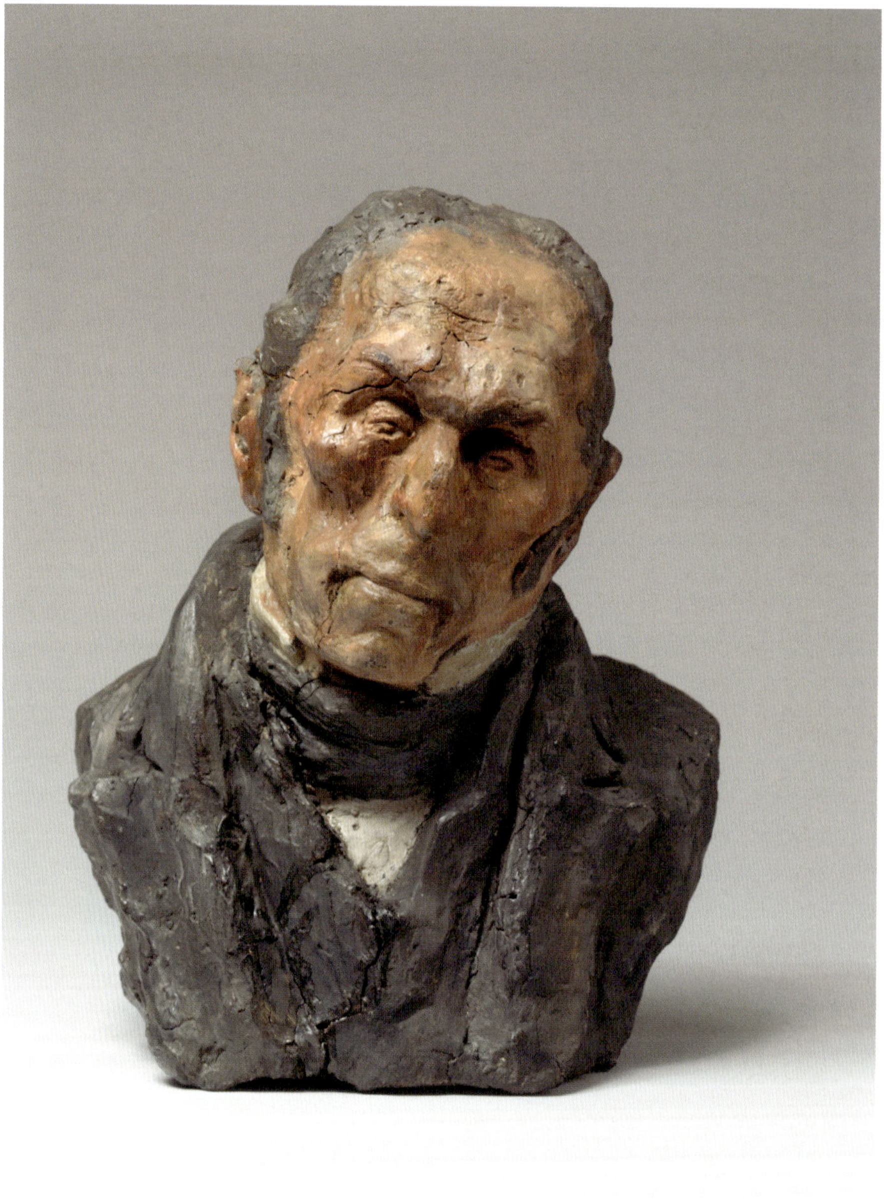

Figure 1.20 Honoré Daumier, *François Guillaume Guizot*, 1833

seem to signal sins of excess or untrustworthiness. Indeed, phrenology was 'an eminently sculptural theory', where one was meant to interpret permanent character types as well as shifting emotions through physiognomic traits.[68] Daumier's clay models also initiated a profound stylistic shift in Daumier's illustrated work. His explorations of permanent physical attributes and fleeting facial expressions in three dimensions gave his drawings

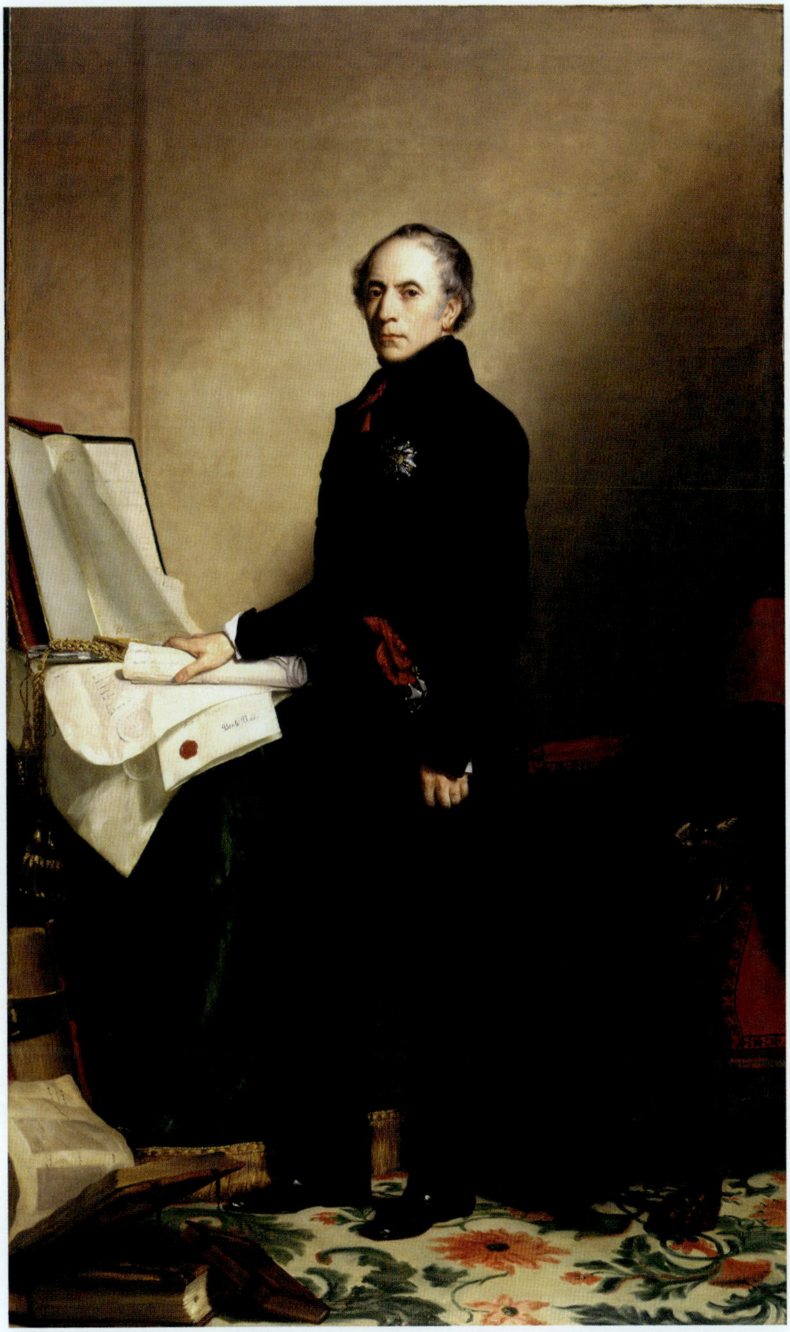

Figure 1.21 George Peter Alexander Healy, *François Pierre Guillaume Guizot*, 1841

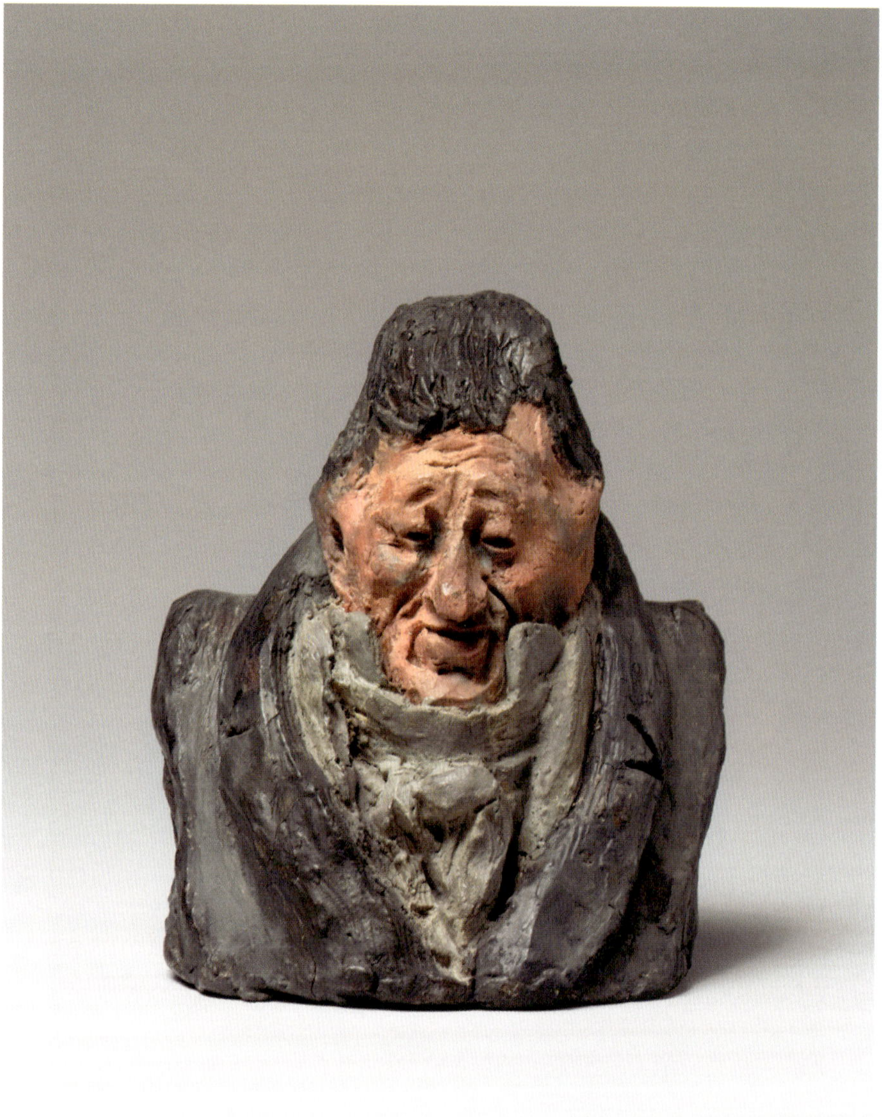

Figure 1.22 Honoré Daumier, *Pierre-Paul Royer-Collard*, 1833

a new sense of dimensionality and self-assurance, particularly when compared to early work like 'Les bons gendarmes'.

It is hard to overestimate the boldness of Daumier's technical experiment of sculpting the clay busts, particularly given that he had no formal training in sculpture. The bust of comte Charles-François-Malo de Lameth is likely the first *portrait-charge* Daumier sculpted. It shows Daumier's technical facility; the clay remains in excellent condition, lacking the fissures that plague some of the other unbaked clay portraits.[69] This is perhaps owed in part to the artist's friendship and possible collaboration with the sculptor

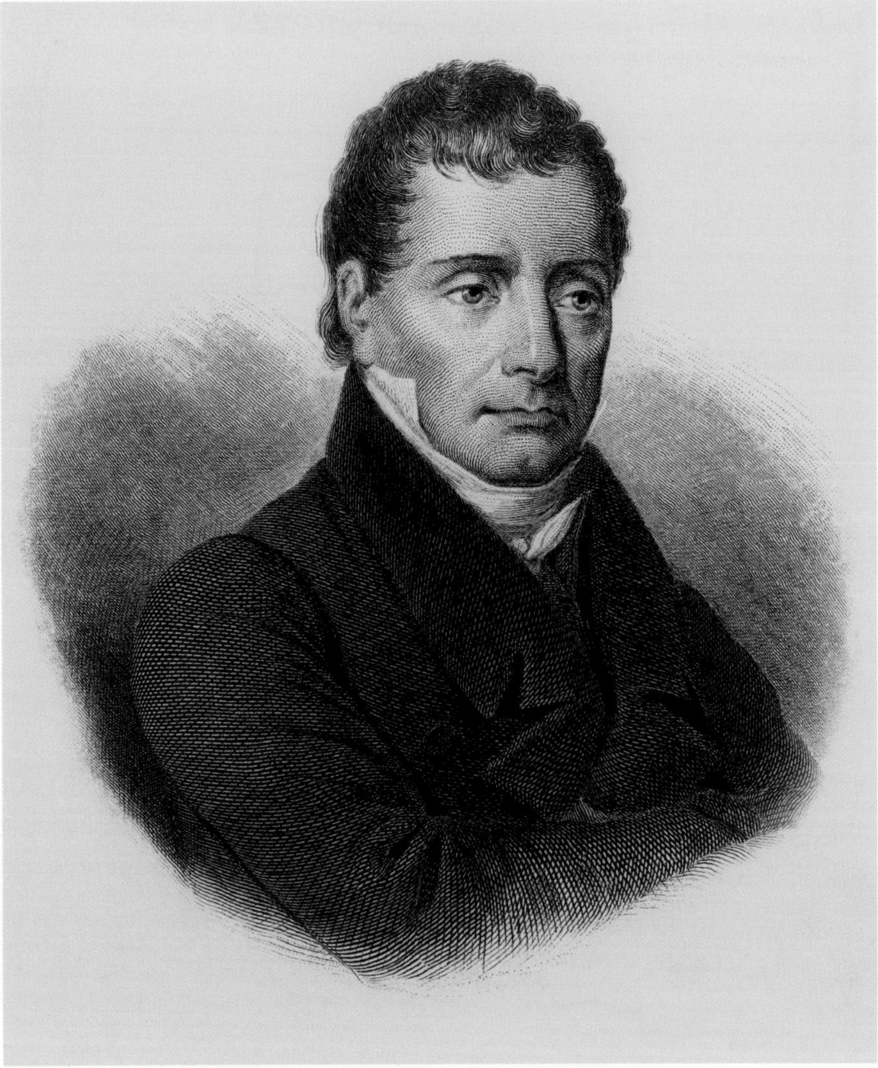

Figure 1.23 François Giroux, *Portrait of Pierre-Paul Royer-Collard*, 1844

Auguste Préault, whom Daumier met in 1823. Indeed, the *livret* for the Salon of 1830 lists Daumier as a co-creator of Préault's bas-relief *Two slaves cutting the throat of a young Roman actor*.[70] Préault likely helped Daumier with basic techniques in clay modelling. Around this time, Préault tended to leave scores from the teeth of his tools on the surfaces of his sculptures, a strategy Daumier also employed in the *Celebrities of the juste milieu* series. This is particularly evident in Lameth's hat, which shares the same short scrapes of a knife that appear in the background and scroll elements of Préault's *Model for the Schoelcher tomb* (c. 1832, Figure 1.24). These marks of the artist's hands and tools would not have been acceptable for public exhibition. Even in Préault's expressive Romantic sculptures,

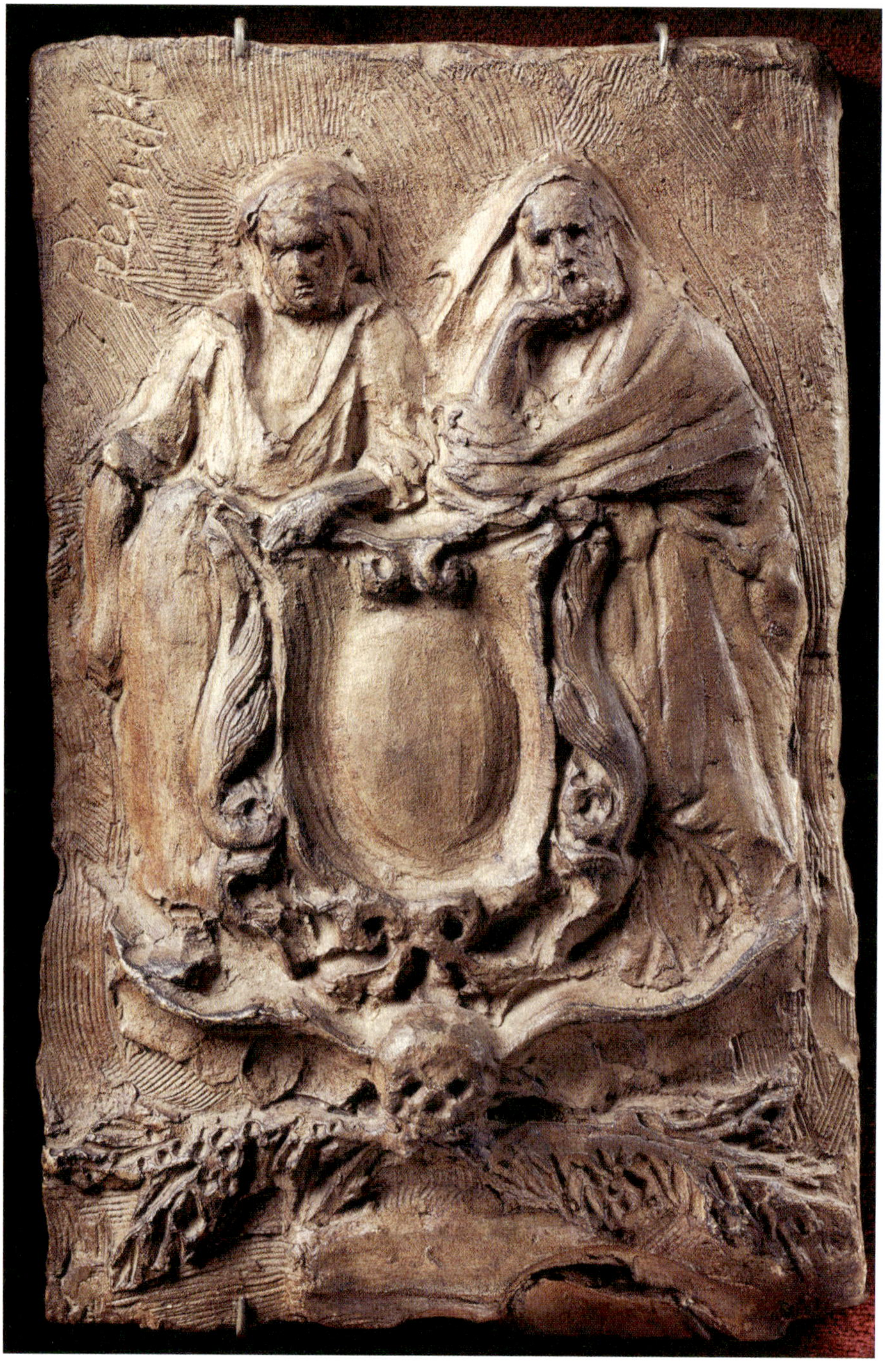

Figure 1.24 Auguste Préault, *Model for the Schoelcher tomb*, c. 1832

the technique of scoring a surface with parallel serration lines appears only in the background. Daumier's *Lameth* lacks a careful symmetry or a polished surface, as was fitting for a rough or unfinished clay maquette. Daumier's sculptures are considered maquettes, hasty sketches or scale models, and in fact a technical analysis by the Musée d'Orsay from 2005 determined that Daumier completed each of these portrait busts quickly, applying the paint while the clay was still tacky.[71]

Comte Charles-François-Malo de Lameth was from a distinguished military family and, after suffering a wound at Yorktown, was also a hero of the war of American Independence. During the French Revolution, he was part of the left-leaning coalition of the National Assembly, advocating for the freedom of the press and of religion. He was exiled in 1792 and restarted his political career after finally returning to France in 1809. Replacing his brother Alexandre-Théodore-Victor, he took a seat in parliament with the Royalist-Constitutionalists in 1829. Soon after, in the early days of Louis-Philippe's reign, the newly re-elected Lameth stood for conservative ideals, advocating for the country to maintain a hereditary system for the Chamber of Peers.[72] For Daumier, Lameth represented a betrayal of the Great Revolution and as a result his sculptural bust appears deflated and perhaps burdened with regret. For Champfleury, this inversion of the heroic ideal was 'a revelation'.

> At that time, art had raised the flag of violence: the movement was opposed to peace, the passionate to the cold, and ugliness to beauty. Such is the nature of revolutions to act on both art and politics. This portrait of old Lameth was a revelation. Henceforth, Daumier looked over the major peers of France, making reliefs that seemed to have been detached from a Trajan's Column of constitutional monarchy. It is not a pencil nor chisel, but a sarcastic stigmata that marked the peerage so deeply.[73]

With *Lameth*, Daumier considered the representative's legacy of disappointment and the responsibility of art to adjust to the messy narratives of living men. In doing so, he took a conventional object of celebrity culture – the statuette – and brutalized it.

Daumier's small busts were part of a wider craze in early nineteenth-century France for celebrity portraits in the round. By 1845, celebrity statuettes were so popular that the journal *Paris comique* published the following commentary:

> Nowadays, the statuette is submerging us; it is an epidemic; a public calamity. Statuettes are made with the same facility as are caps for guns and sealing wax. They are made of plaster, of cast iron, of papier mâché, of biscuit, of colored glass; they are sold by ironmongers, by stationers, by print sellers and by tobacconists. The time is past when barely one saint or one dancer in marble was issued in six months; at the present time it is enough to advise your artist twelve hours in advance to have a whole museum of celebrities delivered; it takes no more time than a quarter of an hour to bake a dancer or five minutes to cast a diplomat.[74]

Statuettes were appealing because they were tradable, decorative, and easily made. They could be found in modest materials and commissioned to create a bespoke gallery in one's home. Time is once again at issue. The article emphasizes the incredible – almost industrial – speed of production, a speed that threatened institutions and reputations. Ubiquitous and affordable, small portrait statues democratized the idea of a museum of great men.

The tactility of celebrity statuettes appealed to the democratic ideals of a post-revolution generation. As Gustave Planche stated in 1835, in a review of sculpture in that year's Salon,

> It is Plutarch who said, 'The images of great men give us a powerful excitation to do good', and indeed, we cannot see this too closely, and it is even necessary that the blind can touch their hands to these sacred images, so that the blind themselves can have an idea of the human form that takes virtue from the earth.[75]

For Plutarch and Planche, art had ethical and didactic missions. Portraits in particular could inspire feelings of aspiration and moral certainty. Planche further reasoned that the tactility of three-dimensional objects could be a metaphor for access and erudition. Particularly after the iconoclasm of the late eighteenth century, proximity to objects and to the images of men was political. The tactility and smallness of the celebrity statuette meant possibilities for owners to demonstrate allegiance and understanding with certain values through their domestic presentation.

In the early decades of the nineteenth century, Napoleon promoted the cultivation of heroic personalities. This, coupled with the promotion of isolated individualism by the Romantic generation, led to an obsessive veneration of public figures in the first half of the century.[76] The press was a new and essential force for immortalizing the public image of writers and cultural figures, and the reassessment of the biographical tradition led to a new anchoring in the present and a celebration of living figures.[77] Emerson Bowyer describes this 'age of pantheons' thusly: 'Eulogies, collective biographies, dictionaries of celebrated contemporaries, series of portrait prints, and even waxwork museums – all these probed the category of the *grand homme*, rushing to fill its borders with a litany of exemplary names.'[78] Among the new celebrants of the *grand homme* were such sculptors as Dantan jeune and Pierre-Jean David, who would become famous as David d'Angers (1788–1856).

Around 1830–31, just before Daumier would begin his *Celebrities of the juste milieu* series, David d'Angers wrote about his growing project of small portraits: 'I continually pursue my gallery of great men.'[79] His *Gallery of contemporaries* was a more private version of another memorializing sculpture project in the 'age of pantheons', Louis-Philippe's plan for a museum at the Château de Versailles. In the early years of the July Monarchy Louis-Philippe imagined a project for collecting the busts of famous men, a custom linked to the traditions of Roman sculpture.[80]

Daumier's sculptural busts satirized the stateliness of such memorials, chronicling the yawns, squints, and hanging jowls of politicians, thereby making the members of a new political class recognizable. During the first public exhibition of the *Juste milieu* sculptures at Daumier's retrospective in 1878, Champfleury made this connection explicit even at a distance of many decades, writing that the 'portraits are more real than the majority of those in the galleries in Versailles'.[81] The series drew on common strategies for memorialization in order to parody the cult of great men.

We can also link Daumier's *Celebrities* series to a tradition of engraved portraiture in the eighteenth century as well as a growing fad for *dictionnaires des contemporains*, encyclopedic books of lithographic portraits of contemporary figures, often including short biographical sketches.[82] For instance, François Delpech began his project the *Iconography of contemporaries* in 1823, publishing two lithographic portraits per month for nine years. By 1832, when *Celebrities of the juste milieu* appeared in print, Delpech had published around 200 portraits and the series had become so popular that it was republished in book form.[83] Delpech's prints feature lithographic portrait busts, carefully modelled with detailed costumes and identified by names in both script and signature, as is evident in Delpech's print of Dubois (Figure 1.25).[84] Daumier almost certainly would have known of this popular series, and his prints would follow closely in this model, but in parody. They include abbreviated names or revealing titles below detailed, three-dimensional lithographic portraits, seizing upon the subject's physical flaws with cruel exaggeration (Figure 1.26).

Like David d'Angers, Philipon imagined his commission as an answer to the galleries of great men, and like David d'Angers and the *dictionnaires des contemporains*, he aimed to create a portrait series of specifically *contemporary* figures. As he refined the conception of this project, he called it both a 'gallery' and a 'monument', emphasizing its memorializing ambitions and contemporaneity:

> This great gallery to the dishonoured, for whom the talent of Mr Daumier is a guarantee of resemblance ... will be so interesting for our customers when it will be complete and include everything that needs to be distinguished among potbellied gluttons. It is a monument that we raise to contemporary stupidity.[85]

Philipon set the series in *La Caricature* apart from other prints in the illustrated press by dramatizing the sculptural basis of the portraits reproduced, which also distinguished it from the other celebrity dictionaries and illustrated galleries. He also followed the tradition of Molière, who wrote of his ambition 'to present a general picture of all the defects of men, and especially of the men of our own age'.[86]

Caricatures of the king sufficed when there was an absolute monarchy. However, when the July Monarchy ushered in a parliamentary system with real power, a new group of political players became important to the public and to caricature. Finding ways for a public figure to be instantly recognizable in mass representation, even when drawn by

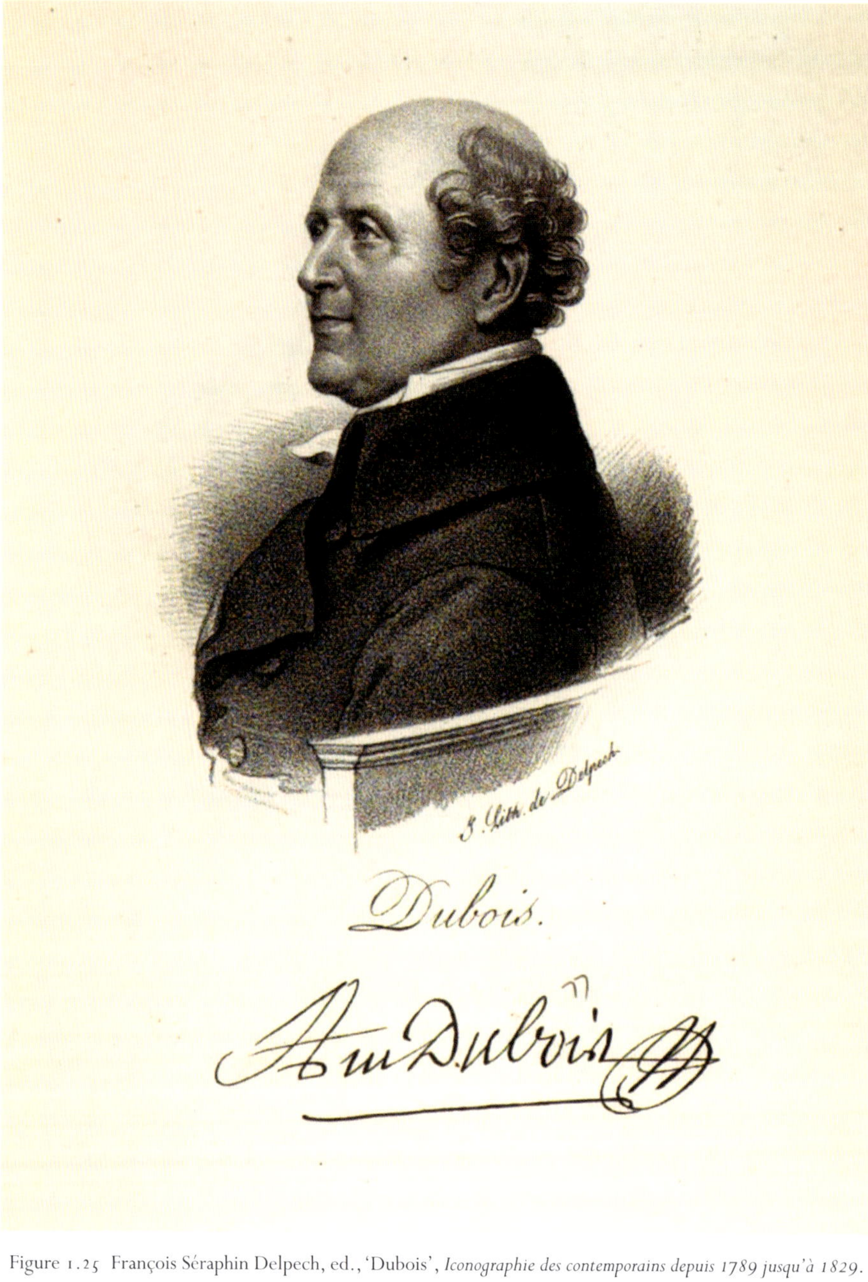

Figure 1.25 François Séraphin Delpech, ed., 'Dubois', *Iconographie des contemporains depuis 1789 jusqu'à 1829*. Paris: Delpech, 1832.

numerous artists, is a problem that persists in caricature today, and it was an ingenious solution by Philipon to create a fixed set of typologies for many artists to work from.

One of the largest of the *Celebrities* sculptures and one of the first of the series is *Unknown, called Frédéric Alfred, comte de Falloux?* (c. 1832, Figure 1.27).[87] Daumier modelled a rough bust and then removed sections of clay in order to build the features of 'Falloux's'

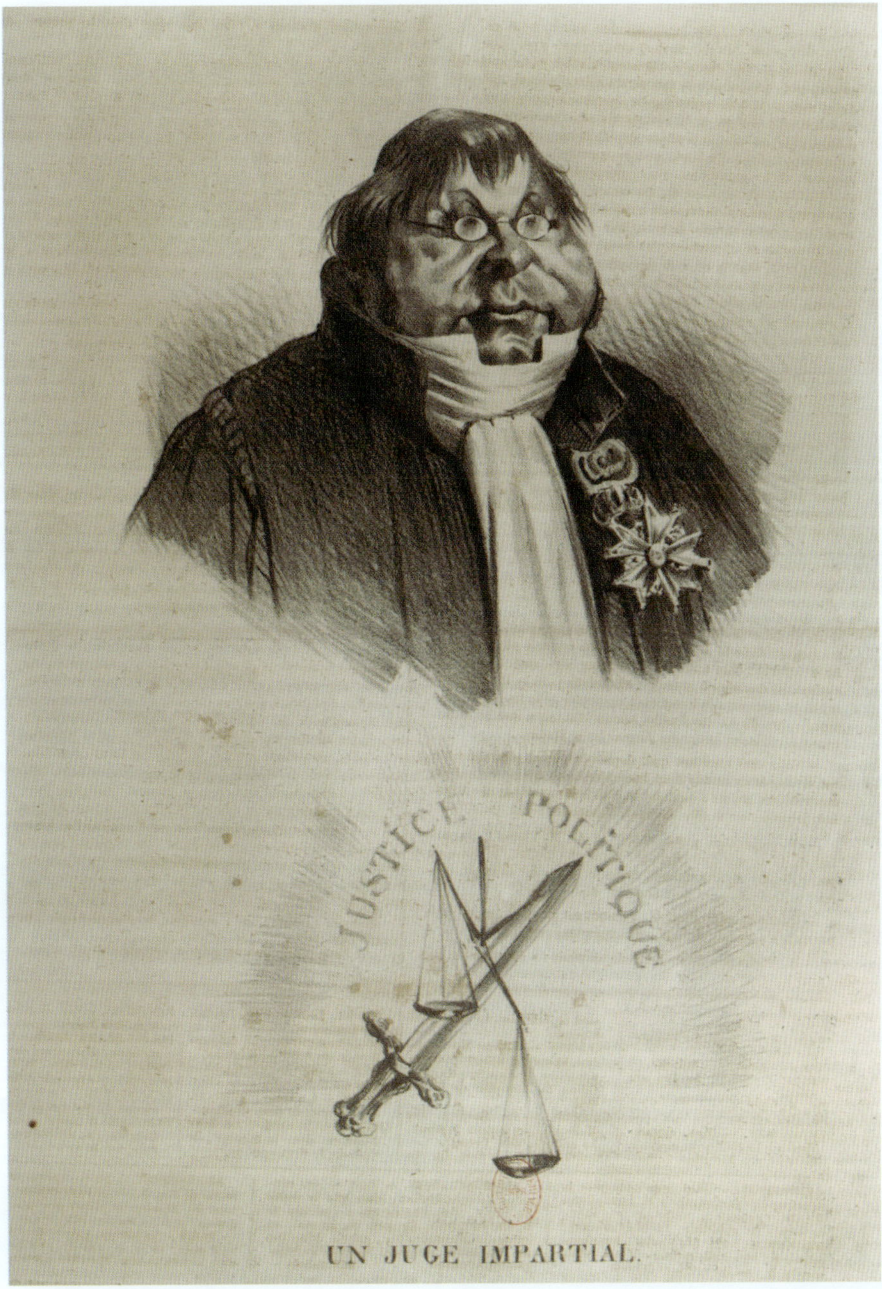

Figure 1.26 Honoré Daumier, 'Mr Tu-Bois: An impartial judge' ('M. Tu-Bois: Un Juge impartial'), *Le Charivari*, 25 March 1833

narrow face. The artist emphasized the length of the subject's visage with deep, vertical trenches on either side of his nose, in parallel to those stretching from the corners of his mouth to his chin, and mirroring the gashes next to his fanning sideburns. Shallow, serrated divots create pinched wrinkles below Falloux's eyes and in three rhyming V-shaped

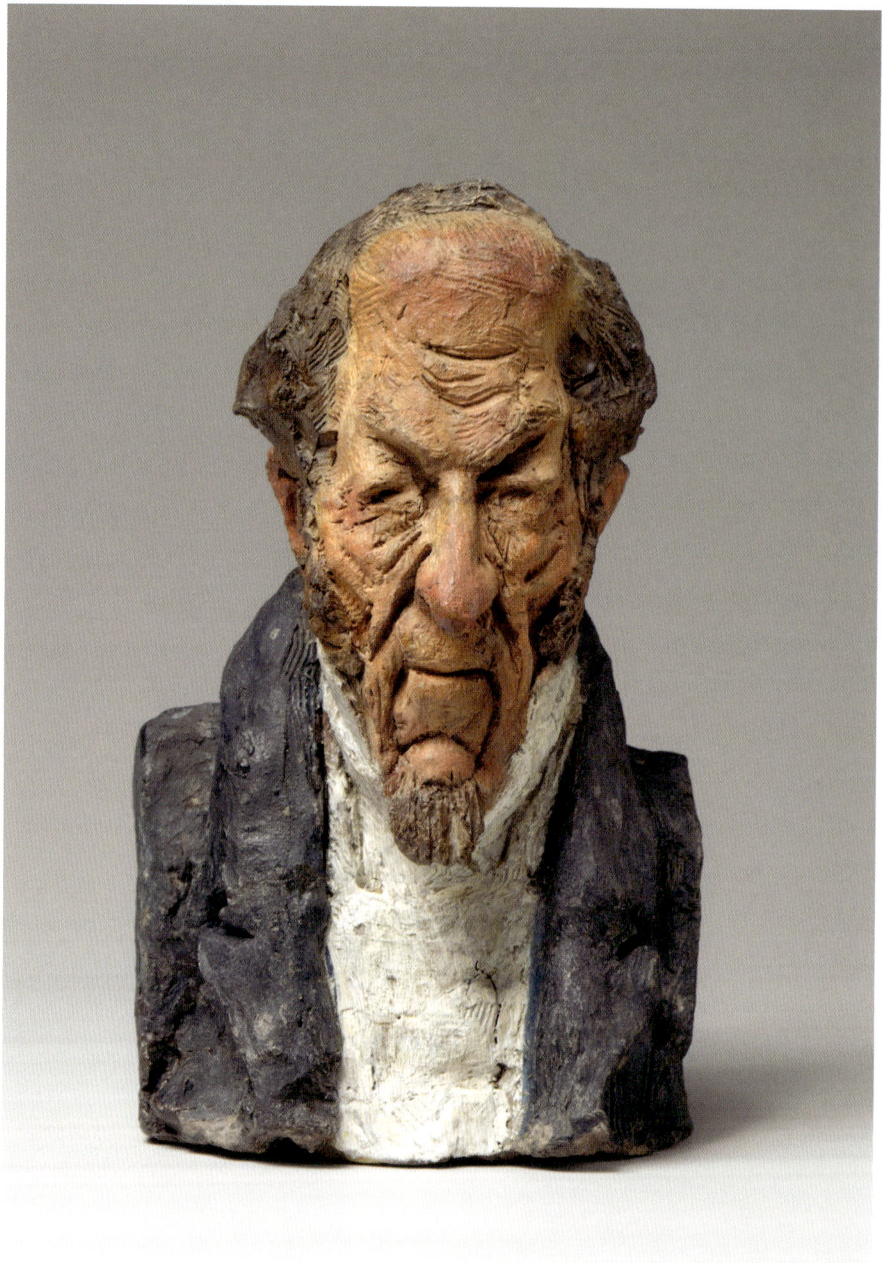

Figure 1.27 Honoré Daumier, *Unknown, called Frédéric Alfred, comte de Falloux*, c. 1832

lines above his eyebrows. Even the collar of the sitter's coat has been scooped away from the clay around his shoulders in order to define the height of the starched cloth. Daumier removes matter in order to define physiognomy, a very different process than the positive lithographic application of crayon to stone. However, his method shares with lithography a demonstrable speed of execution. The clay of the *Juste milieu* sculptures reserves the traces of Daumier's hand and suggests a material immediacy.

Daumier's rapid gestures in these portrait busts suggest not a formal sitting, but a hurried impression. The exact circumstances of production remain unclear, but the series has inspired two telling origin myths, both establishing Daumier's caricatural authority in terms of his direct observation and in-person occupation of the parliamentary space. Champfleury, writing a generation after the sculptures were made, claimed: 'So I would only say that Daumier attended the meetings of the Chamber of Peers, a piece of modelling clay in hand, moulding from life some small busts, after which he would lithograph his plates.'[88] A similar account by Bernadille added that Daumier sculpted the clay busts clandestinely inside his hat.[89]

That Daumier took wet lumps of clay into the Chamber of Peers is unlikely from a practical standpoint, but it is not surprising that Champfleury, an early champion of Realism, promoted a narrative of objects being constructed *sur nature*. Two decades later, journalist and art historian Gustave Geffroy observed the *Juste milieu* series when they were in the possession of Philipon's grandson. Geffroy's account, published in 1905, emphasizes Daumier's speed of construction. He cites Champfleury's account but corrects the timeline slightly. According to Geffroy, Daumier visited the chamber, but instead of kneading the clay inside its walls he sculpted the figures immediately after departing:

> Champfleury, in his *History of Modern Caricature*, speaks of the cartoonist's strange approach and claims that Daumier attended the meetings of the Chamber of Peers, a piece of modelling clay in hand, moulding some small busts *sur nature* ... He kneaded some figurines in just a few seconds with a small bit of modelling clay, and with quick encouragement he brought out the characteristic traits of the subjects that he wanted in an astonishing fashion ... [I]n reality it was by memory, but an immediate memory in leaving the meetings, where the investigative and ruthless eyes of Daumier trained their predatory vision on his victims.[90]

Geffroy championed Cézanne, Monet, and the Impressionist movement, so he emphasized the freshness of Daumier's impression, the *souvenir immédiat*, and his speed of execution ('Il pétrissait alors en quelques secondes').

The dual origin stories and conspicuous facture of Daumier's *Celebrities of the juste milieu* imply both access to, and scrutiny of, the parliament. The king's likeness was easily available in oil paintings or engraved reproductions, and Dantan jeune – like James Gillray in England – could use those official portraits to create his caricatures. Historically, it was harder to access or recognize parliamentary deputies.[91] In 1830, sittings of the Chamber of Deputies were made public, turning visibility into a new liberty.[92] The citizen's observation of a legislative body in both Champfleury and Geffroy's narratives bolsters Daumier's Realist credentials, but also provides a small fable of an ideal republic. The caricaturist becomes a kind of conduit for the larger public, his physical proximity to government dramatizing the promise of democratic access. These sculptures memorialized Daumier's observation of the *juste milieu* and also allowed for the possibility of its re-creation, generating a kind of perpetual opportunity for scrutiny by journalists and artists in Philipon's office.[93] Daumier's clay statuettes were also, in this way, a testament to and a hedge against the instability of the political climate. They allowed Daumier, Grandville, and Traviès to continue to make caricatures of the *juste milieu* in spite of the whims of the parliament and its eventual shuttering to dissenting observers.

Daumier's technical facility as a caricaturist, even in the early 1830s, meant that he could execute lithographs quickly, at the pace required by the routinized work of Philipon's commercial practice. Daumier had the ability to create *portraits-charges* of politicians without the kind of inconvenient labour of observation or the intermediary step of creating a sculptural model that, as Philipon stressed, delayed the debut of the *Celebrities of the juste milieu* in the paper. Daumier's clay busts solidified the derisive distortion of a caricatural sketch, preserving the precious liberty of democratic scrutiny in three dimensions. The size of these statuettes, about as tall as the palm of your hand, linked them to cults of celebrity, debasing the so-called great men of the day with low-class entertainments and commercial 'epidemics'. Daumier appropriated the portability and visibility of popular sculpture, expanding the project into the illustrated press. The prints particularized the crimes of the *juste milieu* and, through detailed modelling and invented iconographic systems, claimed the authority of direct observation. Handed a window of visibility into parliamentary disorder, Daumier seized it, constructing a new set of terms that would become the foundation for subversive political speech in the years to come.

Conclusion

In addition to celebrity portraits, the tidy grouping of detached heads in *Masks of 1831* also hints at an intersection with the popular culture of sculpted and grotesque heads, particularly displays of wax figures and guillotined bodies at the turn of the eighteenth and nineteenth centuries. A print by Jean-François Janinet shows Madame Tussaud's mentor, Dr Philippe Guillaume Mathé Curtius (né Creuz or Kurtz), holding wax busts of the duc d'Orléans and Jacques Necker (Figure 1.28). Curtius's presentation of the heads stirs excitement in the room, and Janinet leaves some ambiguity about whether the reaction is driven more by the likeness of the duke or the novelty of this popular reproductive technology. These wax heads were taken from Curtius's museum and carried through the city in effigy.

News of Necker's dismissal had just reached Paris, and the procession of his wax head was a defiant act of political protest triggering the first act of bloodshed in the French Revolution.[94] This political pageant and display of heads would be eerily repeated not long afterwards with the severed head of Louis XVI, represented in images such as 'Food for thought for the crowned jugglers' ('Matière à reflection pour les jongleurs

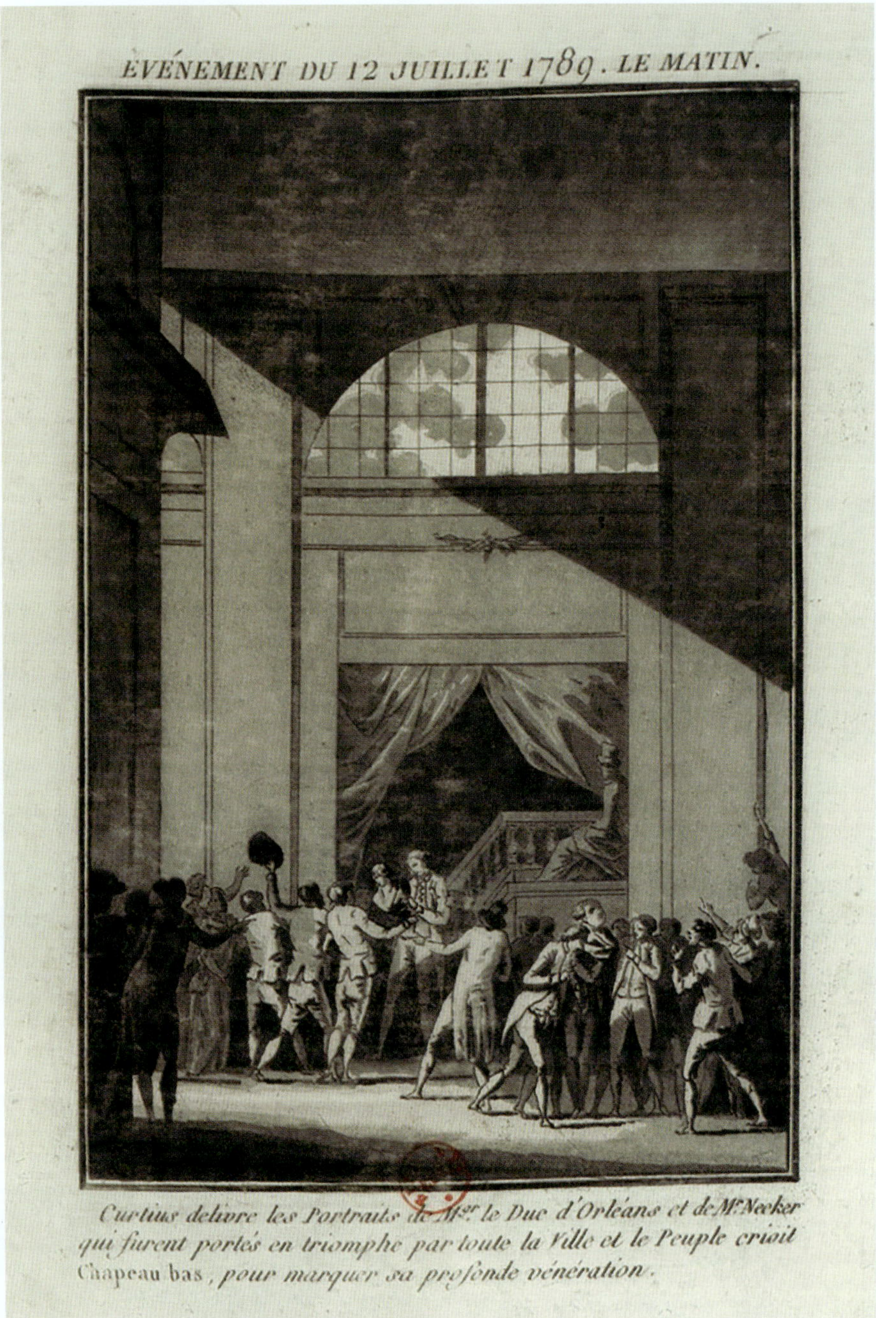

Figure 1.28 Jean-François Janinet, 'Événement du 12 juillet 1789 – le matin: Curtius délivre les portraits de Mgr le duc d'Orléans et de Mr Necker qui furent portés en triomphe par toute la ville et le peuple criait chapeau bas, pour marquer sa profonde vénération', 1789–91

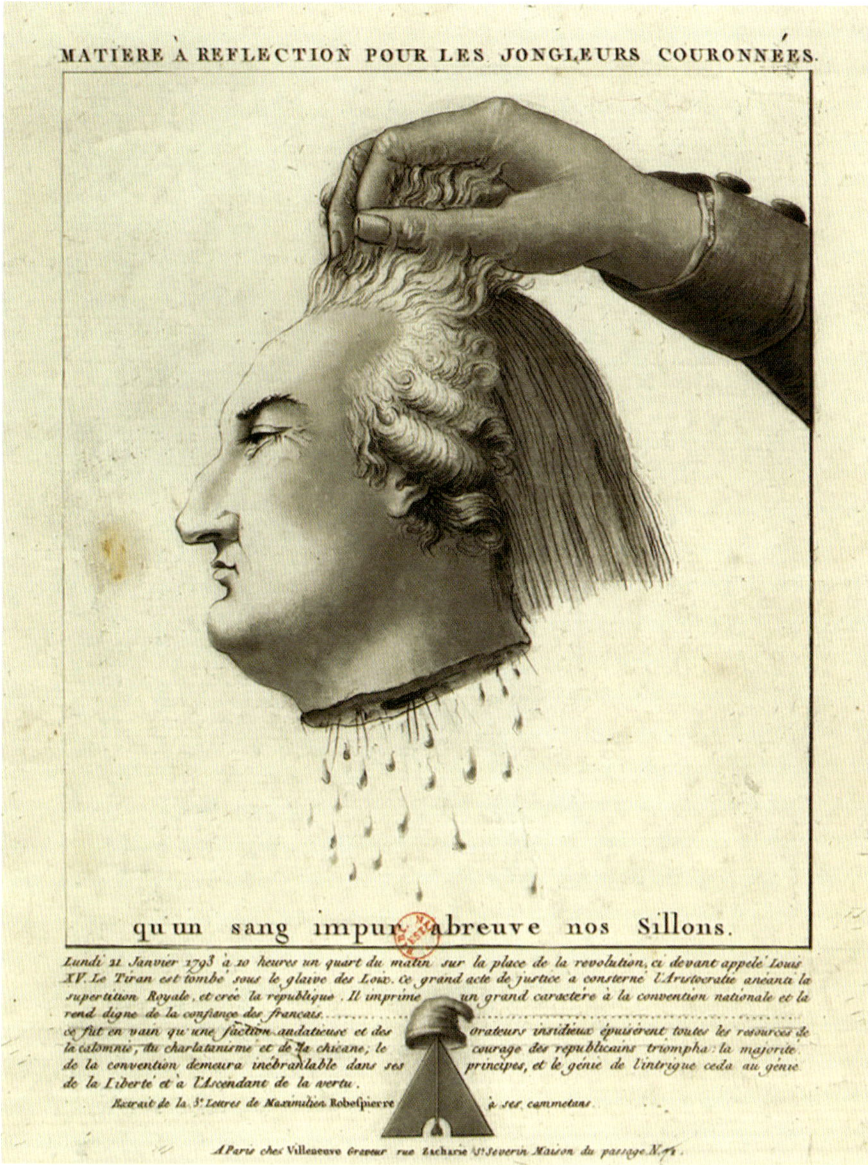

Figure 1.29 [Villeneuve publisher], 'Food for thought for the crowned jugglers' ('Matière à reflection pour les jongleurs couronnés'), 1793

couronnés') of 1793 (Figure 1.29). The objectification and detachment – the *skinning* effect – of Daumier's *Masks of 1831* carried some of these associations. It held a threat that Daumier would soon transfer into the safer spaces of puns and invented crests. This displacement of violence from *Masks of 1831* to Persil's crest, for instance, would also, critically, place cruelty and injustice in the hands of the government, not in the imagination of the caricaturist.

Because of the two masks behind the making of Persil, there was a sense of detachment, or mortification, that lingered. After all, underneath the masks of Charles X and Persil, the referent was not reality; it was the dead matter of clay and another layer of representation that offered deniability in libel suits. Philipon chose to sketch a cartoon of Dantan jeune's *sculpture*, not the king himself. His image was already removed from reality by a layer of mediation and interpretation, a process analogized by the mask. Daumier's clay busts similarly blurred the lines between referent and translation – dead matter and imitated flesh – until the repetition became a kind of disorientation. This was the point: train your eyes to distrust representations and you may train yourself to distrust representatives. Politics, like caricature, was a world of exaggeration and hollow ideas, a grotesquerie. After an initial investigation of masking procedures in Philipon and Daumier's political caricature of the 1830s, which followed the subversive political revival of Molière in the 1820s, Daumier would return more forcefully to the playwright's theatrical satire in another period of censorial conflict with the state.

Daumier would continue to exploit and parody the age of pantheons and the cult of the *grand homme* as he took up subjects from literary great men such as La Fontaine, Molière, and Cervantes in the decades that followed. Memorialized in the eighteenth century as proof of Louis XIV's good government, the first two of these authors were the subjects of government sculpture contests and panegyrics at the Académie Française.[95] La Fontaine's *Fables*, Molière's theatrical works, and Cervantes's *Don Quixote* were three of the best-selling books during the formative years of Daumier's life. Between 1815–25 La Fontaine's *Fables* was top of the bestseller list, with forty-four editions published at global print runs of around 95,000–105,000. There were twenty-one editions of Molière's plays in these four short years, a print run of 28,000–35,000, and six editions of Cervantes's novel, where about 19,000–21,000 copies were published at a moment when there were rarely more than 1,000 editions of a novel in print.[96] These popular texts, from authors embroiled in their own censorship restrictions, would replace the cruel likenesses of politicians as the thin scrims covering the contours and sharp edges of subversive political speech.

Notes

1 'La censure / Seule est sûr / Pour gouverner, je l'assure; / La censure / Sans blessure / Guérit le mal / Libéral'. Félix Auguste Duvert, Etienne-Vincent Arago, and Joseph Xavier Boniface, *Cagotisme et liberté, ou les Deux semestres, revue de l'année 1830* (Paris: J.-N. Barba, 1830), 6.

2 Elizabeth C. Childs, 'Big trouble: Daumier, Gargantua, and the censorship of political caricature', *Art Journal* 51, no. 1 (1992): 26–7. Daumier, Aubert, and Hippolyte Delaporte were brought to trial on 22 February 1832 for designing, exhibiting, selling, and printing the lithograph that had been submitted to the *Dépot legal* on 16 December 1831.

3 For more on the trials, see Childs, 'Big trouble', Elise Kenny and John Merriman, *The Pear: French Graphic Arts and the Golden Age of Caricature*, exh. cat. (South Hadley, MA: Mount Holyoke Art Museum, 1991), and Sandra Petrey, 'Pears in history', *Representations* 35 (Summer 1991): 52–71.

4 Charles A. Knight, *The Literature of Satire* (Cambridge: Cambridge University Press, 2004), 119–20.
5 David H. Pinkney, 'Conflict without compromise', in *French Revolution of 1830* (Princeton, NJ: Princeton University Press, 1972), 42–3.
6 'Mais ce serait nier l'évidence que de ne pas voir dans les journaux le principal foyer d'une corruption dont les progrès sont chaque jour plus sensibles, et la première source des calamités qui menacent le royaume.' 'Rapport du roi', *Le Moniteur universel* 207 (26 July 1830): 813. These new policies were announced in *Le Moniteur universel* 207 (26 July 1830): 813–15.
7 H. A. C. Collingham and R. S. Alexander, *The July Monarchy: A Political History of France 1830–1848* (New York: Longman, 1988), 6–8.
8 Collingham and Alexander, *The July Monarchy*, 25–9.
9 Pinkney, 'Conflict without compromise', 42–3.
10 Karen F. Beall, 'The interdependence of printer and printmaker in early 19th-century lithography', *Art Journal* 39, no. 3 (Spring 1980): 196.
11 James Cuno, 'Charles Philipon and la Maison Aubert: The business, politics, and public of caricature in Paris, 1820–40' (PhD diss., Harvard University, 1985), 67–9.
12 David S. Kerr, *Caricature and French Political Culture 1830–1848: Charles Philipon and the Illustrated Press* (Oxford: Clarendon Press, 2000), 8.
13 Richard Terdiman, *Discourse / Counter-Discourse: The Theory and Practice of Symbolic Resistance in Nineteenth-Century France* (Ithaca, NY: Cornell University Press, 1985), 47. Theodore Zeldin, *France 1848–1945*, vol. 2 (Oxford: Clarendon Press, 1977), 540.
14 Kerr, *Caricature and French Political Culture,* 9.
15 Kerr, *Caricature and French Political Culture*, 10.
16 Alex Djordjevic et al., 'New results for DR6', Daumier Register, www.daumier.org/fileadmin/daumier_reference/DR6_E.htm (accessed 11 December 2015). Djordjevic makes this argument based on the figure's beard and, most persuasively, on the striped shawl detail which likely references the coat of arms of Polignac's family.
17 Bruce Laughton, *Honoré Daumier* (New Haven: Yale University Press, 1996), 60. See also: Bruce Laughton, 'Some Daumier drawings for lithographs', *Master Drawings* 22, no. 1 (1984): 56–133.
18 Maurice Gobin, *Daumier sculpteur 1808–1879: avec un catalogue raisonné et illustré de l'œuvre sculpté* (Geneva: Pierre Cailler, 1952), 21.
19 Kerr, *Caricature and French Political Culture*, 11–13. Kerr notes that Philipon used the 'Jesuit' scandal to establish revolutionary credentials in the prospectus for this journal, even though before the 1830 Revolution he was preparing to work for the royalist weekly *Le Lys, chronique de la Cour*.
20 *La Silhouette* was not exclusively left-leaning. Diverse political viewpoints were represented and satirized in its pages. Kerr, *Caricature and French Political Culture*, 11.
21 J. R. Pole, 'Representative institutions 1776–1876: Ideology, estates and interests', *Parliaments, Estates and Representation* 27, no. 1 (2007): 26.
22 Judith Wechsler, *A Human Comedy: Physiognomy and Caricature in 19th Century Paris* (Chicago: The University of Chicago Press, 1982), 69–70.
23 Gerd Unverfehrt, Westfälisches Landesmuseum für Kunst und Kulturgeschichte Münster, Universität Göttingen, and Gutenberg-Museum Mainz. *La Caricature: Bildsatire in Frankreich 1830–1835 aus der Sammlung von Kritter: [Ausstellung] Westfälisches Landesmuseum für Kunst und Kulturgeschichte Münster 16 März–10 Mai 1980 Kunstsammlung Der Universität Göttingen 26 Oktober–7 Dezember 1980 Gutenberg-Museum Mainz 20 April–7 Juni 1981*, exh. cat (Göttingen: Kunstgeschichtliches Seminar der Universität, 1980), 29.

24 Alain Vaillant, 'Les sociétés d'auteurs et la censure au XIXe siècle', in *La Censure en France à l'ère démocratique, 1848-* (Brussels: Éditions Complexe, 1997), 105.

25 'Les Français ont le droit de publier et de faire imprimer leurs opinions, en se conformant aux lois. Le censure ne pourra jamais être rétablie.' 'Déclaration de la Chambre des Députés', *Le Moniteur universel* 222 (10 August 1830): 877.

26 Unverfehrt, *La Caricature*, 27–8.

27 Édouard Papet, 'Les Célébritiés du Juste Milieu (1832–1835)', in *Daumier: Les Célébritiés du Juste Milieu (1832–1835): Étude et restauration* (Paris: Réunion des musées nationaux, 2005), 15. The catalogue notes that for a long time the series was considered as Daumier's idea and that it began with the artist's portrait sculpture of Philipon. However, it seems more reasonable to assume that the series was at least partially the initiative of Philipon. Papet also notes the existence of other lithographs in this style, suggesting that there were more than forty statuettes in total. He believes that not all of the sculptures were conserved by Philipon and therefore some have gone missing or were destroyed (35).

28 Kenny and Merriman, *The Pear*, 21; and Kerr, *Caricature and French Political Culture*, 11.

29 Robert Justin Goldstein, 'The debate over censorship of caricature in nineteenth-century France'. *Art Journal* 48, no. 1 (Spring 1989): 15; and Kerr, *Caricature and French Political Culture*, 11–12.

30 Sheryl Kroen, *Politics and Theater: The Crisis of Legitimacy in Restoration France, 1815–1830* (Berkeley, CA: University of California Press, 2000), 4.

31 Kenny and Merriman, *The Pear*, 9–21.

32 Janet Seligman, *Figures of Fun: The Caricature-Statuettes of Jean-Pierre Dantan* (New York: Oxford University Press, 1957), 37–41.

33 Florence Quideau, 'Origins of modernism in French romantic sculpture: David d'Angers, Dantan-Jeune, Daumier and Préault' (PhD diss., Rutgers, The State University of New Jersey, 2011), 229. For the use of this verb, see also: 'Trois nouveaux Dantanisés', *Le Vert-Vert* (14 November 1833).

34 Jean-Pierre Dantan, Philippe Sorel, Musée Carnavalet, and Maison de Balzac. *Dantan Jeune: Caricatures et portraits de la société romantique: Maison de Balzac* (Paris: Direction des affaires culturelles de la Ville de Paris: Paris-Musées, 1989), 27–32.

35 Dantan jeune made two sculptures of Charles X, one in the costume of a Jesuit and the other *à la française*. Some authors allege that Dantan jeune also made two sculptures of Louis-Philippe which are not extant today. If they had existed, they were likely backdated from around 1848 to 1830. See Quideau, 'Origins of modernism in French romantic sculpture', 211–12, and Dantan et al., *Dantan Jeune*, 32.

36 Quideau, 'Origins of modernism in French romantic sculpture', 212–14. This dating could be self-serving. It is possible Dantan did not anticipate the revolution by so many months.

37 Quideau, 'Origins of modernism in French romantic sculpture', 221.

38 For a comparison of Jesuit imagery with the *poire*, see also: Fabrice Erre, 'The "King-Jesuit" and the "King-Pear:" The proliferation of seditious "mischief" against Charles X and Louis-Philippe (1826–1835)', *Romanticism* 150, no. 4 (2010): 109–27.

39 Kerr, *Caricature and French Political Culture*, 16–17.

40 While the lithograph 'Encore un petit moment' was not published, it was likely exhibited at La Maison Aubert, the publishing house Philipon established with his brother-in-law Gabriel Aubert in the Passage Véro-Dodat in the Passage des Panoramas. In December of 1829, Aubert went bankrupt and was forced to sell his notary practice. Philipon offered to set up a print business with him to keep his family out of financial insolvency, and La Maison Aubert opened

on 15 December 1829. La Maison Aubert sold lithographs that Philipon commissioned, including prints like 'Encore un petit moment', and its windows served as a site of public access and commercial enticement '*Encore un petit moment, je vous en prie ...*' Daumier Register, http://daumier-register.org/werkview.php?key=4 (accessed 8 April 2014), and Kerr, *Caricature and French Political Culture*, 7–10.

41 The French association of the pear with Louis-Philippe began at the trial of Daumier's editor, Charles Philipon. In November 1831, Philipon went to trial for violating the press laws of 1830 by publishing 'Replastering (Dupinade)', or 'The Mason' ('Le Replâtrage [Dupinade]', or 'Le Maçon'). In his statement to the court before his conviction, he constructed two arguments. On the one hand, Philipon insisted on the audacious overreach of a law that would condemn a print based on loose resemblance. He also claimed that in order to communicate abstract ideas in pictorial formats, the artist must often turn to symbols and personification. Philipon's step-by-step transposition of an image from portrait to pear dramatically demonstrates the challenge in finding a clear line between satire and resemblance. Charles Philipon, *Les Poires faites à la cour d'assises de Parie [sic] par le directeur de* la Caricature *vendues pour payer les 6,000 francs d'amende du journal* (Paris: Auffray, 1833). Also Wechsler, *A Human Comedy*, 71–5.

42 Papet, *Daumier*, 43–5.

43 Papet, *Daumier*, 20–1.

44 See, for example, the defence for the 25 June 1830 trial of Victor Ratier and Benjamin Louis Bellet for offending the person of the king. The attorney Woolis questioned the government's certainty about the portrait's resemblance. Goldstein, *Censorship of Political Caricature*, 115–16.

45 Emmanuel Bénézit, *Dictionnaire critique et documentaire des peintres, sculpteurs, dessinateurs et graveurs: de tous le temps* ... 4 (Paris: Gründ, 1976), 238. The few exceptions involved a few comical portrait statues of the aristocracy in England. In Paris, Dantan jeune seemed to begin his practice of 'caricature sculptée' around 1829 and treated personalities like Victor Hugo, Rossini, Balzac, Dumas, Frédérick Lemaître, and Paganini. Dantan et al., *Dantan Jeune*, 27–32.

46 Childs, 'Big trouble', 26–37.

47 Pole, 'Representative institutions', 27.

48 Papet, *Daumier*, 15.

49 Victor E. Starzinger, *Middlingness:* Juste Milieu *Political Theory in France and England, 1815–48* (Charlottesville, VA: The University Press of Virginia, 1965), viii–55. There are many complexities surrounding the parties and personalities in government after 1830. However, Guizot and Royer-Collard are exemplary in that having lived through the Great Revolution. Royer-Collard was a member of the convention in 1793 and nearly lost his life in the Terror, and Guizot's father died by the guillotine. They were extremely wary of threats to order and blocked reform in its name (20, 55). Although Guizot led a liberal current, seeking to end theocracy by limiting the influence of the church in education, he also led attacks on associations and could not tolerate opposition after 1830. Robert Alexander, *Rewriting the French Revolutionary Tradition: Liberal Opposition and the Fall of the Bourbon Monarchy* (New York: Cambridge University Press, 2003), 299–311. See also Pierre Rosanvallon, *Le Moment Guizot* (Paris: Gallimard, 1985) for a detailed analysis of Guizot and the crucial question of the relationship between liberalism and democracy.

50 Alexis de Tocqueville, *The Recollections of Alexis de Tocqueville*, ed. J. P. Mayer, trans. Alexander Teixeira de Mattos (New York: Meridian Books, 1959), 2–3.

51 Laughton, *Daumier*, 10.

52 De Tocqueville, *Recollections*, 8.

53 De Tocqueville, *Recollections*, 3.

54 'Nous donnons le portrait du plus cruel ennemi de la Liberté, et surtout de la presse.' L. Derville, 'Planches, *La Caricature* 127 (11 April 1833): 1015.

55 Delaporte mistakenly identifies the censor as Persil. He is actually d'Argout. Christian Delporte, '"Anastasie:" L'imaginaire de la censure dans le dessin satirique (XIXe–XXe siècles)', in *La censure en France à l'ère démocratique, 1848–* ..., ed. Pascal Ory (Brussels: Éditions Complexe, 1997), 91.

56 'Un portrait moral', Papet, *Daumier*, 96–7.

57 'M. Persil fut une puissance ce n'est plus qu'un masque. Un jeune artiste avec son crayon arrive au relief des médailles, et ce crayon, rien ne peut l'effacer. La politique du temps est oubliée, la royauté disparaît, l'homme meurt; reste une feuille de papier avec un masque de procureur générale. Toujours, dans les moments de trouble, la foule veut voir dans l'accusateur public une figure qui ressemble à ce portrait. L'individu s'efface pour faire place à un type.' Champfleury claims to quote Saint-Beuve in the above passage. Champfleury [Jules Husson], *Exposition des peintures et dessins de H. Daumier* (Paris: Gauthier-Villars, 1878), 14–15.

58 Georges Buraud, *Les Masques* (Paris: Encre Marine, 2015), 9–11.

59 D. B. Wyndham Lewis, *Molière: The Comic Mask* (New York: Coward-McCann, 1959), 180.

60 See for example: Louis Émile Dieudonné Moland, *Molière et la comédie italienne* (Paris: Didier et cie, 1867), 23–4, 140. Édouard Fournier understands Molière's mask to be both a strategy of costuming and a common metaphor for deception and social performance in his plays. Édouard Fournier, *Études sur la vie et les œuvres de Molière* (Paris: Laplace, Sanchez, et Cie, 1885).

61 Molière's incorporation of *commedia* themes is well documented. See, for example, Moland, *Molière et la comédie italienne*; and Pierre Louis Duchartre, *The Italian Comedy: The Improvisation, Scenarios, Lives, Attributes, Portraits, and Masks of the Illustrious Characters of the Commedia dell'Arte*, trans. Randolph T. Weaver (New York: Dover Publications, 1966).

62 Duchartre, *The Italian Comedy*, 20–2.

63 '*La Caricature* avait, dans le temps, promis à ses abonnées une galerie de portraits des célébrités du Juste-Milieu, dont les ressemblances, consciencieusement étudiées, devaient posséder en outre ce caractère énergique, ce trait burlesque, connu sous le nom de *charge*. Habituée à porter dans ses publications toutes les conditions possibles du succès, *la Caricature* a différé quelque temps la réalisation de ce projet, parce qu'elle a fait modeler chaque personnage *en maquette*. C'est ensuite d'après ces moules [sic] de terre que les dessins ont été exécutés.' 'Planches', *La Caricature* 78 (26 April 1832): 622.

64 Pinkney, 'Conflict without compromise', 42–3.

65 Gérard Unger, 'Daumier et Gizot: le choc inévitable', *Cahiers Daumier: bulletin de l'Association des amis d'Honoré Daumier* 2 (spécial 2008): 61–3.

66 Roy Howard Brown, 'The formation of Delacroix's hero between 1822 and 1831', *The Art Bulletin* 66, no. 2 (June 1984): 248.

67 Wechsler, *A Human Comedy*, 137.

68 Emerson Bowyer and Frick Collection, *David d'Angers: Making the Modern Monument* (New York: Frick Collection, 2013), 36. The difference between type (Physiognomics) and feeling (Pathognomics) is explained in Wechsler, *A Human Comedy*, 15, 139–145, 179.

69 Papet, *Daumier*, 80–2. Lacking definitive archival evidence, the order of construction is under debate. Quideau's 'Origins of modernism in French romantic sculpture' suggests the sculpture of Daumier's editor Charles Philipon was the first, a joke that launched the series (231).

70 Papet, *Daumier*, 14–15. For the date Daumier met Préault, see: *La sculpture des peintres: Honoré Daumier, Edgar Degas, Paul Gauguin, Pierre-Auguste Renoir ... 2 juillet–19 octobre 1997* (Saint-Paul: Fondation Maeght, 1997), 28. In 1856, Théophile Silvestre lists this work as being

in Daumier's collection: Théophile Silvestre, *Histoire des artistes vivants, français et étrangers, études d'après nature* (Paris: E. Blanchard, 1856), 302. Its location is not presently known.

71 Papet, *Daumier*, 20.

72 Adolphe Robert, Edgar Bourloton, and Gaston Cougny, *Dictionnaire des parlementaires français …: depuis le 1er mai 1789 jusqu'au 1er mai 1889*, vol. 3 (Paris: Bourloton, 1889), 565–6.

73 'A cette époque, l'art avait inscrit la violence son drapeau: le mouvement était oppose au calme, le passionné au froid, le laid au beau. Tel est le propre des révolutions d'agir à la fois sur l'art et sur la politique. Ce portrait du vieux Lameth fut une révélation. Dès lors, Daumier passa en revue les principaux pairs de France, en faisant des reliefs qui semblent détachés d'une colonne Trajane de la royauté constitutionnelle. Ce n'est plus un crayon, non plus un ébauchoir, c'est un stigmate sarcastique qui marque profondément la pairie.' Champfleury, *Histoire de la caricature moderne*, 3rd ed. (Paris: E. Dentu, 1885), 33–4.

74 Quoted in Seligman, *Figures of Fun*, 13. Translation is Seligman's.

75 'C'est Plutarque qui l'a dit: "Les images des grands hommes nous sont une puissante excitation à bien faire"; et en effet, nous ne pouvons pas le voir de trop près, et il faut même que les aveugles puissent toucher de leurs mains ces images sacrées, afin que les aveugles eux-mêmes aient une idée de la forme humaine que peut prendre la vertu sur la terre.' Gustave Planche, 'La sculpture: Salon de 1839', *L'Artiste* 2, 2nd ed. (1839): 309, quoted in Laurent Baridon, 'Jean-Pierre Dantan, le caricaturiste de la statuomanie', Robert, et al. *Dictionnaire des parlementaires français …*, 127–43.

76 Seligman, *Figures of Fun*, 52.

77 Jean-Claude Bonnet, *Naissance du Panthéon: essai sur le culte des grandes hommes* (Paris: Fayard, 1998), 146–9.

78 Bowyer and Frick Collection, *David d'Angers*, 27.

79 Pierre-Jean David d'Angers, *Les Carnets de David d'Angers* I (Paris: Plon, 1958), 99, quoted in Bowyer and Frick Collection, *David d'Angers*, 65.

80 'Partie officielle: Rapport au roi' *Le Moniteur universel* 248 (5 September 1833): 1. This project was to include 'la suite des portraits de tous les personnages qu'on peut considérer comme historiques, et dont la carrière a obtenu une célébrité quelconque'.

81 Champfleury, *Exposition*, 10.

82 Anne McCauley, *A. A. E. Disdéri and the Carte de Visite Portrait Photograph* (New Haven: Yale University Press, 1985), 56, 237. McCauley reviews a few of these illustrated volumes, including L. G. Michaud's 52 volume *Biographie universelle – ancienne et moderne* (1811–28), reissued in a 45-volume edition (1854–65), *Un homme de rien, Galerie populaire des contemporains illustrés* (Paris, 1840), *Iconographie des contemporains* published by Delpech in 1832 and reissued as *Célébrités contemporains* in 1842, both with lithographic portraits and text, Sarrut and Bourg's illustrated *Biographie des hommes du jour* (Paris 1835–43), Lalanne, Remer, and Bernard's *Biographie portative universelle* (1844 and 1852).

83 Patricia Mainardi, *Another World: Nineteenth-Century Illustrated Print Culture* (New Haven: Yale University Press, 2017), 34.

84 François Séraphin Delpech, ed., *Iconographie des contemporains depuis 1789 jusqu'à 1829* (Paris: Delpech, 1832), NP.

85 '[C]ette grande galerie d'improstitués dont le talent de M. Daumier est un gage de ressemblance … sera si intéressant pour nos abonnés, lorsqu'elle sera complète et qu'elle comprendra tout ce qui mérite d'être distingué parmi les ventrigoulus. C'est un monument que nous élevons à la sottise [sic] contemporaine.' 'M. Odieux', *La Caricature* 137 (20 June 1833): 2.

86 Andrew Calder, *Molière: The Theory and Practice of Comedy* (London: The Athlone Press, 1993). From Scene 4 of *L'Impromptu de Versailles.*

87 This is almost certainly a misattribution. Falloux was a legitimist and a Catholic; however, he was elected to the Chamber of Deputies in 1846 and born in 1811, so he would have been too young and unimportant when Daumier sculpted this portrait bust. The attribution is made because of a resemblance to the figure in Daumier's lithograph 'Saint-Ignatius of Falloux' from 1849. I do not agree with Wasserman's (1983) conjecture that this might be from an addition to the *Juste milieu* series during the Second Republic. National Gallery of Art (US), Ruth Butler, Suzanne G. Lindsay, and Alison Luchs, eds., *European Sculpture of the Nineteenth Century* (Washington: National Gallery of Art; Oxford University Press, 2000), 147.

88 'Si je ne disais que Daumier assistait aux séances de la Chambre des pairs, un morceau de terre glaise en main, modelant sur nature de petits bustes, d'après il lithographiait ses planches.' Champfleury, *Histoire de la caricature moderne*, 34.

89 Victor Champier, *L'Année artistique. Année 1878(–1882)* 1 (Paris: A. Quantin, 1879), 359, quoting Bernadille in *Le Français* (26 April 1878).

90 'Champfleury, dans son Histoire de la caricature moderne, parle de l'étrange façon de procéder du caricaturiste, et prétend que Daumier assistait aux séances de la Chambre des pairs, un morceau de terre glaise en main, modelant sur nature de petits bustes ... Il pétrissait alors en quelques secondes, avec un peu de terre glaise, des figurines, et en rapides coups de pouce il accentuait d'une étonnante façon les traits caractéristiques des sujets qu'il voulait des ... en réalité, été fait de souvenir, mais de souvenir immédiat, en sortant des séances où les yeux investigateurs et impitoyables de Daumier avaient exercé leur vision de proie sur ses victimes.' Gustave Geffroy, 'Daumier sculpteur', *Les Arts et les artistes* 1, no. 3 (June 1905): 102.

91 McCauley writes that because the average lithographic portrait tended to idealize the faces of famous figures, even an avid consumer of the biographical press would not have been able to identify them on the street. McCauley, *Disdéri*, 57.

92 Pole, 'Representative institutions', 27.

93 Quideau asserts that because of occasional visits from censoring officials, Philipon would not have displayed them in his office, but this claim is unsupported by available evidence. 'Origins of Modernism in French Romantic Sculpture', 237. Geffroy, on the other hand, reports that the sculptures occupied two vitrines in the office at the time they were photographed by Philipon's grandson and were thus likely similarly displayed in the 1830s. Geffroy, 'Daumier sculpteur', 104.

94 David McCallam, 'Waxing revolutionary: Reflections on a raid on a waxworks at the outbreak of the French Revolution'. *French History* 15, no. 2 (June 2002): 153–73.

95 Bonnet, *Naissance du panthéon*, 391–6.

96 Roger Chartier and Henri-Jean Martin, *Histoire de l'edition francaise: Le temps des éditeurs* (Paris: Fayard/Promodis, 1990), 416–17.

2

Fables and La Fontaine

Daumier first explored intersections between great art and laughter in his early paintings inspired by Jean de La Fontaine, establishing himself as an artist in line with celebrated satirists of the French literary canon. The fables of La Fontaine allowed Daumier and his fellow caricaturists to make allusions to contemporary political issues in the 1830s when direct political speech was restricted in the illustrated press. La Fontaine later became the subject of Daumier's first painting submission to the Salon, *The miller, his son, and the ass* from 1849 (Figure 2.1). This chapter establishes *The miller, his son, and the ass* as an early and profound exploration of the intersection between humour and the fine arts in Daumier's oeuvre, and here we can see the artist finding form for political dissent in paint. This case study will be instructive for investigations of his later engagement with Molière and Cervantes and sheds light onto the artist's broader engagement with seventeenth-century satire, balancing the revival of a well-known literary motif and the contemporaneity of critical speech.

The miller, his son, and the ass was not only Daumier's first artwork accepted to the Salon but also the only work he exhibited in the Salon of 1849 and only his second painting shown to a broad public.[1] Ambitious in size and compositional drama, the painting depicts a raucous trio of barefoot village women calling back to a miller and his son who are taking their donkey to market in the painting's middle ground. Daumier represents figures from a fable by Jean de La Fontaine (1621–95), the seventeenth-century French poet and writer whose *Selected fables put into verse* took the form of twelve books published between the years of 1668–94 that explored morality, satire, and intermittently reflected contemporary politics.

The miller, his son, and the ass sets two groups into conflict with each other. In the foreground, a tangle of three women march forward towards the viewer. A central woman with fair hair bends her neck backwards as her body spills forward in a long stride, creating a crescent shape that ties her to the women on either side of her. One elbow covers the arm of a dark-haired woman at right who seems to shout loudly behind her, turning her face from the viewer almost entirely, even as her weight shifts to her right foot downhill and towards us. Her arm reaches back at a dramatic diagonal that mirrors the hill behind

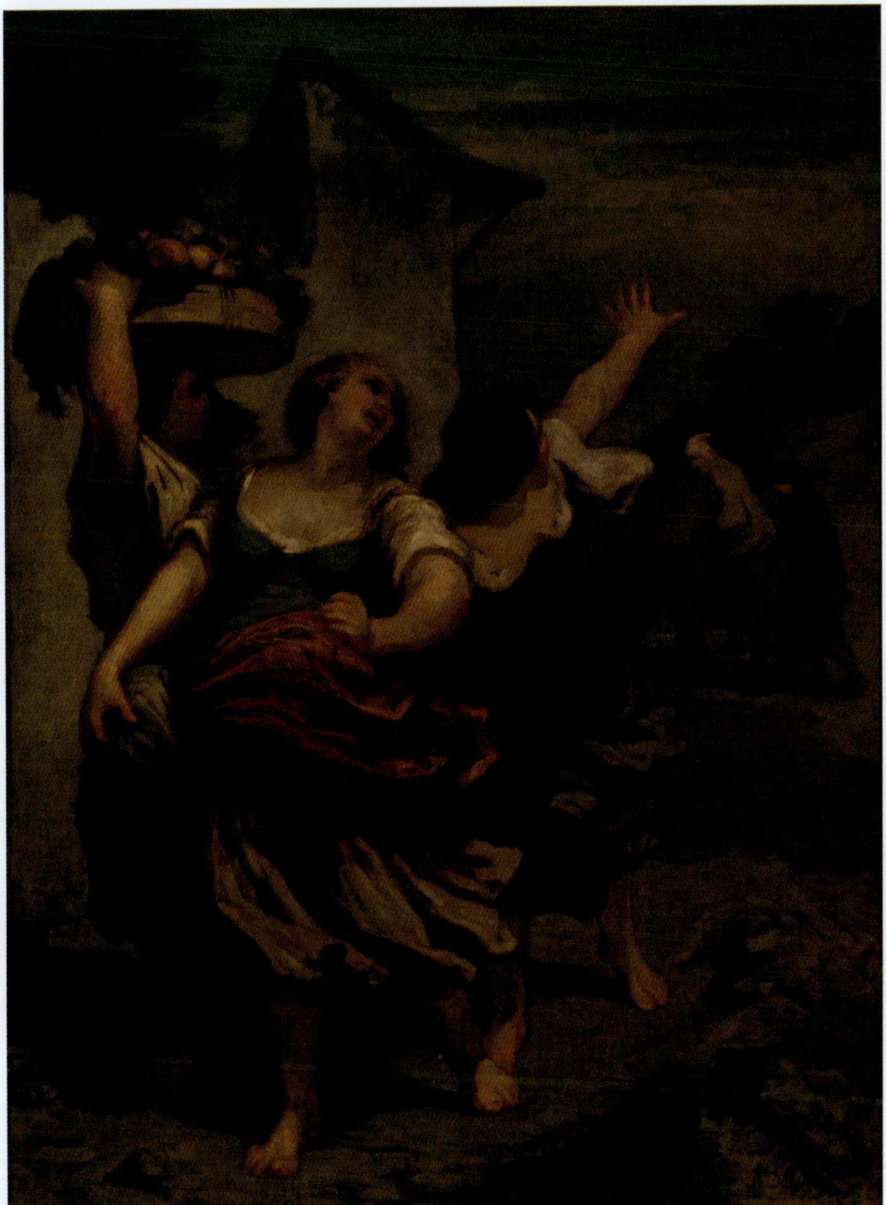

Figure 2.1 Honoré Daumier, *The miller, his son, and the ass*, 1849

her, a sleeve billowing wildly in the air, creating a Baroque sense of swirling motion. The third woman stands upright on the left side of the canvas balancing a basket of fruit on her head. Her muscular body is somewhat hidden by the central woman, whose arm cuts down across her torso. The calves and feet of all three appear below their skirts as a tangle of movement and connection. The women are utterly self-possessed as they overlap,

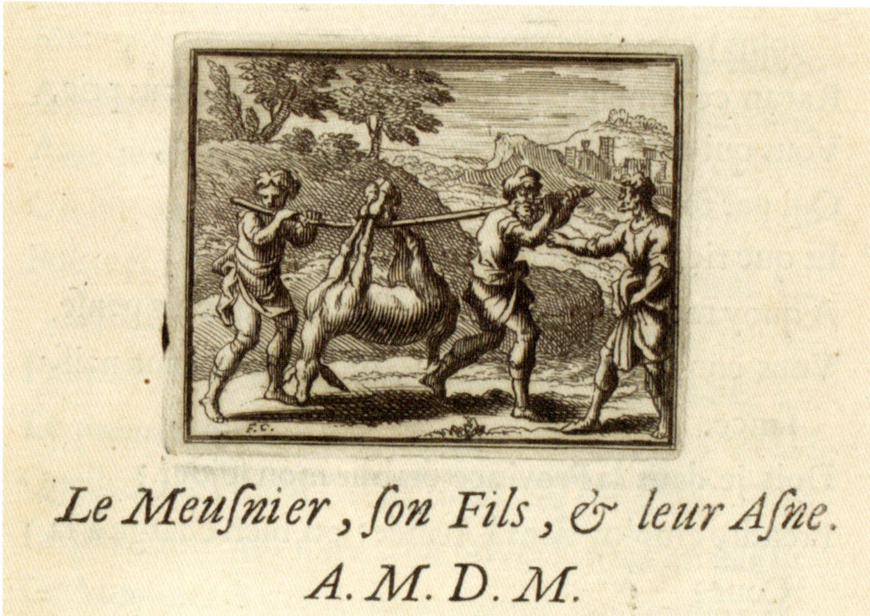

Figure 2.2 François Chauveau illustrator, 'The miller, his son, and the ass' ('Le Meunier, son fils et leur asne'), wood engraving

move, and touch. The miller and his son are relegated to the background even though it is their trip to the market – punctuated with judgements from passers-by – that is the central narrative in the fable.[2]

While many of Daumier's later realist paintings show the development of a form of visual satire that is evacuated from comic lightness, one that becomes more tragic, more violent, and more profound, *The miller, his son, and the ass* is funny, capturing the absurd comedy of La Fontaine's fable. In the story, a miller and his son set out to sell their donkey at the market. First, they string the beast up on a rope 'like a chandelier' to save it from tiring out (Figure 2.2). They are mocked mercilessly along the way, first for this initial formation, and then with each change they make (donkey with no rider, donkey with son riding on top, miller riding the donkey). In Daumier's painting we see the moment when women mock the miller, who was at that moment riding on the donkey's back, for mistreating his son by making him walk.

A passage from La Fontaine's fable was included along with the title of Daumier's work in the Salon brochure published in June 1849. It excerpts the story just after the miller has taken his place on the donkey:

> Three girls next passed: 'Oh, what a shame!' says one,
> 'A father treating like a slave his son!
> The churl rides like a bishop's calf.' 'Not I',
> The Miller made the girls a sharp reply:

> 'Too old for veal, you hussies, and ill-famed.'
> Still with such jesting he became ashamed,
> Thought he'd done wrong; and changing his weak mind,
> Took up his son upon the croup behind.[3]

The women in Daumier's painting twist to shout behind them even as their movement carries them beyond the miller's reproaches. The rightmost figure reaches her arm back, her breasts nearly spilling out, suggestive of the insult that will be hurled back by the miller, shown in Daumier's painting in initial silent shock. The contrast between the two trios, between movement and stillness, noise and silence, confidence and humiliation, communicates some of the humour in the fable. Daumier paints the women launching forward in tethered, swirling motion towards the viewer's space, ready to shift their attention to the next source of shared laughter. Frozen and stilted, the miller and his son will be hurt enough by these admonitions to switch places, a weakness in self-certainty which provides the eventual moral lesson of the story. In *The miller, his son, and the ass*, literature becomes a useful source for an artist balancing commitments to representing profound moral truths (as was expected of paintings) and voicing contemporary – and temporary – political ideas. This was utterly in line with the reception of La Fontaine in the opposition newspapers that he would work at for four decades. Through this painting, we can understand more about the breadth of his political project and uncover a creative strategy for subversive expression in moments of government repression.

La Fontaine's legacy

Though written in the seventeenth century, La Fontaine's works were a part of the French curriculum and a popular subject in French culture and the visual arts in the nineteenth century. *Fables* was used as a pedagogical text, and many eighteenth- and nineteenth-century editions explicitly declare its usefulness 'to facilitate intelligence', 'for the usage in lower level classes', and for student instruction in grammar, mythology, and morality.[4] The vernacular language of the *Fables*, children's love of animals, and La Fontaine's canny humour made them ubiquitous in public instruction and deeply familiar to nineteenth-century audiences. Biographers have speculated that a young Daumier likely would have encountered La Fontaine among his father's small collection of books at home, perhaps the edition published by Engelmann and illustrated by the Vernet brothers.[5]

In the final decades of the *ancien régime*, La Fontaine was marshalled as one of the great men of France, elevated as part of a larger effort to build secular nationalism by worshipping a pantheon of illustrious Frenchmen.[6] We can distinguish the eighteenth-century valorisation of great men from Renaissance versions of this project by its emphatically patriotic messaging and the degree to which credit was given to the patronage of French monarchs. In state architectural projects, plans for galleries of paintings and sculptures of important cultural and historic figures often centred around a portrait of the king, offering a record of good governance through evidence of vibrant cultural production.[7] La Fontaine was frequently included in this wave of 'great men' celebrations in the 1770s and 1780s. For example, Louis XVI's Minister for the Arts, the marquis d'Angiviller, named La Fontaine and Molière as the subjects of major sculpture commissions for the Salon of 1783.[8] In this moment, La Fontaine was framed as one of the nation's literary great men, a genius who flourished under the exemplary rule of Louis XIV.

In the nineteenth century, La Fontaine was increasingly understood to be at odds with the monarch, who by most accounts should have been his enthusiastic patron. Though La Fontaine's contemporary Molière had some struggles with Louis XIV, he certainly received much more state support and institutional recognition than the fabulist. Nineteenth-century biographies described how Louis XIV was hostile to La Fontaine's advancement following the arrest of his early patron Nicolas Fouquet, the king's former Superintendent of Finances, to whom the writer remained loyal.[9] In the 1820s Charles-Athanase Walckenaer argued that La Fontaine's responses to the king's scandals circulated in ways that annoyed Louis XIV, who kept him far from the court.[10] He believed that La Fontaine influenced public opinion in Fouquet's favour more than any other person at the time and that his fables embedded recognizable responses to contemporary political events.[11] Indeed, La Fontaine remained just outside the highest echelons of official recognition for most of his career and was not admitted to the Academy until he was in his sixties (and only after Colbert's death). Later in the nineteenth century, the literary critic and historian Louis Moland (1824–99) framed this quasi-outsider status as suiting La Fontaine's love of freedom and distrust of absolute and suffocating authority.[12] He wrote that the fabulist could not have expressed direct opposition to the king, especially after Fouquet's fall, but that his refusal to be dazzled by royal splendour and his inclusion of fables that were profoundly unflattering to masters in the human or animal worlds demonstrated a 'secret dissent'.[13]

Hippolyte Taine (1828–93) went further, calling La Fontaine's distrust of royal authority practically Saint-Simonian.

> He understands what royal egotism is better than Saint-Simon himself. He sees through it, mocks it … he is without a doubt the most courageous rebel of the century … No one spoke less respectfully to 'the powers that be'. He seems particularly to be happy mocking the greats … He found the time to toss 'people eaters' in passing against the nobles.[14]

This is quite a radical view of La Fontaine's rebelliousness towards the king and the nobility, one that whatever its historical accuracy reflected and constructed the reputation of La Fontaine for nineteenth-century thinkers. The frequent use of La Fontaine's *Fables* in caricatures in the nineteenth century similarly reflects a persistent association of the author with subversive leftist politics and critiques of power within systems of state oppression.

La Fontaine was a popular subject in the visual arts in the nineteenth century.[15] Along with a growing publishing industry, an interest in France's literary golden age continued to flourish during this period. While only 125 editions were published between 1700 and 1800, more than 1,200 editions of La Fontaine's *Fables* were printed between 1800 and 1900.[16] The *Fables* were a favourite subject for book illustrators including Achille Devéria, Tony Johannot, J. J. Grandville, Jules David, Cham (Amédée de Noé), Gustave Doré, Seurre (aîné), Auguste Delierre, and Gustave Moreau, and a range of Romantic artists, satirists, and Symbolists throughout the century.[17] Some artists seized upon the excitement of animals in conflict (Eugène Delacroix and Rosa Bonheur) or amusing vignettes (Victor Schnetz), and in the late 1820s and 30s La Fontaine's *Fables* became a conduit of more biting and dangerous satire.[18]

These moralizing fables mocked all strata of society, including the powerful, and in this period were commonly used to make thinly-veiled political analogies. Well-known fables were used for political speech in 'caricature-illustrations', where La Fontaine's *Fables* were populated not with playful animals or professional types (teachers or millers) but with identifiable contemporary figures.[19] Henry Monnier (1799–1877), another artist nurtured by Charles Philipon, illustrated *Morality in action from the fables of La Fontaine* in 1828 and 1830 with satiric vignettes or 'caricature-illustrations'.[20] Under the reign of Charles X, censors banned three caricatures of La Fontaine's *Fables* by Monnier. One caricature was described as representing an elderly Napoleon, and another illustrated the fable 'The rat retired from the world'. The censorship of these prints stemmed from powers established in a ministerial circular published on 8 September 1829, which sought to curb anticlerical speech and was likely instantiated because of contemporary worries about the politicization of La Fontaine's material.[21] We may observe in the existing illustration for 'The city rat and the country rat' in Monnier's 1828 volume (Figure 2.3), that the 'rats' were drawn as humans, and the central city rat resembles, with some squinting, the baron d'Argout who would soon become one of Daumier's most biting *charges* in his *Celebrities of the juste milieu* series.

Following the rise of the July Monarchy and Louis-Philippe's quick reversal on his promises of press freedoms, Henri Monnier provided some of these 'caricature-illustrations' for *Metamorphoses of the day, or La Fontaine in 1831*. Written by the author and poet Eugène Desmares (c. 1806–39), the book is a series of scathing reinterpretations of La Fontaine's *Fables* aimed squarely at the new regime. 'The monarch, his son, and the people', an updated fable which parenthetically indicates that it is a reimagining of 'The miller, his son, and the ass', critiques the monarch's treatment of his people (who take the place of the donkey in the story, though the king later calls himself an ass as well) and his handling of international affairs.[22] In the early days of the July Monarchy the fable provocatively asks its reader: who will be made comfortable in the new regime, the king or the people? Who will drive history, and who will be made to obey?

The press is mentioned in the first and last lines of the fable, and the moral is clear that no matter the king's course of action, 'The press will complain; that is the French

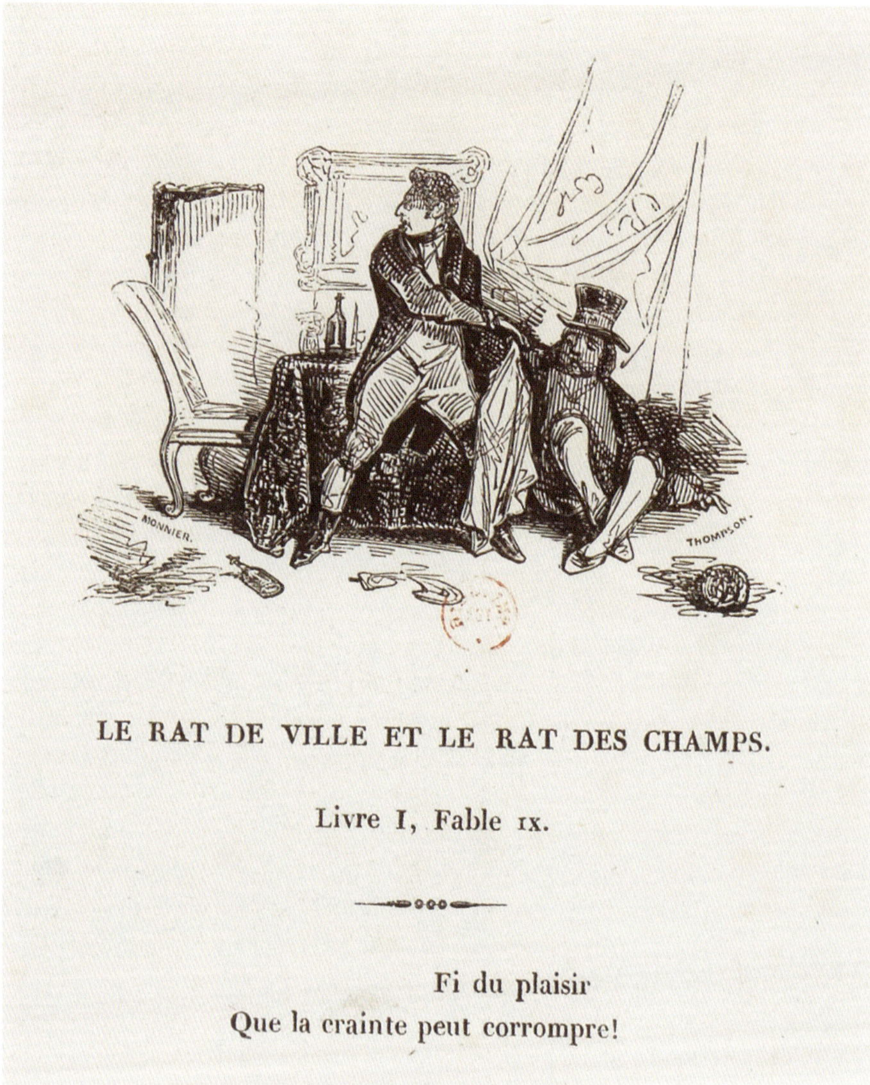

LE RAT DE VILLE ET LE RAT DES CHAMPS.

Livre I, Fable IX.

Fi du plaisir
Que la crainte peut corrompre!

Figure 2.3 Henry Monnier, 'The city rat and the country rat' ('Le rat de ville et le rat des champs'), engraving by Thompson, 1828

spirit'.[23] However, this is no light-hearted parody. In the moment after the son dismounts (the scene Daumier will later paint), the pair are mocked and the king responds: 'When I was a citizen I loved the Republic; / But the role has changed. Carlists [a legitimist movement in Spain], believe me, / It is finally time to execute the law, / Three summations and custom's charge.'[24] In other words, Louis-Philippe may have claimed republican ideals before taking the crown, but was all too happy to shift his values and punish critical voices. Desmares also calls the king a 'usurper' and he and his son 'foolish and quasi-legitimate'.[25] On 22 September 1831, Desmares was sentenced to six months in prison and received a heavy fine of 500 francs for offending the person of the king in *Metamorphoses of the day, or La Fontaine in 1831*.[26] The next year he was acquitted of a second charge for a reinterpretation of another La Fontaine fable, 'The camel and the floating sticks'. In the second trial, the prosecution specifically focused on the phrase 'citizen-tyrant', which the government argued was an extreme and odious offence against the person of the king.[27]

Desmares was Daumier's exact contemporary, though he died quite young, and his parody of La Fontaine was cited in *Le Charivari* as being an explicit, politicized attack on the king: 'The public has not forgotten either the name of M. Eugène Desmares nor the imprisonment which happened just a few years ago, interrupting the young writer parodying La Fontaine for the benefit of his political opinion.'[28] *Le Charivari* revisited Desmares' 1831 intervention and imprisonment to support another politicized parody of La Fontaine's fables, the 1839 *Democratic fables* by Émile Pagès, published by the Bureaux du Charivari, a book that F. T. Claudon acknowledges was necessarily less strident and more abstract than Desmares' because of the intervening September Laws which sought to definitively silence the most damning and direct critiques of the king.[29] Still, Pagès' reinterpretation boldly transforms La Fontaine into a leftist journalist and his animals into the ministers, peers, and deputies of France.[30]

In the pages of *Le Charivari*, Claudon articulates the power of La Fontaine's fables to communicate contemporary political speech. La Fontaine's genius was that he made fables that felt fresh and relevant centuries after they were written, adaptable to the present moment with only small alterations to superficial details. He was easily modernized: '[Writers] could, with this kind of work, offer great service to the contemporary public with little new invention.'[31] Parody, he writes, is just like caricature in this way. Both balance immutable truths and timeless moral lessons with the fleeting specifics of current events. It is easy to imagine Claudon's sentiments being shared by Daumier, and it is likely Daumier knew about Desmares' and later Pagès' reinterpretation of the fables as a lens for political expression through *Le Charivari*, especially because they were embattled in the same conflicts over speech and censorship that he had experienced both before and after the September Laws. It is useful to remember that Claudon wrote that Pagès' fables flirted with the danger of government repression but were necessarily abstracted to a greater degree than Desmares' because of intensified repression of political speech by the government after 1835. We might see a similar process of abstraction from direct political attacks at work when Daumier painted motifs from La Fontaine's *Fables*.

The same year that Desmares published *Metamorphoses of the day, or La Fontaine in 1831*, politicized interpretations of La Fontaine fables also appeared as illustrations in *La Caricature*. For example, 'The donkey loaded with relics', a print attributed to Édouard Wattier, mocks Louis-Philippe who believes it is he who is being worshipped and not the medals and symbols of office burdening the donkey on which he rides (Figure 2.4).[32]

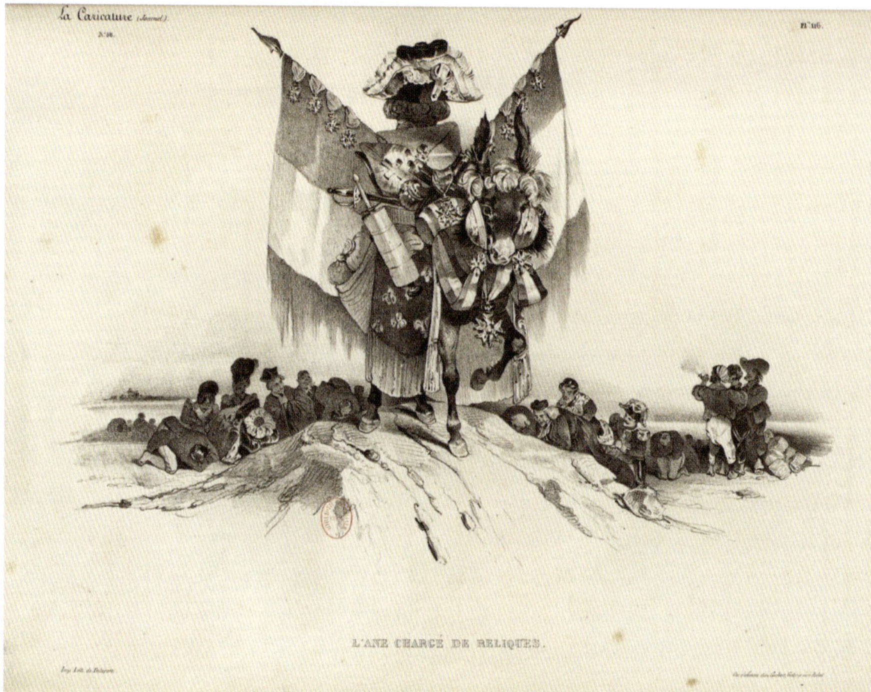

Figure 2.4 Attributed to Édouard Wattier, 'The donkey loaded with relics' ('L'âne chargé de reliques'), *La Caricature* 58 (8 December 1831)

Daumier began to incorporate La Fontaine's *Fables* into his political caricatures around 1834. In 'The lion's lair' (*Le Charivari*, 21 September 1834) a monumental lion lies at the mouth of a cave, resting his massive jowls on a pile of coins delivered by a line of government functionaries (Figure 0.6). The print references La Fontaine's fable 'The sick lion and the fox' (Book 6, Fable 14; hereafter 6:14), derived – as many of his fables were – from Aesop, in which the 'king of the beasts' takes ill and requests visits from his deputies. The foxes refused to send a representative, citing their suspicion about the deputies' tracks going into the cave but not coming back out again. The lion's face adopts the conventions for depicting Louis-Philippe developed by Philipon's stable in the early 1830s; it is pear-shaped, with a mane of hair well-adapted to the lion's. The lion's monumental size also harkens back to Daumier's infamous print of Louis-Philippe as Gargantua, and so in Daumier's hand Rabelais's giant becomes La Fontaine's lion, maintaining the clear allegory for the king's predatory consumption and abuse of taxes, hidden slightly better under the more anodyne and ubiquitous fable.

In 'The lion's lair', the suspicious party watching bureaucrats disappear into the cave takes the form not of a fox but of a strapping man in shirtsleeves at right. His pose mimics the central figure defending press freedoms in Daumier's rousing print from just a few months before, 'DON'T YOU MEDDLE WITH IT!' ('*NE VOUS Y FROTTEZ PAS!*', *L'Association mensuelle*, March 1834). In 'The lion's lair' this figure of tight-fisted resistance is turned into one of suspicion and intransigence. This image of resistance to extractive taxation is likely a response to a new print stamp tax imposed by the administration in 1834, which required a stamp to be affixed to every print sold separately, expanding a law enacted on 14 December 1830 meant for newspapers. This new condition would have the effect of interfering with the aesthetic integrity and profitability of prints sold individually, like those published in *L'Association mensuelle* where 'DON'T YOU MEDDLE WITH IT!' appeared. These collector-quality prints helped offset the legal expenses incurred by Philipon's papers, and so the stamp tax was a major blow against the power of the illustrated press to fight their legal battles.[33] Daumier uses La Fontaine as a means of critiquing a specific policy and the king's taxation more broadly while also rewarding Philipon's dedicated readers with references to other prints embedded in the fable's illustration.

That these suspicions are focused on the utility of taxes is confirmed by a loose imitation of La Fontaine's fable that precedes Daumier's lithograph in the edition of *Le Charivari*. This parody makes the royal taxation analogy clearer for the reader. The fox states: 'In the king's coffers, my friend, I am afraid / That my money will be of little value for me. / I believe the prince to be humane and good; but in his den / I see very clearly how gold enters; / I do not see how it comes out.'[34] The analogy between predator and monarch embedded in La Fontaine's Aesopian fable becomes more explicit in *Le Charivari*'s textual interpretation (which mentions the king's coffers and the promised benefits of taxes) and in Daumier's hands a useful cue to communicate mistrust, the disappearance of public money, and government predation. Because of widespread familiarity with La Fontaine, this was an effective reference, placing the press in the role of the shrewd opponent of the king's policies.

In the fall of 1834, continuing a flurry of criticism preceding the September Laws of the following year, we see Daumier again inserting Louis-Philippe into a La Fontaine fable, 'The oak and the reeds' (1:22, Figure 2.5). Louis-Philippe, metamorphosed into a tree, cracks in the middle of his trunk. His much shrewder ministers (many well-known from *Celebrities of the juste milieu*) bend instead to the onslaught of the wind, understood as republican critique in the form of a head with a Phrygian hat. It would have been understood from the familiar fable that though the king wanted to present himself as strong, his inflexibility would be his downfall.

Later that same month, Daumier published two prints that illustrate Louis-Philippe's incompetence through the metaphor of horse riding. Both 'The insect net' and 'The poor beast founders under the burden' were printed in *Le Charivari* in late October 1834 (Figures 2.6 and 2.7). In the former, the king has draped a net over himself and a bony horse on which he rides. The net is there to protect the rider from a swarm of large flies that gather around his body, but the king's portly form identifies him despite his hidden face. With the Tuileries in the background, Louis-Philippe rides an overburdened white horse symbolizing France in 'The poor beast founders under the burden'.[35] The king's massive form, embodying corruption and self-dealing in ways mirroring *Gargantua*, crushes the nation in the form of a horse he is meant to direct and care for.

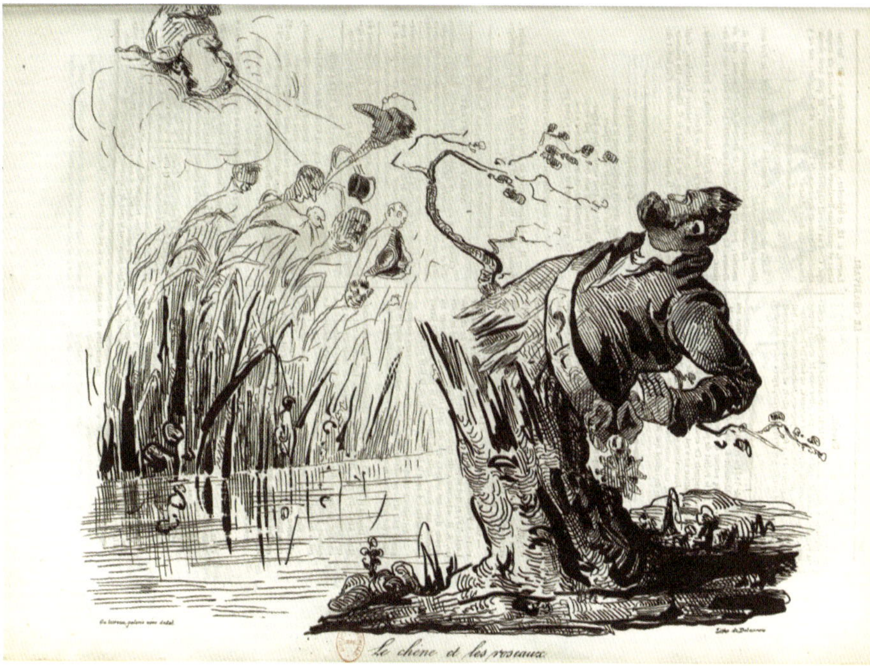

Figure 2.5 Honoré Daumier, 'The oak and the reeds' ('Le Chêne et les roseaux'), *Le Charivari*, 5 October 1834

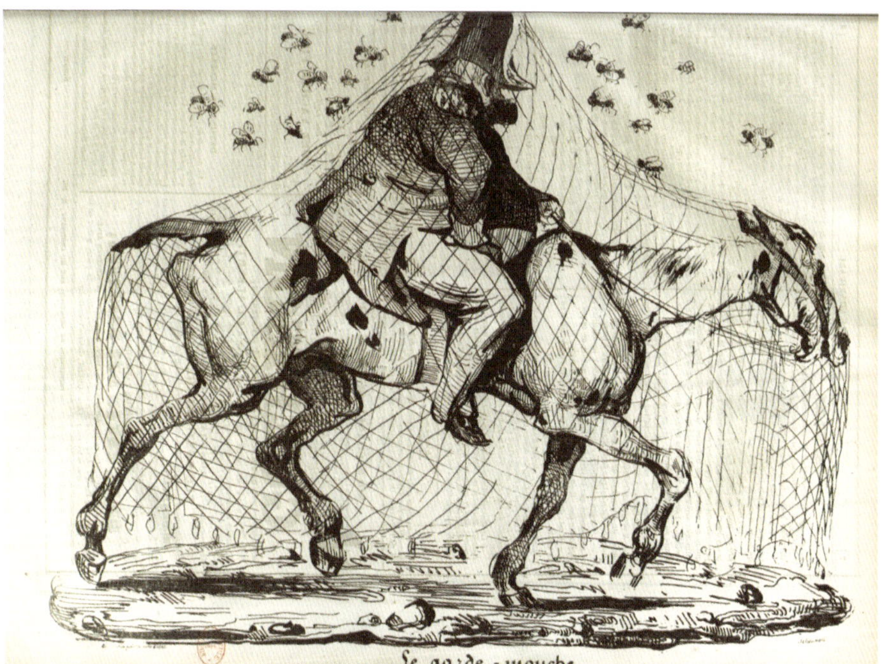

Figure 2.6 Honoré Daumier, 'The insect net' ('Le garde-mouche'), *Le Charivari*, 21 October 1834

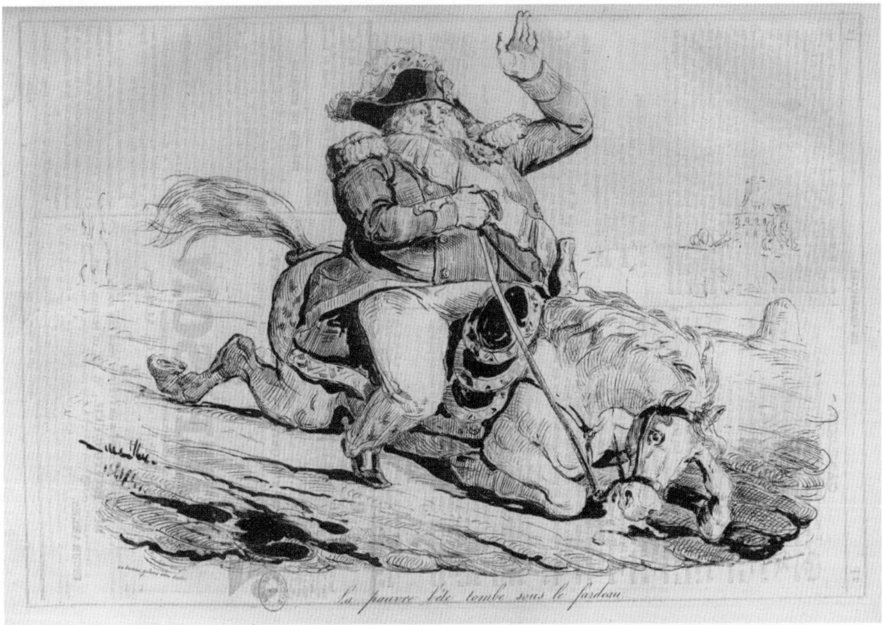

Figure 2.7 Honoré Daumier, 'The poor beast founders under the burden' ('La pauvre bête tombe sous le fardeau'), *Le Charivari*, 30 October 1834

'The cat, the weasel, and the young rabbit' (7:16) appeared in *La Caricature* in May 1835. It is unsigned but likely drawn by Daumier (Figure 2.8).[36] Called upon to settle a quarrel between weasel and rabbit, the cat breaks both of their backs instead. Greater in detail and half-tones than the pen lithograph of a lion's den in 1834, Louis-Philippe is similarly given the head of a man and the body of a cat; a murderous sphinx in the style of Grandville. Rarely has the king looked so demented, violent, and idiotic.

In June of 1835 *Le Charivari* published Benjamin Roubaud's (called 'Benjamin', 1811–47) 'The miller, his son, and the ass' (Figure 2.9). In this reinterpretation, the miller, his son, and the ass become Louis-Philippe, his son Ferdinand, and Joseph Viennet, the vice president of the Chamber of Deputies.[37] Viennet, who has the body and ears of a donkey but a man's head and a dress collar, is strung up on a pole between the two royals in a composition similar to François Chauveau's seventeenth-century illustration of the fable (Figure 2.2). Viennet is identified in an explanation of the image inside the journal, as is the borrowing from La Fontaine.[38] The miller and his son negotiate their relationship with the Chamber of Deputies, and we may assume that the viewer is invited to project judgements on this arrangement. Together, prints from the 1830s establish a practice of La Fontaine's *Fables* being a dynamic and effectual conduit for political speech for Daumier and his colleagues at Philipon's journals. The fables were moral, widely-recognizable, and frequently meditated on power and its mismanagement, and parodies of the fables in the illustrated press established connections to democratic principles and freedom of the press.

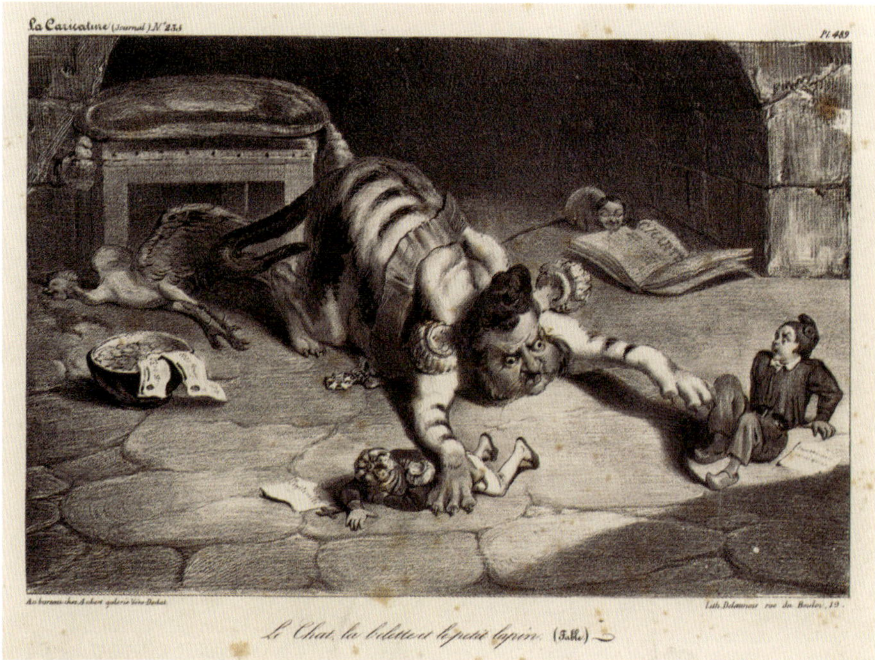

Figure 2.8 Attributed to Honoré Daumier, 'The cat, the weasel, and the young rabbit (Fable.)' ('Le Chat, la belette et le petit lapin (Fable.)', *La Caricature*, 7 May 1835

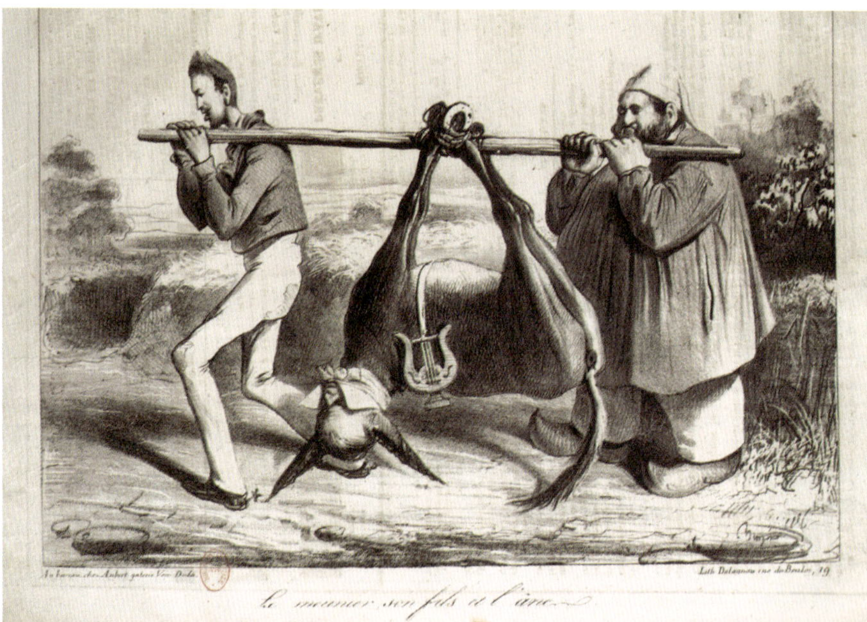

Figure 2.9 Benjamin [Benjamin Roubaud], 'The miller, his son, and the ass' ('Le Meunier, son fils, et l'âne'), *Le Charivari*, 11 June 1835

Painted fables and freedom

Daumier's public foray into painting was likewise political and turned quickly to La Fontaine. The year prior to his first Salon submission of *The miller, his son, and the ass*, Daumier's major announcement of his painting ambitions occurred with his submission of an oil sketch in the competition for the symbol for the Second Republic in 1848 (Figure 2.10). This competition, which began about a month after the revolution (14 March; the Republic was declared on 24 February), included 450 painters, 31

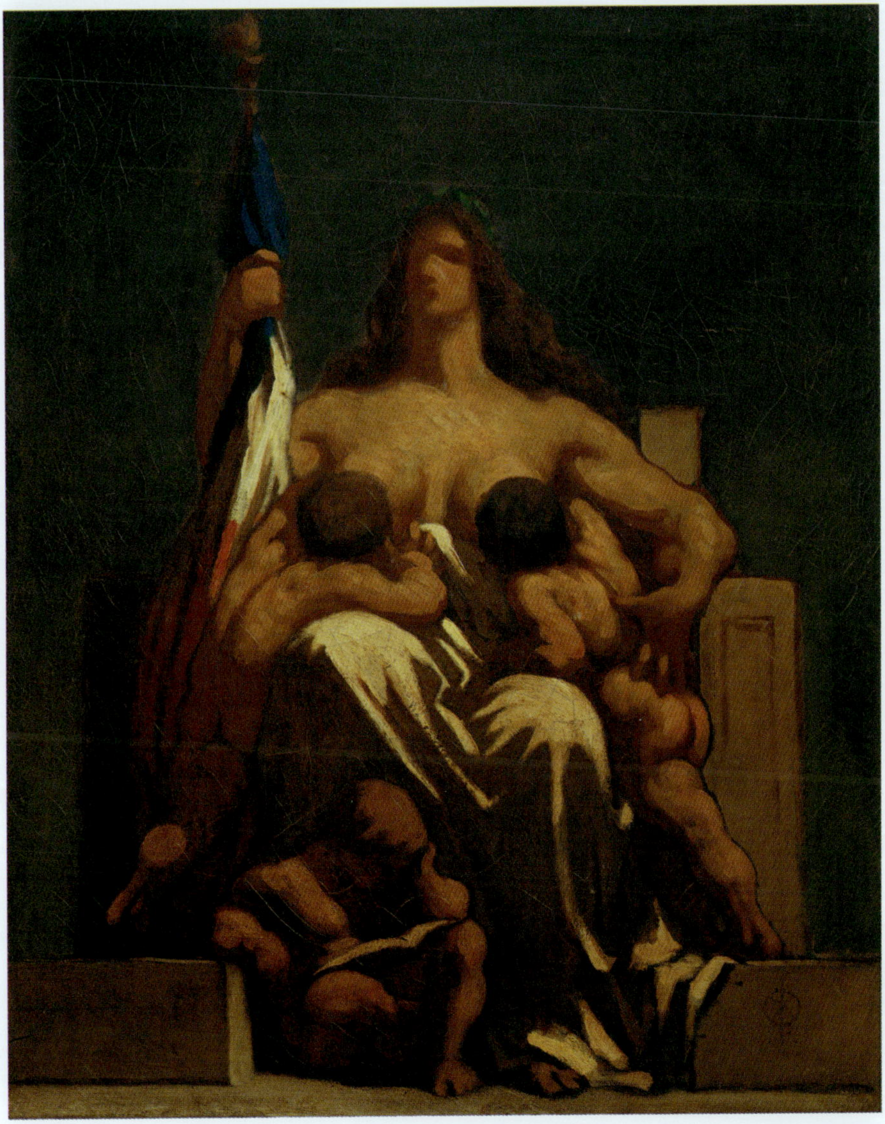

Figure 2.10 Honoré Daumier, *Competition of 1848, sketch of the Republic* (*Concours de 1848, Esquisse de la République*), 1848

engravers, and 173 sculptors, all anonymized.[39] It was a year where several republican painters found great success. The newly-appointed Minister of the Interior, Alexandre-Auguste Ledru-Rollin (1807–74), ordered Paul Chenavard to decorate the Panthéon, Jean-François Millet (1814–75) painted an allegory of Equality, Charles Blanc tapped Eugène Delacroix to paint the central vignette in the ceiling in the Apollo Gallery, and Daumier would receive widespread recognition for his entry into the national competition for a new symbol of state.[40] He made a splash in a crowded field with his painting of a muscular woman breastfeeding two children. A third child reads at her feet, resting an elbow at the foot of her throne. The Republic grasps a tricolour flag in one hand and a baby's back with another, a powerful symbol of the state nourishing and educating French citizens.

Just as with imagery created to represent the new ideals of the First Republic, the 1848 competition used women's bodies as ciphers for the language of allegory. The abstraction and idealization of female figures in the visual arts and in political propaganda at this moment were shaped by forces including the Marian cult, the proclamation of the Immaculate Conception, sentimental depictions of women in Romantic art, Saint-Simonians, Michelet, and discussions about the sanctification of Joan of Arc.[41] Women's bodies emerged as the obvious choice for allegorical representations of the state's power and ideals, but the competition organizers wanted to avoid creating a 'real allegory' like Liberty, which had in recent years been dragged into the gore and smoke of Delacroix's 1830 *Liberty leading the people, 28 July 1830*, desiring instead one that was stable, universal, and peaceful. They mandated that the symbol be a singular figure (children were accessories) so that she would not slide into realism by being folded into a crowd.[42] Daumier's failure to follow through on a final work suggests some discomfort with painting this kind of standalone allegory. Théodore de Banville's memoir praised Daumier but admitted that allegories were not his strength or ultimately his interest: 'And may the devil take the allegories that have neither head nor tail.'[43]

Daumier did not produce a finished painting based on *Sketch for the Republic*, in spite of its critical success.[44] Perhaps he lost motivation to follow through after first conceiving it in the euphoric moment in March of 1848. The provisional government turned quickly to liberating the press from some of the strictest requirements of the September Laws. On 2 March stamp duties were suspended and soon too was litigation against the press, creating the conditions for an explosion of papers – daring, varied, and very often political – perhaps more than 450 in the first few months of the new Republic.[45] The initial promises of freedom soured after the bloody suppression of the June Days uprising, and the second half of 1848 saw a rightward shift and crackdowns on left-wing political expression.[46] Two days after the June insurrection, editors were arrested, eleven presses were sealed, and in August new press laws resurrected many of the restrictions that had only been abolished in March.[47]

The June insurrection of 1848 brought authoritarian powers to General Eugène Cavaignac (1802–57), President of the Conseil des Ministers, who had targeted newspapers as sources of rebellion with his new powers. In spite of his crackdowns, *Le Charivari* publicly supported Cavaignac in the election in December 1848 for a new head of state, vocally opposing Louis-Napoleon Bonaparte's (1808–73) candidacy, perceiving the dictatorial potential of Louis-Napoleon as the greater threat to the Republic.[48] In addition to strident articles in *Le Charivari*, the *Journal pour rire* (1848–55), another of Charles Philipon's papers created in the great frenzy of 1848, published caricatures of then-candidate Louis-Napoleon as an ass. Bertall's 'Here, then, is the people who call themselves the most spiritual on earth' appeared in the journal on 25 November 1848, framing Louis-Napoleon as a heavenly apparition of a donkey surrounded by an adoring crowd, mocking the manic devotion to Napoleon I and portraying the nephew as a brainless pretender.[49]

Rigobert's 'Candidate presented by Nicolas, supported by *La Presse*' (Figure 2.11) exploited perceptions of Louis-Napoleon, who spent most of his life before 1848 exiled from France, as being beholden to foreign powers by showing him as a donkey in Napoleonic costume and propped up by the Russian emperor. An unsophisticated man with donkey ears to the left of Louis-Napoleon represents the rural voter whom republicans worried was in thrall to the Napoleonic legacy, in contrast to the more wary urban worker at right who sees through the charade.[50] Importantly, in the same vein, 'The donkey loaded with relics' emphasized popular devotion to Louis-Napoleon, who rides through adoring crowds as an empty Napoleonic bicorne hat (Figure 2.12). The print was published in the same issue of *Journal pour rire* as Bertall's donkey apparition and also separately and inexpensively by Vial.[51] As with Wattier's 1831 interpretation of the same fable by La Fontaine, Vial's print both mocks an ambitious politician who lacks substantial corporeal form, conflating the ass who believes he is being worshipped and the empty costume of the rider, and the crowds that worship the pageantry of power with a disturbing fervour.

Louis-Napoleon was elected in 1849, and he and the assembly targeted the press, especially the republican or *démoc-soc* (democratic-socialist) press, with more stringent regulations and financial demands. More newspapers were suspended, others were placed under police surveillance, and new laws expanded the list of criminal offences the press could commit.[52] New legislation in the summer of 1849 prohibited attacks on the person of the president, forcing caricaturists to represent him obliquely and with a level of creativity echoing the censorship struggles of the early 1830s.[53] The political context of late 1848 and 1849 helps explain Daumier's turn away from *Sketch of the Republic* and towards his next major painting, *The miller, his son, and the ass*. He returns to La Fontaine for a source to express political criticism and selects a story with an ass, an avatar for power. His decision to foreground the trio of monumental women, the most compelling and idiosyncratic part of the composition, is in this context in dialogue with his monumental allegory for the Second Republic. Daumier failed – or refused – to follow

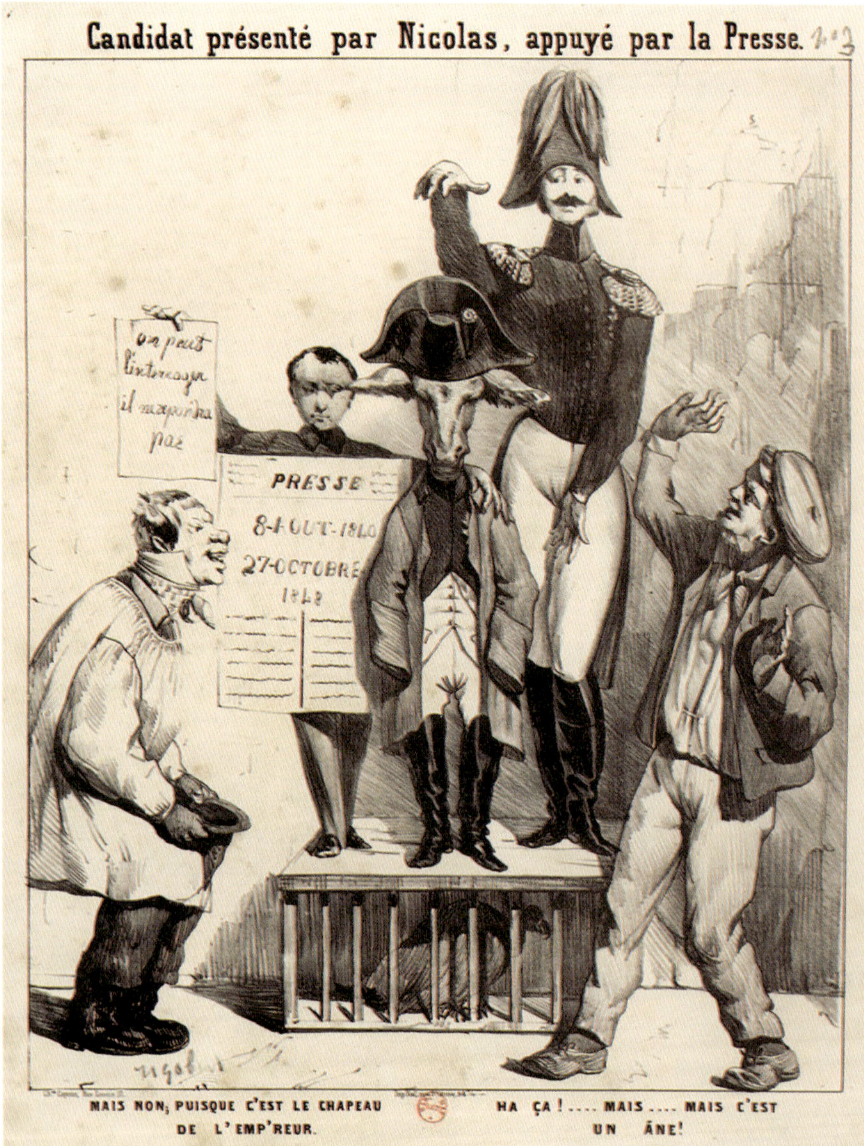

Figure 2.11 Rigobert, 'Candidate presented by Nicolas, supported by the press' ('Candidat présenté par Nicolas, appuyé par la Presse'), published by Ch.es Capron, 1848

through on the formation of a symbol that framed the Republic as the singular, powerful source of care and instruction and instead complicated the allegory of an ideal state with a painting celebrating freedom, noise, and the raucous dissent of a crowd.

He was able to weave humour into *The miller, his son, and the ass* in a way that was perhaps more satisfying to the artist than the ultra-serious *Republic*. He did this both through the invocation of a familiar humorous fable and with the visual devices learned

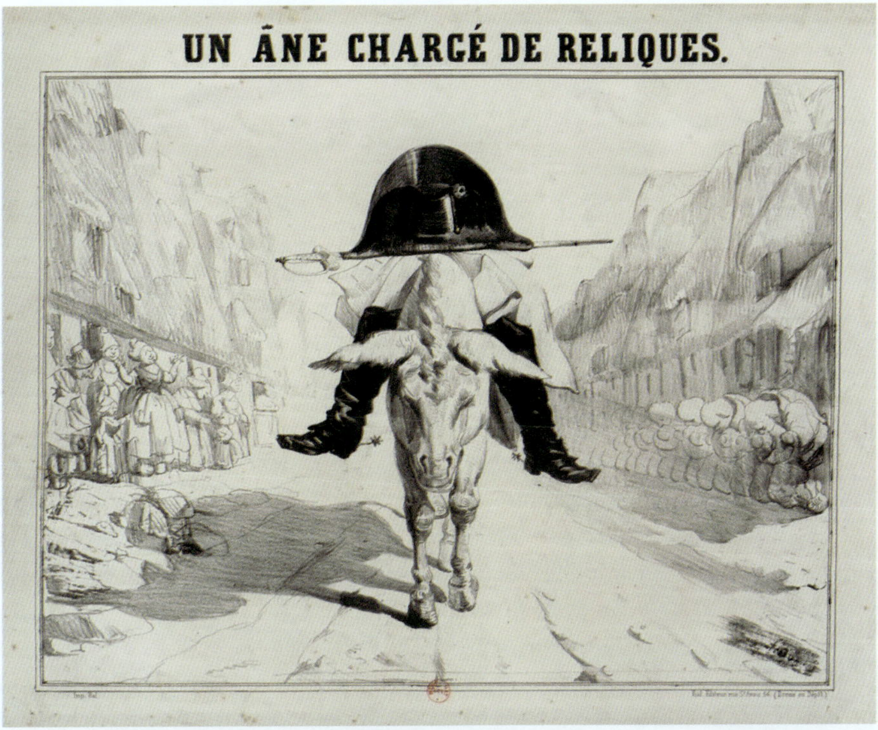

Figure 2.12 Vial, editor, 'The donkey loaded with relics' ('Un âne chargé de reliques')

in caricature: establishing emphatic contrast, creating a sense of bawdiness and noise, and setting the action of one group against the reaction of another. The central woman's fulsome body is emphasized by a narrow second storey of a building rising up beyond her shoulders. The logic of the building's architecture falls apart quite quickly. The women seem to be passing quite close to its white plaster walls, but the rising second storey appears both too far away and too narrow. The building exists to create another contrast, between town and country, culture and nature, setting the miller and his son into a greater humorous contrast with the women. This would certainly make sense in light of Daumier's many cartoons mocking country life. He was happy to poke fun at the backwardness of rural spaces and bourgeois excursions into the country.[54] The white walls of the building frame the trio of women and signal that they belong to a community. The miller and his son, in contrast, seem to travel down this country road alienated from their community and unsure of its shared norms. Daumier puts them at a distinct affective distance from the community of women.

La Fontaine's *Fables* offered legible, familiar, multifigure narratives, moral purpose, and returned to a moment of vibrant cultural production in France during the reign of Louis XIV, so they were well-suited as motifs for nineteenth-century academic painting. Offering an alternative to allegory, they had popular appeal and were accepted by the

Academy. There were numerous examples of representations of La Fontaine's *Fables* at the Salon and other major exhibitions. In 1836 Joseph Guichard exhibited *The miller, his son, and the ass (fable by La Fontaine)* at the exposition of the Society of the Friends of the Arts in Lyon.[55] In 1849, the same year that Daumier submitted *The miller, his son, and the ass*, Marcel Verdier (1817–56) exhibited *The man between two ages and two mistresses*, Jean-Victor Schnetz *Death and the woodcutter*, Auguste-Victor Pluyette *The coach and the fly*, and Auguste-François Ales the engraving *Two fables by La Fontaine*.[56] Verdier exhibited several subjects drawn from La Fontaine at the Salon in the 1840s, including *The women and the secret*, *The man between two ages, and his two mistresses*, and *The miller, his son, and the ass*, among others.[57]

Many scholars have pointed to Peter Paul Rubens' *Lot and his family leaving Sodom* (1625, Figure 2.13), a painting that hung in the Louvre in the 1840s, as an important source for the woman carrying a massive basket filled with fruit and vegetables in Daumier's *The miller, his son, and the ass*.[58] The other two women in Daumier's painting may also have been drawn from *Lot and his family leaving Sodom*, as they echo the powerful overlapping strides and interlocking arms of Lot and the angel, the pair at the rightmost edge of the group fleeing the city of Sodom. We can see, for instance, how the angel's outstretched arm and exposed chest are repeated in the gesture and costume of the woman at the right of Daumier's trio. The central woman imitates Lot's tilted face and his straight right arm and bent left arm, both grasping at the loose fabric of his garments in his hasty retreat. Alexandre Lenoir introduced Daumier to Rubens during his brief apprenticeship, and in Daumier's first few years of making paintings, we see him

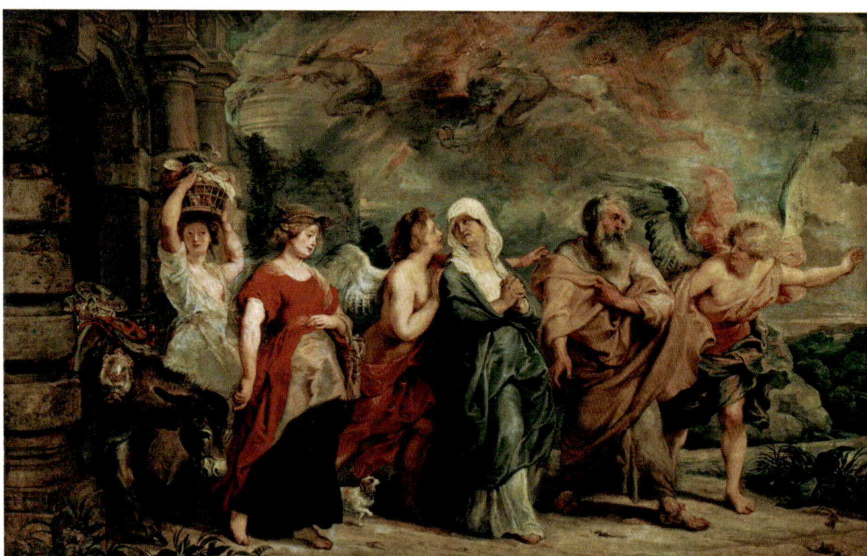

Figure 2.13 Peter Paul Rubens, *Lot and his family leaving Sodom, led by angels*, 1625

looking to Rubens for compelling bodily movement and painterly credibility by means of pastiche.[59]

The biblical story of Lot foregrounds the power of vision, an irresistible story for a young artist translating a text to paint. In *Lot and his family leaving Sodom*, two angels compel a family to leave the city that is about to be destroyed by fire-wielding figures in the sky. Lot's wife is already turning back towards the city gates to look behind her, straining against an intervening angel, just moments before she is turned into a pillar of salt. The story of Lot and his wife titillates with a sense of transgressive vision and embeds a charge of rebellion underneath the three women twisting backwards to look behind them in *The miller, his son, and the ass*. They carry some form of the force or authority of mocking punishment to the miller, whose faltering look back to them mirrors, if anything, the doomed curiosity of Lot's wife in Rubens's painting. In both stories, obedience and hesitation are at issue, though for the miller, the punishment for uncertainty is merely mockery from neighbours, not deadly corporeal transformation.

Daumier's basket-carrier may have also been modelled on a similar figure in Jacob Jordaens' monumental painting *Jesus expelling the merchants from the temple* (c. 1645–50), which was also influenced by Rubens, and was a painting that Daumier would also have seen at the Louvre (Figure 2.14).[60] The basket-carrier figure watches mirthfully as Christ lashes the merchants, a setup that would have resonated with *Miller*'s subject matter, in which women laugh openly at the misfortune of men. By citing two seventeenth-century artists, Daumier does not only add credibility to his new painting

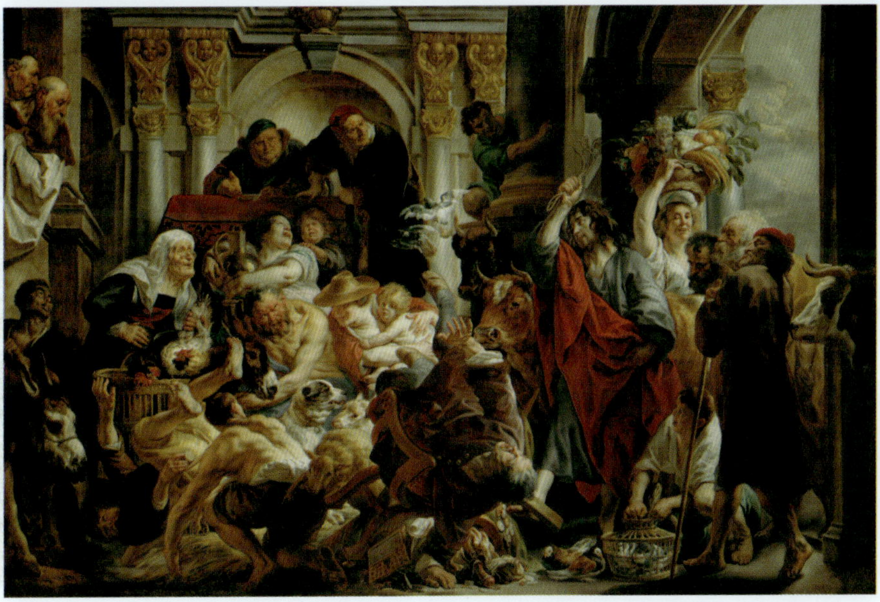

Figure 2.14 Jacob Jordaens the Elder, *Jesus expelling the merchants from the temple*, c. 1645–50

project but also connects style to subject matter. He layers seventeenth-century Baroque techniques over seventeenth-century fables, dramatizing tensions between mutinous vision and derisive laughter.

In *The miller, his son, and the ass*, it was seventeenth-century French literature, not allegory or biblical stories, that would offer the kind of balance Daumier was seeking between serious moral stories and contemporary political concerns. And this reinterpretation of La Fontaine as a means to express present-day politics was aligned with the reception of La Fontaine in *Le Charivari.* In his volume of parodies of La Fontaine published by the bureau of *Le Charivari* in 1839 (a moment when explicit political speech was outlawed), F. T. Claudon's *Democratic fables* examined the ability of literature to speak both to timeless truths and contemporary events. The proper way to make a parody into a work of such evergreen significance, F. T. Claudon insisted, is 'to take up a work after a lapse of time has removed all of the relative truth and to show, with the first faithfully preserved, some truth or some satire that is more current, without changing any or almost any of the original framework'.[61] In *Le Charivari*, the familiar, canonical literature of La Fontaine was used to smuggle subversive content to readers, creating a shorthand to comment on contemporary politics. In 1849, in a way that was both timeless and utterly urgent, Daumier seems to say that freedom (of the press and of speech) was essential to the Republic still finding its feet; that noise, mockery, and the irreverent policing of power dynamics are a sign of a healthy democratic sphere.

Daumier's *The miller, his son, and the ass* sets up a contrast between laughing women and the bewildered miller and his son. But the miller, son, and donkey do not have equal weight, and an earlier oil sketch, *The ribalds* (1848–49) from the Barnes Foundation, shows the artist working out the tangle of the women's bodies and leaving the miller out completely (Figure 2.15). Daumier foregrounds the swirling group of Rubenesque women in a way that was ichnographically unique to depictions of this fable in France. As we have seen, some illustrations revelled in the absurdity of the miller stringing the donkey up like a chandelier. J. J. Grandville illustrated a book of La Fontaine's *Fables* published in 1838, an intuitive choice for an artist who had made his name through his celebrated human–animal hybrids in the 1829 *Metamorphoses of the day* (Figure 2.16).[62] His rendition of *The miller, his son, and the ass* unifies multiple scenes in the fable by surrounding an embarrassed miller with several of the parties who mocked him along his travels. We see the women's backs retreating in the middle distance. Another strategy for illustrating the fable emphasized a confrontation between two sexes, setting the women into conflict with the miller riding his donkey.[63] This gendered contrast between certainty and hesitation is exaggerated in Daumier's construction, as he pushes the women forward and sets them into motion. His painting broke from conventions that had previously illustrated the fable, blew the women up to the monumental proportions of *Sketch of the Republic*, and emphasized the power of vision and the force of righteous mockery using Baroque forms.

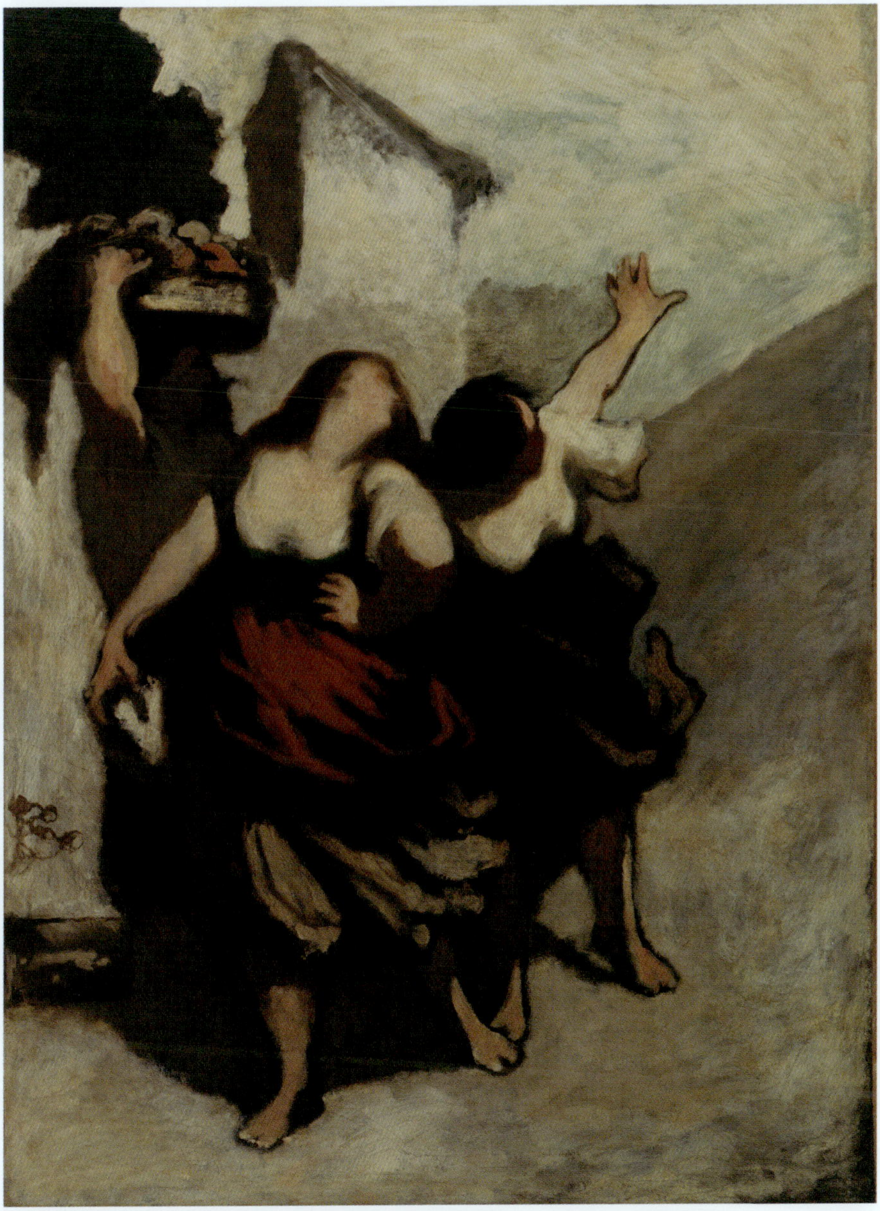

Figure 2.15 Honoré Daumier, *The ribalds* (*Les Ribaudes*), 1848–49

Contemporary responses to Daumier's *Miller* both by his supporters and those disappointed with his showing at the Salon commented on the liberties the artist took representing the familiar fable. A representative review from *L'Artiste* noted: 'Mr Daumier and Marcel Verdier translated the good La Fontaine, but, in our opinion, a bit too freely.'[64] The critic Champfleury (Jules François Felix Fleury-Husson), a particularly insightful

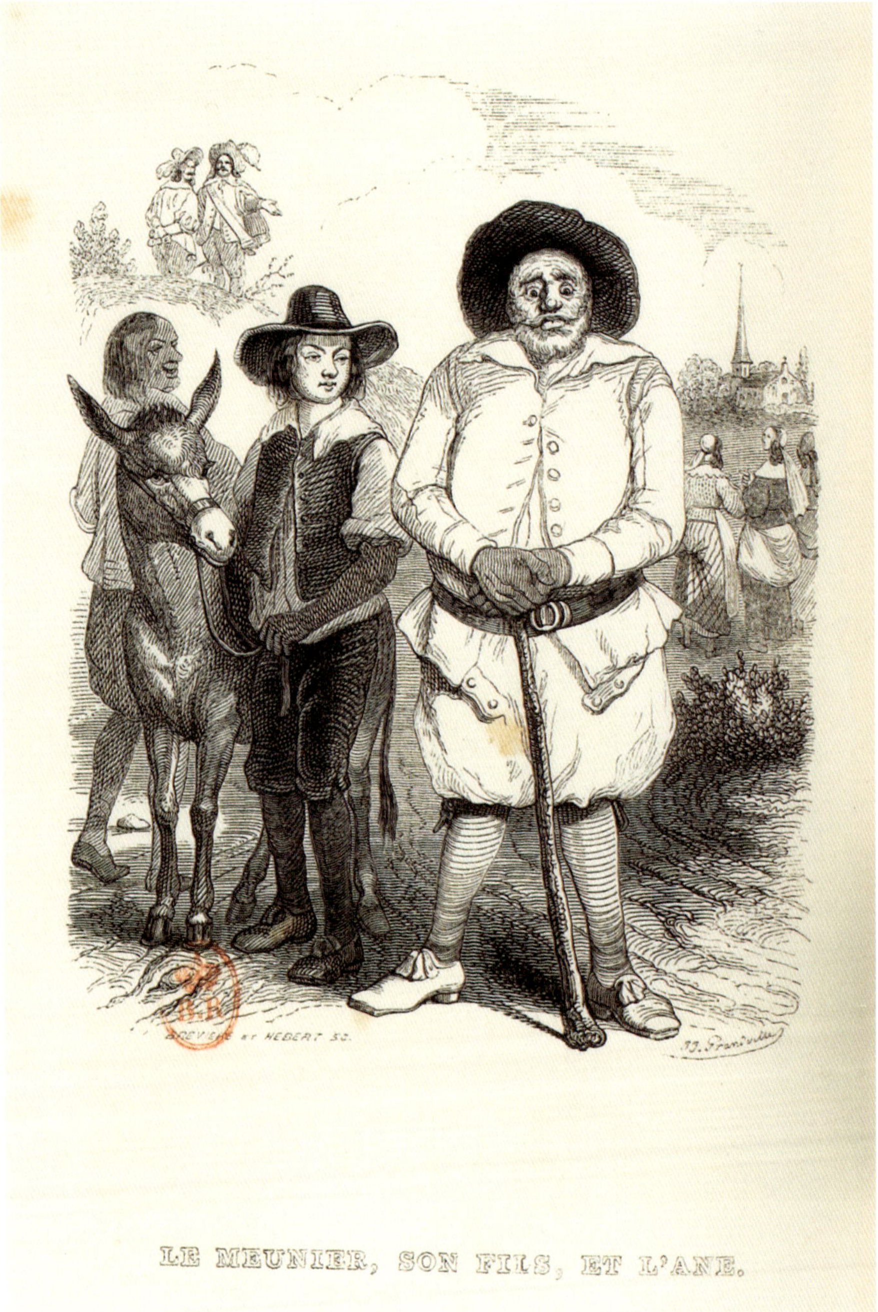

Figure 2.16 J. J. Grandville, 'The miller, his son, and the ass,' in Jean de La Fontaine, *Fables de La Fontaine* 1 (Paris: H. Fournier, 1838–40)

reader of Daumier's work, described this painting in his review of the Salon of 1849, emphasizing the artist's ambitious transition from caricature to painting:

> The author of the drawings of *Charivari*, the illustrious and serious artist ... Daumier, attacked painting with the courage and the verve we know him to have. It is *The miller, his son, and the ass* that serves as a text on canvas *(qui sert de texte au tableau)*; but the painter has left the three actors in the distance, so staging three fat creatures who scream with laughter while looking at the ass basking like an archbishop.[65]

We see an acknowledgement in this analysis of Daumier's interest in translating a story from text to paint. Champfleury indicates that Daumier's surprising compositional choices serve to preserve the humour of the fable. The artist foregrounds the three women rather than the fable's protagonists, highlighting their exaggerated muscularity and loud mocking calls. He suggests that Daumier draws from the caricatural tradition of exaggerating gesture and expression in his new painting project and believes his reversal of the typical configuration of this scene is a declaration of Daumier's aesthetic autonomy. He continues later: 'I was consoled at his moment of weakness when I saw the fable of La Fontaine by Daumier, painted with great freedom; some may not find this canvas French enough', perhaps referring to Rubens's Flemish influence.[66] Freedom is emphasized twice in the brief passage above. In Champfleury's mind, this sense of independence and creative expression is essential to Daumier becoming a 'serious' artist.

Freedom is also key to the fable itself. Daumier tethers his decision to place the women so frontally in a wild convergence of noise and movement to the story represented, a story that stresses liberation from social pressures and constraints. Freedom, in other words, is the whole point of both subject and style. La Fontaine's telling of the fable addresses a young person worried about choosing his career, encouraging the reader to resist strict dictates and think freely. Painted during a right-wing turn in the French Second Republic when press freedoms were being rolled back, newspapers shuttered and surveilled, and punishment meted out to parties offending the new president, it is useful to frame this painting as a celebration of dissent. There are no heroes in La Fontaine's fable, but in Daumier's hand the hecklers are the more compelling party. Critique should not necessarily dictate policy, but competing opinions are healthy. Dissent is inevitable, moral, and a delight.

Some art historians have argued that because Daumier had so frequently used La Fontaine as a device to filter speech critical of the king, and because his colleagues placed Louis-Philippe on a donkey in a La Fontaine fable, Daumier's interpretation of *The miller, his son, and the ass* may stand in for the departure of the king, who was forced into abdication and exile in February of 1848. I agree with K. E. Maison and Kirsten H. Powell that had Louis-Philippe been the specific target of the fable's moral lesson, Daumier could not have resisted making a *portrait-charge* of the king that he had lampooned for so many years. At the very least, Daumier would have gestured to the pear-shaped physiognomic type that he had helped to make so familiar.[67] Instead of Louis-Philippe's abdication, it is better to understand the ass in *The miller, his son, and the ass* as a metaphor for the conservative turn and substantial changes to censorship under Louis-Napoleon in the Second Republic and for misused political power as a principle.

The French word *âne*, or ass, had been a linguistic signifier for donkey since the tenth century and was used in a figurative sense since the thirteenth century as a description for a person of low intelligence. Literary satirists helped colour new shades of meaning for the ass: Molière is credited with the invention of *âne bâté*, or jackass (1670), Rabelais for *faire de l'âne pour avoir sur bren* (*son*), or to play the fool to achieve one's ends (1534), and La Fontaine for a number of proverbial phrases including *l'âne chargé de reliques*, *l'âne vêtu de la peau du lion*, and *le plus âne des trois*. That last phrase, 'the biggest ass of the three', entered into the French lexicon from his fable *The miller, his son, and the ass*.[68]

For La Fontaine and the journalists at *Le Charivari*, the ass was frequently the victim of unfair power dynamics and extractive labour.[69] In Eugène Desmares' *Metamorphoses of the day, or La Fontaine in 1831*, the donkey's mistreatment was a clear proxy for the monarch's poor behaviour towards his people. So, too, in fifteen of La Fontaine's *Fables*, the fabulist used the donkey to tell tales of mismanaged mastery, domination and subordination, and imprisonment.[70] Political analogies are made by La Fontaine himself. In 'The thieves and the ass' (1:13), a fable painted by Daumier in 1858 with a violence matching the fabled brawl (Figure 2.17), two thieves argue over whether to sell a donkey, and during the confusion it is stolen by a third.[71] The second stanza does the analysis for the reader:

> This ass is, by interpretation,
> Some province poor, or prostrate nation.
> The thieves are princes this and that,
> On spoils and plunder prone to fat,—'
> As those of Austria, Turkey, Hungary.
> (Instead of two, I've quoted three—
> Enough of such commodity.)
> These powers engaged in war all,
> Some fourth thief stops the quarrel,
> According all to one key,
> By riding off the donkey.[72]

Seventeenth-century literature taught largely through symbol and allegory, and La Fontaine's *Fables* translated current events through barely-abstracted stories.[73] Many of his references were about foreign affairs, as we see in 'The thieves and the ass'. Readers also understood there was domestic political commentary embedded as well, even if it needed to be obscured to avoid censorship:

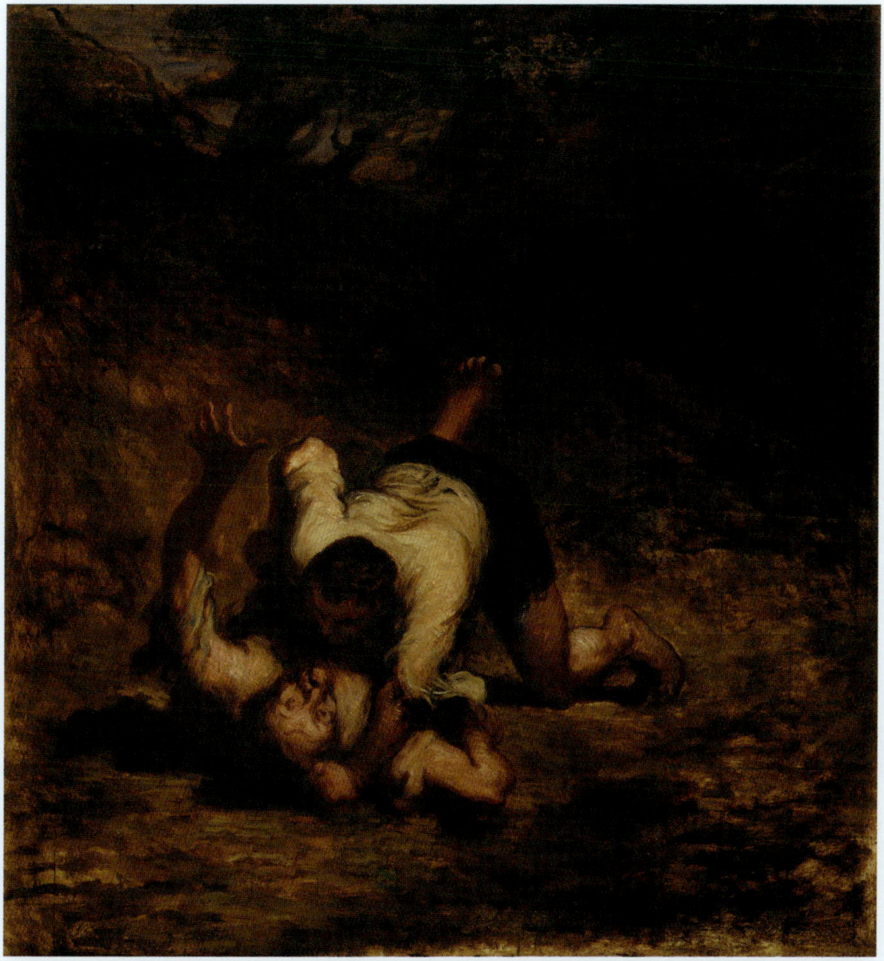

Figure 2.17 Honoré Daumier, *The thieves and the ass* (*Les Voleurs et l'âne*), c. 1858

> I would willingly use Baudelaire's word and speak of the 'modernity' of the Fables … [A] word here and there puts us back in the climate of the time, warning us that animal masks barely conceal men, and, what is more, exact contemporaries of the fabulist: poor recluses, court spies, guessers; but it is rare for the fabulist to allow anyone to guess what incident of internal politics inspired him.[74]

Power is the most potent axis in the Baudelairean balance between the eternal and ephemeral in La Fontaine's works. The *Fables*, particularly those involving an ass, were a meaningful channel for Daumier to explore the exchange of power, its seizure and manipulation.

La Fontaine belonged to a current of pacifism in seventeenth-century literature and was deeply suspicious of power. 'Our enemy is our master', he wrote in 'The Old man and the donkey'.[75] It is a theme that recurs in the moralities of fables, defanged of some of their danger by the use of animals and silly men, but nonetheless subversive to publish under an absolute monarchy. La Fontaine warns his readers: do not rely on kings, do not attract them to your lands, do not participate in their wars.[76] In fact, it was these very meditations on power (in addition to some subtle anticlerical allusions) in La Fontaine's earlier *Contes* that kept him outside of Louis XIV's favour.[77]

In the middle ground of Daumier's painting, the donkey crosses to the right of the trio of women, its head intersecting with the waist of the woman twisting backwards, drawing a connection between the two groups. While the donkey is not staged as the funny part of Daumier's painting (the women are), it does signal an awareness of humour, mockery, and how power is wielded. It is likely, too, that the artist would have been aware that for both La Fontaine and his colleagues writing for the leftist press the domestic animal was an analogy for the condition of slavery. In the journal *Le Charivari*, the ass was cited in abolitionist appeals.

Le Charivari reported on debates about the 'eternal embarrassment' of the institutionalized enslavement of human beings throughout the 1830s and 1840s.[78] In the years preceding the abolition of slavery under the Second Republic, there was widespread support for emancipation, though there were ongoing debates about the method (gradual or simultaneous), and various commissions and groups competed to lobby for a range of solutions.[79] These articles frequently referenced asses. An 1836 issue of *Le Charivari* discussing the morality and legitimacy of the practice of slavery and the position of the Chamber of Deputies relayed: 'We have never heard donkeys braying such comical reasonings ... Therefore, men are more asses than asses themselves.'[80] In this impassioned article, the donkey is invoked with merciless regularity to drive home the point that men who support slavery had a brutality and intellectual deficiencies unsurpassed by the dull beast, qualities that would find echoes in 1848 caricatures of Louis-Napoleon in *Journal pour rire*.

In 1838, *Le Charivari* reworked 'The miller, his son, and the ass' with 'The miller, the farmer, and the ass (fable)' with a clear antislavery message.[81] In it, a donkey that has been mistreated and overburdened by a miller one day bucks the man off. The miller falls, hits his neck, and the donkey frolics and dislodges from his halter. The ass is soon convinced by a neighbouring farmer to take back the yoke in exchange for protection, and the food he was long denied is dangled in front of him as he walks, a torture that is increased by the lash. The fable ends, 'I know such was the case in a corner of the world', a clear nod to contemporary events.[82] Britain voted to abolish slavery in 1834 under a law which took effect in 1838, though extractive colonial practices continued. As a result of abolition in Britain and popular opposition in France, the July Monarchy felt pressure to dial back its practice, causing a deluge of impassioned debate from the late 1830s until France finally abolished slavery for the second time in the Second Republic.[83]

In 1843 Marcel Verdier, formerly a pupil of Ingres, submitted a painting *Punishment of four stakes in the colonies* (*Châtiment des quatre piquets dans le colonies*) to the Salon of

1843, which was rejected, likely because it would have reflected poorly on the treatment of enslaved people in French colonies at a moment when slavery was deeply unpopular and embarrassing.[84] A graphicly violent painting, it foregrounds a moment during the brutal lashing of a man and indicts the white landowner, who appears nonplussed by the inhumanity of the scene. Verdier was able to show the rejected canvas at the Bazar Bonne-Nouvelle and the painting was reproduced in *L'Illustration* that year.[85] It is believed that Verdier post-dated the painting to 1849 after the abolition of slavery in France in order to shift the scene away from the French context.[86] Verdier also started painting motifs from La Fontaine beginning in 1846. Perhaps this too was part of a broad exploration of subjugation and power when disagreements about slavery were at such a fever pitch.[87]

Daumier's 1849 *The miller, his son, and the ass* is likely not an explicitly abolitionist painting, but it does meditate on power relations, exploitative labour, and the selling of a labouring body. The fable traces a miller's confusion about whose body should be exhausted and whose labour should be extended. Exhibited the year after slavery was abolished in French colonies for the second time, the question of violent, extractive colonial labour was certainly not settled, as systems of indentured work would continue to support plantation economies in the French Caribbean.[88] Perhaps more importantly for Daumier, in the 1830s and 1840s in France chattel slavery was frequently deployed as a metaphor for the exploitation of the working class. Socialists in the first half of the nineteenth century saw clear parallels between the treatment of enslaved persons abroad and the exploitation of urban workers. Political texts from the period describe the struggle of French workers using metaphors and explicit historical comparisons with chattel slavery.[89] This is, for instance, the pivotal comparison in the popular 1839 book *Of modern slavery* (*De l'esclavage moderne*) written by the Christian socialist Félicité Lamennais (1782–1854), an embattled priest who established key theories for liberal Catholicism and social justice practice. Lamennais claimed that under capitalism the proletariat is enslaved not by physical chains but by hunger.[90]

Lamennais would have been known to Daumier. Revered by the writers and editors of *Le Charivari*, in 1844 the journal called him 'the greatest writer of the century' and wrote about his unfair imprisonment as a key moment in the government's growing crusade against the press.[91] The repressive press laws passed following the June insurrection caused the closing of many of the newspapers that had sprung up in the heady days of March, including Lamennais' *Le Peuple constituant* (27 February to 11 July 1848), which published as its final death rattle 'Silence to the poor'.[92] In the 1840s alone, Lamennais was mentioned around 150 times in *Le Charivari*. It celebrated his radical political positions as well as his creativity and resistance during his year-long incarceration in Sainte-Pélagie, where Daumier had been jailed a decade earlier.[93] In this journal, Lamennais became associated with unfair censorship and imprisonment, and it is likely that Daumier would have associated humanitarian discourses on slavery with the treatment of the labouring classes in France.

It is notable that Daumier selected a specific vignette from La Fontaine's fable 'The miller, his son, and the ass' that made an allusion to slavery, however glib. The women yell back to the miller that they see 'A father treating like a slave his son!' Foregrounding these women in a composition without direct precedent, Daumier offers a scene of strident critique of the administration of power, an antecedent of more direct explorations of the conditions of urban wage labourers in later paintings including the *Laundress* series and *Man on a rope*. In a period of disappointing reversals to the promises of the Second Republic and in one of Daumier's earliest experiments in paint, La Fontaine's fables were a powerful lens from which to comment on the unsatisfying treatment of the working classes and the press by the newly-elected Louis-Napoleon.

La Fontaine was a dangerous conduit for political speech in the theatre in the 1840s as well. We see evidence of this in the scripts for plays registered with the Minister of the Interior and marked up with corrections. The changes imposed on plays reflect the morals, values, and anxieties of the government officials working in this period. Censors heavily redacted a vaudeville of *La Fontaine's Fables* written in 1842, forcing the playwrights to eliminate references to 'poor people' and the king to avoid politicized commentary.[94] 'King' is changed to 'prince', and 'monarch' to 'autocrat'.[95] There are many instances where other unpleasant references to 'prince' or 'master' are struck from the script altogether. Class and power were pivotal ideas in reinterpretations of La Fontaine in theatrical adaptations of the *Fables* in this period. Later, an anonymously published 1863 vaudeville, *The animals sick of the press*, marks itself as a 'fable in verse, a parody of M. Lafontaine', a play on the fable 'The animals sick of the plague'.[96] The play makes light of the censors' fear of the press and their strict guidelines and harsh punishments, and whole passages were eliminated that argued that the press had important critical or judiciary functions.[97] Clearly, like the illustrated press in the 1830s, there continued to be a tradition in the performing arts of using La Fontaine's fables as ciphers for speech about press freedoms, power, and censorship.

So, an avatar for shifting power structures is set against a group of noisy women, and noise – we will see – was central to the self-conception of the radical leftist press. In the engraved head strip Daumier designed for *Le Charivari* that was published on 24 November 1833, artists become musicians, banging percussive instruments and playing string and brass (Figure 2.18). We understand that they are not meant to harmonize but to produce loud, attention-grabbing noise, conjuring the crash of cymbals and a dramatic drumbeat; inelegant, democratic, and uproarious. The title of the journal *Le Charivari* refers to a rural folk tradition of noisy civic disturbance. Originally a serenade for a newly married couple, a *charivari* eventually became a sort of satirical inversion of this tradition, where a crowd would call attention to the inappropriate sexual behaviour of members of the community (dalliances, second marriages, and large age gaps between partners, for example) by congregating at their residence and making a ruckus by banging pots and pans.[98] The noise of the *charivari* was a popular regulatory mechanism, a strategy of disorganized, cacophonous critique, and Daumier stages artists and journalists of the illustrated press (the staff of *Le Charivari*) not just as musicians but also as people enacting

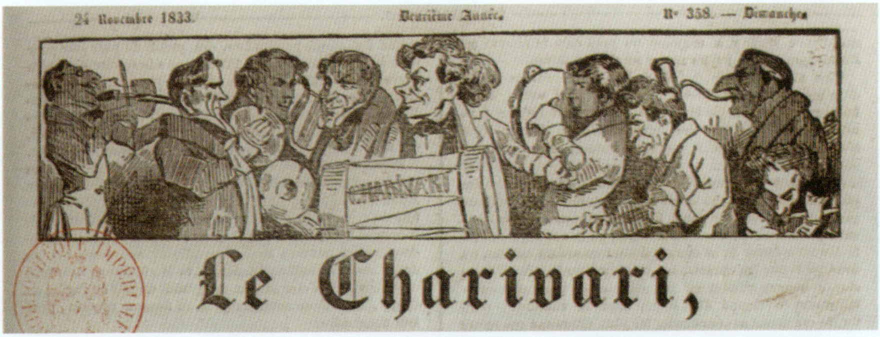

Figure 2.18 Honoré Daumier, Head strip for *Le Charivari*, 24 November 1833

a *charivari*. The three shouting women in *Miller* join this tradition, shouting mockery back to a miller who is struggling with how to manage his power.

The popular shouts carry more weight just after the republican insurrection of 1848 and its attendant debates about how state power should be wielded. The women move through a street, yelling at a man for favouring himself over the next generation. With some hope that gender equality would be baked into the social and political reforms attending the uprising against the Orléanist regime in February of 1848, feminists were one of the contingents soon disappointed by the Second Republic. Women writers such as Marie d'Agoult, George Sand, Delphine Gay de Girardin, and Hortense Allart condemned first the provisional government and then the Second Republic for the disappointing lack of progress regarding the status of women and the betrayal of the working class.[99] Though admittedly many intellectual and political concerns of the feminist movement were skewered in Daumier's lithographs for Philipon's papers, the composition, source text, and context surrounding the reception of La Fontaine suggest that instead of seeing Daumier's trio of women in *The miller, his son, and the ass* as the butt of his joke, they are better understood as dynamic sources of mockery and contumacious speech.[100] Closer to the abstracted allegory of *Sketch of the Republic* than his bluestockings in the illustrated press, we should not see the women in *Miller* standing in for the voices or concerns of contemporary women – towards whom Daumier held little sympathy – but instead for the idea of both mockery and the popular dissatisfaction of the working classes and the opposition press.

This is not to say that this early attempt at painting for the public was successful at balancing the eternal and ephemeral elements or achieving the verve and legible subversive content of his lithographs. A review of *The miller, his son, and the ass* in *L'Union* calls the painting a 'travesty' and pleads with Daumier to go back to caricatures: 'My God! What a strange mistake our excellent cartoonist Mr Daumier has just fallen into! … Now dear Monsieur Daumier, no more bad jokes like this. Make caricatures! Make caricatures! Make caricatures!'[101] Champfleury, too, begged Daumier to go back to his caricatures: 'I was consoled at his moment of weakness when I saw the fable of La Fontaine by Daumier, painted with great freedom; … let him worry no longer about old masterpieces; let him turn inward and he will leave painting behind.'[102] Perhaps the artist thought that the contemporary resonance of La Fontaine would be more obvious based on caricatural precedents. At the very least, he was still working out the balance between timeliness and timelessness, and though there is evidence that he was continuing to investigate press freedoms, power, and popular dissent in this work – themes that persisted throughout his career – these were not made obvious, and the abstract or eternal elements of the story have lent themselves to other interpretations.

Following closely on the heels of *The miller, his son, and the ass*, *Sketch for the martyrdom of Saint Sebastian*, c. 1849–51 is another early experiment by Daumier (Figure 2.19).[103] It is a strange painting that fails in many ways to translate the artist's expertise in bodily gesture into convincing bodily agony. T. J. Clark partially excuses Daumier's experiment by acknowledging the disappointment following the failed revolution of 1848–51. He writes:

> I found the artist's dealings with the state, in the years following the revolution, most unfortunate, and on the whole embarrassing … But I truly never anticipated that the painting would be as unfortunate as the one I illustrate [*Saint Sebastian*] – its modelling so rubbery and half-inflated, its fall of light so perfunctory, its saint's expression so louche.[104]

After the finished painting's rediscovery in a parish church in 1979, art historians have noted that it likely references *Le Charivari*'s battles over press freedoms, primarily through the quill-like palm frond held by a flying putto.[105] Both the sketch and the final painting clearly draw from Daumier's lithograph 'The new St. Sebastian: Virgin and martyr', published in *Le Charivari* on 25 December 1849, a print attacking Doctor Louis-Désiré Véron (1798–1867), who sued the journal in a defamation case that month (Figure 2.20).[106] In the lithograph, Doctor Véron is bound to a tree, and a small archer identified as the journal *Charivari* is about to loose his next arrow into his overextended torso. Véron's face is covered, as Daumier is adhering to restrictions on the representation of 'portraits of celebrated men', one of the reversals to the initial freedoms granted in 1848 (along with the return of security deposits). Press laws tightened because the government saw dangers 'principally born from the deplorable direction which the press has followed for some time'.[107]

Some of Daumier's painterly ambivalence can be linked to his decision to fulfil a commission for a religious subject by layering underneath it an iconography rooted in disgust and indignation, a strike of retribution in a defamation battle. The saint in Daumier's painting is neither ecstatic nor visibly suffering and is instead focused on the approaching angel, which seems to whisper to him. The visual power and rhetorical clarity of 'The new St. Sebastian' was stripped in this confused sublimation of a political idea, and the painting languished in a parish church for over a century, unidentified as the work of the famous visual satirist. *Saint Sebastian* helps us see that the 'failures' of Daumier's early paintings are better understood as an unsteadiness about how to gesture to contemporary politics in paint. We can see him straining between modes of representation, against tendencies towards satire. In the early years of his painting practice, he tested motifs drawn from allegory and

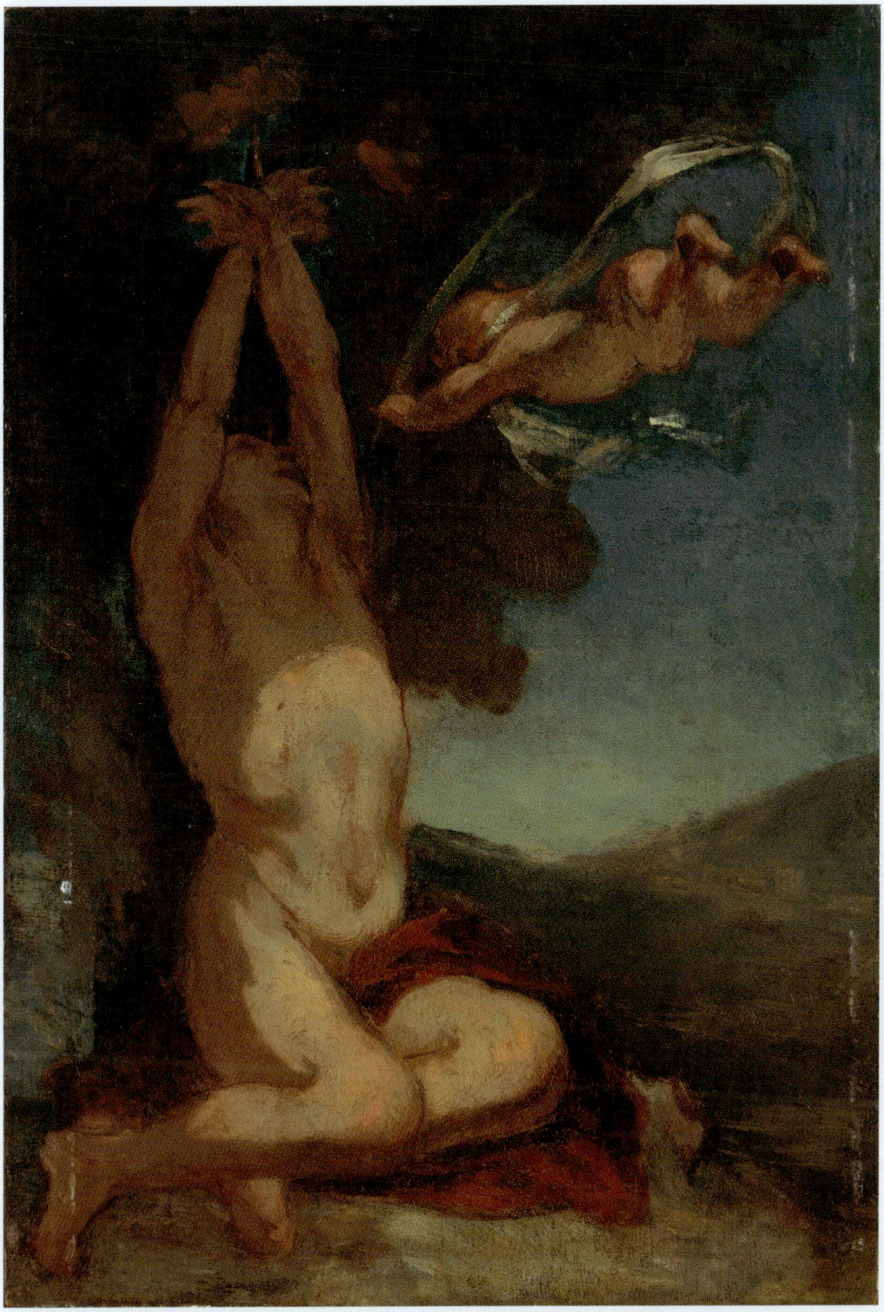

Figure 2.19 Honoré Daumier, *Sketch for the martyrdom of Saint Sebastian*, c. 1849–51

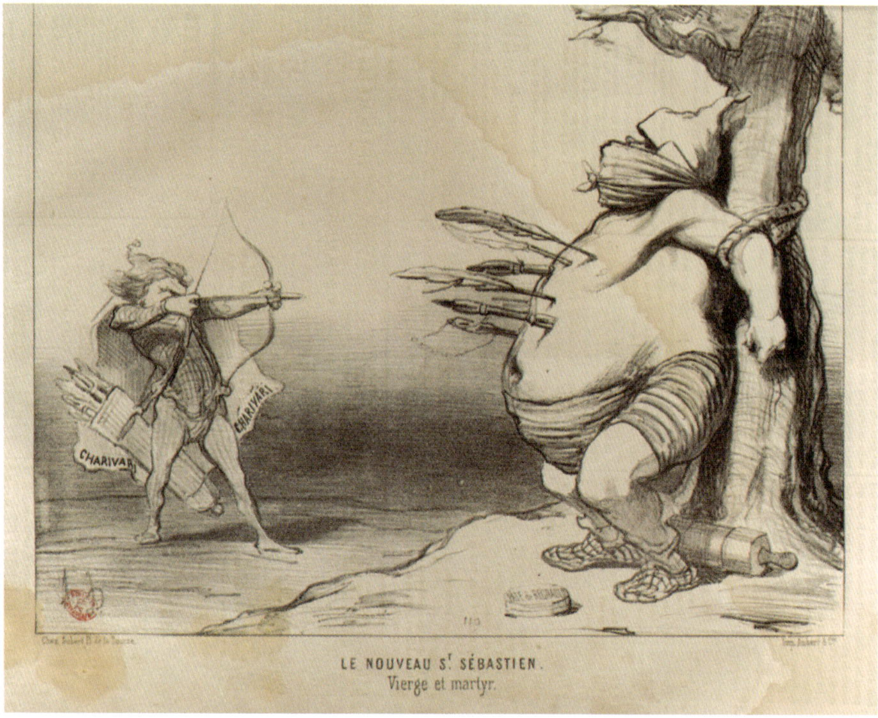

Figure 2.20 Honoré Daumier, 'The new St. Sebastian: Virgin and martyr' ('Le Nouveau St. Sébastien. Vierge et martyr'), *Le Charivari*, 25 December 1849

religious subjects but found more utility in familiar literary sources. La Fontaine carried associations with the navigation of censorial power and his *Fables* were humorous, lessons Daumier would carry forward in his explorations of Molière and Cervantes in paint.

The interest in La Fontaine persisted. In 1855, Daumier was part of a group of Barbizon artists that planned to collectively illustrate a volume of his *Fables*. Along with works by Théodore Rousseau, Martin Etcheverry, Millet, Narcisse Diaz de la Peña, Antoine-Louis Bayre, Jules Dupré, and Eugène Delacroix, Daumier was tasked with contributing designs for seven fables, 'The gardener and his lord', 'The swan and the cook', 'The schoolmaster and the boy', 'The astrologer who fell into a well', 'The cobbler and the financier', 'The oyster and the litigants', and 'The drunkard and his wife', with the desire specifically to draw on his skills representing irony and working-class morals.[108] The project was stalled in its planning stages, but Daumier did produce six drawings in preparation for the illustration of three fables (Maison nos. 394–400). He turned two of these drawings into watercolours.[109]

The Second Empire's Article 22 had tight restrictions on material that could offend the king or political persons, repeating some of the most forceful language from the September Laws of 1835. However, beginning in 1866, while the laws did not change, enforcement became looser and less predictable, and censors were given greater autonomy about what kinds of images they might refuse. In this period, we see Daumier making political caricatures again; as many as 463 between 1866 and 1872.[110] Some of these returned to La Fontaine. 'La Fontaine renewed' ('Renouvelé de Lafontaine') from 10 October 1867 reinterprets 'The wolf as shepherd' (3:3), placing a Prussian as the predator wolf guarding sheep marked as the states of Hesse, Baden, and others (Figure 2.21). Similarly, 'IN SPAIN. The frogs asking for a king.' ('EN ESPAGNE. Les grenouilles qui demandent un roi.' *Le Charivari*, 3 December 1868 (3:4) shows Spanish factions supplicating to an almighty god-king.

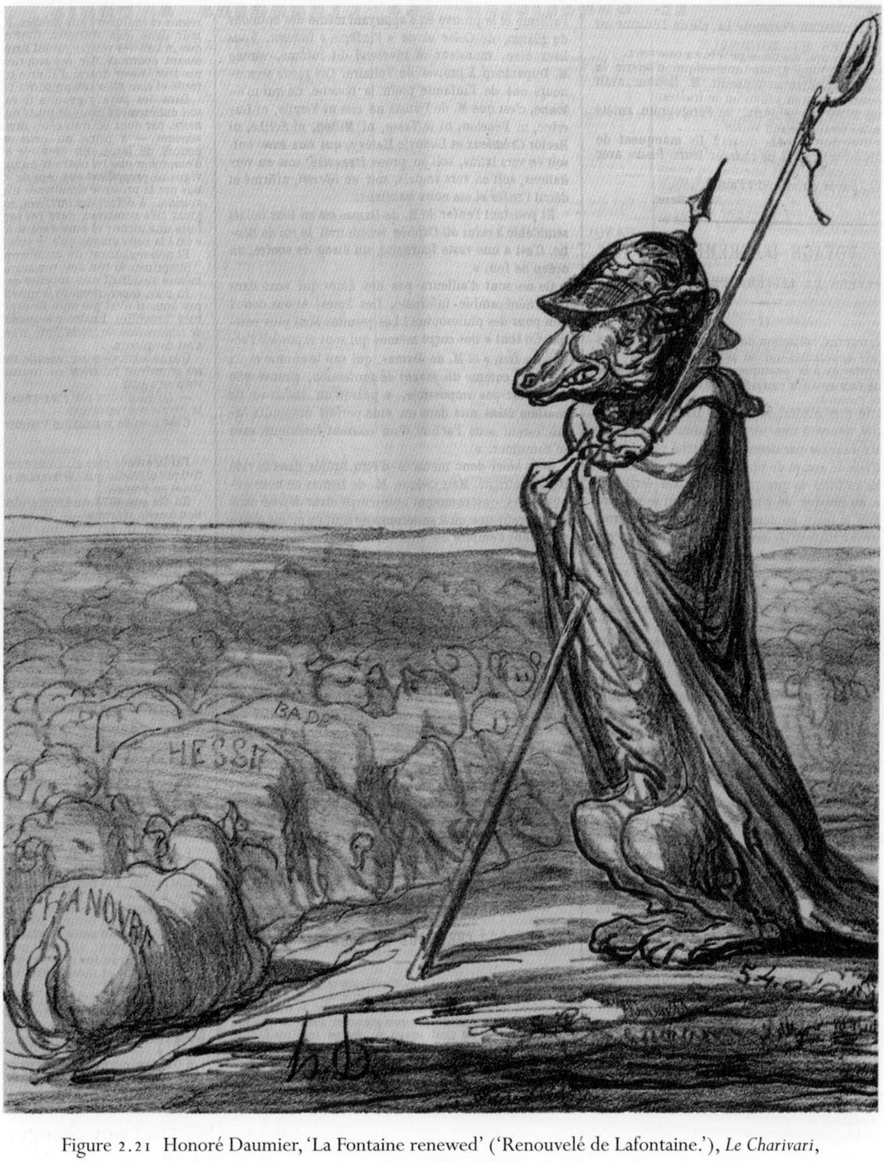

Figure 2.21 Honoré Daumier, 'La Fontaine renewed' ('Renouvelé de Lafontaine.'), *Le Charivari*, 10 October 1867

In 1869, after a new constitutional monarchy was established, censorship of domestic political material was loosened.[111] *Le Charivari* published a *portrait-charge* of Émile Ollivier, who had been formerly allied with the opposition voices of Philipon's papers (Figure 2.22). Ollivier switched alliances to become a liberal monarchist, and the lithograph 'I am a bird, see my wings. I am a bat, long live the rats.' from 1869 paraphrases La Fontaine's 'The bat and the two weasels' ('La Chauve-souris et les deux belettes', 2:5) in a campaign to ruin Ollivier's reputation. The print suggests he is willing to pretend to be any number of loathsome creatures to ensure his own survival. In 1870, Daumier tried to publish 'Revival of the "Fable of the astrologer"' ('Renouvelé de la

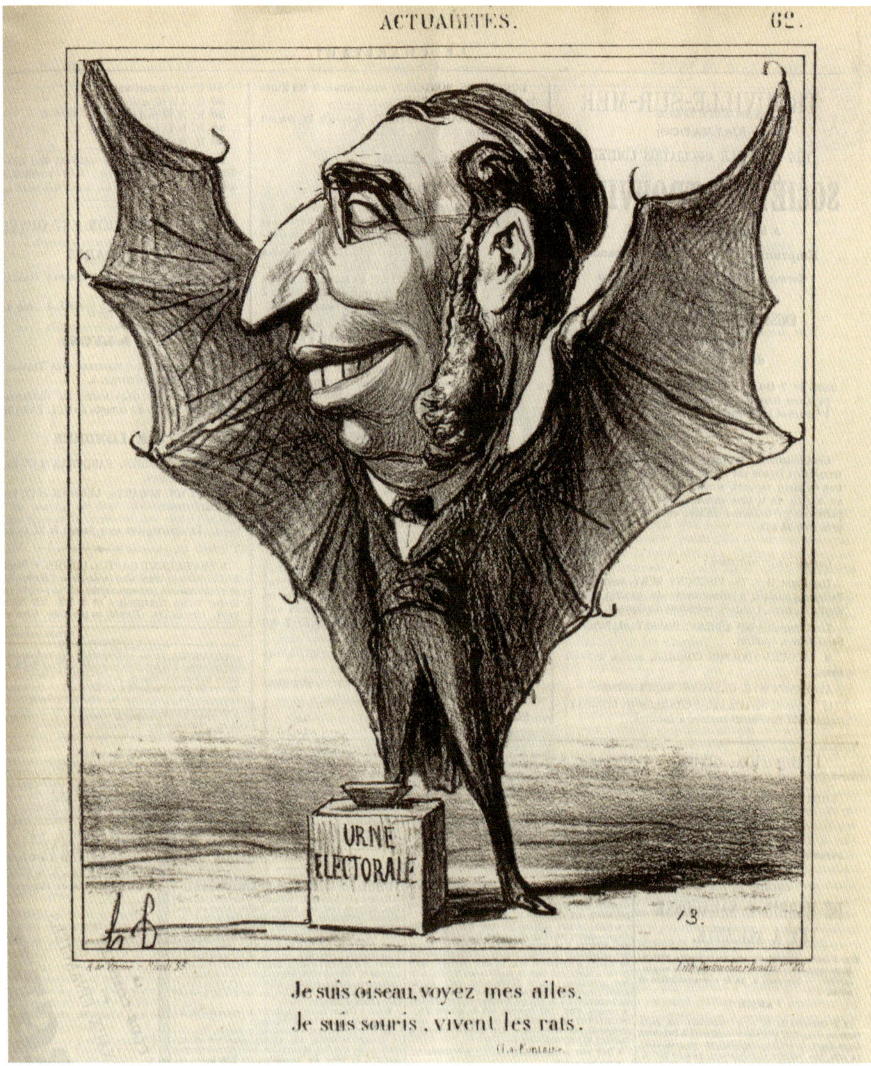

Figure 2.22 Honoré Daumier, 'I am a bird, see my wings. I am a bat, long live the rats (La Fontaine),' ('Je suis oiseau, voyez mes ailes. Je suis souris, vivent les rats. (La Fontaine)'), *Le Charivari*, 24 March 1869

fable de l'astrologue'), a lithograph placing Otto von Bismarck as the astrologer in La Fontaine's fable, but it was deemed too insulting to Prussia at a sensitive political moment and was prohibited by the censors.[112] Daumier's 'The oysters and the suitors' ('L'huitre et les plaideurs', *Le Charivari*, 7 December 1871) targeted domestic politics under the new freedoms in the French Third Republic. Therefore, throughout Daumier's career, La Fontaine remained an important subject in his visual arts practice and a powerful conduit for political speech.

Like *Sketch of the Republic*, *The miller, his son, and the ass* foregrounds powerful, monumental women and organizes its composition around the triangulation of figures. In this move from *Sketch of the Republic* to *Miller*, women go from being a source of sacred and profound national nourishment to figures voicing criticism. They are not stoic, symbolic abstractions that were not supposed to be tainted by realism but lively, noisy figures mined from literary and painterly sources. Departing from the mandates of the competition to create a symbol of the new Republic, *Miller* examined gesture and expression more fully and with Baroque drama, capturing a seventeenth-century artistic sensibility with a seventeenth-century literary source. Daumier gained confidence through pastiche, excerpting figures from Rubens to more fully absorb what he may have perceived as the vocabulary of painting. And he differentiated the subject from traditions of illustration with a dramatic compositional reversal.

Daumier continued to explore humorous literary subjects in paint for nearly three more decades. *The miller, his son, and the ass* sets the scene for the artworks examined in the next two chapters, when Daumier continued to subvert state repression by drawing on the seventeenth-century literary giants Molière and Cervantes, who were understood to have embedded political resistance into their satiric works and to have navigated their own censorship restrictions. Just as we saw La Fontaine emerge in nineteenth-century performances, texts, and the visual arts, there was a cross-fertilization of creative responses to censorship as artists responded to restrictions on new material and integrated the satire of Molière and Cervantes into their work.

This was part of a broader cultural shift towards increased popular expression. The brief freedoms unleashed at the beginning of the July Monarchy and then the Second Republic not only gave French citizens a new appetite for political speech, but they were also given time to develop a vocabulary of effective critique. As Daumier and others first worked out in the precarious moment of the early 1830s and then returned to when state repression started to seep back over the briefly held press freedoms in 1849, La Fontaine's *Fables* were a powerful and legible way to use popular literary humour to excoriate unfair power dynamics. The subject Daumier chose for his Salon debut, 'The miller, his son, and the ass', is a story about community self-policing and the diversity of public opinion. The artist layered stylistic liberties over a narrative celebrating the cacophony of democratic ideas, and we can liken the kind of noise these women make to the work of fables, plays, and cartoons. They project the values of the community in a moment of raucous, untamed, public mockery.

Notes

1 *Explication des ouvrages de peinture, sculpture, architecture, gravure et lithographie des artistes vivants, exposés au Palais de Tuileries le 15 juin 1849* (Paris: Vinchon, 1849), 46. The first painting Daumier exhibited in a major public forum was his entry sketch for the 1848 competition for a symbol for the new Second Republic, *Competition of 1848, sketch of the Republic*. See Albert Boime, 'The Second Republic's contest for the figure of the Republic', *The Art Bulletin* 53, no. 1 (March 1971): 68–83.

2 Jean Adhémar calls La Fontaine's story merely a 'pretext' for the Rubensesque trio of women in the foreground. Jean Adhémar, *Honoré Daumier* (Paris: Tisné, 1954), 41.

3 'Quand trois filles passant, l'une dit: c'est grande honte / Qu'il faille voir ainsi clocher ce jeune fils, / Tandis que ce nigaud, comme un évêque assis, / Fait le veau sur son âne et pense être bien sage; / Il n'est, dit le meunier, plus de veaux à mon âge; / Passez votre chemin, la fille, et m'en croyez. / Après maints quolibets coup sur coup renvoyés, / L'homme crut avoir tort et mit son fils en croupe ...' *Explication des ouvrages de peinture, sculpture ... le 15 juin 1849*, 46. Translation: Jean de La Fontaine, *La Fontaine's Fables*, trans. Walter Thornbury (New York: Cassell, Petter, and Galpin, 1886), 108–9.

4 René Bray, *Les Fables de La Fontaine* (Paris: Malfère, 1929), 150–5. Examples include: *Fables choisies, mises en vers par M. de La Fontaine, avec la Vie d'Ésope, nouvelle édition, augmentée de petites notes pour en faciliter l'intelligence* (Paris: David, 1715); M. Mongez, *Fables choisies de La Fontaine, à l'usage des enfants* (Paris: Agasse, 1797); M. N. S. Guillon, *La Fontaine et tous les fabulistes, ou La Fontaine comparé avec ses modèles et ses imitateurs, nouvelle édition avec des observations critiques, grammaticales, littéraires, et des notes d'histoire naturelle* (Paris: Veuve Nyon, 1803); and F. Roger, *Excerpta, ou Fables choisies de La Fontaine, avec des notes nouvelles; édition prescrite et adoptée par la commission d'instruction publique pour les lycées et les écoles secondaires* (Paris: Delalain, 1805). See too: Antoine-Alexandre Barbier, *Notice des principales éditions des Fables et des œuvres de Jean de La Fontaine* (Paris: Rignoux, n.d.), 5–7.

5 Oliver Larkin, *Daumier: Man of His Time* (New York: McGraw-Hill, 1966), 3–5, 189.

6 David Avrom Bell, *The Cult of the Nation in France: Inventing Nationalism, 1680–1800* (Cambridge, MA: Harvard University Press, 2001), 107–8. See also: Jean-Claude Bonnet, *Naissance du panthéon: Essai sur le culte des grandes hommes* (Paris: Fayard, 1998).

7 Bell, *The Cult of the Nation in France*, 109.

8 Bonnet, *Naissance du panthéon*, 395–6. Albert Boime identifies La Fontaine and Molière in Ingres's grand painting in *Art in the Age of Counterrevolution, 1815–1848* (Chicago: University of Chicago Press, 2004), 226–7.

9 Louis Moland, 'La Fontaine: Sa vie et ses ouvrages', in *Œuvres complètes de La Fontaine*, vol. 7 (Paris: Garnier frères, 1872–76), 26–7.

10 Charles-Athanase Walckenaer, *Histoire de la vie et des ouvrages de J. de La Fontaine*, vol. 2 (Paris: A. Nepveu, 1821), 9–15.

11 'Mais personne ne contribua plus que La Fontaine à intéresser le public en faveur de Fouquet'. Charles-Athanase Walckenaer, *La Fontaine en estampes, ou Nouvelle édition des Fables ... précédée de la vie de l'auteur, extrait du nouvel ouvrage de M. Walckenaer* (Paris: Nepveu, 1821), ix, xxiij–xxv.

12 Moland, 'La Fontaine: Sa vie et ses ouvrages', 27.

13 Moland, 'La Fontaine: Sa vie et ses ouvrages', 27. Moland attributes this phrase to Saint-Beuve.

14 'Il comprend ce qu'est l'égoïsme royal aussi bien que Saint-Simon lui-même. Il le perce à jour, le raille, et n'est jamais la de recommencer son persiflage. Il est sans en douter le plus hardi frondeur du siècle ... Ils sont couverts du monarque pour railler le reste. Il ouvre sa galerie de ridicules par le portrait du roi. Et ce portrait-là ne nuit pas aux autres. Personne n'a

parlé moins respectueusement “de puissances”. Il semble particulièrement se plaire à railler les grands ... Il trouve le loisir de lancer en passant des traits contre les nobles “mangeurs de gens”, contre les “volereaux” qui font les voleurs, contre les seigneurs “qui one belle tête, mais point de cervelle”, ou “qui n'ont que l'habit pour tout talent.”' Hippolyte Taine, *La Fontaine et ses fables* (Paris: Hachette, 1888), 28. This was originally published in 1853.

15 See Wolfgang Drost, *Jean de La Fontaine dans l'univers des arts* (Heidelberg: Carl Winter Universitätsverlag, 1991).

16 Bray, *Les Fables de La Fontaine*, 140.

17 Roger Chartier and Henri-Jean Martin, *Histoire de l'édition francaise: Le temps des éditeurs* (Paris: Fayard/Promodis, 1990), 353.

18 Drost, *Jean de La Fontaine dans l'univers des arts*, 55–71.

19 Drost, *Jean de La Fontaine dans l'univers des arts*, 72–3.

20 Jean de La Fontaine, *La Morale en action des fables de La Fontaine: collection de vignettes dessinées par Henry Monnier et gravées par Thompson* ..., vols. 1–2 (Paris: Urbain Canel, 1828); and Jean de La Fontaine, *La Morale en action des fables de La Fontaine: collection de vignettes dessinées par Henry Monnier et gravées par Thompson* ..., vols. 3–4 (Paris: Perrotin, 1830). Chartier and Martin, *Histoire de l'édition francaise*, 353.

21 Robert Justin Goldstein, *Censorship of Political Caricature in Nineteenth-Century France* (Kent, OH: Kent State University Press, 1989), 113–15. *La Silhouette* defended against the war on caricaturists, including Monnier, in an anonymous article on 24 June 1830.

22 Eugène Desmares, 'Le Monarque, son fils et le peuple', *Les Métamorphoses du jour, ou La Fontaine en 1831* (Paris: Delaunay, 1831), 91–4.

23 'La presse se plaindra; tel est l'esprit français'. Desmares, 'Le Monarque, son fils et le peuple', *Les Métamorphoses du jour, ou La Fontaine en 1831* (Paris: Delaunay, 1831), 94.

24 Desmares, 'Le Monarque, son fils et le peuple', 93.

25 'usurpateurs'; 'Couple sot et quasi-légitime!' Desmares, 'Le Monarque, son fils et le peuple', 91, 92.

26 *Le Moniteur universel* (25 September 1831): 1

27 'Cour d'assises de la Seine', *Journal des débats politiques et littéraires* (26 January 1832): 2.

28 'Le public n'a oublié ni le nom de M. Eugène Desmares ni la prison qui vint il y a quelques années, interrompre ce jeune écrivain parodiant Lafontaine au profit de son opinion politique.' F. T. Claudon, 'Fables démocratiques par Émile Pagès', *Le Charivari* (23 October 1839): 4.

29 Claudon, 'Fables démocratiques par Émile Pagès', 2. This text is largely the same as Claudon's preface for the 1839 book, which also acknowledges that most of the fables in the published volume had already appeared in *Le Charivari* or *Le Journal du peuple* before that date.

30 'J'ai donc tout simplement métamorphosé Lafontaine en journaliste démocrate, et ses bêtes en ministres constitutionnels, en pairs de France et on députés de tous les centres.' Louis Bergeron and François Théodore Claudon, *Fables démocratiques par Emile Pagès* (Paris: Aux bureaux du Charivari, 1839), 13. Claudon wrote the preface. Some of the fables shift their focus to international issues (Spain features prominently), but some mention deputies and ministers like Guizot, Thiers, and Persil by name.

31 'Si tous les écrivains l'entendaient, et surtout s'ils l'exécutaient comme M. Emile Pagès, ils pourraient, par ce genre d'ouvrage, rendre à peu de frais d'invention, de très grands services au public contemporain, et quelquefois même aux ouvrages anciens, qu'ils rajeuniraient, dans leur partie changeante, en les appropriant à des choses, à des mœurs et à des institutions nouvelles.' Claudon, 'Fables démocratiques par Émile Pagès', 2.

32 Kirsten Powell, *Fables in Frames: La Fontaine and Visual Culture in Nineteenth-Century France* (New York: Peter Lang, 1997), 79.

33 Goldstein, *Censorship of Political Caricature in Nineteenth-Century France*, 146–7. See also Edwin de T. Bechtel, *Freedom of the Press and L'Association Mensuelle: Philipon Versus Louis-Philippe* (New York: The Grolier Club, 1952).

34 'Dans la caisse du roi, mon ami, j'appréhende / Que mon argent pour moi soit de mince rapport. / Je crois le prince humaine et bon; mais dans cet antre / Je vois fort bien comme l'or entre; / Je ne vois pas comme il en sort.' 'Dessin. Le Roi Lion et le fin renard. Imitation libre de la fable de Lafontaine, intitulée: *Le Lion malade et le Renard*'. *Le Charivari* (21 September 1834), 2.

35 Daumier Register.

36 Daumier Register.

37 Powell, *Fables in Frames*, 79.

38 'Dessin', *Le Charivari* (11 June 1835): 2.

39 Boime, 'The Second Republic's contest', 68. See also: Bernard Lemann, 'Daumier and the Republic', *Gazette des Beaux-Arts* 27 (February 1945): 104–20.

40 Adhémar, *Honoré Daumier*, 36.

41 Maurice Agulhon, 'Preface', in Marie-Claude Chaudonneret, *La Figure de la République* (Paris: Éditions de la Réunion des musées nationaux, 1987), 8.

42 Agulhon, *La Figure de la République*, 5–7; Chaudonneret, *La Figure de la République* 36–9. Chaudonneret traces the iconographic origins of many of these female symbols to Roman art as well as Ripa's *Iconologia* (1593) and Gravelot and Cochin's manual *Iconologie par figures*, n.d [1789–91], 35. The first call to artists was made on 14 March 1848 in *Le Moniteur universel*: 634 outlining the single-figure guideline, among others. The Phrygian cap was required to identify the symbol as the Republic, yet in 1848 it put many ill-at-ease as a symbol too close to their bloody republican predecessors and so, the programme stated, it could be transformed. Many painters chose to alter it to become a crown of leaves. Chaudonneret 42–3.

43 'Et que le diable emporte les allégories qui n'ont ni queue ni tête.' Théodore de Banville, *Petites études. Mes souvenir: Victor Hugo, Henri Heine, Théophile Gautier, Honoré de Balzac, Honoré Daumier, Alfred de Vigny ... etc.* (Paris: G. Charpentier, 1882), 166.

44 Passeron, *Daumier*, 159–60.

45 Irene Collins, *The Government and the Newspaper Press in France 1814–1881* (London: Oxford University Press, 1959), 101–2.

46 Chaudonneret, La Figure de la République, 65–6.

47 Collins, *The Government and the Newspaper Press in France 1814–1881*, 105–10.

48 Collins, *The Government and the Newspaper Press in France 1814–1881*, 104–7.

49 Laura O'Brien, *The Republican Line: Caricature and the French Republican Identity* (Manchester: Manchester University Press, 2015), 205–17.

50 O'Brien, *The Republican Line*, 211–20.

51 O'Brien, *The Republican Line*, 217.

52 Collins, *The Government and the Newspaper Press in France 1814–1881*, 105–10. See too: Henry Izambard, *La Presse parisienne: Statistique bibliographique et alphabétique de tous les journaux, revues et canards périodiques nés, morts, ressuscités ou métamorphosés à Paris depuis la 22 février 1848 jusqu'à l'Empire ... Précédé des lois actuelles qui régissent la presse, et suivi de la liste exacte de tous les journaux des départements* (Paris: P.-H. Krabbe, 1853).

53 O'Brien, *The Republican Line*, 246–8.

54 His exploration of themes around country life include the *Album la chasse*, *Album pastorales*, *Émotions de chasse*, and others. He would also soon demonstrate profound sympathy with rural labour in paintings like *The boat hauler* (c. 1850–55), drawing from Jean-François Millet's social realism.

55 *Explication des ouvrages de peinture, de sculpture, dessin, gravure etc. faisant partie de l'exposition de la Société des amis des arts de Lyon, en 1836* (Lyon: Société des amis des arts de Lyon, 1836), no. 172, 25.

56 *Explication des ouvrages de peinture, sculpture, architecture, gravure et lithographie des artistes vivants, exposés au Palais de Tuileries le 15 juin 1849* (Paris: Vinchon, 1849), no. 1993, 174; no. 1825, 160; no. 1678, 148; no. 2467, 221.

57 These titles are listed in 'Nécrologie: Marcel Verdier'. *Le Pays: journal des volontés de la France* (19 August 1856): n.p.; *Revue universelle des arts*, vol. 4 (Paris: Paul Lacroix, 1856), 95.

58 Larkin, *Daumier*, 87. K. E. Maison, *Honoré Daumier: Catalogue Raisoneé of the Paintings, Watercolors, and* Drawings 1 (Greenwich, CT: New York Graphic Society, 1968), 64. Maison credits Larkin for the comparison. See also: Gabriele Mandel, 'Catalogue des œuvres', in *Tout l'œuvre peint de Daumier* (Paris: Flammarion, 1972), 90; and Passeron, *Daumier*, 35–7.

59 Many biographers have traced Daumier's admiration for Rubens to his early apprenticeship with Alexander Lenoir. Lenoir owned a sketch by Rubens and had a strong appreciation for the artist's colourism at the time of young Daumier's brief apprenticeship. Passeron, *Daumier*, 35–7, 82, 172. Daumier copied Rubens' grand pastoral celebration of pleasure, *The village fête (La Kermesse)*, in the Louvre between 1846–48. Adhèmar, *Daumier*, 106.

60 Powell, *Fables in Frames*, 89.

61 'Tout l'œuvre se compose de deux élémens [sic] nécessaires, mais bien distincts: l'un généralement et éternellement vrai, l'autre vrai aussi, mais d'une manière relative et par conséquent transitoire. Or, reprendre l'œuvre après un laps de temps qui a enlevé à la seconde partie toute sa vérité, et montrer sur la première, fidèlement conservée, quelque vérité ou quelque satire plus actuelles, sans changer rien ou presque rien au cadre original, c'est faire proprement un parodie.' Bergeron and Claudon, *Fables démocratiques par Emile Pagès*, 8.

62 Jean de La Fontaine, *Fables*, ill. J. J. Grandville (Paris: H. Fornier, 1838), n.p.

63 See: Hippolyte Lecomte (1817) and the classicizing illustrations by Gabriel Bernard Seurre (Seurre aîné) from 1849 as examples.

64 'MM. Daumier et Marcel Verdier ont traduit le bon La Fontaine, mais, à notre avis, un peu trop librement.' Auguste Galimard, 'Examen du Salon de 1849', *L'Artiste* (Paris: n.d.]), 88. Verdier exhibited 'L'homme entre deux âges et ses deux maîtresses' from La Fontaine's *Fables* the same year. *Explication des ouvrages de peinture, sculpture … le 15 juin 1849*, 174.

65 'L'auteur des dessins du Charivari, l'illustre et sérieux artiste qui laissera, comme le monument de l'an 1er de la République de 1848, sa galerie de *Représentants représentés*, Daumier, a attaqué la peinture avec le courage et la verve qu'on lui sait. C'est le *Meunier, son fils et l'âne* qui sert de texte au tableau; mais le peintre a laissé ces trois acteurs dans le lointain, afin de mettre en scène trois grasses créatures qui s'égosillent de rire à regarder l'âne se prélassant comme un archevêque.' Champfleury [Jules-François-Félix Husson], *Œuvres posthumes. Salons 1846–1851* (Paris, 1894), 176.

66 'J'ai été consolé de ce moment de faiblesse en voyant la fable de La Fontaine de Daumier, peinte avec une grande liberté; quelques-uns ne trouveront peut-être pas ce tableau assez *français*. Il est vrai que les trois joyeuses commères me rappellent de belles Maritornes espagnoles, plutôt par la physionomie que par la manière de peindre; mais ceci ne vaut pas la peine d'être

discuté. Désormais Daumier appartient à la famille de maîtres; qu'il ne s'inquiète pas trop des chefs-d'œuvre anciens; qu'il se regarde en dedans, et il laissera de la peindre.' Champfleury, *Œuvres posthumes. Salons 1846–1851* (Paris, 1894), 178. Maritornes is a comically ugly servant in Cervantes's *Don Quixote*.

67 Powell, *Fables in Frames*, 79–83. Powell believes this painting criticizes feminist activists of the period.

68 *Le Robert. Dictionnaire historique de la langue française*, ed. Alain Rey, vol. 1 (Paris: Dictionnaires Le Robert, 1998), 133.

69 Susan Tiefenbrun, 'The art and artistry of teaching in the fables of La Fontaine', *L'Esprit créateur* 21, no. 4 (Winter 1981): 58.

70 Pierre Boutang, *La Fontaine politique* (Paris: J.-E.. Hallier/Albin Michel, 1981), 198. In addition to 'Le meunier, son fils, et l'âne' (3:1), some of these include 'L'âne et ses maîtres' (6:11); 'Le cheval et l'âne' (6:16); 'L'âne et le chien' (8:17); 'Le vieillard et l'âne' (1.8); 'Le voleurs et l'âne' (1:13); 'L'âne et ses maîtres' (6:11); 'Le cheval et l'âne' (6:16); and 'L'âne et le chien' (8:17).

71 Maison I-116, the painting now at the Musée d'Orsay, was the first of Daumier's paintings accepted into the Louvre's collections. It is related to Maison I-115, a smaller canvas in a private collection, and is likely based on two lithographs from 1844 and 1845 of hunters and their dogs and a street fight. 'I tell you, I made him leave' ('Je te dis que je l'ai fait partir') *Le Charivari* (10 January 1844) and 'But what's worse, I tell you, they're friends' ('Mais pis que j'vous dis qu'c'est des amis') *Le Charivari* (23 August 1845). Michael Pantazzi, 'The Thieves and the ass', in Honoré Daumier, J. Douglas Campbell, Usher Caplan, National Gallery of Canada, Galeries nationales du Grand Palais (France), and Phillips Collection Daumier, Honoré, J. Douglas Campbell, Usher Caplan, National Gallery of Canada, Galeries nationales du Grand Palais (France), and Phillips Collection, *Daumier 1808–1879: National Gallery of Canada, Ottawa, 11 June–6 September 1999; Galeries nationales du Grand Palais, Paris, 5 October 1999–3 January 2000; Phillips Collection, Washington, 19 February–14 May* 2000, exh. cat. (Ottawa: National Gallery of Canada, 1999), 334–6.

72 'The Thieves and the ass' (1:13), *The Fables of La Fontaine*, trans. Elizur Wright (London: Bell, 1892), 15. 'L'âne, c'est quelquefois une pauvre province: / Les voleurs sont tel et tel prince, / Comme le Transilvain, le Tuc, et le Hongrois. / Au lieu de deux, j'en ai rencontré trois: / Il est assez de cette marchandise. / De nul d'eux n'est souvent la province conquise: / Un quart voleur survient qui les accorde net / En se saisissant du baudet.' Jean de La Fontaine, *Fables (Nouvelle éd. précédée d'une notice biographique et littéraire, accompagné de notes)* (Paris: Hachette, 1843), 16.

73 Georges Couton, *La politique de La Fontaine* (Paris: Société d'édition 'les Belles lettres', 1959), 7.

74 '[J]'emploierais volontiers le mot de Baudelaire et parlerais de la "modernité" des Fables ... Il est des fables qui font très ouvertement allusion à la politique extérieure. Dans d'autres, un mot de ci de là nous remet bien dans le climat du temps, nous avertissant que les masques animaux dissimulent à peine des hommes, et, qui plus est, contemporains exacts du fabuliste: pauvres reclus, espions de cour, devineresses; mais il est rare que le fabuliste laisse deviner quel incident de la politique intérieure l'a inspiré.' Couton, *La politique de La Fontaine*, 9–11.

75 'Notre ennemi, c'est notre maître.' Jean de La Fontaine, 'Le Vieillard et l'âne' (6:8), *Fables* (Paris: Hachette, 1843), 130. This strain of pacifism includes Louis Petit's *Discours satiriques et moraux* (1686) and the writings of La Bruyère. Couton, *La politique de La Fontaine*, 95.

76 Couton, *La politique de La Fontaine*, 99–100.

77 Bray, *Les Fables de La Fontaine*, 110–11.

78 'A question de l'esclavage, cet embarras éternel des gouvernements qui ne veulent pas l'aborder de front, revenait hier à la chambre des députés, sous forme de rapport d'une pétition adressée par les ouvriers de Paris en faveur de l'émancipation ...' *Le Charivari* (6 May 1844): 1. In the 1860s French newspapers continued to criticise slavery but shifted focus to the American context. See: George M. Blackburn, 'Paris newspapers and the American Civil War', *Illinois Historical Journal* 84, no. 3 (1991): 177–93.

79 Frédéric Régent, *La France et ses esclaves: de la colonisation aux abolitions, 1620–1848* (Paris: Pluriel, 2012), 284–5. For example, in 1843 the Commission pour l'examen des questions relatives à l'esclavage produced a report offering two solutions: simultaneous emancipation on the first day of 1853 or progressive emancipation spread over twenty years. See also: Nelly Schmidt, *Abolitionnistes de l'esclavage et réformateurs des colonies (1820–1851)* (Paris: Karthala, 2000).

80 'Eh bien! je vous prie de me dire si, parmi les ânes dont nous rabaissons tant les facultés intellectuelles, il y en a qui se lassent réduire, par leurs semblables, à l'état de chardon; qui se laissent posséder, vendre, torturer, mener à la foire ou au moulin par d'autres ânes? Cela ne s'est jamais vu chez les ânes. Donc, les hommes sont plus ânes que les ânes eux-mêmes ... Nous n'avons jamais entendu braire aux ânes des raisonnements si cocasses que celui-ci, dont la discussion du budget de la marine nous procure annuellement le retour. Donc les ânes, même ayant d'être tannés, raisonnent beaucoup mieux que les hommes.' 'Comment nos honorables ... à propos de l'affranchissement des Négres', *Le Charivari* (27 May 1836): 1–2.

81 'Le Meunier, le fermier et l'âne (Fable)', *Le Charivari* (17 October 1838): 2.

82 'Je connais tel était dans un coin de la sphère / A qui de ce pauvre âne on fait subir le sort ...' 'Le Meunier, le fermier et l'âne (Fable)', 2.

83 Schmidt, *Abolitionnistes,* 527.

84 Hugh Honour, David Bindman, and Henry Louis Gates, *The Image of the Black in Western* Art, vol. 4, part 1 (Cambridge, MA: Belknap, 2012), 123–4. Britain voted to abolish slavery in 1834 and it took effect in 1838, though extractive colonial practices continued. As a result, the July Monarchy felt pressure to dial back its practice and agreed to ship inspections by the British.

85 *L'Illustration* (20 May 1843): 197.

86 Honour et al., *The Image of the Black in Western Art*, 127–8.

87 'Nécrologie: Marcel Verdier', *Le Pays: journal des volontés de la France* (19 August 1856): n.p.

88 Frédéric Régent, *La France et ses esclaves: De la colonisation aux abolitions (1620–1848)* (Paris: Bernard Grasset, 2007), 286–7.

89 Naomi J. Andrews, 'Selective empathy: Workers, colonial subjects, and the affective politics of French Romantic socialism', *French Politics, Culture & Society* 36 (2018): 3–4.

90 Félicité Robert de Lamennais, *De l'esclavage moderne* (Paris: Pagnerre, 1839), 36. An article from *Le Charivari* notes that *De l'esclavage modern*'s editor had his home raided by the commissaire of police and his papers destroyed that same year. *Le Charivari* (9 March 1840): 4.

91 'Lamennais, le plus grand écrivain du siècle', 'Académie français', *Le Charivari* (10 February 1844): 1. 'Il parait, du reste, que la saisie de l'ouvrage de M. Lamennais est le prélude d'une croisade générale contre la presse.' *Le Charivari* (21 October 1840): 1–2.

92 Collins, *The Government and the Newspaper Press in France 1814–1881*, 106.

93 See for example Alphonse Esquiros, 'La Prison', *Le Charivari* (4 July 1841): 1 as well as mentions of Lamennais' imprisonment in issues (17 October 1840): 1 and (13 August, 1841): 1–2, among others.

94 Archives nationales, Pierrefitte-sur-Seine, France (hereafter AN), F/18/788, manuscript of a play by Langlois, Vanderburch, Pittaud de Forges, *Les Fables de La Fontaine* (1842), 5, 4, 10.

95 For example, 'Roi pour rire, monarque infiniment trop fatiguons, tu vas nous fiche le camp tous de suite … voilà notre ultimatum', becomes 'Prince pour rire …' AN F/18/788, 94.

96 AN F/18/762, manuscript of play by unknown author ('after La Fontaine'), *Les Animaux maladies de la presse* (25 April 1863).

97 AN F/18/762. The three passages struck from the text all liken the press to 'une magistrature'.

98 Emma Dillon, *The Sense of Sound: Musical Meaning in France, 1260–1330* (Oxford: Oxford University Press, 2012), 93. See also *Le Robert* 1:707, which dates this tie between disturbance and discordant music to 1690.

99 Whitney Walton, 'Writing the 1848 revolution: Politics, gender, and feminism in the works of French women of letters', *French Historical Studies* 18, no. 4 (Autumn 1994): 1001–24.

100 Daumier's *Bluestockings* (Les Bas-bleus), *The Divorced women* (Les Divorceuses), and *Socialist women* (Les Femmes socialistes) series were made up of almost 60 plates. Mocking suffragettes and feminist ideas, these prints show clear hostility to women's liberation, suffrage, and intellectual empowerment. Interestingly, Janis Bergman-Carton observes that the working class or Saint-Simonian feminist newspapers were largely left out of the attacks on women intellectuals by Philipon's papers. Bourgeois *bas-bleus* were not so lucky, so this neglect may indicate some acknowledgement of class solidarity or political affinity. Janis Bergman-Carton, 'Conduct unbecoming: Daumier and les bas-bleus', in *Reclaiming Female Agency: Feminist Art History after Postmodernism*, ed. Norma Broude and Mary D. Garrard (Berkeley, CA: University of California Press, 2005), 205. See too: Kirsten Powell, Elizabeth C. Childs, Christian A. Johnson Memorial Gallery, and Neuberger Museum, *Femmes d'esprit: Women in Daumier's Caricature* (Middlebury, VT: C. A. Johnson Memorial Gallery, Middlebury College, 1990); Louis Provost, *Honoré Daumier: A Thematic Guide to the Œuvre*, ed. Elizabeth C. Childs (New York: Garland, 1989); and Honoré Daumier and Jacqueline Armingeat, *Lib Women: Bluestockings and Socialist Women* (Paris: L. Amiel, 1974).

101 'A regret, nous n'en dirons pas autant du *Meunier, son fils, et l'âne*; cette *délicieuse moralité* si souvent traduite avec esprit par le crayon, qui pourra la reconnaître ainsi travestie? Mon Dieu! Dans quelle étrange erreur vient de tomber notre excellent caricaturiste, M. Daumier! Pour lui, les années se suivent et se ressemblent, à l'Exposition, du moins; car, en 1848, l'auteur de tant de charges parfaites, qui stigmatisent les fous et les sots, ne s'avisa-t-il pas de concourir pour aime statue symbolique de la République? Pour punir d'un tel écart, peu s'en fallut, assure-t-on, qu'il ne remportât le prix: son nom lui fit tort. Maintenant, cher monsieur Daumier, plus de mauvaises plaisanteries comme celle-là. Faites des caricatures! Faites des caricatures! Faites des caricatures!' Ch. De. B., 'Exposition des ouvrages d'art aux Tuileries en 1849', *L'Union* 205 (24 July 1849): [n.p. (1)].

102 'J'ai été consolé de ce moment de faiblesse en voyant la fable de La Fontaine de Daumier, peinte avec une grande liberté; quelques-uns ne trouveront peut-être pas ce tableau assez *français*. Il est vrai que les trois joyeuses commères me rappellent de belles Maritornes espagnoles, plutôt par la physionomie que par la manière de peindre; mais ceci ne vaut pas la peine d'être discuté. Désormais Daumier appartient à la famille de maîtres; qu'il ne s'inquiète pas trop des chefs-d'œuvre anciens; qu'il se regarde en dedans, et il laissera de la peindre.' Champfleury, *Œuvres posthumes. Salons 1846–1851* (Paris, 1894), 178.

103 The artist received the first payment in April of 1849, a few months before he painted *The miller, his son, and the ass*. *Daumier 1808–1879* [Ottawa], 553. Daumier's painting was one of two commissions for religious paintings by the state at that time. *Mary Magdalene in the desert* (1848–49) was never delivered but the state accepted a gouache of *The drunkenness of Silenus* (Salon of 1851) in its place in 1863. Laughton identifies the period Daumier was painting

his *Saint Sebastian* as 11 April 1849 to 30 June 1852. Bruce Laughton, *Honoré Daumier* (New Haven: Yale University Press, 1996), 21–4.

104 T. J. Clark, *The Absolute Bourgeois: Artists and Politics in France 1848–1851* (London: Thames & Hudson, 1973), 6.

105 Laughton, *Honoré Daumier*, 24.

106 Véron sued in the sixth chamber of the correctional police. The lawsuit was described on the front page of *Le Constitutionnel*, which Véron owned and directed: *Le Constitutionnel* (23 December 1849): 1. He sued over the 12 December 1849 article in *Le Charivari*, 'Au seigneur Fontanarose'. The Daumier Register offers background into the 'Véron-series' and this print's connection to the defamation suit between *Le Charivari* and the owner of *Le Constitutionnel*, 'New research results for DR1917', Daumier Register, www.daumier.org/fileadmin/daumier_reference/DR1917_E.htm (accessed 1 November 2022). See also: 'Véron, ce saint homme, a des ennemis qui ne rendent pas à son admirable piété toute la justice qu'elle mérite!' 'Circulaire-Rouher: À tous les bedeaux des paroisses de France', *Le Charivari* (20 December 1849): 2. A preparatory sketch in charcoal at the Metropolitan Museum in New York makes this source even clearer, the saint closely mirroring the left-facing orientation of Véron, his standing position, and the attachment of ropes to his elbows, not his wrists. Colta Feller Ives, Margret Stuffmann, Martin Sonnabend, Klaus Herding, and Judith Wechsler, *Daumier Drawings* (New York: Metropolitan Museum of Art, 1992), 102–3.

107 Goldstein, *Censorship of Political Caricature in Nineteenth-Century France*, 171–5.

108 Alfred Sensier, *Souvenirs sur Th. Rousseau* (Paris: Leon Techener, 1872), 230–2. 'Le Villageois et son seigneur' (4:4), 'Le Cygne et le cuisiner' (3:12), 'L'Écolier et le pédant' (1:19), 'L'Astrologue qui se laisse tomber dans un puits' (2:13), 'Le Savetier et le financier' (8:2), 'l'Huître et les plaideurs' (9:9), and 'l'Ivrogne et sa femme' (3:7).

109 Maison, *Honoré Daumier* II, 137.

110 Judith Wechsler, 'Daumier and censorship. 1866–1872', *Yale French Studies*, no. 122, Out of Sight: Political Censorship of the Visual Arts in Nineteenth-Century France (2012): 53–5.

111 Wechsler, 'Daumier and censorship', 64.

112 Laughton, *Honoré Daumier,* 189 n33.

3

Molière's whisper / Daumier's clamour

It's quite difficult to get one's bearings from the wings of a theatre;
– statesmen suffer from the same blindness.

(Gérard de Nerval, *The Salt Smugglers, 1850*)[1]

On 11 September 1834, a year before devastating restrictions on speech made Daumier's publication of political caricatures all but impossible, *La Caricature* published his lithograph captioned 'Lower the curtain. The farce is over' (Figure 3.1). Louis-Philippe, recognizable by an overfed, pear-shaped face, commands a great stage. He gestures theatrically towards a statue of blind justice – here hollowed out to a prop – with his right arm extending across a heavy theatre curtain. Behind the curtain, the curved amphitheatre of parliament is seen from above, at some distance. Drawing its title from Rabelais's dying words, this is the same space from Daumier's 'The legislative belly' of January 1834, the Chamber of the Palais Bourbon which served as the seat of the French legislature (Figure 1.10).[2] A stage light at lower left casts dramatic shadows in the upper right behind Louis-Philippe's face, making his looming figure all the more sinister as he slowly lowers the curtain on the farce of French parliamentary authority and legislative checks on his power.

The basic joke in 'Lower the curtain. The farce is over' is meant to illuminate the disingenuous performance of democracy and the charade of shared power. Louis-Philippe is a kind of puppet master, signalling the end of one act in political history and stepping from the shadows into the spotlight. He is dressed as a clown from the *commedia dell'arte*, wearing a costume similar to the trickster Harlequin (Figure 3.2). He removes his hat, as if about to bow, revealing either a face or a mask-like plaster membrane frozen in a smug grimace. The comic mask, like Daumier's caricatural abstractions, simplifies and exaggerates Louis-Philippe's portrait into a *charge*. Combining this satirical portrait with a stock character from an ancient theatrical tradition, Daumier cues questions about the line between archetype and individual, disguise and recognition.

'Lower the curtain' establishes an association between theatre and contemporary politics, using theatre as a lens through which politics is refracted, refocused, made entertaining, and

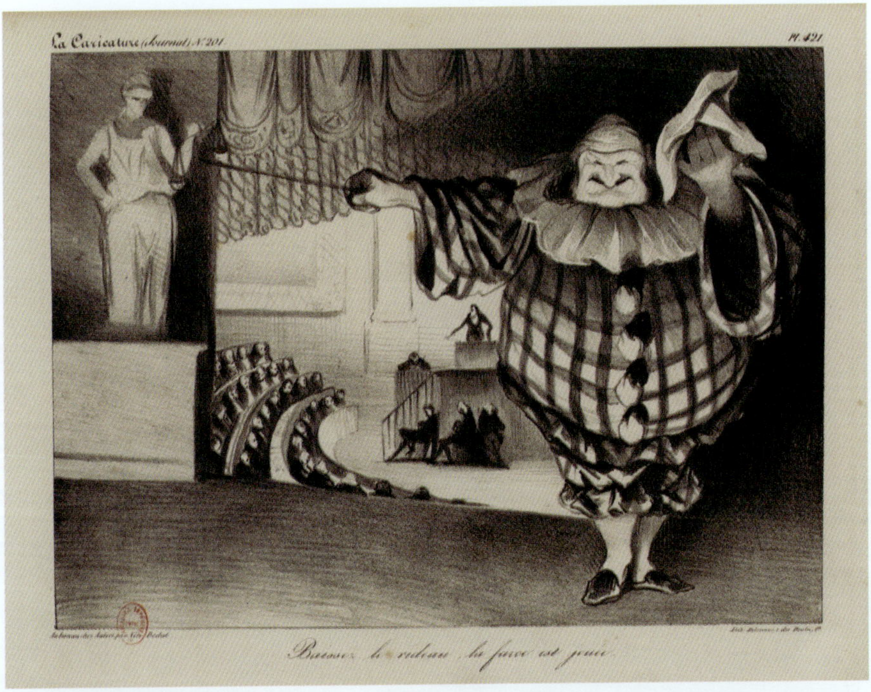

Figure 3.1 Honoré Daumier, 'Lower the curtain. The farce is over'. *La Caricature*, 11 September 1834

critiqued. By setting up the viewers of his print as an audience of political theatre, Daumier poses questions about their level of engagement or passivity. Louis-Philippe gestures towards the scales of justice, inviting the audience to react and evaluate. Do we applaud as the curtain falls? Audience response was not only a metaphor for public judgement of contemporary events. It was also used, quite radically and at precisely the moment Daumier drew this lithograph, to define media and to restrict their expression. Caricature and theatre were censored not because of their material form, but because of the audience reaction they were said to incite. Daumier would be drawn to a caricatural style in his depictions of the theatre in the decades that followed, in part because of these links.

This print puts both the legislative chamber and Daumier's famous satirical image of it behind a curtain. Drawing on *poire* imagery as well as 'The legislative belly', the artist creates a self-reflexive *mise en scène*. He reveals the ensemble of signs that construct a theatrical performance, including actors, costumes, props, controlled lighting, and a backdrop that extends the pictorial space of the shallow stage. He also includes citations of his own prints, as if to emphasize the representation's distance from the real. Like the comic mask, this theatrical *mise en scène* signals not only the king's artificiality but also the artist's awareness of his work's materiality, blending theatrical tradition with graphic illustration in ways that provoke an increased awareness of the layered, playfully subversive devices used in both print and performance.

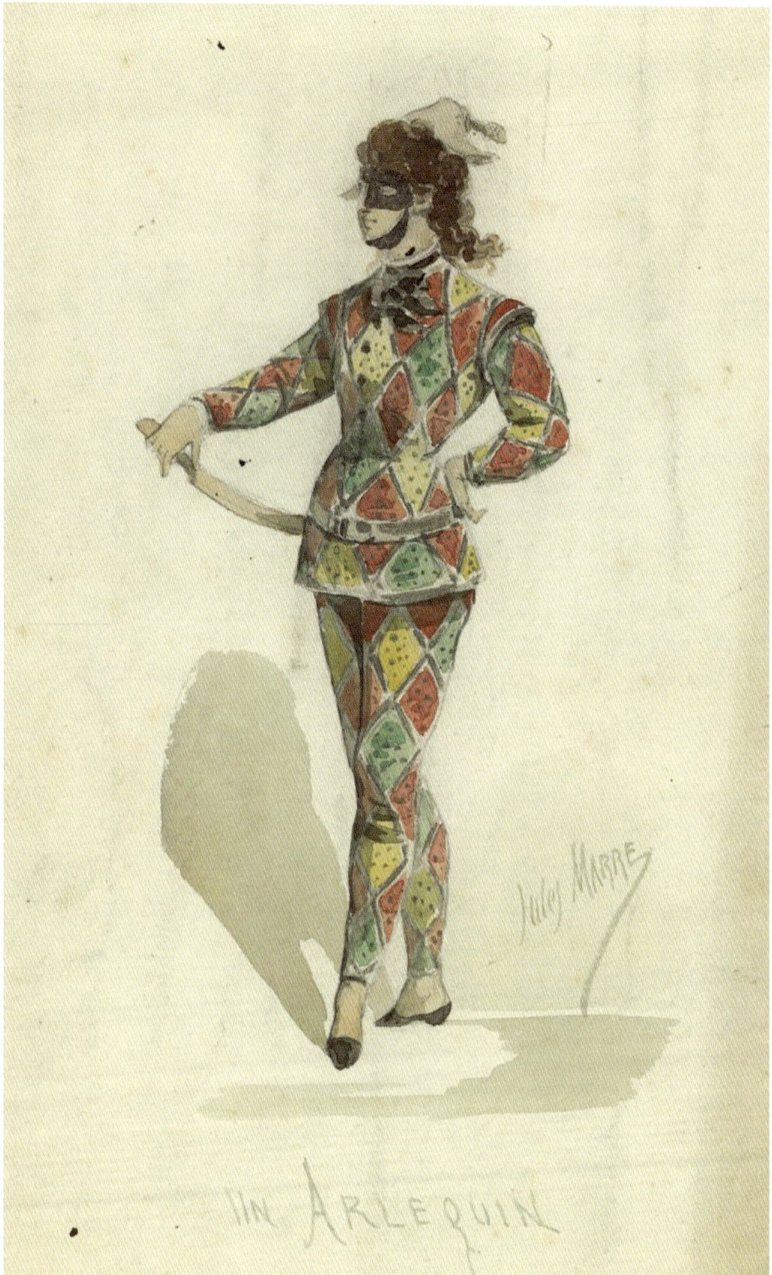

Figure 3.2 Jules Marre, *Harlequin (Arlequin)*, 19th century

Over two decades after 'Lower the curtain. The farce is over' Daumier would revisit the motif of a stage as a space of political speech in paint. In March of 1860, after thirty years with the illustrated press, he was fired from his job at *Le Charivari* following a new wave of Second Empire censorship. In an editorial about the dismissal, 'L'abdication de

Daumier' in *Le Journal amusant*, Philipon seems to critique the rationale of the paper he used to run for getting rid of an artist because of public opinion, which had perhaps turned against Daumier because his interest seemed to be turning to painting and because of perceptions of his failing imagination in print, a 'laziness' that caused the artist to treat the same subject twenty or thirty times. Philipon defends his old friend:

> the crowd ignores the level of talent necessary for an artist to return so often to the same theme, and each time to create a different drawing, a new drawing; all they see is repetition of the same subject, and from that repetition, they assume the artist has run out of ideas.[3]

Forced once again to abandon explicitly political material in print, Daumier turned more of his labour to painting and intensified his deep and abiding engagement with the seventeenth-century playwright Molière, retracing the same scenes with variations that explored the range of pathos and absurdity they were able to contain. This was the moment where Daumier's previous invocations of the *commedia dell'arte* and his experimentation with Molière's characters and the comic mask consolidated more forcefully in the form of paintings and watercolours of Molière's theatrical satires. This chapter will concentrate on Daumier's representation of scenes from Molière's comedies *The imaginary invalid* (*Le malade imaginaire*) written in 1673 and *Scapin the schemer* (*Les Fourberies de Scapin*, 1671), subjects that Daumier painted in fevered numbers. We can say that at least fifteen paintings and oil sketches by Daumier depict figures from Molière's plays, along with four watercolours, and numerous drawings.[4]

But why, besides a 'lack of imagination', would Daumier interrogate Molière so obsessively in paint in the last twenty years of his career? What does it mean to make a painting theatrical? Is it a matter of graphic immediacy? Of narrative or its absence? Can satire – a mainstay of both caricature and theatre – have a life in painting? In this chapter I will argue that for Daumier the operations of theatre were linked to caricature in part because of censorship laws that created an equivalence between the two.

Daumier's firing and the pressures of censorship on political speech help contextualize his interest in Molière. Nineteenth-century theatres revived works by the beloved seventeenth-century dramaturge at moments when new material was being heavily censored, in order to stage oblique attacks on the government. Daumier – who had himself been incarcerated for violating press laws – was drawn to Molière at a key moment in his career when explicitly political speech was prohibited. In what follows I will outline the specific restrictions on speech that prompted Daumier to paint theatrical subjects in a caricatural style, formally connecting theatre to caricature because censorship laws conjoined the two. I propose that these works emerge from his larger commitment to political dissent by intervening in the contested space of speech in Second Empire France. They function as critiques of the repressive authority of the government in large part because of contemporary associations between Molière and subversive artistic practice in the nineteenth century.

'A deed, an action, a behaviour': Censorship of caricature and the theatres

The Charter of 1830 that established the July Monarchy declared a categorical abolition of censorship. However, the regime maintained several tools to continue their suppression of subversive speech even from the beginning: the *cautionnement*, a security bond guaranteeing financial penalty in case of wrongdoing, a stamp tax known as the *timbre*, and criminal sanctions.[5] The government became increasingly reactionary as caricatures turned from the former king, Charles X, to Louis-Philippe, newly enthroned in 1830. Censors targeted Charles Philipon's political caricatures in particular. Between November 1831 and April 1832, he was arrested three times, fined 4,600 francs, and sentenced to thirteen months in jail. His journal *La Caricature* was seized twenty times.[6] In August of 1835, a Corsican named Giuseppe Fieschi and two members of the Leftist Society for the rights of man attempted to assassinate the king.[7] Fieschi constructed a dramatic machine of twenty-five guns propped on a frame on the boulevard du Temple next to the Théâtre Lazari in the heart of Paris's theatre district. While the king escaped with his life, eighteen people were killed and twenty injured.[8] After this, Louis-Philippe's government expanded censorship even further. Freedom of expression was quickly restricted in two specific media: caricatures and theatrical productions.

While the July Monarchy's 1830 Charter promised that the regime would never re-establish censorship, its September Laws of 1835 criminalized speech offensive to the king specifically in drawings, caricatures, and theatrical pieces by claiming that they operated differently than the printed word. 'When opinions are converted *into actions*' by the circulation of drawings or a play, 'it is a question of speaking to the eyes. That is something more than the expression of an opinion; it is *a deed, an action, a behaviour*' not covered under the Charter's protections, or so claimed Jean-Charles Persil, the government's head censor.[9] The law demanded that works on paper, including drawings, lithographs, engravings, and prints secure prior approval by the Minister of the Interior or the Prefect of the Provinces before their exhibition or sale and detailed strict surveillance of the theatres using nearly identical terms and rationales. They required theatres to seek authorization before opening shows and allowed the government to shutter any plays that caused 'trouble' or 'scandal', an ambiguity that would allow for broad policing. The September Laws introduced prohibitions on images or performances that would disparage the king or any act of government directly or indirectly, any act of perceived disloyalty, any use of the name 'Republican', and any implied desire for the restoration of the Bourbon monarchy or the destruction of the constitutional monarchy, all of which would be considered treasonous.[10]

Fears that illustrations and performances were exceptional because they were unmediated, more direct and therefore potentially incendiary in their impact on an audience, drove their dramatic repression relative to the written word. Gesture and expression in both caricature and theatre relied on the legibility of the body and were therefore more threatening to the repressive authority of the government than texts, which were seen as less immediate in their impact, not to mention inaccessible to significant (illiterate) portions of the population. By circumventing text, the graphic arts were not only more persuasive, but inflammatory too.

After a brief reprieve during the Second Republic, the Second Empire reinstated the strict censorship of prints and performances. An edict by Louis-Napoleon (Charles-Louis-Napoléon Bonaparte, or Napoleon III, 1808–73) enacted on 17 February 1852 reinstated prior censorship for journals, targeting any drawings, engravings, or lithographic images found within, echoing the language of the September Laws.[11] The language in Article 22 was as expansive as possible, preventing the publication or sale of drawings, engravings, lithographs, medals, prints, or emblems. It should be noted here that although *gravure* literally meant engraving, by the mid-nineteenth century it was understood to mean prints as a general term much like the English word 'print'; also at this time, book and periodical illustrations were largely done by wood engraving, but cartoons were mostly lithographs.[12]

A ministerial memorandum dated 30 March 1852 written by the Minister of Public Police further outlined prefects' obligations to control images. According to the police, even the worst page of the most offensive book needed a certain degree of intelligence and discernment to be threatening, whereas prints were 'within the reach of all minds' ('*à la portée de tous les esprits*'), and were thus 'the most dangerous of all seductions' ('*la plus dangereuse de toutes les séductions*').[13] Artists were legally obligated to secure prior authorization from censors as well as from persons being caricatured between 1852 and 1866, suppressing most political cartoons.[14] Indeed, though Louis-Philippe and the July Monarchy are more famous for zealous censorship, there were more illustrations forbidden annually during the Second Empire.[15]

Theatres were also targeted. They had long been places of diverse public assembly, which made them dangerous. Like cartoons, theatrical performances could address illiterate populations and in doing so they held powerful didactic potential. Famously, the dramaturge and director of the Opéra-Comique, René-Charles Pixérécourt, said 'I write for those who cannot read.'[16] In August of 1789, mayor Bailly of Paris believed that theatres should be exempt from the revolutionary proposal for a total abolition of censorship:

> I believe that we should exclude the theatre … everything that may tend to corrupt the mores or the morals of the government. The performance is one part of public instruction which should not be left to everyone and that the administration should monitor … this is not an attack on the freedom of some, it is respect for the freedom and moral security of others.[17]

As a result of this kind of exceptional influence, the revolutionary government placed theatres under the surveillance of municipalities, who were zealous in their attempts to monitor any seditious public instruction from the stage, a pattern of repression that continued in the next century.

In the early nineteenth century, theatre became the principal source of entertainment for Parisians. Under Napoleon's 1807 decree theatrical performances were limited to just nine venues in order for the state to control both the influence and revenue of theatrical performances. These theatres were le Français, l'Odéon, l'Opéra, l'Opéra-Comique, l'Opéra-Bouffe, le Vaudeville, les Variétés, la Gaîte, and l'Ambigu-Comique. Under the Bourbon Restoration, some small theatres cropped up, but they too remained under strict surveillance. Regardless of attempts to control the ideology of *les spectacles*, one can speak of a truly 'popular theatre' in the first half of the nineteenth century.[18] Theatrical audiences remained quite diverse until Haussmann's destruction of many popular theatres on the boulevard du Temple and orders to eliminate the *parterre*, or pit, in those remaining, in part because of fears of class mixing. After this, collective experience of the theatre was Balkanized as citizens of the *faubourgs* and *banlieues* tended to attend proliferating *café-concerts*.[19] Interestingly, it was the longer plays with the higher production values in the large, state-subsidized theatres such as the Odéon and Comédie-Française that tended to risk content that questioned conventions of morality or systems of government.[20]

Louis-Napoleon's February 1852 decree expanded theatre censorship, reviving Louis-Philippe's 1844 prohibition on depictions of religious figures or objects and targeting plays with perceived hostility to monarchies. In 1852, the censors only accepted 246 out of 682 plays without substantial revisions or being subjected to a ban and prohibited a number of plays allowed during the July Monarchy.[21] Like the drawn image, the theatre was thought to communicate ideas directly. According to Baron Taylor,

> There is produced, among those present, a sort of *electric communication* much more stirring for the masses than parliamentary speeches, and a thousand times more dangerous than the most vehement of articles in the daily press.[22]

Electricity was also used as a metaphor for the relationship between content and audience in the repression of the theatre by Victor Hallays-Dabot, who claimed in his 1862 book *Histoire de la censure théâtrale en France* that the energetic power of the theatre 'controls a room like an electric current'.[23] Baron Taylor and Hallays-Dabot likened the theatre to something reactive, dangerous, unpredictable, and even seductive. Taylor's comparison to parliamentary speeches betrayed a fundamental fear: that entertainment could usurp the influence of government. Meaning in performance could be transmitted as if with a jolt, uninsulated. This notion that the ideas in plays were unmediated by the written word and activated by a live performance was for them best described by electricity's invisible force. Rather than material support, media were defined by the shock of impact and the activation of the viewer.

Comedies from the 'ancien répertoire' were revived during periods of increased scrutiny over new material. Older plays were generally considered safer, so in 1835, when stricter censorship was imposed on theatres and the illustrated press, the Théâtre-Français staged plays by Molière with great frequency and popularity. The *Journal des débats* described this craze that year: 'I advise modern authors not to venture to put on a new work during the week when the *L'Impromptu de Versailles* (1663) and *Les Fâcheux* (1661) will be revived. You must take part in it. Molière is in vogue.'[24] However, reinterpretations of his work were also censored during Daumier's lifetime. Most famously, perhaps, censors demanded that a passage from George Sand's (Amantine-Lucile-Aurore Dupin, 1804–76) 1851 *Molière* be eliminated because it valorised the poor and thus touched on the sensitive issue of class conflict.[25] The French National Archives list at least forty-one manuscripts of censored performances of Molière's plays and plays dedicated to Molière during Daumier's career. Ten of these censored performances took place in the 1860s in large theatres like the Théâtre-Français (now the Comédie-Français) alone, the moment when Daumier took up these motifs with a kind of fervour.[26]

Similarly, we remember that in justifying the constitutionality of the new censorship restrictions imposed on performances and prints in 1835, the French Minister of Justice Jean-Charles Persil explained that these media constituted 'a deed, an action, a behaviour' capable of operating directly on collective opinion.[27] The government's redefinition of medium was based not on material support but on collective response, leading to the strange equivalence between cartoons, plays, and 'behaviour'. Implicit was the issue of access. Caricature and theatre were popular art forms, and Persil's comments betray a fear that the consumption of these media by common citizens could translate into political action. Daumier tested the boundaries of this law as well as its claims about the impact and immediacy of various media by translating motifs between lithography, painting, watercolour, and sculpture, and by drawing often on theatre and literature for subject matter. Exploiting the stated equivalence between caricature and spectacle, he represented theatrical subjects with the gesture and expressiveness of political cartoons.

Lower the curtain

As a result of this renewed pressure on the illustrated press, social satires proliferated, and Cham and Gavarni published with increased frequency beginning in 1852.[28] Then, in events eerily echoing the conservative response to Fieschi's attack on Louis-Philippe in 1834, an assassination attempt on Napoleon III in January 1858 drove the government to increase censorship restrictions yet again. Ostensibly as a result of this intensified pressure on the illustrated press, Daumier was fired from the journal *Le Charivari* in March of 1860.[29] Before 1860, he had produced a number of unfinished and unexhibited canvases since his submission of *Competition of 1848, sketch of the Republic* and had found some modest commercial success selling watercolours of subjects his buyers recognized from his most popular lithographic series, including lawyers and domestic life.[30] After he was fired, Daumier continued to shop watercolours to some loyal patrons and also began working more seriously and ambitiously in oil.

Daumier's paintings of theatrical satires, in particular Molière's plays, began at this moment in the early 1860s.[31] His interest in theatrical motifs seemed to intersect with the *commedia dell'arte*, filtered not only through the pantomime of the Théâtre de Funambules but also by way of Thomas Couture.[32] Couture served on various art committees with Daumier and influenced his technical development as a painter.[33] Couture likely came to the *commedia dell'arte* through George Sand and her son Maurice (Jean-François-Maurice-Arnaud Dudevant, 1823–89) as early as the 1840s. They published several pieces on the *commedia* tradition, including George Sand's 1852 article on the history of Harlequin and Maurice's two-volume *Masques et bouffons* of 1860 (George Sand wrote the introduction). In the former article, George Sand discusses Dominique, the actor who brought the role of Harlequin to life in Molière's lifetime. Couture was deeply affected by the story of Dominique and insisted that he had had visions of the clown during a project at the church of Saint-Eustache in 1856, where Dominique and Molière were buried.[34]

Maurice and George Sand brought the *commedia dell'arte* to life with puppet shows in the 1840s (Figure 3.3). Maurice created the puppets with Eugène Lambert, and George constructed the costumes.[35] Likewise, in the summer of 1861, Edmond Duranty created a puppet theatre in the Tuileries, the théâtre de Polichinelle, which can be seen in

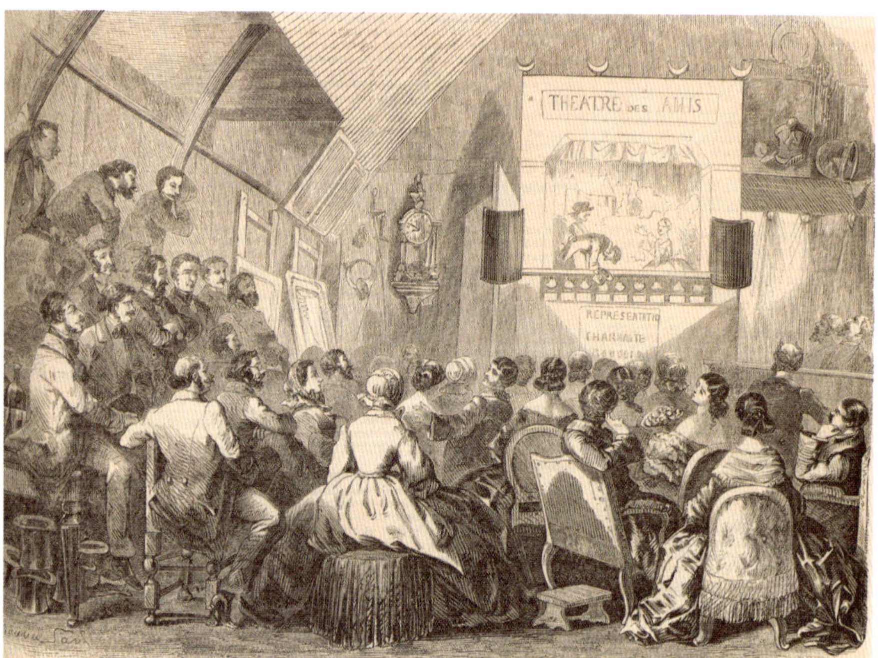

Figure 3.3 Engraving after Maurice Sand, 'Marionette theatre (representation in the studio of Mr Maurice Sand)' ('Théâtre des Marionnettes (représentation dans l'atelier de M. Maurice Sand)'), *Le Monde Illustré*, 24 April 1858

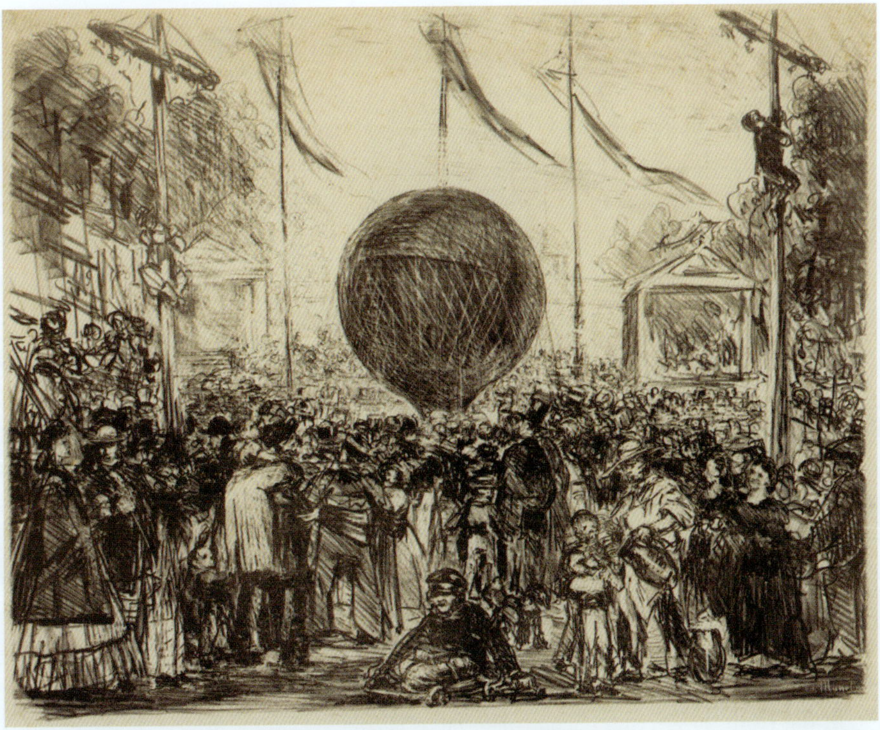

Figure 3.4 Édouard Manet, *The balloon*, 1862

the right-hand portion of Édouard Manet's *The balloon* of 1862 (Figure 3.4). Just as his mentor Champfleury had written pantomimes for the Théâtre des Funambules, Duranty engaged with the broader revival of seventeenth- and eighteenth-century theatrical traditions and, more specifically, the *commedia dell'arte*.[36]

In 1861, Duranty asked Daumier to sculpt puppet heads for his show.[37] Daumier turned him down just as he was beginning to paint Molière's plays, which were themselves heavily influenced by the Italian *commedia*. This refusal is perhaps even more perplexing considering the theatricality of Daumier's clay maquettes, the *Celebrities of the juste milieu*. Pugnacious and defiant, the plaster heads grab the viewer's attention through vivid expression. Many of them display open mouths, suggesting muffled speech. The colour applied to plaster in these maquettes is brazenly theatrical, a puppet-theatre model of sculpture. Importantly, between these puppet-like sculptures and Daumier's refusal to create actual puppets were the censorship laws that aligned theatre and caricature and defined media by audience response. Theatre and caricature were legally affiliated because they might provoke a 'deed, action, or behaviour' in their viewers, and by the time of Duranty's request, Daumier had shifted that theatrical provocation from sculpture to two-dimensional images of the theatre.

The artist had a longstanding and dynamic interest in the theatre, and although scholarship has largely attended to his images of informal outdoor street performance and *parades*, Daumier produced a number of paintings representing theatrical revivals of Molière's plays in large, state-sanctioned theatres. There is excellent scholarship in the former category, largely exploring an identification between the artist and theatrical performers in the informal contexts of the fair or sideshow. These clowns, art historians have generally argued, offer allegorical self-portraits of a disaffected outsider.[38] In a representative and influential analysis, the art historian T. J. Clark has argued that Daumier's clown, or *saltimbanque*, stands in for the figure of the artist in the Second Empire. 'The clown and the lithographer were not so very different', he writes. Both were at war with the repressive authority of the state, both were entertainers and teachers of subversion.[39] On the other hand, although Daumier produced a number of truly impressive paintings representing scenes from classical theatre staged in more formal settings, these have received very little scholarly attention.

Together, Daumier's body of work representing theatrical motifs reflects the bifurcation of theatrical performance in the mid-nineteenth century between large, state-sanctioned institutions on the one hand and *saltimbanques* and *café-concerts* on the other. Putting Daumier's informal *parades* aside for a moment, we will concentrate on his representations of theatrical revivals of Molière's plays. In these paintings, unlike many of the sideshow works, the artist shifts his medium to oil, drawing liberally from his caricatures in print, and immerses the viewer in the narrative drama on the stage.

In the print 'Lower the curtain. The farce is over' Daumier dresses Louis-Philippe in the costume of a *paillasse* (from 'bag of straw'), a clown who appeared in the street shows, or *parades*. The *paillasse* typically wears a checked costume, and is related to Harlequin and Pierrot from the French *commedia dell'arte* tradition. Pierrot, who wears a similar costume but in all white, was often found in the paintings of Jean-Antoine Watteau (1684–1721), as in the large-format painting of the listless *Pierrot* (formerly known as *Gilles*, c. 1718–19) which was in the La Caze collection when Daumier began to take up theatrical subjects in earnest in the 1860s. Daumier could have also seen this painting in the popular seventeenth- and eighteenth-century French painting exhibition at the Galerie Martinet in 1860 (Figure 3.5).[40]

We can also compare the *paillasse* in Daumier's 'Lower the curtain. The farce is over' to Watteau's *The Italian comedians*, painted around 1720 (Figure 3.6). Watteau includes fifteen stock *commedia* characters arranged around Pierrot, who stares out of the picture plane towards a viewer, central and shimmering in a white satin costume. A garland of flowers strewn just below Pierrot's feet and a great red velvet curtain pulled back at the top right of the canvas signal to the viewer that it is a stage, and the actors have just finished their play. Daumier's caricature similarly divides figures from the background with a curtain, but his stage set recedes to the distant amphitheatre of the legislative chamber. Like Daumier's *paillasse*, Pierrot gazes at the audience anticipating applause. The condition for convincing theatrical illusion – the separation of audience from performance – is breached at precisely this moment.[41] Watteau's canvases do not, as some have suggested,

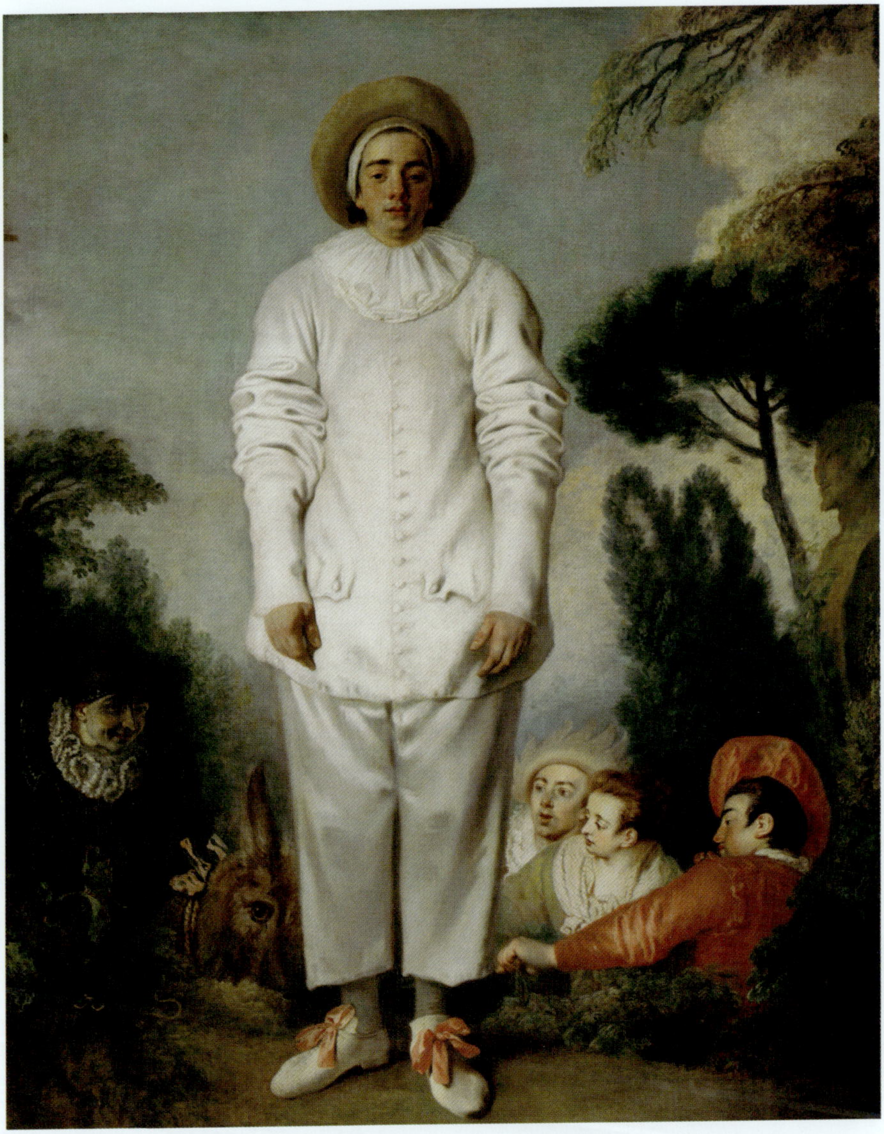

Figure 3.5 Jean-Antoine Watteau, *Pierrot (formerly known as Giles)*, c. 1718–19

extend the mimesis of theatre into the medium of painting; rather, the artist retains the sense that the figures are costumed players in dazzling stage sets, offering the viewer a convincing image of performance.[42]

The garland of flowers that has fallen below the actors' feet in *The Italian comedians* echoes the extended arm of the actor pointing to Pierrot, soliciting applause. The garland is key to the breach of theatrical illusion, having presumably been flung by the audience as congratulation. Daumier caricatures Watteau's wry conceit of audience involvement

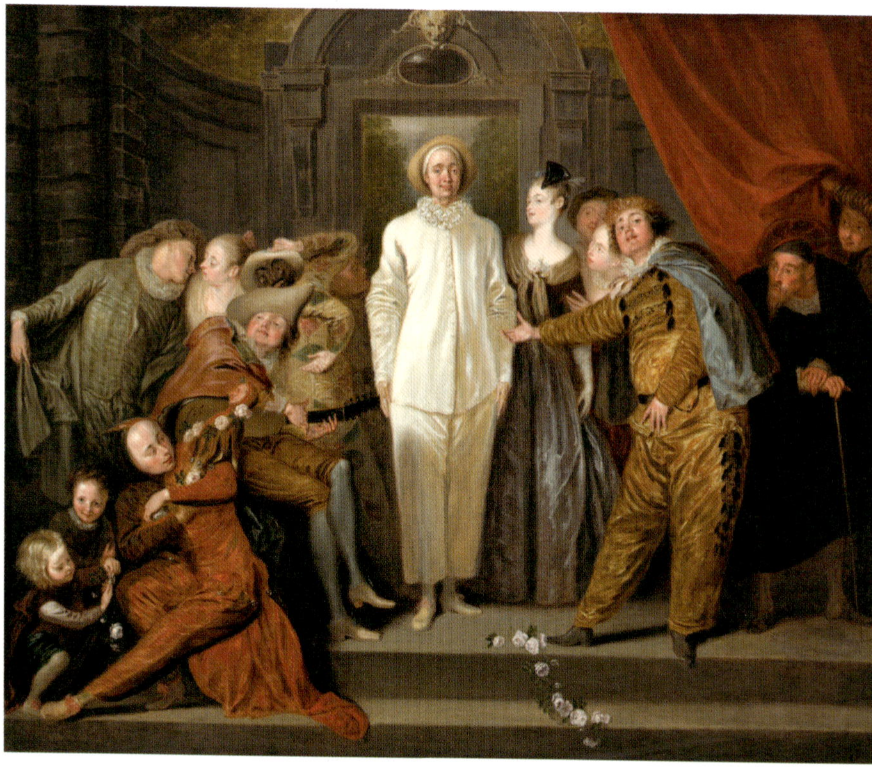

Figure 3.6 Antoine Watteau, *The Italian comedians*, c. 1720

in 'A rather unpleasant role to play onstage, especially in Piedmont', published in *Le Charivari* on 11 May 1859 (Figure 3.7). In the print, an actor dressed as Austrian Emperor Franz Joseph suffers an assault by his audience. In 1859 Piedmont was embroiled in a fight for independence against the Austrians and in this cartoon the audience enact their anger at the emperor by launching projectiles at his substitute on stage. Daumier extends the pictorial plane to include members of the audience, who hurl hats and insults at the performer. He thereby brings Watteau's small breach of theatrical realism to its exaggerated, caricatural end, representing a moment when such a gesture becomes political and even violent.

Like Watteau, Daumier creates an interface between performance and spectatorship in his images of the theatre. Historians of the theatre have called it 'mimesis par excellence'.[43] However, that claim belies the medium's fundamental responsiveness to its changeable audience, a tension that Daumier mined in his caricatures of politicians as actors in the decades following 'Lower the curtain'. In one example, Otto von Bismarck waits in the wings of the parliamentary amphitheatre in 'The Prussian bluebeard getting ready to finish off another Chamber of Deputies', from the series *Album. La Guerre pour rire, Le Charivari*, 13 March 1866 (Figure 3.8). Bismarck is costumed for battle against the Prussian legislature in a composition echoing 'Lower the curtain'. However, the scene is

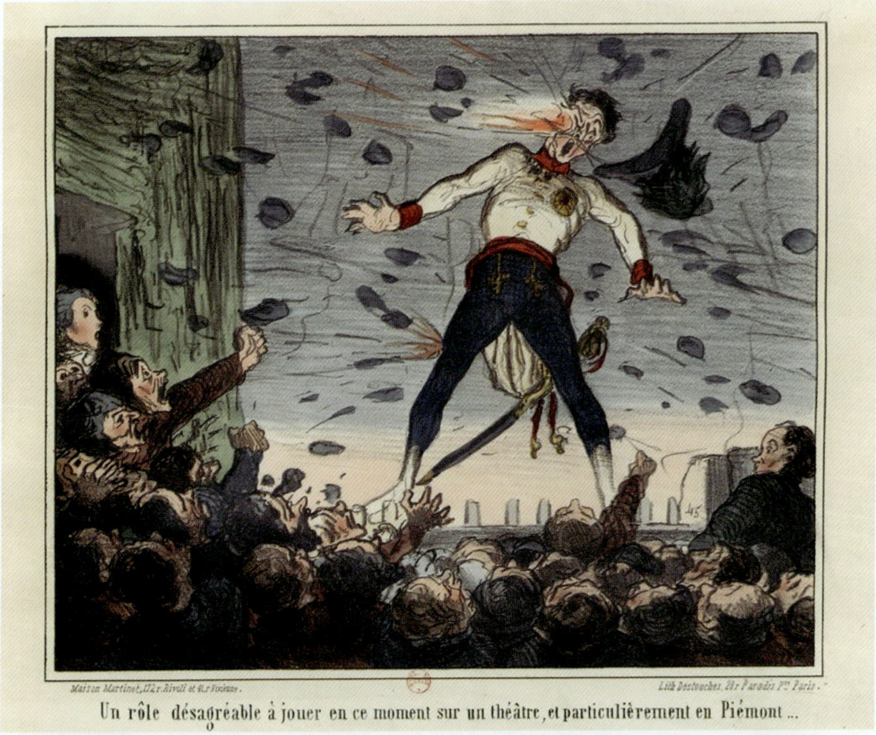

Figure 3.7 Honoré Daumier, 'A rather unpleasant role to play onstage, especially in Piedmont' ('Un rôle désagréable à jouer en ce moment sur un théâtre et particulièrement en Piemont ...'), published by Maison Martine

staged as a prelude to action, not its finale. Bismarck telegraphs his intention to destroy the authority of a legislative body seen in an amphitheatre lit beyond the arched doorway at left. But before Bismarck becomes a spectacle, he is, in a way, its audience.

Daumier layers references to both 'Lower the curtain' and 'The legislative belly' in 'The Prussian bluebeard'. J. J. Grandville also relies on the viewer's familiarity with images from *La Caricature* in 'An audience for "Theatre of Political Madness"' (21 March 1833). Grandville places magistrates in the glaring footlights of the stage, gesturing down towards the play's prompter, or *souffleur*, whose peaked tuft of hair at the bottom hints at a body below both the stage and the pictorial plane (Figure 3.9). The text accompanying the print gestures – quite disingenuously – at anonymity: 'Gentlemen, the author of the piece that we have had the honour of playing for you wishes to remain anonymous.'[44] Although only visible as hair, the prompter is recognizable to any reader of the illustrated journal as Louis-Philippe. The references and allusions are part of the pleasure of theatrical spectatorship. Meaning in both theatre and caricature is collaborative, with rich layers built into the spaces between audience and spectacle. The self-reflexive strategies in caricatures like 'Lower the curtain' nod to the porous interface between performance and spectatorship.

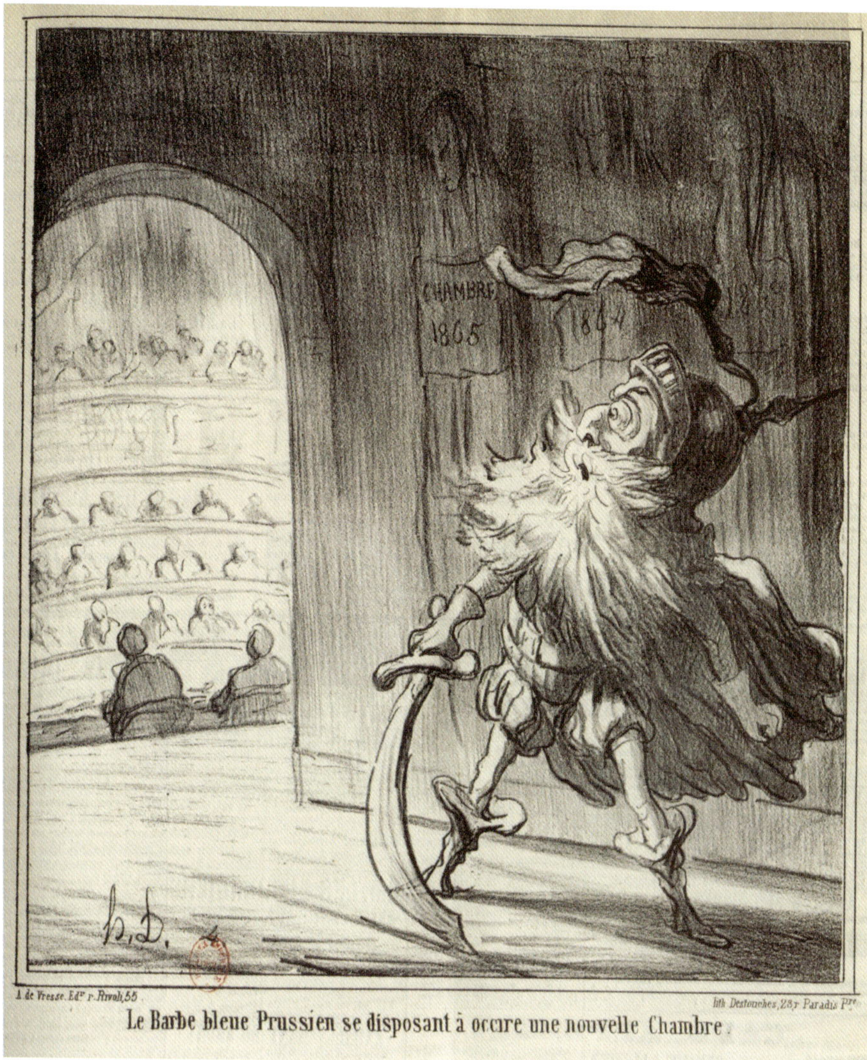

Figure 3.8 Honoré Daumier, 'The Prussian bluebeard getting ready to finish off another Chamber of Deputies'. Series Album. La Guerre pour rire, *Le Charivari*, 13 March 1866

In 'A performance in the theatre of Bordeaux: The annoying thing is you can't see the prompter' (*Le Charivari*, 24 February 1871), Daumier uses a similar trope to Grandville, where an unknown figure feeds lines to a politician/actor (Figure 3.10). However, Daumier broadens the view and aligns the viewer with the audience who cannot see the prompter, but only the hatch that veils his identity. Thiers, elected President of the Republic a year before Daumier's print, stands alone on a stage, his body bent towards the covered prompter vent at the centre. 'A performance in Bordeaux', references Grandville, but also reverses an earlier print published in *Le Charivari* before

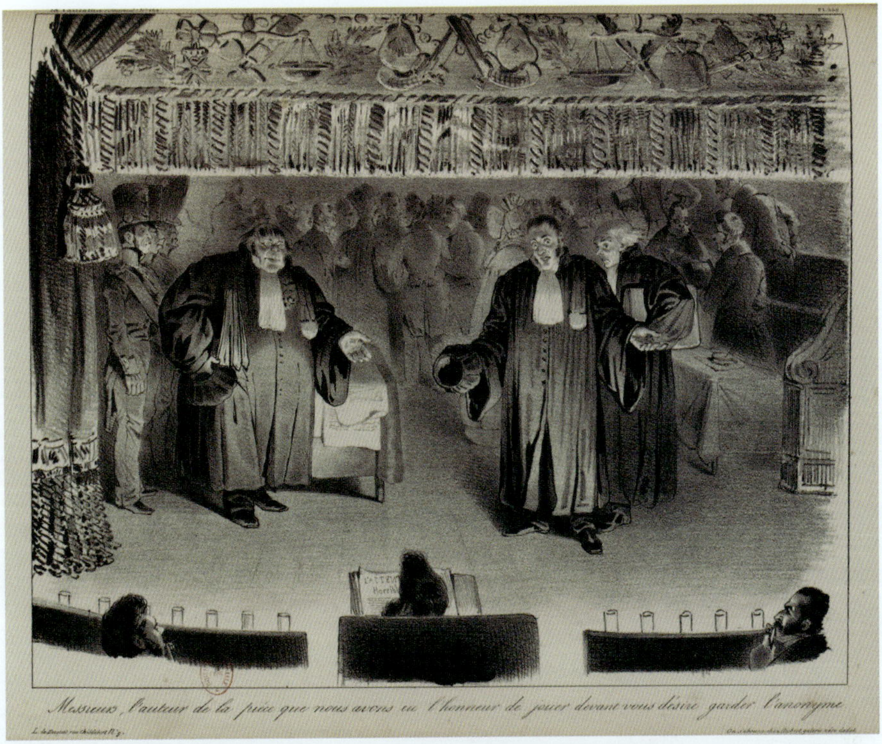

Figure 3.9 J. J. Grandville et Julien, 'An audience for "Theatre of Political Madness"' ('Une audience du "Théâtre des Folies-Politiques"'), *La Caricature,* 21 March 1833

politician Adolphe Thiers (1797–1877) became president, when he was still a confidence man positioning himself near the highest echelons of power (Figure 3.11). This time Thiers is the man whispering lines to the performers in 'The prompter' (*Le Charivari*, 7 February 1870).[45] This print is unusual because instead of aligning the viewer with the audience as Daumier does in 'Bordeaux', 'Piedmont', and 'Lower the curtain', he stages the viewer in the position of the actor, looking out past the floodlights and floorboards at an unnervingly solemn crowd. From this perspective, Thiers as prompter becomes the figurative interface between performance and spectators, becoming – from his privileged and shadowed perch – the point of intersection between performance and viewing. More than this, he is *mediating* the relationship between performance and audience by coaching the actors. He looks towards the stage from the audience's point of view, but has the actor's ear.

Daumier's caricatures of politicians in the guise of actors conditioned viewers to see theatre as a lens through which politics was made entertaining and exposed to critique. In 'Lower the curtain', Louis-Philippe performs the drama of contemporary politics and exposes the false act of democracy. Like Watteau, Daumier breaches the wall of theatrical illusion, emphasizing the artifice of performance. Watteau's garland, Louis-Philippe's

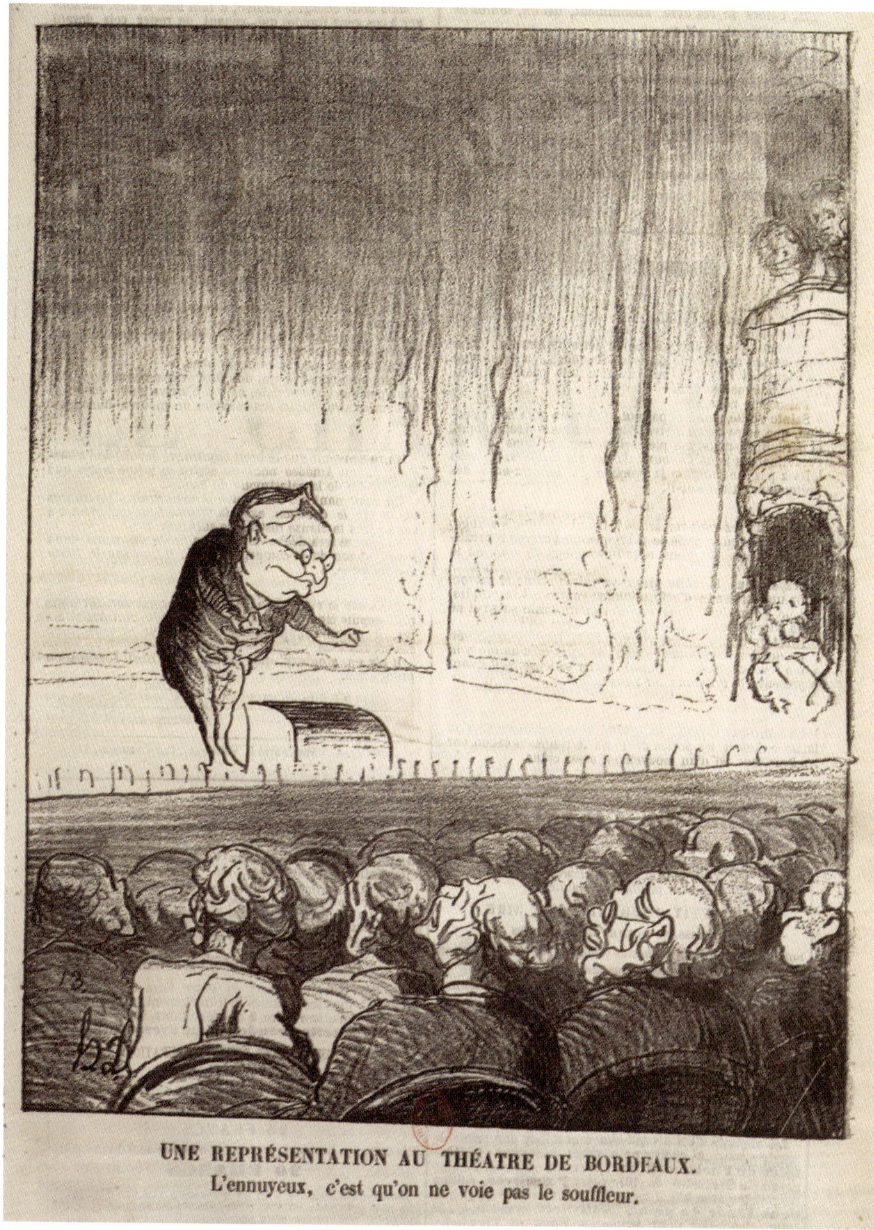

Figure 3.10 Honoré Daumier, 'A performance in the theatre of Bordeaux: The annoying thing is you can't see the prompter.' *Le Charivari*, 24 February 1871

bow, and the audience revolt in 'Piedmont' demonstrate that just as the actor is responsive to his audience, so too is the politician responsible to his public. There can be interference in this relationship – as 'The prompter' demonstrates – however, for Daumier the interaction between performer and audience would persist as a metaphor for political action and democratic response.

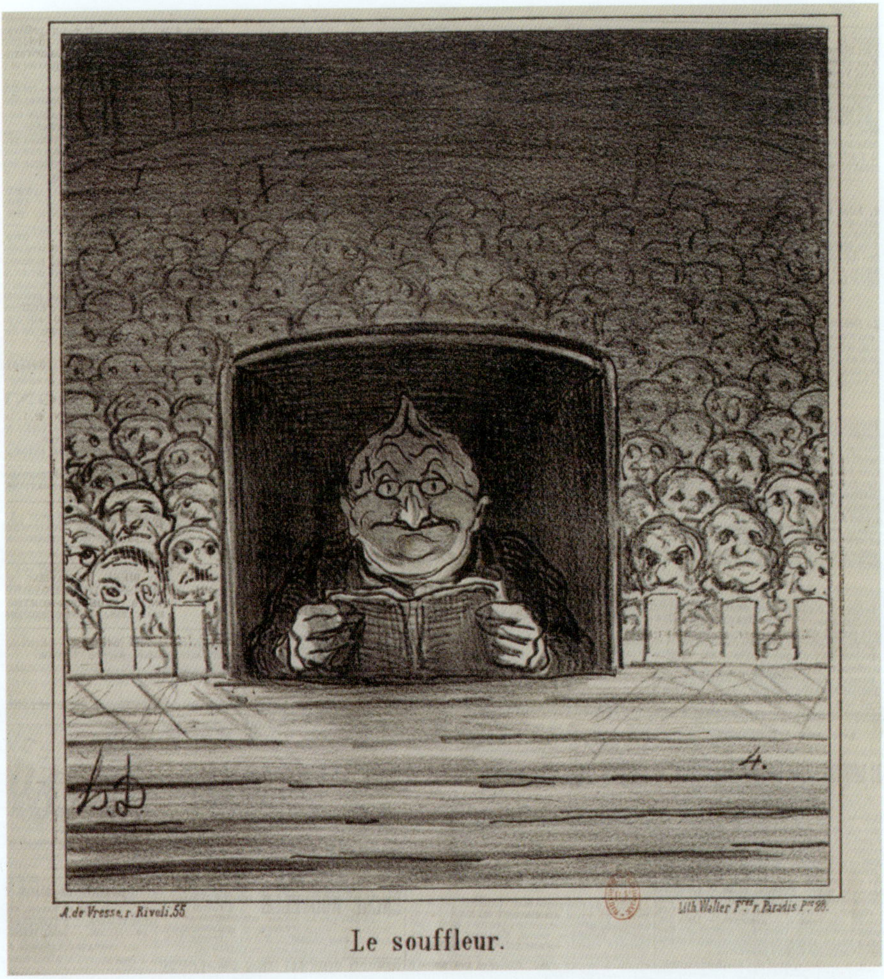

Figure 3.11 Honoré Daumier, 'The prompter' ('Le souffleur'), *Le Charivari*, 7 February 1870

The imaginary invalid and Molière's comic mask

Daumier produced two oil-on-panel paintings in the early 1860s depicting a scene from Molière's play *The imaginary invalid*.[46] The comedy-ballet was written in 1673, a time when Molière was suffering from a pulmonary infection that had killed other Parisians that winter. The play replaces the parody of religious devotion in *Tartuffe* with a devotion to medicine.[47] Daumier's first painting, now in the Barnes Collection in Philadelphia, features a doctor clutching the forearm of a patient swaddled in diaphanous white bed-clothes (Figure 3.12). The patient is propped up in a chair, perhaps having recently lost consciousness. Daumier sets his pale, mottled skin against the unrelenting black paint of the background, the whites of the fabric acting like a boundary to sickness. The dramatic darkness of the interior highlights the pair of figures and the small table of instruments in the foreground. Glimmering brushstrokes describe the transparency of glass in this still

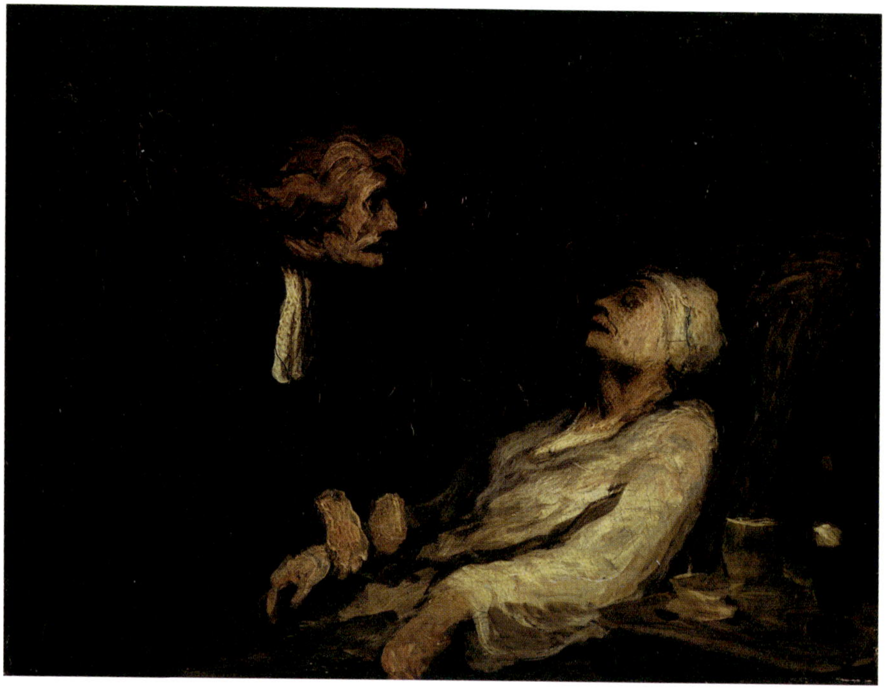

Figure 3.12 Honoré Daumier, *Scene from 'The imaginary invalid'*, 1860–63

life but do not quite anchor the objects to the illusory space of the canvas. In *The imaginary invalid*, the artist clearly draws upon Jacques-Louis David's *Death of Marat* (1793), that masterpiece of unsettling stillness, of fresh blood, and decaying flesh (Figure 3.13). The reference to *Marat* suggests Daumier's ambition to engage and perhaps even compete with the canon of French painting.

The second version of *The imaginary invalid*, now in the Philadelphia Museum of Art, closely imitates the composition of the earlier panel painting (Figure 3.14). A doctor, clad in black with billowing curly hair, grabs the wrist of a reclining patient with two hands. Although the composition and dimensions of this version are nearly identical to the Barnes version, Daumier dramatically changes the tone of the scene. The patient, now conscious, appears more worried about the doctor's interventions than his own illness, and the doctor, in turn, looks intently at the patient. The doctor's expression is analytical and strangely frozen, lacking the empathy or urgency of the former painting. The Philadelphia version also has greater interior detail, including a pair of portrait paintings framed on the wall behind the patient's chair. A similar oval painting is faintly visible in the Barnes painting, but a diptych of rectangular paintings or windows hangs above the patient's chair at odd angles in the corner of the room that in the Philadelphia painting becomes greenish-blue curtains, slightly parted. In his most dramatic shift from the earlier version, Daumier introduces a third figure, a

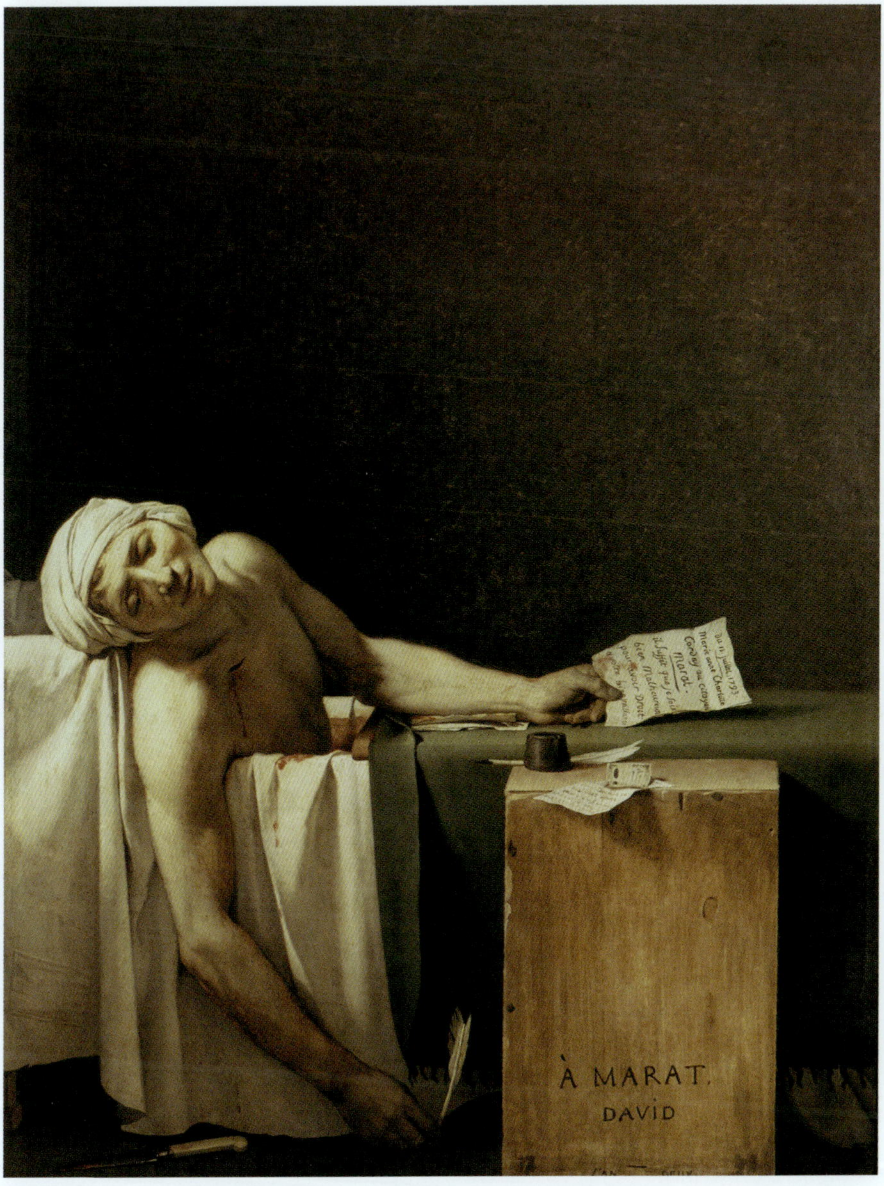

Figure 3.13 Jacques-Louis David, *The death of Marat*, 1793

wide-eyed or perhaps bespectacled man standing behind the doctor, holding a large enema syringe or clyster.

In his second attempt at *The imaginary invalid*, Daumier further defines his figures with graphic black outlines and exaggerated facial expressions and gestures. That is, he introduces procedures from caricature into the medium of painting, testing the heavy facture of the latter against a style that is both more theatrical and more expressive. Together,

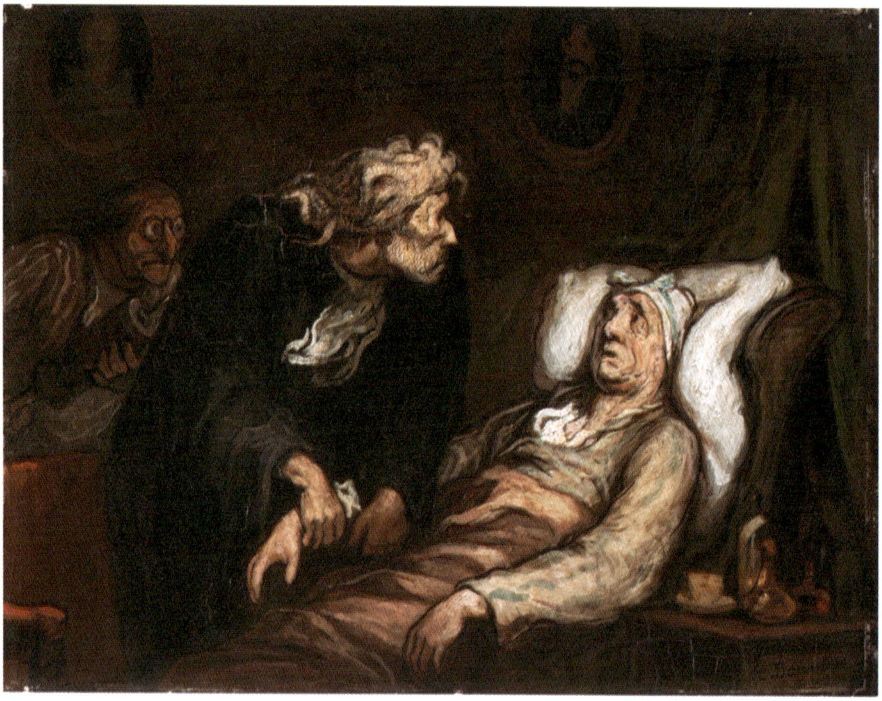

Figure 3.14 Honoré Daumier, *Scene from 'The imaginary invalid'*, c.1860–63

the pair of oils show a critical step in the development of Daumier's practice of producing paintings with print-like qualities. His Philadelphia painting makes evident strategies taken from his works on paper, which include filling in the representational space with incident instead of leaving sombre expanses, incorporating exaggerated facial expressions and dramatic gesture, and refusing to evoke forms that are incomplete or merely suggestive.[48] For Daumier, the operations of the theatre were linked to caricature in part because of Second Empire censorship laws that created an equivalence between the two. Exploiting the legal links between these two media and the redefinition of medium by the government, he represented theatrical subjects with the gesture and expressiveness of political cartoons.

Molière drew many of his characters from the *commedia dell'arte*, which relied on improvisation and a set of stock characters identified by costume, speech, and often masks. There were just a few of these types, or *rôles*, including Pulcinella, Harlequin, Pantaloon, and the Doctor.[49] In the *commedia*, masks provided an understanding of character across time and space, while also linking these characters to a tradition of satire and the grotesque tracing back to antiquity.[50] In her introduction to her son Maurice's two-volume study of the *commedia dell'arte*, *Masques et bouffons*, George Sand wrote that masks helped give characters consistent visual form over time:

> The ancient tradition has been preserved to this day in the clothing of the characters of the Italian comedy. First the mask, which has hardly changed since the main types such as Pulcinella, Harlequin, Brighella, Pantalon, Conviello, Tartaglia all wear masks which have an ancient character, and with the exception of the old men, they all have a headband that hides the hair according to the tradition of the shaved heads of ancient mimes.[51]

Masks offered familiar archetypes to diverse audiences, but they were not completely static. Historian and literary critic Louis Moland documented the pull between the universal and specific qualities of the comic mask in his 1867 book *Molière et la comédie italienne*:

> Jesters and masks created the types who were going to carry on and soon become cosmopolitan. While they preserved the memories and often the costumes and attributes of ancient grotesques, they invented new caricatures and satirical parodies. Each province, each city competed at the party, provided its character. The university cities like Bologna gave birth quite naturally to the doctor, the ridiculous pedant whose every word is delicious nonsense.[52]

Molière incorporated typological characters and masks from the *commedia dell'arte* into his plays, translating established characters into contemporary parodies. Doctor Diafoirus in Molière's *The imaginary invalid* is based on the doctor role in the *commedia*. By playing established types that were recognizable to audiences, actors had more liberty to improvise short plots and jokes. Having appeared in the guise of the clown, the doctor, the captain, or the two old men, for instance, they could play with expectations within or against those typological roles. For instance, Gaspard Debureau (1796–1846), who made the character of Pierrot famous in Daumier's lifetime, had twice assumed the role of the sad clown dressed in the costume of contemporary persons and occupations.[53] Similarly, in the early nineteenth century, it was common for parade clowns to entertain their audiences with jokes and brief skits on topical material.[54] Daumier's print 'Only costume really appropriate for this character', which ran in *Le Charivari* on 6 May 1850 (Figure 3.15), similarly places a caricature of his conservative foe Thiers in the costume of the *paillasse*, suggesting political opportunism, a charge reinforced by the diverse newspapers at his feet. Daumier incorporated this tension between the archetypal role and contemporary politics into his lithographic work and his paintings of *commedia* figures in Molière plays.

In Daumier's first version of *The imaginary invalid*, the doctor could be one of several medical professionals who visit Argan, the hypochondriac at the centre of the comedy first played by Molière himself. Argan tries to marry his daughter to the dim son of the apothecary Doctor Diafoirus and later seeks out another

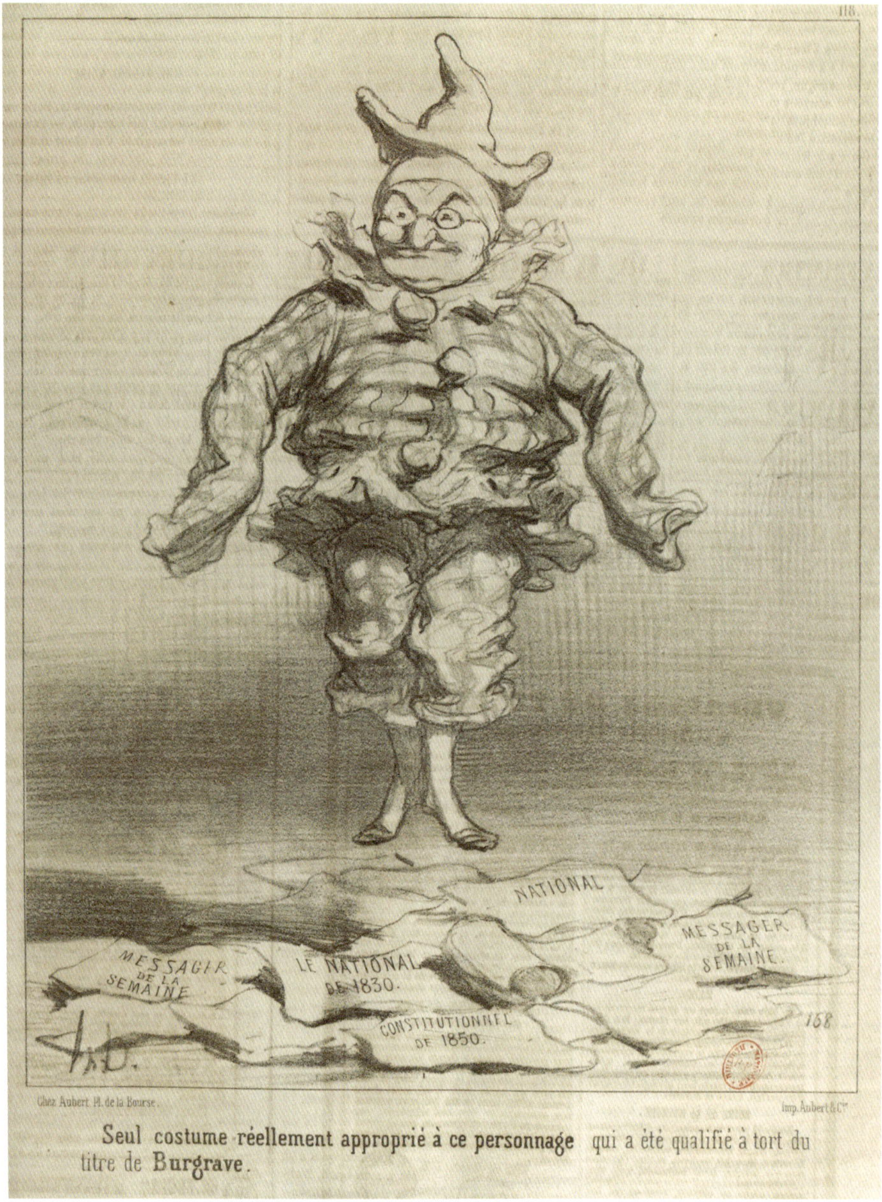

Figure 3.15 Honoré Daumier, 'Only costume really appropriate for this character who was wrongly considered for the title of Burgrave' ('Seul costume réellement approprié à ce personage qui a été qualifié à tort du titre de Burgrave'), *Le Charivari*, 6 May 1850

practitioner – Purgon – for his various ailments. Argan's servant Toinette even dresses as a doctor to counteract some of the distressing advice of the others and prescribes Dutch cheese as a non-lethal solution to his ailments. In Daumier's painting, therefore, the doctor is very much a role in the spirit of the *commedia dell'arte*. His face is indistinct and the precise narrative situation is unclear. He merely tends to the patient in a darkened room.

In the Barnes version of *The imaginary invalid*, Daumier also offers a face that seems sculpted, not painted, the undulations of pink paint giving way to dark recesses in the eyes and mouth. In the Philadelphia Museum of Art's painting, the doctor's face takes on a pale yellowish tone distinct from his neck or his hands. The graphic, caricatural lines are drawn from his jaw to his hairline, in distinct contrast to the gelatinous continuation of cheek and neck in the reclining Argan. Even the doctor's hair seems artificial, wig-like, in contrast to the Barnes version where it emerges from the scalp in wild ochreous undulations. The doctor's face is immobilized, almost stony, recalling the sculptural description of a mask in Lameth's portrait in Daumier's early print *Masks of 1831* (referenced in chapter 1).

This effect is particularly striking if one compares these paintings to the doctor's mask-like visage in Daumier's painting of Dr Diafoirus from perhaps a decade later. *Doctor Diafoirus* (*Le médecin Diafoirus*) from about 1870–75 showcases Daumier's incredible talent for the physiognomic exaggeration and hyperbolic expression that were part of the ancient comic mask tradition. He lays down neighbouring strokes of peach, acrid reds, browns, and pinks so that Diafoirus's skin appears loose, mottled, tugging in all directions. Every twisting paint stroke adds to the sense of facial animation, and Daumier plays with depth, rounding Diafoirus's jowls and carving sunken cheekbones in distinction to the pointed eyebrows that are raised in surprise. The animated flesh of *Doctor Diafoirus* makes the doctors in Daumier's two *Imaginary invalid* paintings seem immobilized and wooden.

Doctors were a popular subject of mockery for both Molière and Daumier, personifying bourgeois power, greed, and professional insincerity.[55] A print from 1847 prefigures the composition of *The imaginary invalid* and shows that the patient could also embody a kind of senseless self-indulgence (Figure 3.16). The joke and the doctor's dubious look in 'Oh doctor, I believe I am consumptive!' both emerge from the contrast between the patient's belief he has a wasting disease and his slightly overfed figure. Daumier drew from many prints in the creation of *The imaginary invalid* paintings, patterning their composition most closely on several lithographs featuring the character Robert Macaire.

Daumier's translation of Macaire lithographs into the *Scene from 'The imaginary invalid'* paintings signals his intensified exploration of the role, or typological figure. The character of Robert Macaire was brought to life in Daumier's lifetime by the actor Frédérick Lemaître. Lemaître had reinterpreted a previously dull drama, *L'Auberge des adrets*, staged initially in 1823, with a new satirical verve. He then produced and starred in the comedy *Robert Macaire*, *'ce cynique scapin du crime'*, increasing the elements of social and political satire. Daumier first drew a Robert Macaire cartoon on 13 November 1834 and continued to use the character of the con man in around 100 lithographs for the next several decades, focusing on Macaire particularly in a series published in *Le Charivari* between

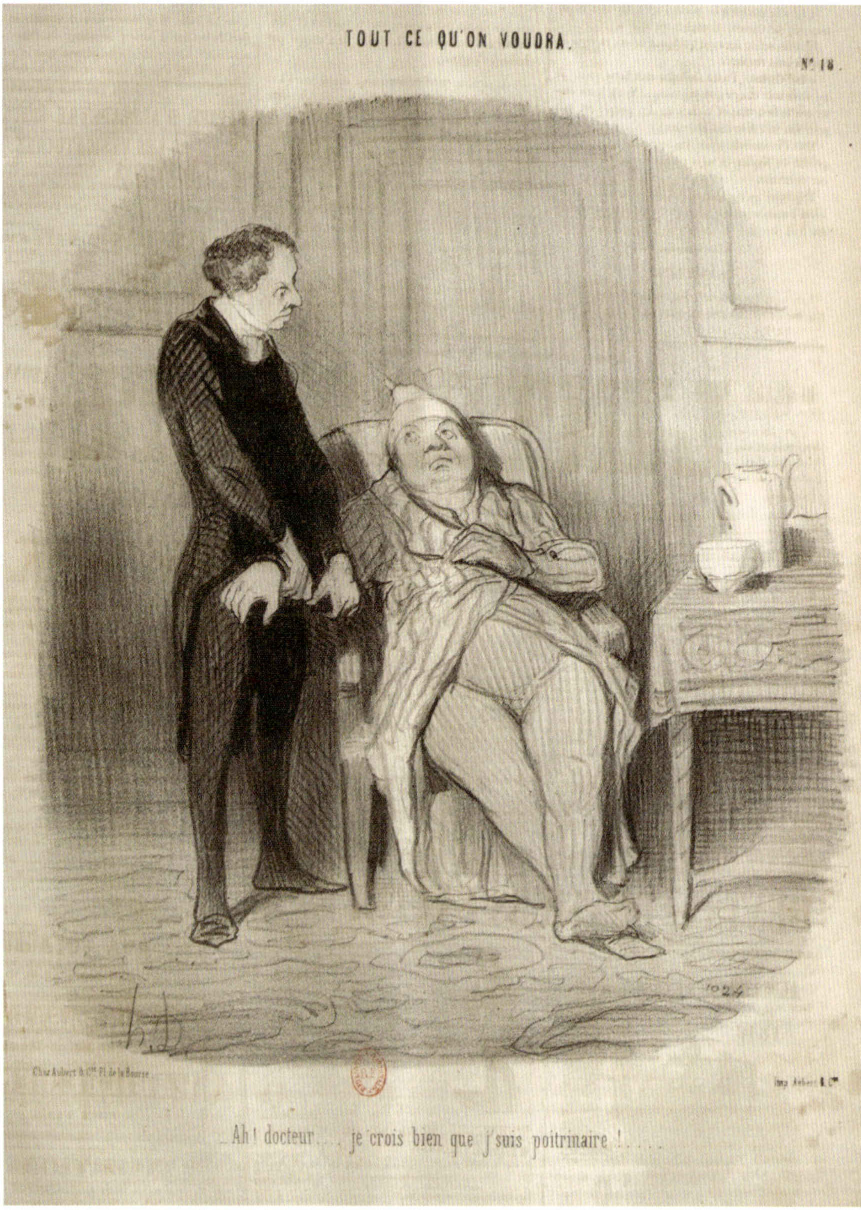

Figure 3.16 Honoré Daumier, 'Oh Doctor, I believe I am consumptive!' (Ah! docteur ... je crois bien que j'suis poitrinaire! ...'), *Le Charivari*, 19 October 1847

1836 and 1838.[56] The critic Victor Fournel described Daumier's reprisal of Lemaître's character in depth:

> Who does not now know by heart this symbolic appearance of the sponsor without cash, the inventor without invention, founder of companies without

> associates, the illustrious doctor without patients, the eloquent lawyer without reason, the financial genius without finances, taking the bait of his anticipated dividends, as telling the legend of caricature ... Robert Macaire, designed by Philipon, translated by Daumier ... you will gather ... words and scenes that make the true and living satirical picture of fever speculation that the time possessed.[57]

Macaire was a character who summed up a period of time, a tendency towards dangerous speculation and urban transformation. A loose avatar for Louis-Philippe and the broader ethos under his regime, he was also changeable, applying the same greed or ineptitude to a number of vocations. Like Lemaître, Daumier's Macaire assumed various costumes with the foundation of an established character, and Macaire's symbolic or typological qualities became an essential tool for Daumier after the September Laws of 1835. The artist could no longer attack Louis-Philippe or the July Monarchy directly, but he could represent their values abstractly or symbolically through the Macaire role.[58]

In Daumier's 1837 lithograph 'Yes, my uncle ...' Macaire's sickly uncle sits in a chair, costumed in a white robe and cap (Figure 3.17). To the right of the frame, a small table holds a wine bottle, a porcelain cup and saucer, and a luminescent glass ampoule, elements that are repeated with surprising fidelity in Daumier's two paintings. Macaire, the nephew in this print, imposes himself on his feeble relative, grabbing the patient's right wrist with both hands, in the very same gesture that Daumier would repeat when representing Molière's doctors nearly three decades later. That double grip on his uncle's wrist is ostensibly an attempt to communicate protection and care but appears to both patient and viewer as a thinly-veiled threat. The deep red of those clutching hands is repeated in the patient's shoes and Macaire's cravat, echoing the discomfiting imposition of physical contact in the print's central gesture.

The similarities between Daumier's *Macaire* lithograph and what I call the Molière revival paintings of *The imaginary invalid* are remarkable. The artist reached back many years into his own oeuvre to find a model for the charlatan and patient pair and selected an image that had not only appeared in the journal *Le Charivari* but whose commercial popularity extended its life into the popular series *Caricaturana* 1838, which was later republished as a book *Les cent et un Robert-Macaire* (1839).[59] Editions centred around Robert Macaire proliferated in the following years, including those under Philipon's direction; in 1848 by the *Journal pour rire* and in 1859 by the *Journal amusant*.[60]

In another lithograph published in *Le Charivari* on 14 January 1838 entitled 'Recipe to cure colic', a theatre director begs his principal actor to go on stage (Figure 3.18). He pleads with arms outstretched, but the performer, Robert Macaire in another guise, has collapsed in a chair on the right side of the picture plane, reaching back to a third figure to call for more hot towels. Instead of a table of tinctures and liquids, in the bottom right corner are a sabre, a glove, and boots, pieces of his costume. The caption reveals that the

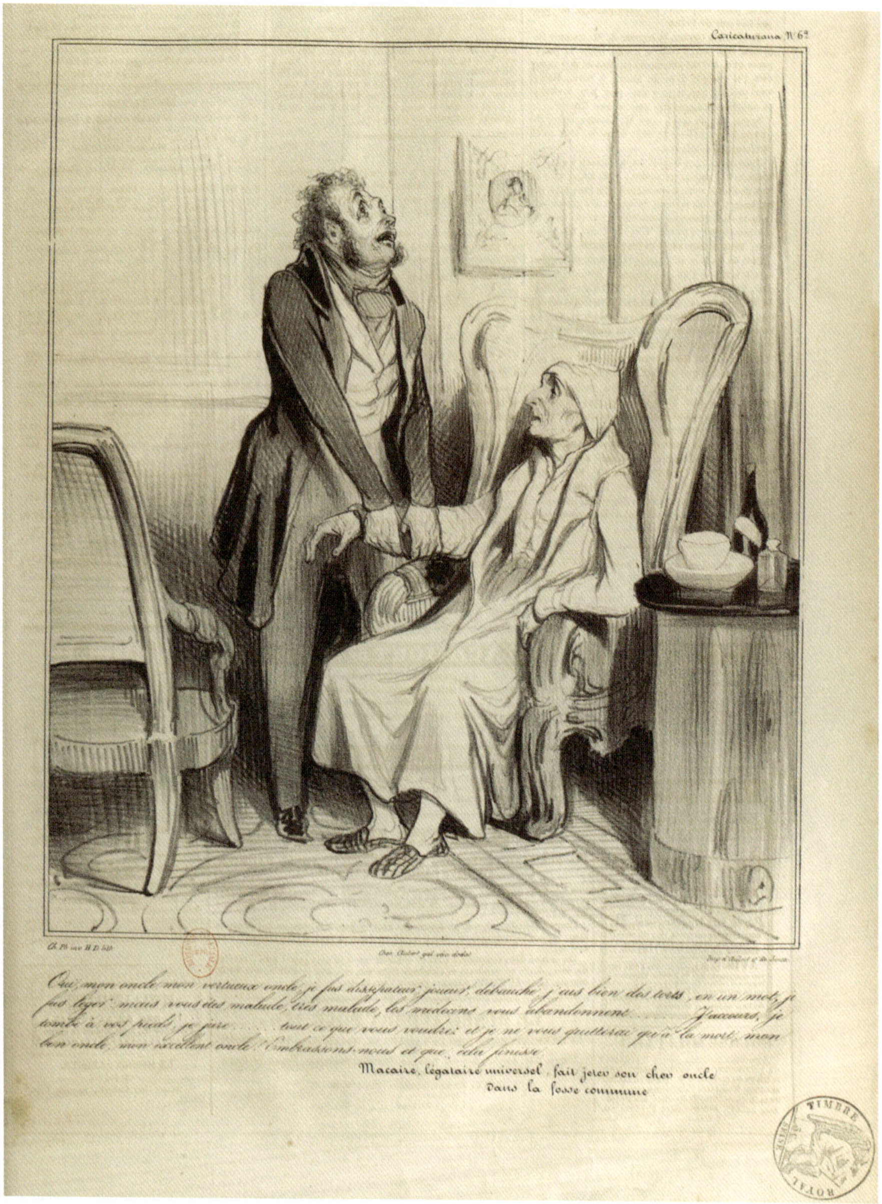

Figure 3.17 Honoré Daumier, 'Yes my uncle, my virtuous uncle ...' ('Oui, mon oncle, mon vertueux oncle ...'), *Le Charivari*, 17 September 1837

actor is faking his illness to negotiate a better cut of the performance's profits. Once the director offers him an even share of the box office receipts, the actor declares: 'The farce has ended and the drama can begin!'

In another close precedent to *The imaginary invalid*, Macaire approaches another startled man from the left in 'It won't be as easy as that, Monsieur!', originally published on

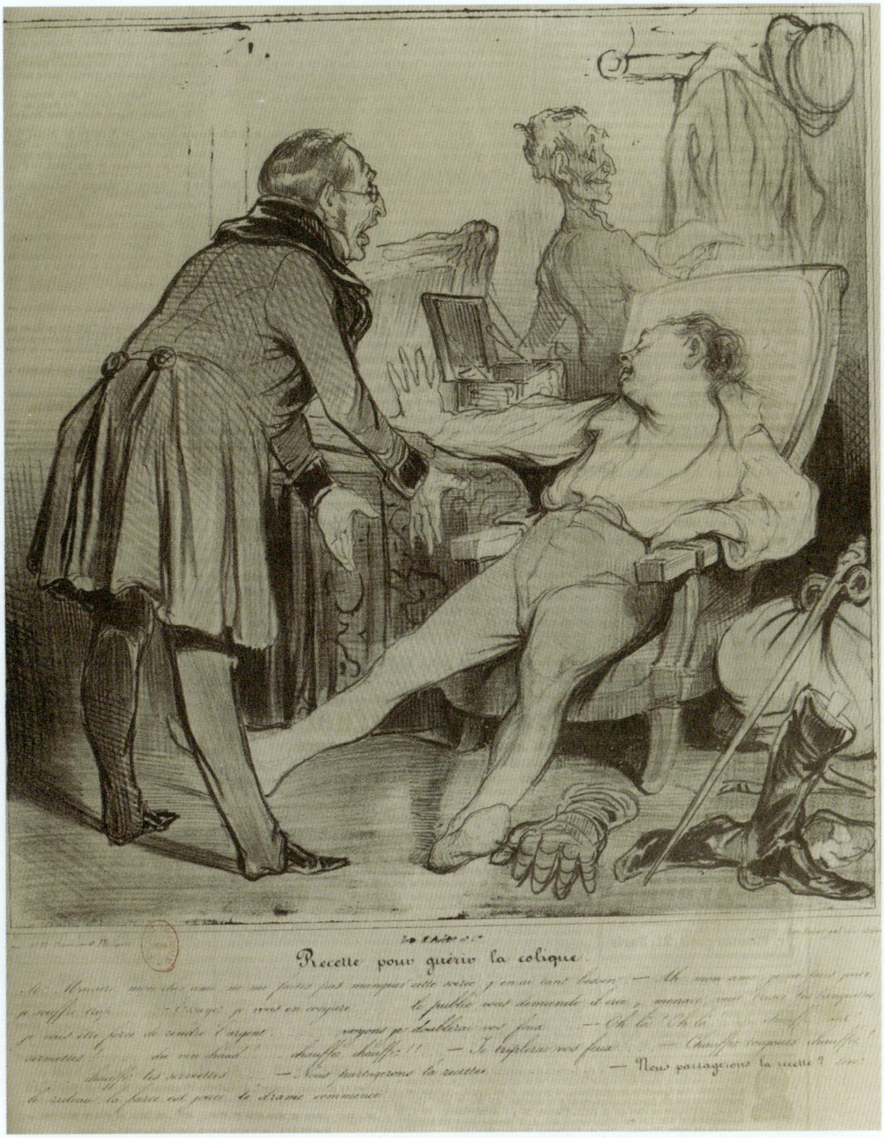

Figure 3.18 Honoré Daumier, 'Recipe to cure colic' ('Recette pour guérir la colique'), *Le Charivari*, 14 January 1838

25 June 1837 (Figure 3.19). In this print, Macaire's creditor sits up in his bedclothes in a bed framing the picture plane. Macaire has stormed into this private space in an absurd early-morning assault to demand an apology for the 'humiliating' request to repay the debt he owes. Maurice Alhoy's satirical story attached to the image in the 1839 book *Les cent et un Robert Macaire* weaves in a reference to Molière by having the crafty Macaire claim to his creditors that an old armchair about to be seized by a bailiff for non-payment was the very chair the dramaturge had died in.[61] That armchair was the site of myth and

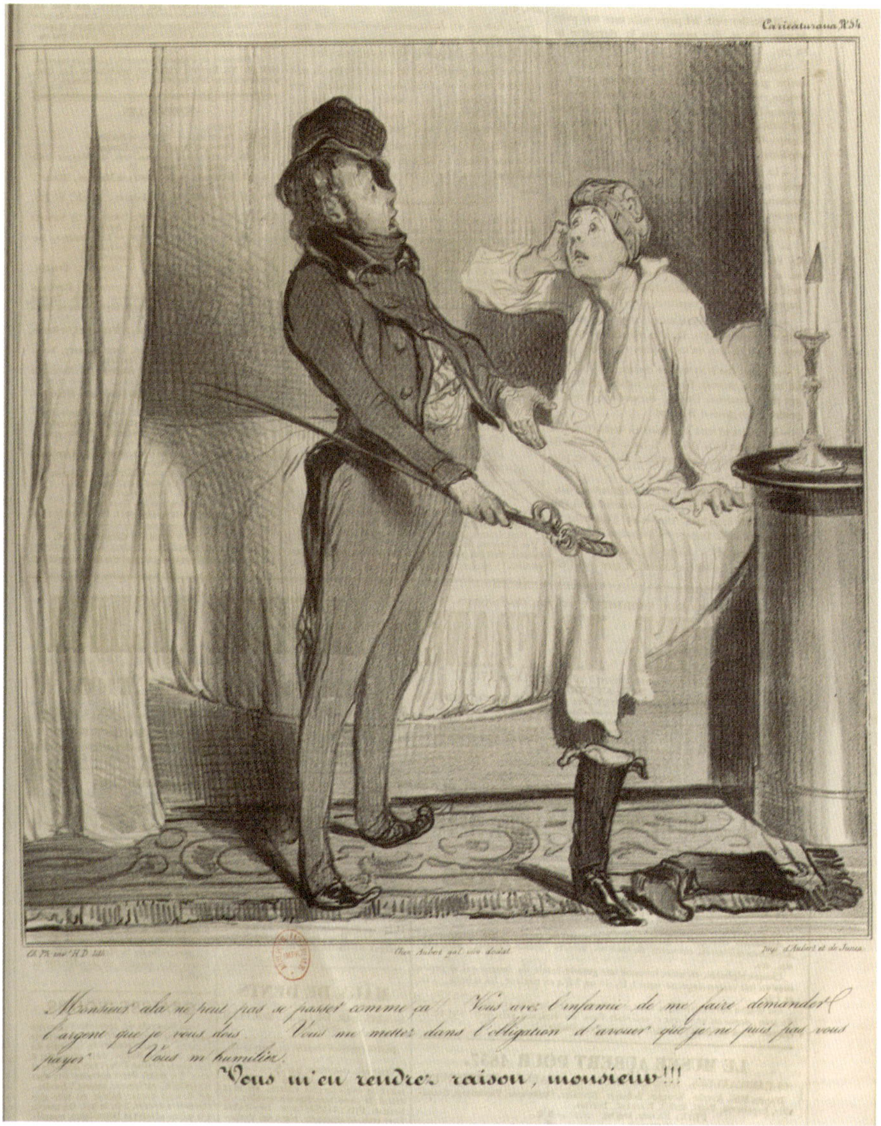

Figure 3.19 Honoré Daumier, 'It won't be as easy as that, Monsieur!' ('Monsieur cela ne peut pas se passer comme ça!'), *Le Charivari*, 25 June 1837

speculation about the dramaturge. Having written a part where he played a hypochondriac who acts out death in a chair on stage at a time when he himself was ill and collapsed during a performance, mythology of Molière's dramatic death often used imagery mirroring Argan's confinement in a chair (see, for example, Pierre Antoine Augustin Vafflard's *Death of Molière*, 1806).[62]

Daumier included translations of the figures of the weak patient or startled mark and predatory charlatan from his lithographs 'Yes, my uncle' and 'It won't be as easy as that, Monsieur!', as well as the hypochondriac from 'Recipe to cure colic', in his renderings of *The imaginary invalid* in paint. Perhaps Daumier wanted to inject some of the commercial success of these illustrated books into his painted work, and the substitution of the doctor for Macaire also helps retain a sense of the original figure's deception. It is notable that he turned to the figure of Macaire instead of modelling the hypochondriac after his earlier representations of Molière's imaginary invalid as a kind of monomaniac (Figure 3.20) or as a con man who used his mental distress to game the criminal justice system (Figure 3.21). In 'The last test' from 1842, a lithograph similar in composition

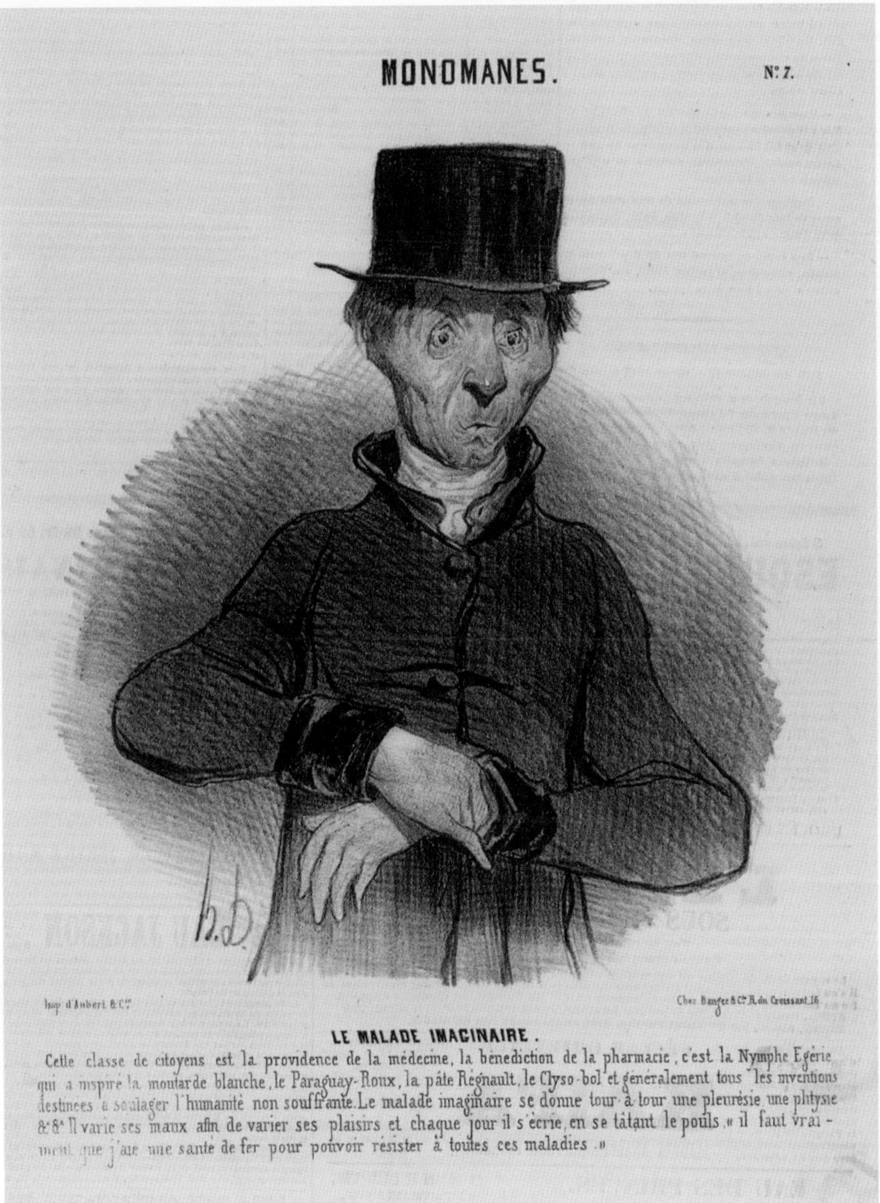

Figure 3.20 Honoré Daumier, 'The imaginary invalid' ('Le malade imaginaire'), *Le Charivari,* 18 January 1841

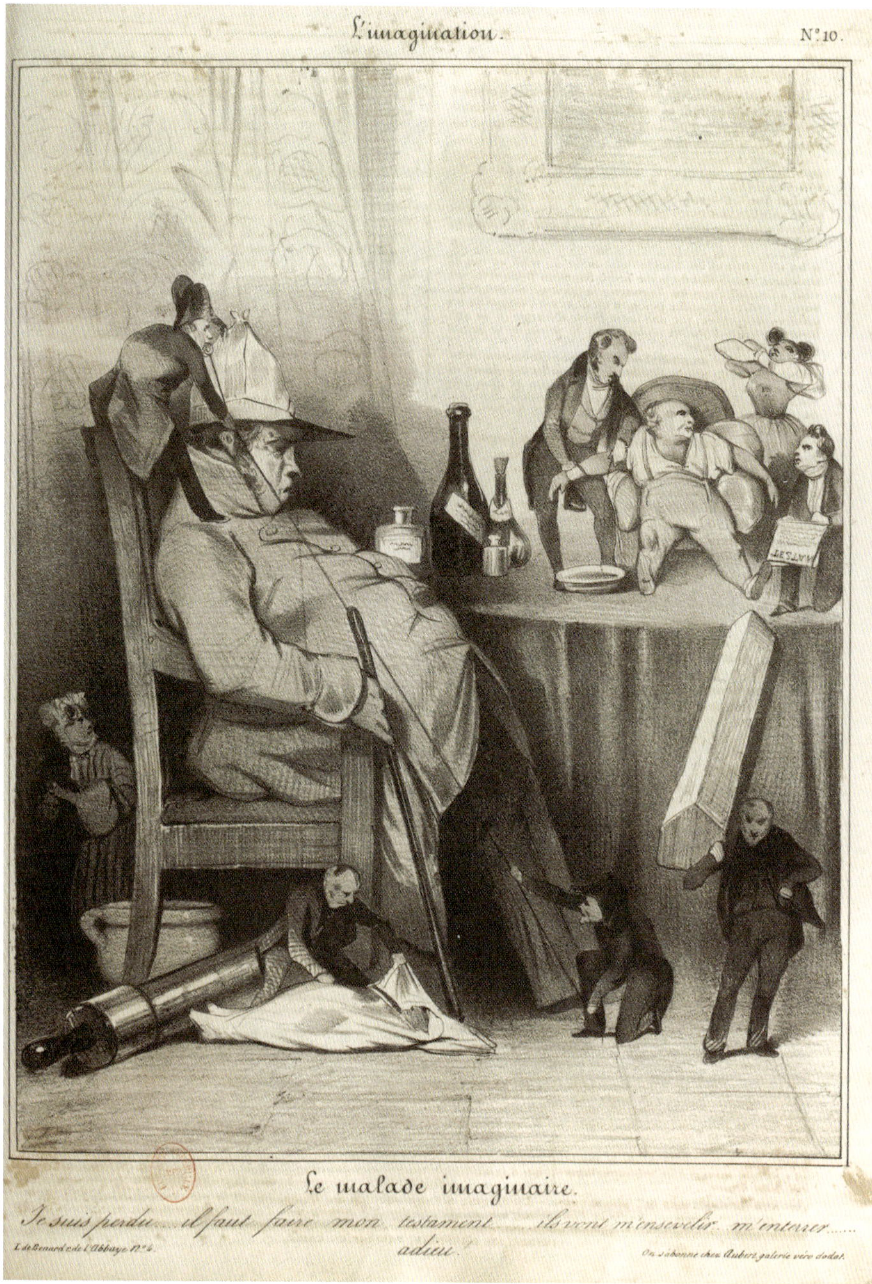

Figure 3.21 Honoré Daumier, 'The imaginary invalid' ('Le malade imaginaire'), *Le Charivari*, 21 May 1833

to Daumier's *Imaginary invalid* paintings, the patient is an allegory for the ailing Royalist journal *Le Constitutionnel*, claiming that his journal's rival and political opponent was in distress (Figure 3.22). Daumier chose not to imitate these images in spite of their closely related motifs. In fact, although Daumier drew similar scenes from Molière's play in

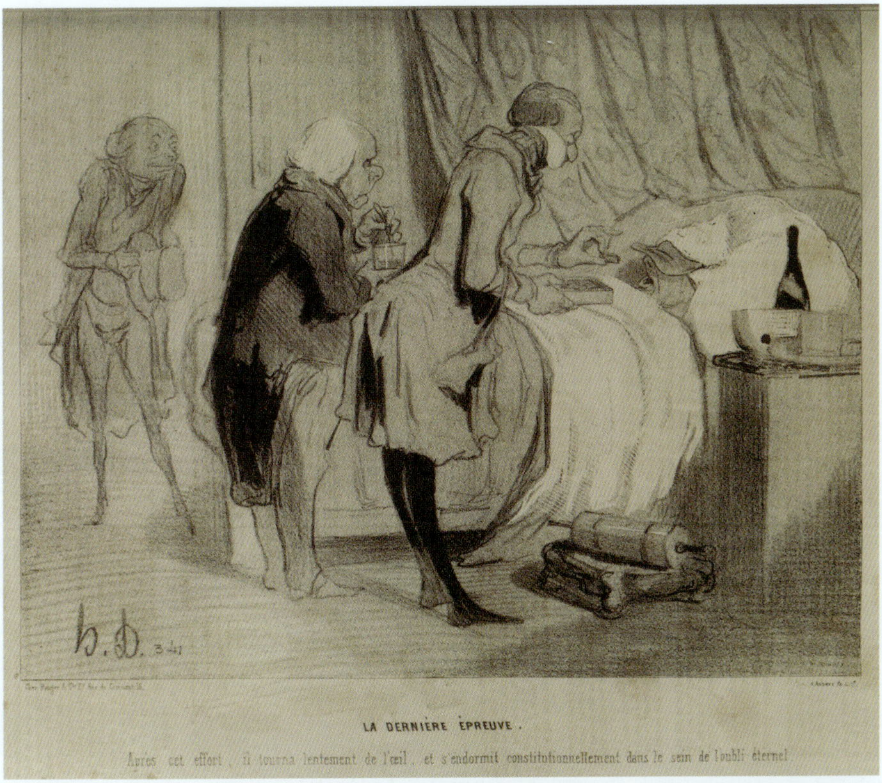

Figure 3.22 Honoré Daumier, 'The last test' ('La Dernière épreuve'), *Le Charivari*, 23 January 1842

watercolour and pen in the years immediately preceding these paintings (Figures 3.23 and 3.24), in the oil compositions he returned to Macaire.

This too was perhaps a response to censorship. Sensitive Second Empire censors forbade the play *Robert Macaire* in addition to all plays dealing with his character, including *L'Auberge des adrets*.[63] Daumier sublimates Macaire into his paintings in order to bring him back, surreptitiously, to the stage from which he has been banished. It is a political act, a bit of defiance against the same regime that has limited the freedom of his lithographic crayon.

The connection between *Robert Macaire* and Daumier's doctor also continues a line of exploration that extends back to the early pear/*poire* figure. Judith Wechsler has argued convincingly that characters like Macaire functioned for Daumier in the exact opposite way to the *poire* of Louis-Philippe. The pear distilled an individual *charge* – an exaggerated and often critical portrait – into a single emblem. I argued in my first chapter that Daumier's *Celebrities of the juste milieu* series similarly solidified *portraits-charge* into types, a process conceptually mediated by the mask. In contrast, Macaire and Joseph Prudhomme (the subject of Wechsler's focus) summarized an entire class of people into a specific, individual character.[64] In Daumier's painted revivals of Molière's plays, the artist once again uses the mask, but this time to investigate the opposite process: type becoming a *charge*.

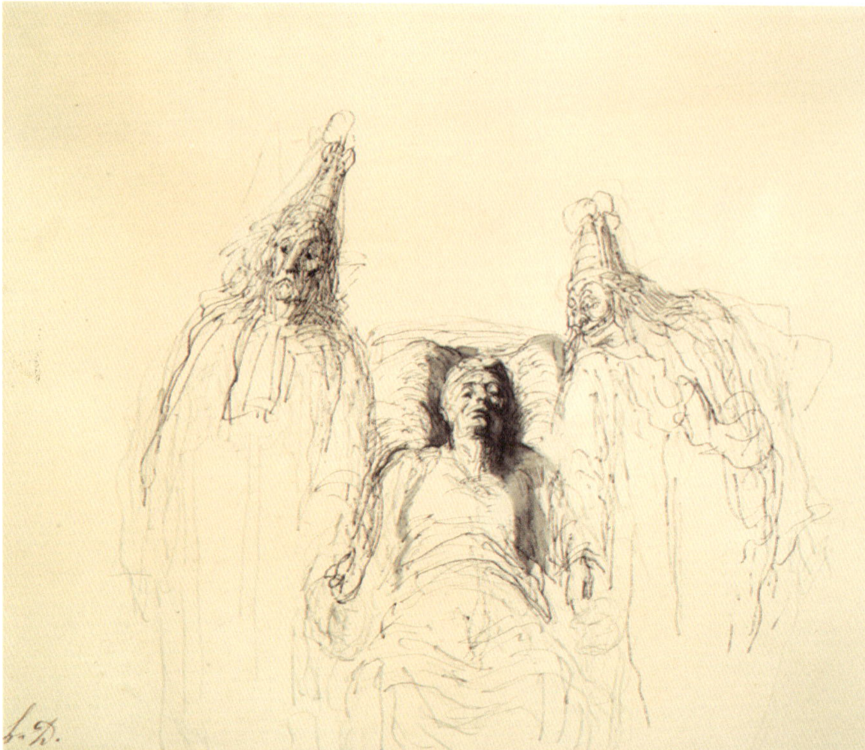

Figure 3.23 Honoré Daumier, *The imaginary invalid* (*Le malade imaginaire*), c. 1860–63

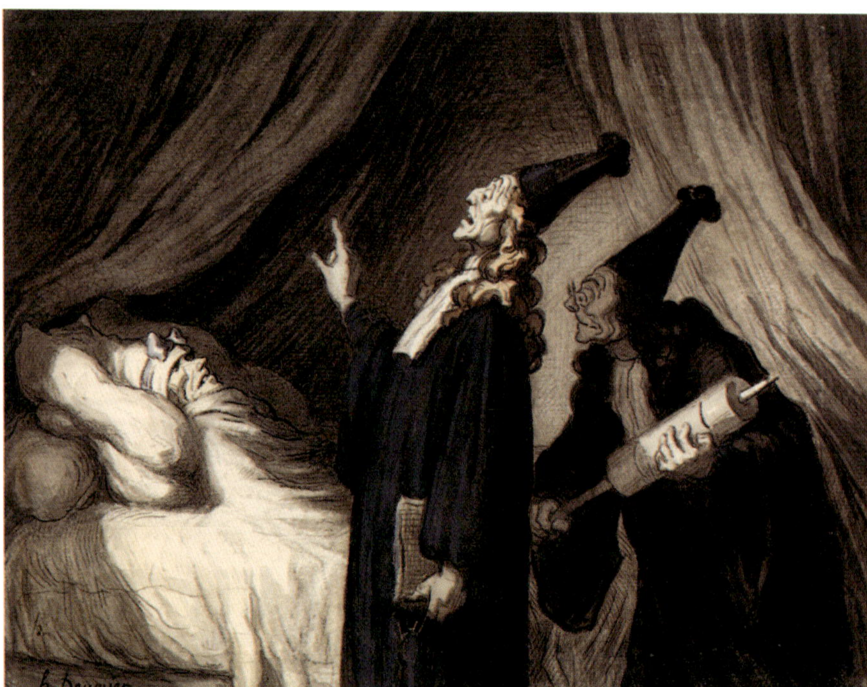

Figure 3.24 Honoré Daumier, *The imaginary invalid* (*Le malade imaginaire*), c. 1850

In the first *The imaginary invalid* painting, Daumier translated elements of composition and the archetypal role from caricatures of *Macaire*. In the second version, he turned again to caricature, but this time for its formal procedures and potential to make contemporary political references. In this painting, the leftmost figure holding the giant syringe clarifies the narrative moment that is so obscure in the Barnes painting. Purgon enters Argan's house with his assistant Fleurant who carries a large clyster, just like the strange looming figure in Daumier's painting. The doctor terrifies the patient with a litany of illnesses leading to death, the sort of chain reaction every hypochondriac fears:

Monsieur Purgon:	In less than four days you will be incurable!
Argan:	Have mercy on me!
Monsieur Purgon:	Then you will develop bradypepsia.
Argan:	Monsieur Purgon!
Monsieur Purgon:	Bradypepsia will lead to dyspepsia.
Argan:	Monsieur Purgon!
Monsieur Purgon:	Dyspepsia will lead to apepsy.
Argan:	Monsieur Purgon!
Monsieur Purgon:	Apepsy will lead to lientery.
Argan:	Monsieur Purgon!
Monsieur Purgon:	Lientery will lead to dysentery.
Argan:	Monsieur Purgon!
Monsieur Purgon:	Dysentery will lead to dropsy.
Argan:	Monsieur Purgon!
Monsieur Purgon:	And dropsy will lead to the loss of life, and that is how far you will have brought yourself by your folly. [65]

The Barnes painting captures Argan's exaggerated expression of horror as he is being delivered his diagnosis by the untrustworthy doctor. Though scholars have noted that Daumier often failed to signal specific narrative moments when translating motifs into oil, instead focusing on expressions and gesture, in this particular painting he provides enough information to signal the identity of Dr Purgon in contrast to Diafoirus or the costumed Toinette.[66] It follows that the doctor's assistant must be Fleurant. Daumier had drawn him before: he is the figure in glasses in the chalk and ink wash *The imaginary invalid*, housed at the Courtauld Gallery (Figure 3.24, c. 1850). The enema Fleurant holds in this work and the Philadelphia painting was a symbol of backwardness and abuses of power for both Daumier and Molière.[67]

The enema joke was an old one and hinged on doctors' resistance to professional modernization while also capitalizing quite effectively on the base scatological humour of 'anal retention'.[68] Molière's *The imaginary invalid* begins and ends with enema jokes. In the beginning of the play, Argan reads through his bloated monthly apothecary bill, halving each charge as he itemizes rhubarb-infused clysters, enemas to cure flatulence, and tonics to clear his bile. The play's finale features a chorus of doctors singing about medicine and emetics in a kind of pig Latin. Like Molière, Daumier found that satirizing doctors appealed to his patrons. In the 1850s and 1860s, Daumier painted watercolours mocking professionals whose specialized costumes might belie a feckless performance of their work in the public interest or sadistic fascinations with bodily fluids. Doctors were a particularly rich subject, offering the potential for body humour, class critique, and processing one's fear of death.

Beginning in the early 1830s, Daumier also used the enema, or clyster, to symbolize political repression. A lithograph from December 1833 shows a wounded messenger (likely an allegory of the embattled French people) subjected to instruments of bleeding, purging, and enemas administered (from left to right) by King Louis-Philippe, Ferdinand Philippe the duc d'Orléans, and General Georges Mouton, comte de Lobau (Figure 3.25). One year earlier, through Maison Aubert, Daumier published a coloured lithograph of Lobau suppressing the riots of May and June 1831 in the Place Vendôme ('Monsignor, if they persist we will put Paris in a state of siege', Figure 3.26). Rather than dramatize the Ministry of Interior's violent attacks on insurgents with city fire hoses, Daumier makes their brutality impotent and debased, the baron spraying the crowd with an enema.[69] In Raymond Escholier's book *Daumier* from 1913, he makes this connection:

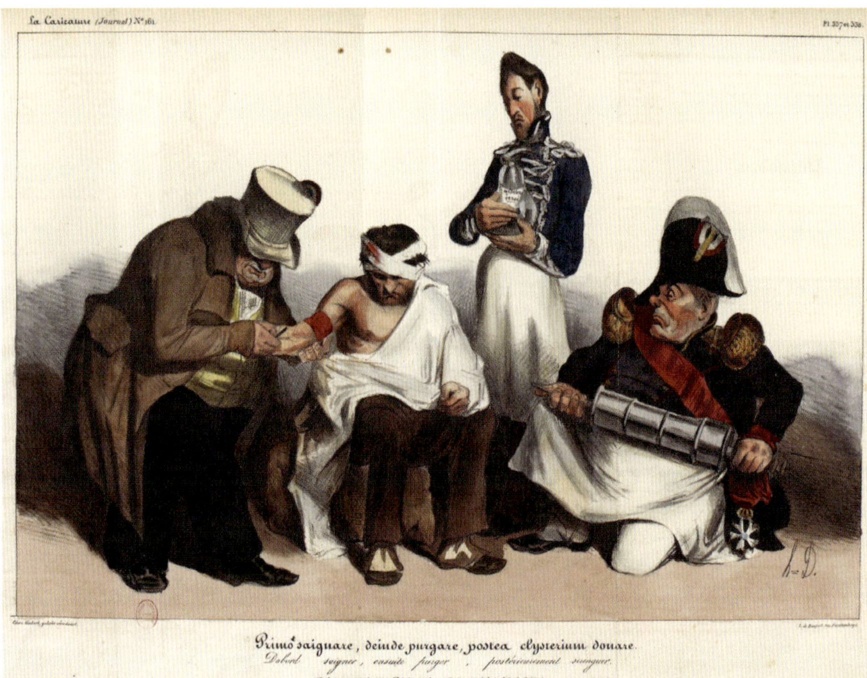

Figure 3.25 Honoré Daumier, 'First bleed, then purge, then use the clyster' ('Primo saignare, deinde purgare, postea clysterium donare'), *La Caricature*, 5 December 1833

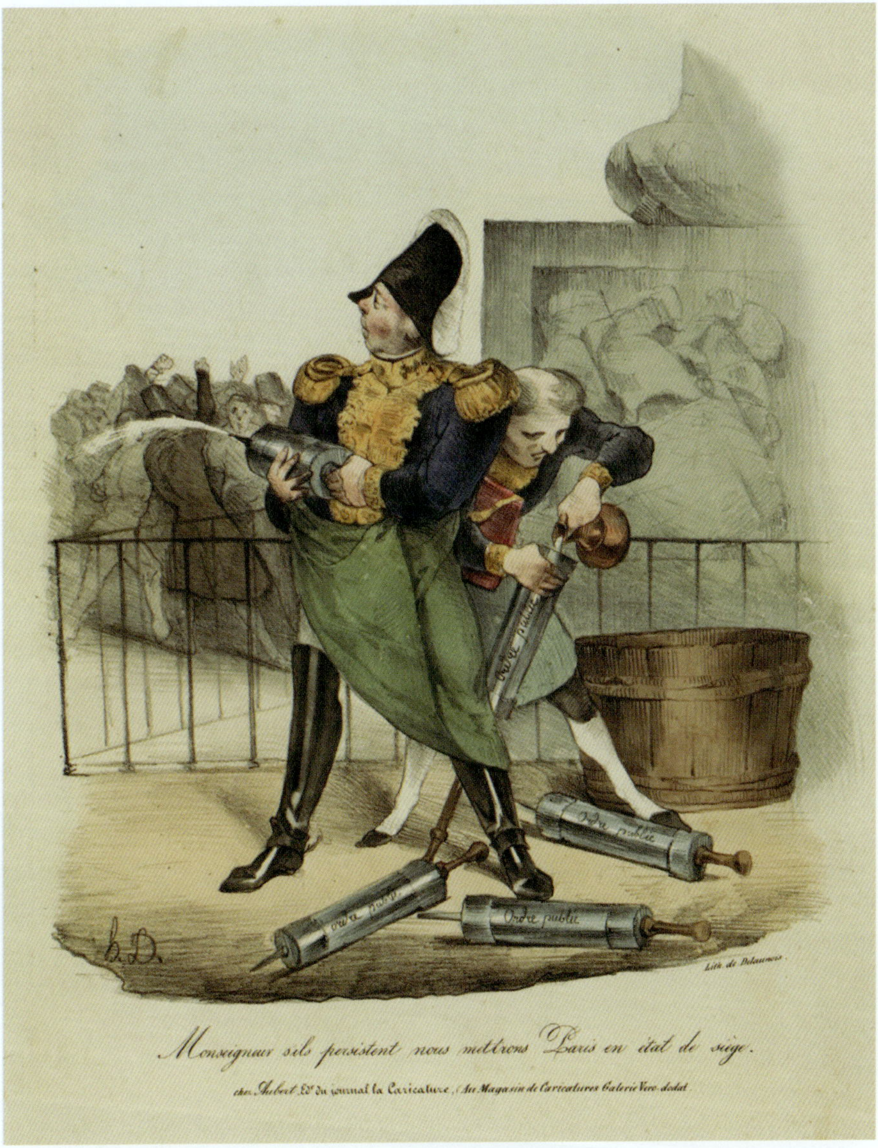

Figure 3.26 Honoré Daumier, 'Monsieur, if they persist we will place Paris under a state of siege' ('Monseigneur, s'ils persistent nous mettrons Paris en état de siege'), 1832

> Who is not familiar with the gesture, so human in short, of Marshal Lobau dispersing the riot by bringing the firehoses into play? ... Since then, there is not a *charge* of Marshal Lobau in which he is not represented decked out like one of Molière's apothecaries.[70]

Thus, in the second version of *The imaginary invalid*, Fleurant and his enema not only insert narrative specificity into the scene but also carry histories of references to contemporary figures and political events.

Doctor Purgon – the doctor in the Philadelphia Museum of Art painting – was modelled, in a way that was recognizable to audiences in Molière's time, after a doctor who had killed his own wife and daughter with an injection of antimony.[71] This was not unusual for the dramaturge. As a young actor, Molière and his troop developed a short farce about doctors, *Le Médecin volant*, and many of his plays continued to make jokes about doctors in general, yet also with specific targets in mind. Molière's 1665 *comédie-ballet*, *L'Amour médecin,* was first performed at Versailles and mocked the medical profession, in particular doctors dedicated to the gruesome practices of bleeding and purging.[72] *L'Amour médecin* made allusions to specific, contemporary doctors by means of recognizable masks that the actors wore. For example, masks made it clear to audiences that one doctor was meant to suggest Tomès, who used bleeding to cure most ills, and another Dr Des Fonadrès, whose adherence to modern chemistry often interfered with the successful treatment of his patients.[73]

Typically, in *commedia* performances or in masquerades, the mask was used to make a particular person (an actor, a dancer) into an archetypal character or to subsume the identity of the wearer beneath another, more generalized identity. However, Molière used masks to particularize, to individualize the typological 'doctor' character. Instead of concealing an identity, the comic mask reveals it. In Daumier's early caricatural portraits of politicians, he used the mask in the way of the *commedia* or the masquerade, transforming a portrait into an image that was typological or symbolic. But perhaps Molière appealed to Daumier in the 1850s and 1860s because he offered a compelling alternative. The playwright made allusions to a contemporary doctor through the archetypal mask, presenting Dr Purgon not as an archetype but a *charge*.

Daumier painted scenes from Molière, whose plays had faced strict censorship restrictions from his royal patron, perhaps most famously from the play *Tartuffe* (1664), at a moment when censorship drove him to work outside of caricature and in paint. Daumier saw *Tartuffe* performed under the Second Empire, a moment when censorship was significantly impacting his career.[74] Molière's mask was therefore a powerful metaphor for an artist working in a time of oppressive censorship. The mask was used by Molière to satirize specific, contemporary figures while obfuscating this contemporaneity from censors by invoking the typological and the eternal. Molière disguised his critique of court doctors, the clergy, and even the monarchy using the masks of the ancient *commedia*, just as Daumier would smuggle serious political criticism under the guise of the archetypal, the symbolic. Daumier's Robert Macaire, like his counterpart in the theatre, was an amalgam of bourgeois tendencies, an archetype given a recognizable face.

***

It is important to note that while some of Daumier's figures appear to be wearing masks, the artist does not fully resolve whether the faces are actually masked or just mask-like. He is interested instead in blurring and crisscrossing the line between living face and mask, taking advantage of the ambiguity made possible with bolder outlines borrowed from the graphic arts. Fleurant's mask-like face has a hard black line dividing his jaw and ear from his neck. His mouth is drawn closed and his eyes are ringed with black frames. The artist mingled expressive portraits with comic masks in *The former Comédie-Français* (c. 1860–65), a clear nod to Watteau's anthology of *commedia* types, *The Italian comedians*, and perhaps Edmond Geffroy's *Molière and the characters of his comedies* (Salon of 1857). Watteau's Harlequin wears a dark mask that somehow, despite the contortions of his body, twists to become parallel with the picture plane. Daumier's Crispin character, the figure with the triangular white collar at the very left of his painting, and the doctor in black on the right both seem to wear masks, an effect that is suggested by their formal and colouristic simplification as well as the graphic black lines that sever their jaws from their necks. From face to face in Daumier's ensemble painting, the eye dances between likeness and type, from flushed cheek to cool planarity. The artist triangulates between the indistinct description of a woman's face at right, the physiognomic specificity of the central figure, towards whom she looks, and the rigid visage of Dr Diafoirus in profile. In this alternation between face and mask, Daumier gives visual form to one of Molière's driving themes. His pictorial revivals of Molière's plays probe tensions between recognition and misrecognition, likeness and disguise.

In a similar trajectory, Daumier repeated Molière's exploration of disguise as both a theme and a vehicle in which persistent, recognizable types might respond to contemporary events. In his works inspired by *Robert Macaire*, Daumier drew a figure originally from the theatre whose tendency to slip on the costumes of many professions gave him legitimacy in none. Macaire's disguises mirrored the sort of doubling that Molière evoked because he was both a figure from the theatre and also a social type.

Moments of comic recognition in Molière's plays were often visual. The audience could see that the doctor prescribing Dutch cheese in *The imaginary invalid* was really Toinette in disguise. The playwright drew associations between characters and contemporary doctors by means of masks designed to be more likeness than type. Molière activated audience complicity with these visual gags, even as his text passed muster with the censors. In caricature, Daumier also plays with familiarity and deviation, recognition and exaggeration. For him, the comic mask was a visual representation of the interface between ancient archetypes and contemporary politics and also between artist and audience. The doubling of the mask also echoed the new doubling of subversive and surface meaning required in the production of caricature and theatre under repressive censorship laws. When Daumier invokes the mask in the context of a Molière painting, implicit is the possible allusion to contemporary figures as well as the resulting *charge* between artwork and audience. Noise, in the Molière revival paintings, would become a similar motif representing audience collusion and, indeed, response.

Barkers, parades, and 'calculated applause': Noise in Daumier's theatres

Noise was critical to Daumier's representations of informal theatrical performances. His paintings, lithographs, and drawings communicate the clamour of parade performers competing with the commotion of the street and the ever-present barker drawing the crowd to his show. The title of the journal *Le Charivari* refers to a rural folk tradition where noise – typically the clash of pots and pans – was used to draw attention to behaviour in breach of community norms. In the medieval period, the *charivari* often involved grotesque masks and costumes.[75] Noise – and specifically a sense of clamour or cacophony – therefore served as a popular regulatory mechanism, a form of community self-policing.

There has been a fair amount of scholarship on Daumier's clowns and comedic performers. Indeed, most of the influential literature on Daumier focuses on his images of outsider comedians and outdoor performances.[76] Bruce Laughton has identified two main themes in this area of Daumier's work: the figure of the clown or *saltimbanque* and outdoor street shows or *parades*.[77] The word *saltimbanque* comes from the Italian derivation for a performer who jumps (*saltare*) on a bench (*banco*) that he carries for his transient show. Helen Borowitz suggests that the figure of such a pathetic, transient clown provided an image of the common man.[78] T. J. Clark writes that Daumier's clown stands in for the figure of the artist in the Second Empire, specifically for those working in illustrated journals, claiming both as outsiders activating laughter as a means to smuggle in subversive politics.[79]

Jesters had historically delivered insights into absolutist regimes that were otherwise insulated from critique. Political caricaturists in the 1830s identified with the jester for this reason. For the Romantic generation and nineteenth-century literature more generally, the figure of the 'sad clown' can be traced to Victor Hugo's dramatic play *Le roi s'amuse* (1832) and his depiction of François I's jester, Triboulet.[80] During the Restoration, Molière was revived as a figure who had, like the jester, earned a kind of creative independence with his king and was able to deliver a measure of subversive comedy along with his flattery.[81]

Paula Harper agrees that the lithographic artists working at Philipon's journals identified with street performers and represented themselves as *saltimbanques* hustling for attention outside the spaces of state-sanctioned entertainment. She cites in particular Daumier's 'Parade du Charivari', published in *Le Charivari*, 6 January 1839 (Figure 3.27).[82] The image is notable for the noise it communicates, the drumbeat, the clash of the cymbals, and the shouts of the barker. The sideshow in 'Parade du Charivari' competes with the discordant sound of the carnival goers gathered below, using noise to draw attention to the static images cordoned off in the rectangular space of printed pages above the stage. A copy of *Le Charivari* acts as the stage upon which the artist-musicians shift and strain to project their auditory assault on the audience.

Parade barkers compete with the discordant sounds of a carnival in a watercolour and pen and ink drawing from the mid-1860s (one of several on this theme). In *The sideshow*,

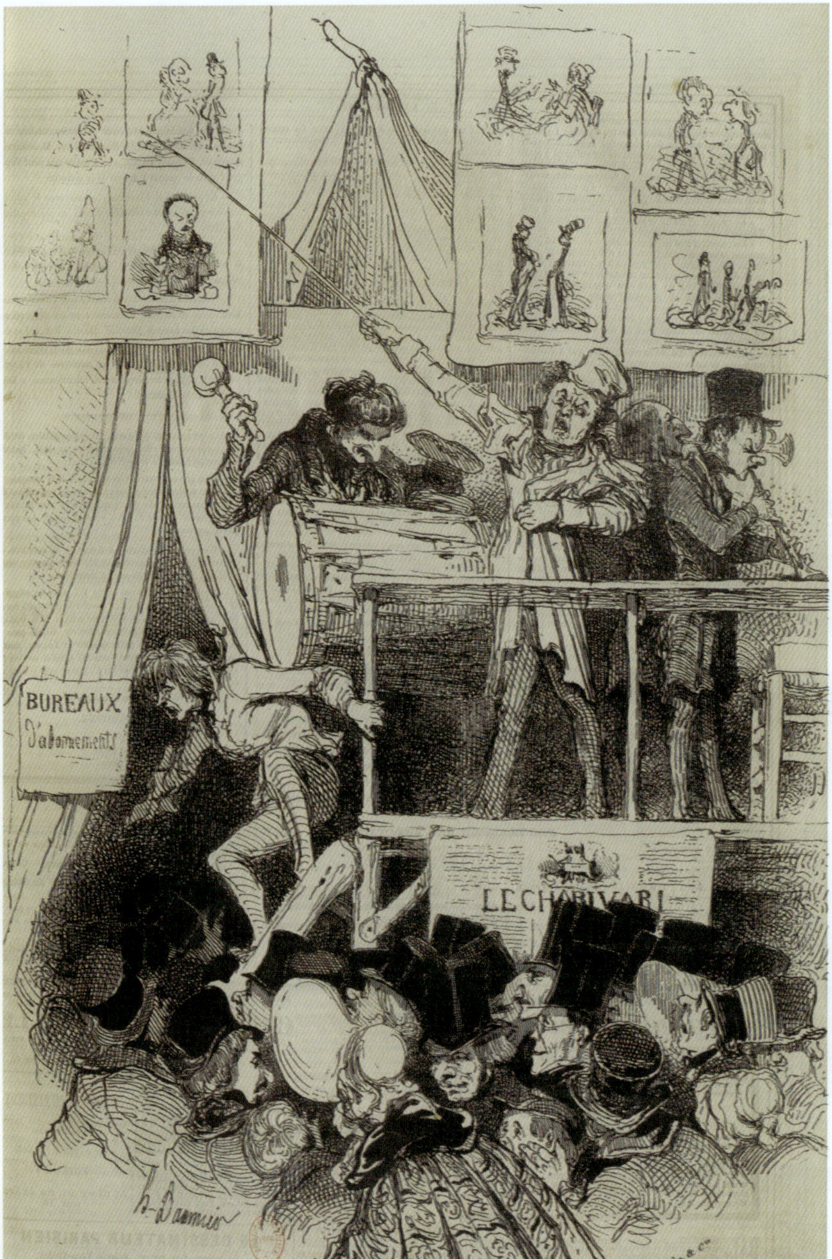

Figure 3.27 Honoré Daumier, 'Charivari parade' ('Parade du Charivari'), *Le Charivari*, 6 January 1839

three out of five figures are bellowing, mouths open, on a makeshift stage and one is holding a clarinet (Figure 3.28). Their bodies pose in exaggerated gestures of shouting and noisemaking.

Although Daumier scholarship has largely attended to his images of outsiders and outdoor performers, his oeuvre reflects the separation between spheres of performance

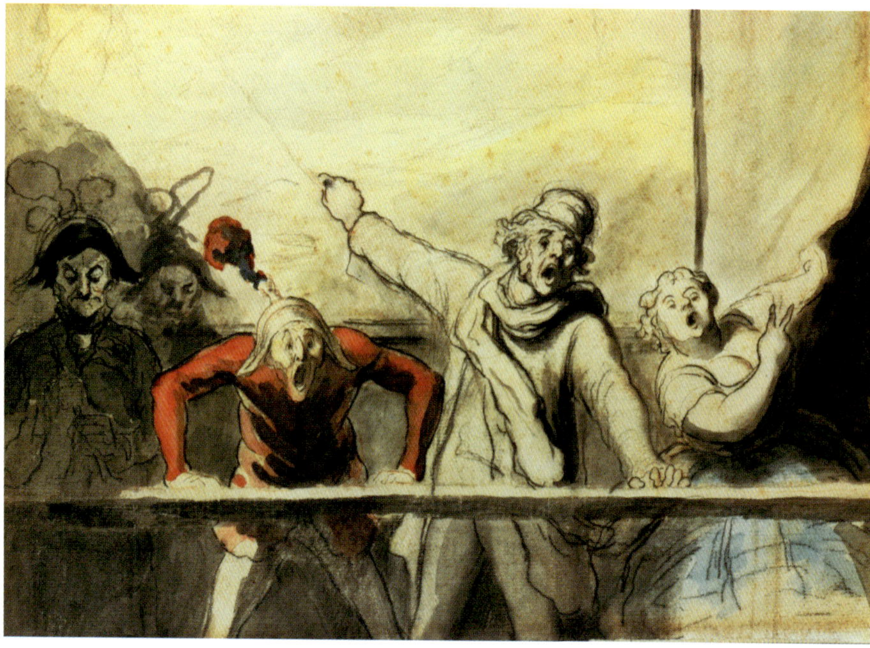

Figure 3.28 Honoré Daumier, *The sideshow* (*La Parade des saltimbanques*), c. 1865

in the mid-nineteenth century between large, authorized theatres on the one hand and informal outdoor performance on the other. Though he produced a number of truly impressive paintings representing scenes from classical theatre, these have received very little scholarly attention. Noise gives us a clue about how these works fit into Daumier's larger investigations into media and his negotiation of censorship laws.

In contrast to Daumier's decidedly noisy images of *saltimbanques*, the stages in his depictions of Molière revivals are silent or full of whispers. In Daumier's *Crispin and Scapin* (c. 1864, Figure 3.29),[83] two figures conspire on a stage. Scapin, the figure at left, wears a billowing white costume and slouchy white hat. He folds his arms across his body, his hands disappearing into the volume of the fabric. Crispin leans in at right, cupping a hand to whisper in Scapin's ear. Under Scapin's sinister eyes are bright, sickly patches of red paint, echoed in his strange reddish ear near the centre of the canvas. This ear, made from two interlocking hooked strokes, is grazed by Crispin's hand, forming a triangle of darkness beneath, a repository for messages unknown. Just below this moment of contact, at the centre of the painting, the two whites of the characters' costumes meet.

Scapin's nose is an enormous pointed beak, the whites of his almond eyes are reddish, and he looks sharply out to the left, away from his friend. A dramatic widow's peak interrupts his white, brightly lit forehead, and his eyebrows arch upwards at the temples like hooks. The undulating paint strokes that make up Scapin's face are like nothing else in the painting and create the impression of thoughts being moulded by secrets shared. Daumier adds a patchy hand, barely described, at left on Scapin's shoulder, an addition

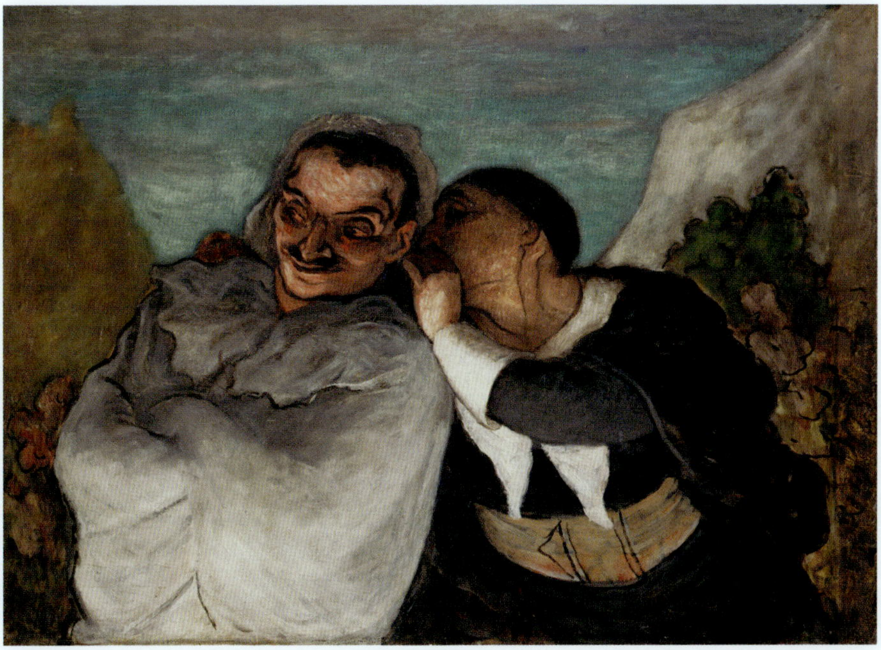

Figure 3.29 Honoré Daumier, *Crispin and Scapin*, c. 1864

that turns the bodies into a closed circuit, linking the two by a secret withheld from both viewer and audience. In contrast to Daumier's informal parades and outdoor barkers, this painting thematizes sound *withheld*.

Crispin and Scapin has a graphic quality and a confident speed of execution more typical of Daumier's lithographs, especially in Crispin's neck, which the artist economically describes in just four vertical slashes and one horizontal jawline. It was only Daumier's second small group painting illustrating a Molière play after *The imaginary invalid*, and he took pains to work out the composition. In the preparatory oil sketch of *Crispin and Scapin* (c. 1863–65) in a private collection, the actors' faces are loose and *informe* in comparison to the final – and much more caricatural – version. Like his work on *The imaginary invalid*, Daumier begins in a painterly style and then ends up moving towards a style reflecting the draughtsmanship, linearity, and mask-like faces of caricature. Typical of his broader oil painting practice, Daumier builds paint from dark to light and highlights Scapin's face in vibrant pink impasto.[84] The red and white are not quite mixed, and this dramatic colour stands in stark contrast to the chilled grey-blue sky behind the figures. This background is flattened, schematic, a painted stage set layered into Daumier's painting. Graphic scrawls of flowers and trees might be movable panels at the stage edges. The set's artificiality is further emphasized by the precision of the meeting points between the yellow and white mountains and the collars of Crispin and Scapin, which not only frame these figures but seem to extend contiguously with them. This scene is illuminated from below, evoking the theatrical lighting of oil or gas lamps at the edge of stages.

Just as he had translated the composition of *The imaginary invalid* from print to painting, Daumier transferred the figural composition of *Crispin and Scapin* from an earlier 1858 lithograph of two men whispering in a butcher's shop (Figure 3.30).[85] The electric communication of the theatre was legally aligned to, and most closely described by, the improvisational hand of the caricaturist: 'when opinions are converted into actions by the circulation of drawings … it is *an incitement to action*.'[86] For Daumier, the subject matter of classical theatre called for a mode of painting that draws on the direct address of caricature. The translation from stage to painting therefore seemed to require a graphic effect, the scumbled bluish peaches of Scapin's neck abbreviated into four black outlines. We can see too from Daumier's citation of the clown from Molière's play in 'The advice of a political Crispin' published in *Le Charivari* on 12 May 1851 (Figure 3.31) that he was using the *commedia* character as a vessel for political critique. In the print, 'Crispin' is really Louis-Désiré Véron, owner of the rival, right-wing newspaper *Le Constitutionnel* (1819–1914). Véron-as-Crispin offers advice to Louis-Napoleon, gesturing towards a constitution that will be manipulated for the coming *coup d'état*.

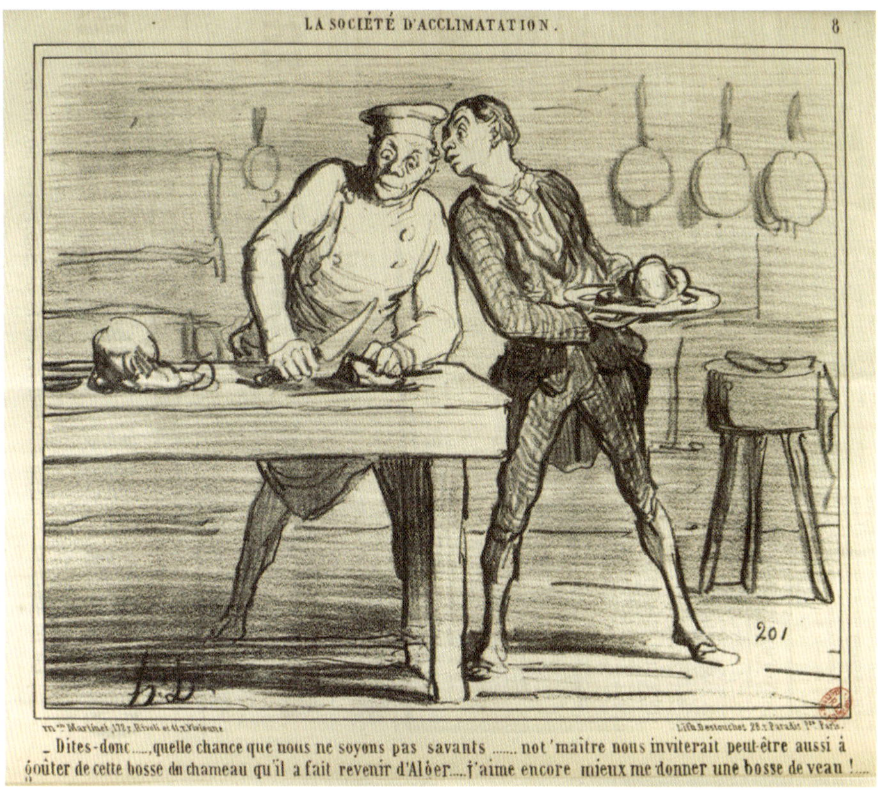

Figure 3.30 Honoré Daumier, 'I am glad we are not scientists …' ('Dites-donc …, quelle chance que nous ne soyons pas savants'), *Le Charivari*, 20 September 1858

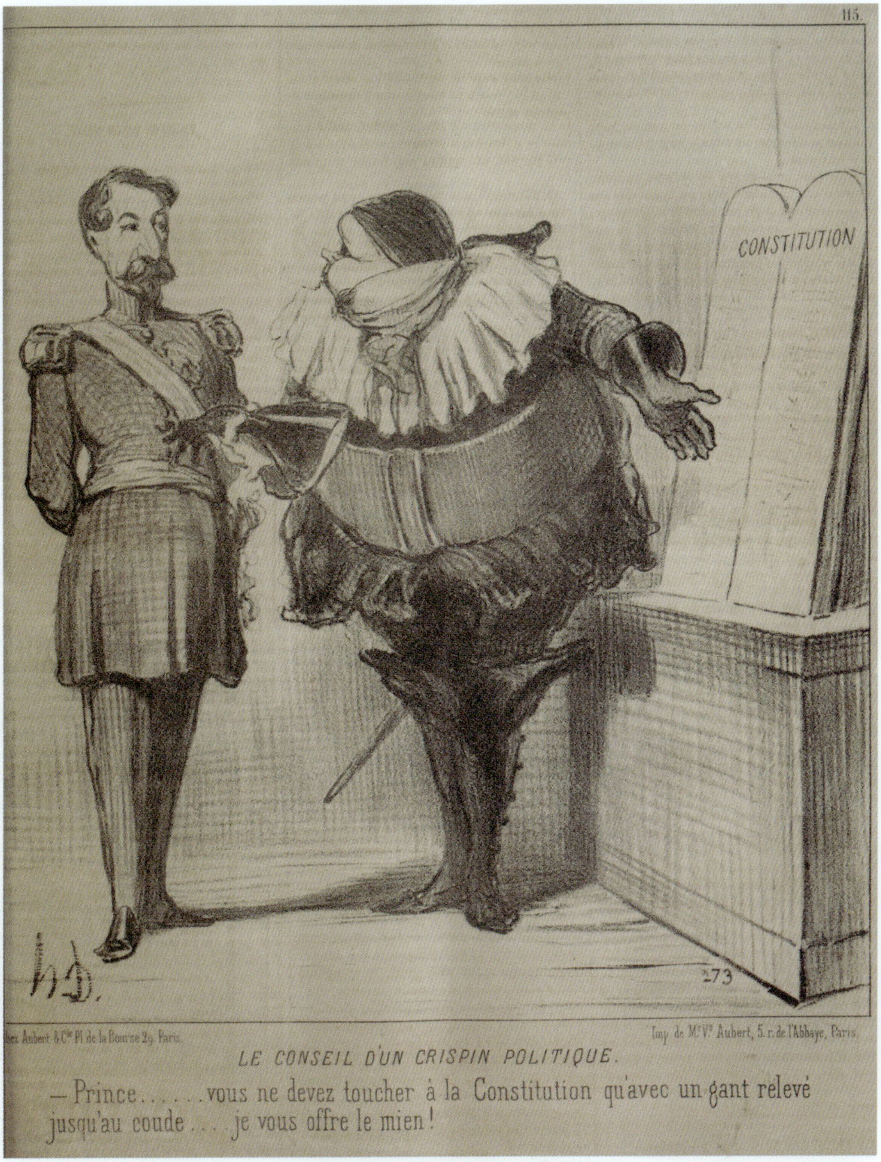

Figure 3.31 Honoré Daumier, 'Advice from a political Crispin' ('Le conseil d'un Crispin politique'), *Le Charivari*, 12 May 1851

Although Daumier appropriates some of the clarity and immediacy of caricature, *Crispin and Scapin* thematizes the withholding of narrative clues.[87] There is no sound emanating from the stage. Crispin visibly muffles his voice in a whisper, eliciting in the viewer of the painting the audience's sense of frustrated listening. Lithographs like 'The tenor's promises' (1842) make it clear that in formalized theatres performers are particularly vulnerable to audience approval, which is primarily indicated

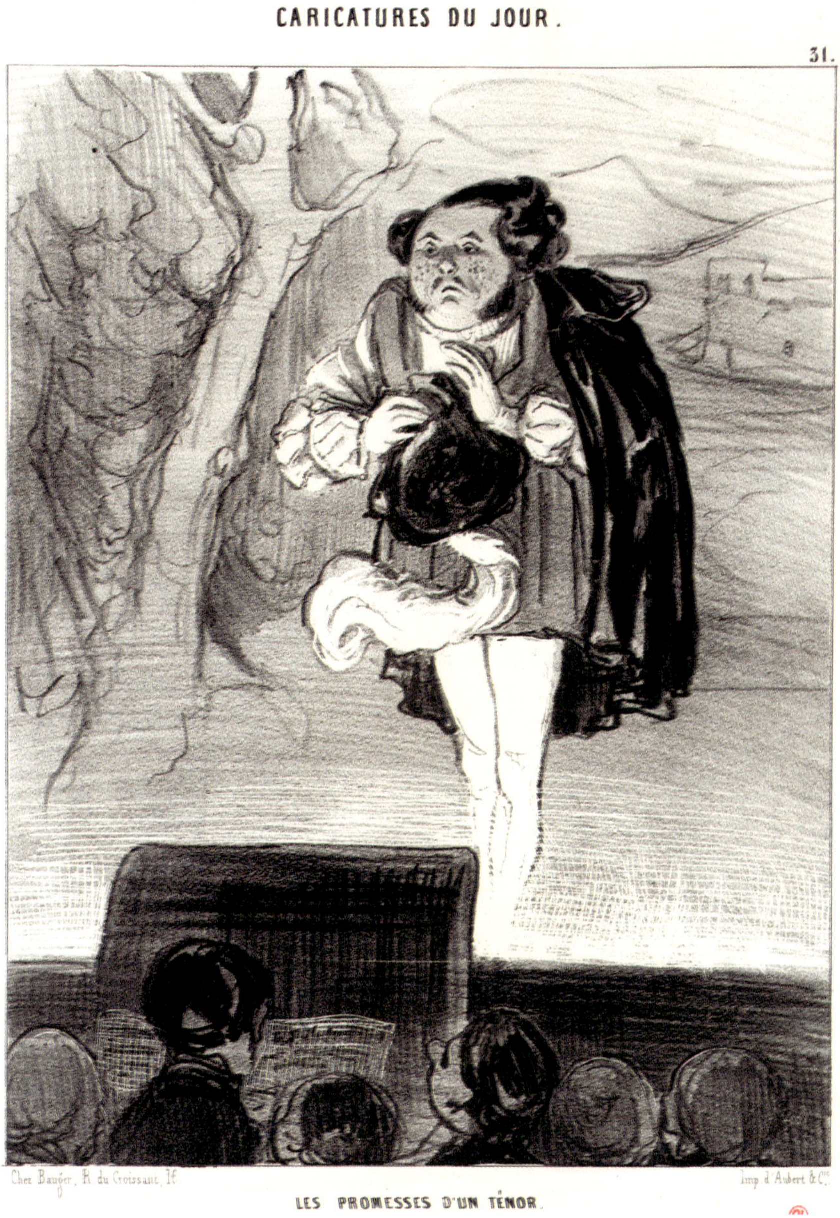

Figure 3.32 Honoré Daumier, 'The tenor's promises' ('Les promesses d'un ténor'), *La Caricature* (Deuxième Publication), 24 July 1842

through noise (Figure 3.32). Unlike the *saltimbanque* pictures, Daumier's paintings of staged productions by Molière displace sound from the performers onto the audience. The lighting and sense of strained listening in *Crispin and Scapin* situates the viewer as if in the theatre, implicating her in the radical response of the pit.

This is the critical difference between these theatre scenes and Daumier's representations of informal street spectacles. In the former, noise is the prerogative of the audience, not the performers, and this can be – as we shall see – a very charged proposition.

F. W. J. Hemmings has argued that the theatre in eighteenth-century France became an effective space for the anonymous expression of ideas otherwise forbidden under an absolute monarchy. Audiences of theatrical performances would respond audibly to a play, signalling approval or disapproval when lines or scenes seemed particularly associated with current events. Hemmings calls this act of subversive applause or audience vocalization 'making applications'. The act was, like the *charivari*, a popular regulatory mechanism that relied on, and inverted, accepted noise-making traditions. The anonymity of the pit and the convention of applause in that space made 'applications' difficult to control. One excellent example took place during a dress rehearsal of Charles Collé's *Partie de chasse de Henri IV* (1764). In the first act, there are rumours that the character Sully is about to be removed as the king's chief adviser, and Henri ends up pardoning him. Collé's play was performed on 19 May 1781, coincidentally the same day as the dismissal of Louis XVI's Finance Minister, Jacques Necker. At the moment when Henri pardons his adviser, a voice in the crowd called out, 'Yes, yes!', leading to a general melee. The audience drew an association between the events portrayed in *Henri IV* and current political events, and their vocalizations during the play allowed them to vent their frustrations about the loss of Necker.[88] Audience applications remained an important method of critique throughout the nineteenth century, especially as restrictions on theatrical performances again mimicked those under the absolute monarchy of the *ancien régime*.[89]

Hemmings also notes that applications decreased during the July Monarchy because of the rise of clappers paid by the house and because of the greater attendance of provincials, who understood fewer political jokes. Louis Véron – who in addition to running *Le Constitutionnel* was a doctor, politician, and director of the Opera in the 1830s – institutionalized the *claque*, a group of clappers planted in the audience in order to ensure applause at key moments in a performance. This was an organized operation, with a strict hierarchy of lieutenants and subordinates, clever signals, and key locations throughout the theatre. Directors attempted to control the voices and applause emerging from the anonymous darkness of a theatre precisely because a bad reaction – the wrong noise – could be devastating, even politically subversive.[90]

***

The iconography used to represent Molière in the first half of the nineteenth century tended to focus on *Tartuffe, ou l'Imposteur*, famously a play that was banned and then rereleased. When *Tartuffe* was first performed for King Louis XIV at a three-day fête, *Les plaisirs de l'île enchantée* at Versailles on 12 May 1664, it was seen as deeply offensive because the distance between satire and piety, between malicious religious hypocrisy and sincere devotion, appeared too close to be represented responsibly.[91] As in *The imaginary invalid*, the conflict in Molière's *Tartuffe* centres on the patriarch of a family falling under the spell of a charlatan. Tartuffe poses as a holy man and talks the unsuspecting Orgon out of his fortune and his daughter's hand, exposing the dangers of pious hypocrisy. The first version of the play was quickly banned in 1664 largely due to pressures from the church. The subject of a hedonist disguised as a pious man may have struck a special chord with a king who was sensitive to the differences between his Christianity and his widely-known tendency to keep mistresses.[92]

By 1669 Molière had cleverly revised the play by adding two acts. Instead of ending the play with Tartuffe – the imposter – seducing Elmire and fooling Orgon, the other characters stage a love scene between Tartuffe and Elmire in order to expose the imposter's deception. In a move intended to flatter the offended king, Molière has the king break the contract and save Orgon's family, and as the Exempt tells Orgon, 'We live under a prince who is the enemy of fraud.'[93] In other words, Molière reassigned *Tartuffe's* original, censored ending to a play-within-the-play. This performance included audience interventions, perhaps a commentary on censorship, and subversively managed to maintain the play's original ending wherein the religious swindler triumphed over the feckless head of the house.[94]

In nineteenth-century visual culture, Molière becomes a cipher for negotiations between artists and repressive state power because he had circumvented the censors' scrutiny and found a means of including critical views of leadership and the clergy. Nicolas André Monsiau's painting of *Molière reading Tartuffe in the apartments of Ninon de Lenclos* (Salon of 1802) shows *Tartuffe*'s controversy and popularity both in its original presentation and its nineteenth-century revival. In Monsiau's painting, Molière's reading stirs up a tittering of discomfort in a salon of his seventeenth-century contemporaries (Figure 3.33). The figures' expressions catalogue a range of reactions, including rapt attentiveness, disturbed dismissal, and exclamatory horror. The group knows the play will be a scandal.[95] In 1829, an English writer and student of the French theatre wrote that Molière 'could apply, when requisite, that delicate flattery, [that] homage which men of genius know so well how to bestow on royalty, and which royalty appreciates too highly to exact at the price of independence'.[96] In the early decades of the nineteenth century, Molière was lauded as an artist who successfully negotiated political repression and the censor's shears.

Works by Édouard Pingret and Jean-François Garneray (1824), Ingres (1857), and Jean-Léon Gérôme (1862) highlighted Molière's relationship with King Louis XIV, a motif that underscored the importance of Molière in the French canon. However, the subject of Jacques Augustin Pajou's *Louis XIV giving Molière permission to play* Tartuffe, 1819, reveals that for nineteenth-century viewers the relationship between king and dramaturge was one not only of mutual promotion but also censorial conflict and imbalanced power.[97]

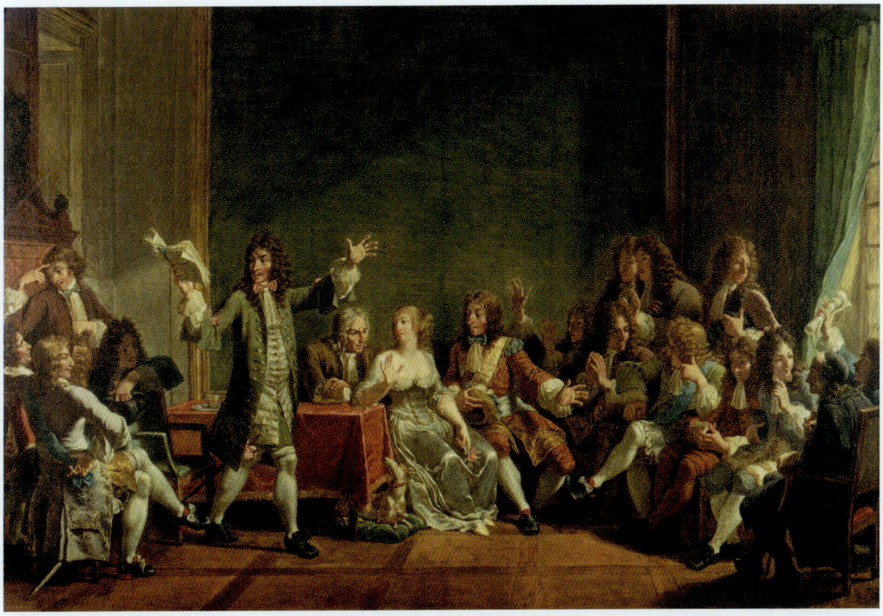

Figure 3.33 Nicolas André Monsiau, *Molière reading Tartuffe in the apartments of Ninon de Lenclos (Molière lisant Tartuffe chez Ninon de Lenclos)*, 1802

Tartuffe remained compelling to French audiences, and during the Bourbon Restoration – another moment of intense censorship over new theatrical material – citizens all over France began to request Molière's play with fresh verve.[98] Patrons called for performances of *Tartuffe*, entreating local theatre directors, distributing brochures, throwing flyers on the stage during other plays, tacking guerilla posters to theatre houses, and simply shouting in the streets.[99] When new plays were tightly regulated in order to prevent political commentary on current events, theatregoers called for Molière and used his plays as vehicles for politicized expression.

The play inspired what became known as the 'troubles of the theatre' in France from 1825–29. When performed, the play became a lightning rod of political disruption and violence. Certain lines became the focus of intense audience applications. Theatregoers took particular umbrage at one of the lines Molière added to appease the king and evade censorship at the play's end, 'We live under a prince who is the enemy of fraud', and would vocalize with hisses and boos at this cue. Sometimes these confrontations would continue into the streets.[100] One such incident broke out on 15 January 1825 in Puy-du-Dôme. It was described in the local newspaper:

> Molière's Tartuffe, which was performed yesterday at our theatre, was for some turbulent spectators an occasion to renew the cries and vociferations which, in a similar circumstance, shook the town of Rouen last year … It seems to us that the frenetic admiration of the parterre should have been satisfied with all of the calculated applause given during each scene.

In April and May 1825 in Rouen the play was the site of a so-called conspiracy for a planned conflict between manufacturing workers and royalists that resulted in the archbishop banning *Tartuffe*. In May 1826 liberal factions from Angoulême erupted in a noisy and violent disturbance during a showing. In Clermont-Ferrand that same year a bust of Molière was crowned on stage with the help of spectators in the loges. And in 1827 in Nîmes, adversaries of the subversive messaging in the play interrupted its performance by throwing rocks at the actors until they were forced off the stage.[101] Crowds clamoured for statues of Molière, for performances of *Tartuffe*, and were encouraged by the press to 'seize with enthusiasm each allusion'.[102] It was by way of these allusions and the responses of 'calculated applause' that Molière's revivals became a lens for contemporary politics and an outlet for critical public response in Daumier's lifetime.

Allusions also pivoted on the suspected clerical plot between the newly ascended Charles X and the Catholic Church. The king sponsored a sacrilege law in 1825, held his coronation at the cathedral in Reims, and hosted a Papal Jubilee in 1826. Perhaps of more local concern to republicans in France, he also allowed Jesuits to rekindle their domestic missionary activity.[103] Molière's play offered a critical vision of a religious con artist who preached asceticism as he feasted from the kitchen of Orgon's bourgeois home. The appeal to anticlerical activists was clear. For instance, in Act I, Scene VI, perceptive Cléante speaks to Orgon about the clergy:

> With forced contortions, and uplifted eyes;
> Who, with an ardour of no common leaven,
> Make fortunes by directing souls to heaven;
> Who live by charities from day to day,
> And canvass favours, while burn and pray;
> Who haunt the court with brow o'erspread with gloom,
> And preach retreat – in the state drawing-room;
> Perfidious, faithless, eager to avenge,
> These make their duty square with their revenge;
> And while they insolently wave the rod,
> Misname their own bad cause, the cause of God.
> More dangerous, since, implacable, severe,
> They, armed with powers which all good men revere,
> The basest passion oft approved reveal,
> And murder with a consecrated steel.[104]

In this passage, Cléante indicts religious institutions whose doctrines of charity and sacrifice offer access to gold and influence. Thus, in the nineteenth century, *Tartuffe* became a means of expressing anticlerical sentiments and examining the legitimacy of monarchy after turns at revolution and Empire. Crowds demanded revivals of Molière in part because excessive restrictions on speech created a climate of self-censorship and stifled the production of new material that could express political discontent.

Over time, censorship creates a rupture between artist and public, author and reader.[105] In Daumier's early career creating political cartoons for the illustrated press, caricature offered a direct connection with popular audiences and a space for biting indictments of clergy and kings. Second Empire censorship broke the collusion between author and audience, and Daumier's paintings in the 1860s sought to explore this lost connection. Daumier's paintings of theatrical performances revive the moment when that collusion was perhaps the strongest in the French tradition, even in a time of strict monarchical censorship: the age of Molière. The playwright developed a series of comedies – *Tartuffe*, *Le Malade imaginaire*, *Les Fourberies de Scapin* – that incorporated critique in a manner that was acutely self-conscious about the connection between theatre (as entertainment) and the performance of social and political life. Molière's use of the play-within-the-play satirized this connection, cracking open divisions between performance and spectatorship. Daumier, similarly, tried to draw the crowd back into the scene, invoking popular regulatory mechanisms like applause and the *charivari* to once again breach the space between passive viewing and participation in contemporary events.

By setting up the viewers of his paintings as an audience of Molière's plays, Daumier invites the audience to react and evaluate. Do we applaud as the patriarch is duped? Do we boo when the imposter swindles? Audience response in the nineteenth century was, quite radically, used not only as an act of critique by popular audiences but also as the measure used to define media and to restrict their expression legally by the government, which is why illustrations and plays were tethered together so tightly in Daumier's lifetime. Daumier was thus drawn to a caricatural style in his depictions of Molière's plays, and he used these artworks to investigate the links between the impact and immediacy of theatrical performance and graphic satire.

Of course satire, Daumier's favoured method of critique, relies upon the distance between a referent and its representation, on familiarity with an image or an idea and also its subversion. This distance is both the material and the motivation of dramatic satire.[106] Theatre is particularly effective at spotlighting the limitations of language and the fragility of social positions; indeed, much of the humour in satirical performance is built on misunderstandings between meaning and language, costume and identity. By calling attention to these distances and deficits, satire provokes an awareness of the performance of the play itself, of the assumption of roles, and the construction of language that contribute to theatrical illusion.[107] For Daumier, unveiling the mechanisms of the medium held particular appeal. Like his early lithograph of Louis-Philippe as a *paillasse,* his theatrical works of Molière revivals respond to the government's attacks on political speech.

Daumier's paintings of Molière's plays are generally seen by art historians as standing outside his broader political commitments. His decision to represent Molière's seventeenth-century plays appears on first analysis to be uncharacteristically anachronistic, an almost nostalgic tribute to a national cultural hero who was popular with the general public and sanctioned by deeply conservative national institutions. However, in

Daumier's lifetime, and particularly in those moments when scripts for new performances – like political caricatures – were being intensely censored, Molière's plays were revived as lightning rods for public commentary about censorship and government overreach. Molière, who himself had faced censorship restrictions from his royal patron, used the mask – a visual screen outside of the text that would have appealed to a painter testing his merit – as a means to incorporate subversive content and evade the censor's shears, a strategy Daumier recalls in the mask-like visages in his paintings of Molière's characters. We can therefore see that in representing the comic mask, formally linking caricature and theatre in ways that mirrored censorship laws, and displacing sound onto the audience, Daumier was activating powerful strategies of subversive artistic collusion with audience during a time of oppressive censorship and contested speech. Far from being departures from his larger political project, Daumier's painted revivals of Molière's plays are fundamental to understanding its breadth.

Notes

1 Gérard de Nerval, *The Salt Smugglers: History of the Abbé de Bucquoy*, trans. Richard Sieburth (Brooklyn, NY: Archipelago Books, 2009), 30.

2 Honoré Daumier, J. Douglas Campbell, Usher Caplan, National Gallery of Canada, Galeries nationales du Grand Palais (France), and Phillips Collection, *Daumier: 1808–1879: National Gallery of Canada, Ottawa, 11 June–6 September 1999; Galeries nationales du Grand Palais, Paris, 5 October 1999–3 January 2000; Phillips Collection, Washington, 19 February–14 May* 2000, exh. cat. (Ottawa: Musée des Beaux-Arts du Canada, Ottawa, 1999), 179.

3 'Il projetait toujours de quitter la lithographie pour la peinture. Était-ce paresse? On est si volontiers paresseux pour faire ce qu'on n'aime pas! Il ne cherchait pas ses sujets, et n'en trouvait jamais la légende. De là tant de motifs traités vingt fois, trente fois par lui, à son grand préjudice pour l'opinion de la foule, car la foule ignore la somme de talent qu'il faut à un artiste pour traiter aussi souvent le même motif, et, à chaque fois créer un dessin différent, un dessin nouveau; elle n'est frappée que de la répétition du sujet et, de cette répétition, elle conclut que l'artiste est, comme elle dit, *au bout de son rouleau.*' Charles Philipon, 'L'abdication de Daumier 1er', *Le Journal amusant: journal illustré, journal d'images, journal comique, critique, satirique, etc.*, no. 297 (7 September 1861): 7.

4 The paintings include *Head of Scapin* (*Tête de Scapin*), c. 1850 oil on panel, Private Collection, Maison I-34; *Theatre scene* (*Scène de théatre*), c. 1858–62, oil on panel, Kunsthaus Zürich, M I-127; *Scene from a comedy* (*Scène de comédie*) c. 1863–65, oil on panel, Fogg Art Museum, Cambridge, MA, Maison I-128; *Scene from a comedy (Un Scapin*, also known as *Scène de comédie),* c. 1863–65, oil on panel, Paris, Musée d'Orsay, M I-129; *Portrait of Charles Debureau,* c. 1861, oil on canvas, Private Collection, M I-144; *Crispin and Scapin (Crispin et Scapin),* c. 1863–85, oil on canvas, Paris, Musée d'Orsay, M I-162; *Scene from 'The imaginary invalid' (Scène du Malade imaginaire),* c. 1860–63, oil on panel, Barnes Foundation, Maison I-153; *Scene from 'The imaginary invalid' (Scène du Malade imaginaire),* c. 1860–63, oil on panel, The Philadelphia Museum of Art, Maison I-154; *Head of Pasquin* (*Tête de Pasquin*), c. 1862–63, oil on panel, Geneva, Mr Emery Reves, M I-156; *Two actors (Scène de comédie),* c. 1870–73, oil on panel, Los Angeles, UCLA at The Armand Hammer Museum of Art and Cultural Center, Maison I-237; *Scapin and Silvester* (also known as *Arlequin et Cassandre),* c. 1863–65, oil on panel, Private Collection

(formerly Fuchs), Maison I-161; *The former Comédie Française (L'ancienne Comédie Française)*, c. 1860–65, oil on canvas, Private Collection, Maison I-164; and *Doctor Diafoirus (Le médecin Diafoirus)*, c. 1870, oil on panel, Maison I-223; *Head of a clown (Pierrot) (Tête de paillasse (Pierrot))*, c. 1870, oil on panel, Oxford, Private Collection, M I-224; *On the stage (Sur la scène)* or *Pierrot et docteur*, c. 1870–73, oil on canvas, Winterthur, Collection of the late Dr Oskar Reinhart, M I-230. This list excludes paintings of more generalized actors and audiences as well as the informal barkers and *saltimbanques*.

5 Alain Vaillant, 'Les sociétés d'auteurs et la censure au XIXe siècle', in *La censure en France à l'ère démocratique, 1848-* (Bruxelles: Éditions Complexe, 1997), 106.

6 James Bash Cuno, 'Charles Philipon and La Maison Aubert: The business, politics, and public of caricature in Paris, 1820–1840' (PhD diss., Harvard University, 1985), 11–14.

7 Cuno, 'Charles Philipon and La Maison Aubert', 132; and Judith Wechsler, *A Human Comedy: Physiognomy and Caricature in 19th Century Paris* (Chicago: The University of Chicago Press, 1982), 80.

8 John McCormick, *Popular Theatres of Nineteenth-Century France* (New York: Routledge, 1993), 105.

9 'Qu'un auteur se contente de faire imprimer sa pièce, il ne pourra être assujetti à aucune mesure préventive; que le dessinateur écrive sa pensée, qu'il la publie par la voie de l'impression et que de cette manière il s'adresse seulement à l'*intelligence*, il ne rencontrera aucun obstacle. C'est dans ce sens qu'on dit que la censure ne pourra jamais être rétablie. Mais lorsque les opinions sont converties *en actes*, lorsque, par la représentation d'une pièce ou l'exposition d'un dessin, on s'adresse aux hommes réunis on parle à leurs yeux, il y a *un fait, une mise en action, une vie* dont ne s'occupe pas l'article 7 de la Charte, et qu'il confie par cela même à la haute direction des pouvoirs établis.' *Archives parlementaires de 1787 à 1860: recueil complet des débats législatifs & politiques des chambres françaises imprimé par ordre du Sénat et de la Chambre des Députés sous la direction de J. Mavidal et al.*, 2nd ser., vol. 98 of 127 (Paris: P. Dupont, 1898), 257–8. Emphasis in original.

10 *Archives Parlementaires de 1787 à 1860*, 98: 256–60. For more on the parallel repressions of caricature and the theatre see: Robert Justin Goldstein, 'Censorship of caricature and the theatre in nineteenth-century France: An overview', *Yale French Studies* 122, Out of Sight: Political Censorship of the Visual Arts in Nineteenth-Century France (2012): 14–36; and Odile Krakovitch, *Les pièces de théâtre soumises à la censure (1800–1830)* (Paris: Archives nationales: diffusé par la documentation française, 1982), 12.

11 'Décret organique sur la presse', *Le Moniteur universel: Journal officiel de la République Française* 49 (18 February 1852): 273.

12 *Le Robert. Dictionnaire historique de la langue française*, ed. Alain Rey, vol. 2 (Paris: Dictionnaires Le Robert, 1998), 1633. This outlines this more expansive use of *gravure*, which emerged around 1829. Patricia Mainardi's *Another World: Nineteenth-Century Illustrated Print Culture* (New Haven: Yale University Press, 2017) offers a rich history of the technological innovations and common print practices in each of these areas of illustrated print culture.

13 Odile Krakovitch, *Censure des répertoires des grands théâtres parisiens (1835–1906). Inventaire des manuscrits des pièces F/18/669 à F/18/1016 et des procès-verbaux F/21/966 à F/21/995* [finding aid] (Paris: Centre historique des Archives nationales, 2003), 49–50.

14 Robert Justin Goldstein, *Censorship of Political Caricature in Nineteenth-Century France* (Kent, OH: Kent State University Press, 1989), 179–80.

15 Krakovitch, *Censure des répertoires des grands théâtres parisiens*, 51.

16 Krakovitch, *Censure des répertoires des grands théâtres parisiens*, 52.

17 'Je crois qu'on doit exclure du théâtre ... tout ce qui peut tendre à corrompre les mœurs ou l'esprit du gouvernement. Le spectacle est une partie de l'enseignement public qui ne doit pas être laissée à tout le monde et que l'administration doit surveiller ... ce n'est point une atteinte à la liberté des uns, c'est le respect pour la liberté et la sûreté morale des autres ...' Krakovitch, *Les pièces de théâtre soumises à la censure (1800–1830)*, 12. Extract of *Mémoires de Bailly*, cited in Henri Welschinger, *Le théâtre de la Révolution* (Paris: 1888), 94.

18 Krakovitch, *Les pièces de théâtre soumises à la censure (1800–1830)*, 18.

19 Robert Justin Goldstein, ed., *The Frightful Stage: Political Censorship of the Theatre in Nineteenth-Century Europe* (New York: Berghahn Books, 2009), 102.

20 McCormick, *Popular Theatres of Nineteenth-Century France*, 100.

21 Goldstein, 'France', in The Frightful Stage, 98–9.

22 'Il se produit, entre tous les assistants, *une sorte de communication électrique* bien plus entraînante pour les masses qu'un discours de tribune, et mille fois plus dangereuse que les articles les plus véhéments de la presse quotidienne.' *Conseil d'état, enquête et documents officiels sur théâtre*. Survey conducted by Baron Taylor, Paris, 1843. Cited in Krakovitch, *Les pièces de théâtre soumises à la censure (1800–1830)*, 12.

23 'Il règne, à travers une salle, comme un courant électrique qui, passant du comédien au spectateur, les enflamme tous deux d'une ardeur soudaine et leur donne une audace inattendue.' Victor Hallays-Dabot, *Histoire de la censure théâtrale en France* (Paris: E. Dentu, 1862), viii–ix.

24 'Je conseille aux auteurs modernes de ne pas s'aventurer à faire jouer un ouvrage nouveau dans la semaine où l'on reprendra l'Impromptu de Versailles et les Fâcheux. Il faut en prendre son parti. La vogue est à Molière.' 'Théâtre Français: Le Menteur, comédie de Corneille', *Journal des débats politiques et littéraires* (27 December 1835): n.p.

25 Goldstein, 'France', 97–8.

26 Archives nationales, Pierrefitte-sur-Seine, France (hereafter AN), F/18/680, manuscript of a play by Bornier, *Le Quinze janvier – propos pour l'anniversaire de la naissance de Molière*, 1860, Théâtre français; AN F/18/714, manuscript of a play by Martin, *La Fête de Molière*, 1860, Théâtre de l'Odéon; AN F/18/715, manuscript of a play by unknown author, *Poème pour Molière*, 1862, Théâtre de l'Odéon; AN F/18/717 and F/21/967, manuscript of a play by Fournier, *La Fille de Molière*, 1863, Théâtre de l'Odéon and verbal report; AN F/18/681, manuscript of a play by unknown author, *À Molière*, 1865, Théâtre-Français; AN F/18/682, manuscript of a play by Du Boys, *Anniversaire de la naissance de Molière*, 1867, Théâtre-Français; AN F/18/682, manuscript of a play by Bayeux, *Stances à Molière*, 1868, Théâtre-Français; AN F/18/682, manuscript of a play by Fournier, *La Valise de Molière*, 1868, Théâtre-Français; AN F/18/682, manuscript of a play by Carcassonne(?), *À Molière*, 1869, Théâtre-Français; AN F/18/719, manuscript of a play by Laluyé, *Scapin marié*, 1869, Théâtre de l'Odéon. Odile Krakovitch, *Censure des répertoires des grands théâtres parisiens (1835–1906). Inventaire des manuscrits des pièces F/18/669 à F/18/1016 et des procès-verbaux F/21/966 à F/21/995* [finding aid] (Paris: Archives nationales, 2003). Retrieved www.siv.archives-nationales.culture.gouv.fr/siv/rechercheconsultation/consultation/ir/consultationIR.action?formCaller=GENERALISTE&irId=FRAN_IR_059673&gotoArchivesNums=false&defaultResultPerPage=&frontIr=&optionFullText=&fullText=&udId=&consIr=&details=false&page=&auSeinIR=false (accessed 21 January 2024).

27 *Archives parlementaires de 1787 à 1860*, 98:258.

28 Goldstein, *Censorship of Political Caricature in Nineteenth-Century France*, 182.

29 Charles Philipon, 'L'abdication de Daumier 1er', *Le Journal amusant: journal illustré, journal d'images, journal comique, critique, satirique, etc.*, no. 297 (7 September 1861): 7. Daumier was rehired at *Le Charivari* in 1863.

30 Bruce Laughton, *Honoré Daumier* (New Haven, CT: Yale University Press, 1996), 49.

31 Many authors have cited the closing of the Théâtre de Funambules in 1862 as the inspiration for these paintings. However, by 1860 the popular theatres of the boulevard du Temple were in decline and had already begun to inspire nostalgia for their better days. See Paula Harper, *Daumier's Clowns, Les Saltimbanques, et Les Parades: New Biographical and Political Functions for a Nineteenth Century Myth, Outstanding Dissertations in the Fine Arts* (New York: Garland, 1981).

32 Wechsler, *A Human Comedy*, 42–56.

33 Laughton, *Honoré Daumier*, 68.

34 Helen O. Borowitz, 'Painted smiles: Sad clowns in French art and literature', *The Bulletin of the Cleveland Museum of Art* 71, no. 1 (January 1984): 31.

35 Wechsler, *A Human Comedy*, 58.

36 Michael Fried, *Manet's Modernism: Or, The Face of Painting in the 1860s* (Chicago: University of Chicago Press, 1998), 51–5.

37 Wechsler, *A Human Comedy*, 63.

38 T. J. Clark, *The Absolute Bourgeois: Artists and Politics in France, 1848–1851* (Berkeley, CA: University of California Press, 1999), 122–3. See too: Harper, *Daumier's Clowns*, 183–6. Margret Stuffman, 'Sideshows and saltimbanques', in *Daumier Drawings*, by Colta Feller Ives (New York: Metropolitan Museum of Art: Distributed by Harry N. Abrams, 1992), nos. 113–115; Henry James, *Daumier, Caricaturist* (London: Rodale Press, 1954), 36.

39 Clark, *The Absolute Bourgeois*, 119–213.

40 Margret Stuffman, 'Sideshows and saltimbanques', 204. Stuffman also includes an etching of Watteau's *Gilles* that was etched by Edmond Hedouin and published in the *Gazette des beaux-arts* in 1860 (260–1).

41 Josephine Touma, 'From the playhouse to the page: Visual sources for Watteau's theatrical universe', *Studies in Eighteenth-Century Culture* 40 (2011): 93.

42 Touma, 'From the playhouse to the page', 97.

43 Ben B. Halm, *Theatre and Ideology* (Selinsgrove, PA: Susquehanna University Press, 1995), 14, quoted in Touma, 'From the playhouse to the page', 97.

44 'Messieurs, l'auteur de la pièce que nous avons eu l'honneur de joueur devant vous désire garder l'anonymat.' J. J. Grandville, 'Une audience du 'Théâtre des Folies-Politiques', *La Caricature* (21 March 1833): n.p. [Pl. 258].

45 'DR number 3764', Daumier Register, www.daumier-register.org/hintergrundlist_popup.php?key_m=3764 (accessed 15 September 2015).

46 The title for these works and their connection to Molière's play were established with the exhibition of the painting now in the Philadelphia Museum of Art's collection at the 1878 retrospective exhibition of Daumier's artwork, which took place a year before the artist's death. The painting was listed as 'Scène du *Malade imaginaire*'. *Exposition des peintures et dessins de H. Daumier* (Paris: Gauthier-Villars, 1878), 57n31. In addition to the characterization of the figures, this title helps us to contextualize the painting within Daumier's many representations of doctors, understanding that they were an ancient and often generalized subject of satire in the graphic arts, print, and theatre.

47 Georges Forestier, '"Portraits" de Molière', in *Molière [Exposition organisée par la Bibliothèque nationale de France, Comédie-Française, Opéra national de Paris du 27 septembre 2022 au 15 janvier 2023]*, ed. Laurence Decobert, Joël Huthwohl, and Agathe Sanjuan (Paris: Bibliothèque nationale de France, 2022), 43.

48 For some of the stylistic elements of print, it was helpful for me to look to a catalogue on Felix Vallotton's multimedia practice: Christian Rumelin and Cabinet d'art graphique, *Félix*

Vallotton: De la gravure à la peinture [Exposition organisée par Le Cabinet d'arts graphiques des musées d'art et d'histoire Genève du 7 octobre 2010 au 10 janvier 2011]. (Gèneve: Musées d'art et d'histoire Geneve, 2010), 10–26. The authors contend that Vallotton sometimes took woodblocks, watercolours, and lithographs as points of departure for his paintings.

49 Pierre Louis Duchartre, *The Italian Comedy: The Improvisation, Scenarios, Lives, Attributes, Portraits, and Masks of the Illustrious Characters of the Commedia dell'Arte*, trans. Randolph T. Weaver (New York: Dover Publications, 1966), 20.

50 Duchartre, *The Italian Comedy*, 41.

51 'La tradition antique s'est conserve jusqu'à nos jours dans l'habillement des personnages de la comédie italienne. D'abord le masque, qui s'est peu modifié, car les types principaux, comme Pulcinella, Arlequin, Brighella, Pantalon, Conviello, Tartaglia, portent tous le masque, qui a un caractère ancien, et, à la exception des vieillards, ils ont tous un serre-tête qui cache les cheveux, par tradition de la tête rasée des mimes antiques.' Maurice Sand, *Masques et bouffons (comédie italienne)* (Paris: Michel Lévy frères, 1860), 36.

52 'Les bouffons et les masques créèrent les types qui allaient se perpétuer et devenir bientôt cosmopolites En même temps qu'ils conservaient les souvenirs et souvent les costumes et les attributs des grotesques antiques, ils inventaient des caricatures nouvelles, des parodies satiriques. Chaque province, chaque ville concourait à la fête, fournissait son personnage. Les villes d'université comme Bologne enfantèrent tout naturellement le docteur, le pédant ridicule, dont chaque mot est une délicieuse ânerie …' Louis Moland, *Molière et la comédie italienne* (Paris: Didier et cie, 1867), 12.

53 Debureau became a celebrity in 1832, around the time of the inauguration of Daumier's *Celebrities of the juste milieu* series, and often played at the Théatre de Funambules. Daumier painted Debureau's son in 1861, around the time he began painting *commedia* themes and *saltimbanques* in earnest, though the theatre was long gone. Laughton, *Honoré Daumier*, 129. Judith Wechsler calls this Daumier's only non-caricatural portrait. Wechsler, *A Human Comedy*, 56. She also describes the pantomimes in the Théâtre des Funambules, including an act by Leclerq, a *grimacier* or *physiomane*, that consisted of showcasing a catalogue of human expressions by grimacing in candlelight (42).

54 Harper, *Daumier's Clowns*, 38.

55 Laughton, *Honoré Daumier*, 89.

56 Stanislav Osiakovski, 'History of Robert Macaire and Daumier's place in it', *The Burlington Magazine* 100, no. 668 (November 1958): 389.

57 'Qui ne sait par cœur aujourd'hui cette physionomie symbolique du bailleur de fonds sans caisse, de l'inventeur sans invention, du fondateur de compagnies sans associés, de l'illustre médecin sans malades, de l'éloquent avocat sans cause, du financier du génie sans finances, prenant à l'hameçon de ses dividendes anticipés, comme disait la légende de la caricature, ces Gogos naïfs qui sont de Robert Macaire, conçues par Philipon, traduites par Daumier, et où le crayon et la plume épanchent à l'envi des flots de verve, parois un peu grossière, mais toujours entraînante, vous recueillerez des traits d'observation, des mots et des scènes qui en font le véritable et vivant tableau satirique de la fièvre d'agiotage dont l'époque était possédée.' Victor Fournel, *Les artistes français contemporains* (Tours: Alfred Mame et Fils, 1884), 505.

58 Osiakovski, 'History of Robert Macaire and Daumier's place in it', 390.

59 Maurice Alhoy, Louis Huart, and Charles Philipon, *Les cent et un Robert-Macaire, composés et dessinés par M. H. Daumier sur les idées et les légendes de M. Ch. Philippon; réduits et lithographiés par MM. ***; texte par MM. Maurice Alhoy et Louis Huart* (Paris, 1839). This title makes the issue of captions quite clear, at least for this series.

60 See the advertisements in *Album du journal pour rire, Charles Philipon [Directeur de publication], ill. de Gustave Doré, Henry Emy, Nadar, … [et al.]*, no. 51 (January 1848). The next edition is advertised in *Le Journal amusant* on 24 December 1859.

61 Maurice Alhoy, 'Robert-Macaire débiteur', *Les cent et un Robert-Macaire, composés et dessinés par M. H. Daumier sur les idées et les légendes de M. Ch. Philippon; réduits et lithographiés par MM. ***; texte par MM. Maurice Alhoy et Louis Huart* (Paris, 1839), n.p.

62 Christophe Gauthier, 'Portraits cinématographiques de l'artist en grand homme', in *Molière [Exposition organisée par la Bibliothèque nationale de France, Comédie-Française, Opéra national de Paris du 27 septembre 2022 au 15 janvier 2023]*, ed. Laurence Decobert, Joël Huthwohl, and Agathe Sanjuan (Paris: Bibliothèque nationale de France, 2022), 170–1.

63 Goldstein, *The Frightful Stage*, 100. See also Odile Krakovitch, 'Robert Macaire ou la grande peur des censeurs', *Europe: Revue litteraire mensuelle* 65 (1987).

64 Wechsler, *A Human Comedy*, 114–16.

65 Robert W. Goldsby, *Molière on Stage: What's So Funny?* (New York: Anthem Press, 2012), 174. Translated by Goldsby.

66 Laughton, *Honoré Daumier*, 91. Laughton argues that this is Doctor Diafoirus and that Argan's recoil was 'generic' (87) but I propose that it is actually Dr Purgon. There is the small issue of Argan kneeling for Purgon's delivery of the lines above, but I believe that Daumier prioritized composition, which he translated from his own *Robert Macaire* lithographs, over this detail.

67 Henri Loyrette also identifies this figure as M Fleurant and notes the possible political connotations of the enema and its association with the Count de Lobau, who turned hoses against French citizens. Henri Loyrette, 'Scene from "The imaginary invalid"', in *Daumier: 1808–1879* (Ottawa: Musée des Beaux-Arts du Canada, Ottawa, 1999), 356–7.

68 Laughton, *Honoré Daumier*, 80–3.

69 'DR 24 and DR 73 Background Details', Daumier Register, www.daumier-register.org/hintergrundlist_popup.php?key_m=73 and www.daumier-register.org/hintergrundlist_popup.php?key_m=24 (accessed 8 May 2015).

70 'Qui ne connaît le geste, très humain en somme, du maréchal Lobau, dispersant l'émeute, en faisant jouer les pompes à incendie? … Dès lors, il n'est plus de charge du maréchal Lobau, où l'on ne le représente, accoutré à la façon des apothicaires de Molière.' Raymond Escholier, *Daumier* (Paris: L. Michaud, 1913), 34–5.

71 Goldsby, *Molière on Stage*, 174.

72 D. B. Wyndham Lewis, *Molière: The Comic Mask* (New York: Coward-McCann, 1959), 80–2.

73 Andrew Calder, *Molière: The Theory and Practice of Comedy* (London: The Athlone Press, 1993), 128.

74 Arsène Alexandre, *H. Daumier. L'Homme et l'œuvre* (Paris: H. Laurent, 1888), 168.

75 Emma Dillon, *The Sense of Sound: Musical Meaning in France, 1260–1330* (Oxford: Oxford University Press, 2012), 93. See also: *Le Robert* 2:707, which dates this tie between disturbance and discordant music to 1690.

76 See, for example: Jean Adhémar, *Daumier* (Marseille: Arts et livres de Provence, 1948); and Léon Rosenthal, *Daumier* (Paris: Librairie central des beaux-arts, 1912).

77 Bruce Laughton, *The Drawings of Daumier and Millet* (New Haven: Yale University Press, 1991), 202.

78 Borowitz, 'Painted smiles', 23.

79 Clark, *The Absolute Bourgeois*, 119–213.

80 Borowitz, 'Painted smiles', 24.

81 E.-F., *Translations Into Verse From Comedies of Molière and Casimir Delavigne, Preceded by a Cursory View of French Dramatic Literature, to Which Are Added Original Poems, Imitations, School Exercises, and the Magic Lantern, a Satire* (Paris: A. and W. Galignani, 1829), 4–7.

82 Harper, *Daumier's Clowns*, 16.

83 I will be using the Musée d'Orsay's title here. At Daumier's 1878 retrospective exhibition, this painting was listed as simply *Scapin*, the Rouart collection listed it as *Crispin et Scapin*, and Jean Adhémar suggested the correct title should be *Scapin et Silvestre*. Loyrette, *Daumier: 1808–1879*, 355.

84 For more information on Daumier's technique of scumbling reddish brown layers of painting before adding on lighter layers, a practice largely inherited from Thomas Couture, see: Laughton, *Honoré Daumier*, 68 and 180. Couture opened his atelier to students in 1847. He also wrote the textbook *Méthode et entretiens d'atelier* (Paris 1867).

85 Laughton, *Honoré Daumier*, 41. Laughton suggests that Daumier may have even traced the cartoon for the construction of the oil painting, perhaps at the suggestion of Geoffroy-Dechaume, Daumier's friend and the painting's first owner. He considers such a compositional transfer to be quite abnormal.

86 Oliver W. Larkin, *Daumier: Man of His Time* (New York: McGraw-Hill, 1966), 29. Emphasis is mine.

87 Laughton, *The Drawings of Daumier and Millet*, 202. Laughton has said that Daumier's representations of street performances and *saltimbanques* are expressive rather than narrative, and it is clear to me that many of his images of formal stage productions are similarly non-narrative, for example the first version of *Le malade imaginaire*. The non-narrative quality of *Crispin and Scapin* is also evidenced in the longstanding debate over what to name this painting based on confusion about the identity of the figure on the right (see footnote 83).

88 F. W. J. Hemmings, *Theatre and State in France, 1760–1905* (New York: Cambridge University Press, 1994), 123–4.

89 Hemmings, *Theatre and State in France*, 136.

90 James H. Johnson, *Listening in Paris: A Cultural History*, Nachdr., Studies on the History of Society and Culture 21 (Berkeley, CA: University of California Press, 2008), 246–8.

91 Julia Prest, *Controversies in French Drama: Molière's* Tartuffe *and the Struggle for Influence* (New York: Palgrave Macmillan, 2014), 37–8.

92 Prest, *Controversies in French Drama*, 68–70.

93 Prest, *Controversies in French Drama*, 68–9. 'Nous vivons un Prince ennemi de la fraude.'

94 Michael Spingler, 'The king's play: Censorship and the politics of performance in Moliere's "Tartuffe"', *Comparative Drama* 19, no. 3 (Fall 1985): 240–1.

95 Krakovitch, *Les pièces de théâtre soumises à la censure (1800–1830)*, 15. The repression of Molière's *Dom Juan*, *l'École des Femmes*, and *Tartuffe* were some of the most famous examples of the censorship of actors and theatrical performances in the seventeenth century.

96 E. F., *Translations Into Verse From Comedies of Molière*, 6.

97 *La Comédie-Française s'expose au Petit Palais [Paris 13.10.2011 – 15.01.2012]*, ed. Gilles Chazal, Agathe Sanjuan, and Musée du Petit Palais (Paris: Paris-Musées [u.a.], 2011), 22.

98 Louis XVIII maintained Napoleon's same strict system of censoring plays whereby houses needed authorization to open new shows and even went so far as to carry over the same administrators. Eugène Lintilhac, *Histoire générale du théâtre en France. La comédie: de la Révolution au Second Empire*, vol. 5 of 5 (Paris: E. Flammarion, [1904–10]), 7–9.

99 Sheryl Kroen, *Politics and Theater: The Crisis of Legitimacy in Restoration France, 1815–1830* (Berkeley, CA: University of California Press, 2000), 250.

100 Kroen, *Politics and Theater*, 1–2.

101 Alain Corbin, 'L'Agitation dans les théâtres de province sous la Restauration', in *Popular Traditions and Learned Culture in France from the Sixteenth to the Twentieth Century*, ed. Marc Bertrand (Saratoga, CA: AMNA Libri, 1985), 107.

102 Corbin, 'L'Agitation dans les théâtres de province sous la Restauration', 251–2.

103 Kroen, *Politics and Theater*, 4.

104 E.-F., *Translations Into Verse From Comedies of Molière*, 13.

105 Vaillant, 'Les sociétés d'auteurs et la censure au XIXe siècle', 111.

106 Charles A. Knight, *The Literature of Satire* (Cambridge: Cambridge University Press, 2004), 119.

107 Knight, *The Literature of Satire*, 199–20.

4

Painting Quixote

> Once we found a dead mule, bones picked about clean, ants streaming through the eyes.
>
> The stench was too much for us and after poking the corpse we ran away, gasping for breath.
>
> We talked about that mule for weeks. What was its fascination?
>
> (Frank Conroy, *Stop-Time, 1965*)[1]

Miguel de Cervantes Saavedra's novel *The ingenious gentleman Don Quixote of La Mancha* (*El ingenioso hidalgo Don Quijote de la Mancha*, Part I 1605, Part II 1615) was an enormously popular cultural phenomenon in nineteenth-century France, appearing in numerous translations as well as plays, operas, and illustrations. In the last two decades of his life, Daumier created around thirty paintings and forty drawings inspired by *Don Quixote*. They are strange works – Don Quixote and Sancho Panza plod quietly through evacuated, loosely-brushed landscapes – and they do not narrate moments of delusion or high conflict in the book. This was an intensely private exploration; few of the paintings were publicly exhibited or intended for commercial sale. The oil-on-canvas *Don Quixote and the dead mule,* 1867, is indicative of the broader tone in Daumier's *Don Quixote* series: melancholy, experimental, spare (Figure 4.1). Many of these works focus on slow navigation, arrested attention, or capture the moment just before Quixote's literary remembrances confront the obstinate matter of nature. The 1867 *Don Quixote and the dead mule* serves as the pivot for an analysis of Daumier's engagement with Cervantes's satire. As with his caricature, Daumier abstracts a complex set of narrative and connotative associations into the barest of visual terms. In *Don Quixote and the dead mule*, Daumier blends expressionistic brushstrokes with the stark lines of popular art, echoing the kind of reflexive reference to representation that made Don Quixote the first 'modern' novel. The facture of this painting poses questions about individual expression, illusion, deception, and delusion in ways that parallel the themes of Cervantes's novel. Daumier understood that the drama and humour of *Don Quixote* depend on the same distance between

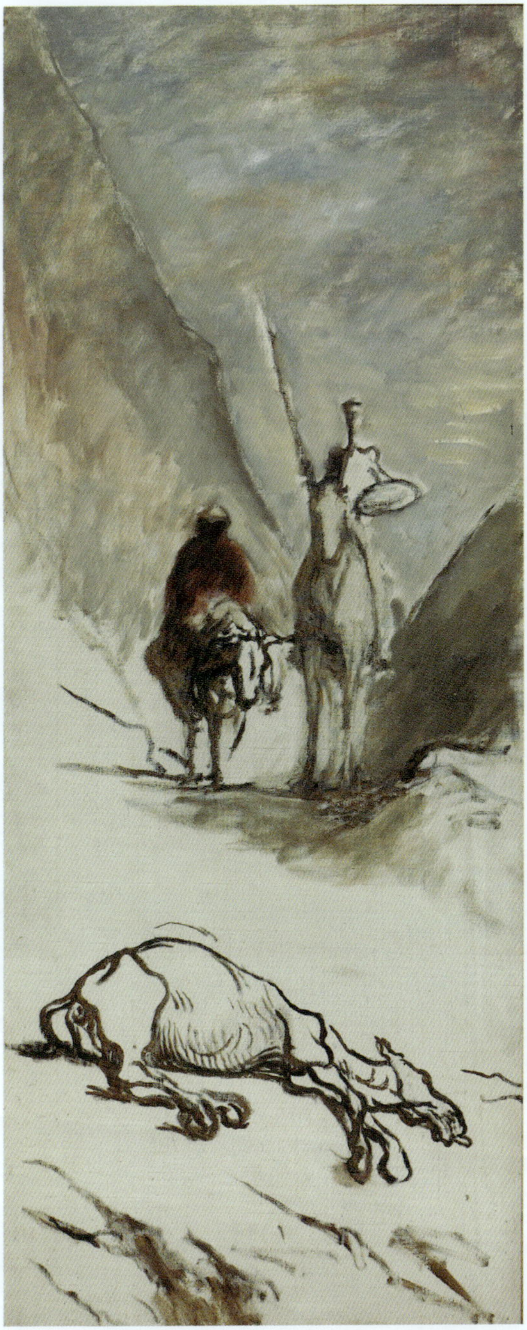

Figure 4.1 Honoré Daumier, *Don Quixote and the dead mule (Don Quichotte et la mule morte)*, 1867

reality and perception that was at the centre of nineteenth-century debates about art and political expression. Completing the arc of this book's investigations of Daumier's painted motifs of literary subjects and the ways in which they embed subversive political ideas, this chapter shows Daumier exploring what satire looks like without lightness; that is, when it is brutal, intensely self-reflective, and violent.

The rage of Cervantes

The first datable version of Daumier's *Don Quixote* motif was a painting accepted at the Paris Salon of 1850–51 titled *Don Quixote and Sancho Panza going to Camacho's wedding feast*, likely now lost.[2] This was the only oil-on-canvas painting in Daumier's second group of accepted works at the Salon in the year following his submission of *The miller, his son, and the ass* in 1849. His interest in *Don Quixote* accelerated in the 1860s and 1870s and coincided with his exploration of scenes from Molière's plays in paint, but went beyond that series in the sheer number of works. Like Molière and La Fontaine's works, Cervantes's *Don Quixote* was a seventeenth-century text that reached large audiences in nineteenth-century France through illustrated translations, staged performances, music, and the fine arts.

In the seventeenth century *Don Quixote* was already being adapted to the stage in France. In 1638, Guyon Guérin de Bouscal put on the play *Don Quixote of la Mancha*, followed by a second part in 1640. In Paris in 1642 a comedy titled *The government of Sancho Panza* was performed. In 1660, Molière's troop put on *Don Quixote, or the enchantments of Merlin*, with Molière perhaps playing Quixote himself.[3]

Daumier's Salon entry *Don Quixote and Sancho Panza going to Camacho's wedding feast* first appeared during the Second Republic, at first a period with expanded legal freedoms and a more inclusive arts administration.[4] On 5 March 1848 around one hundred playwrights and composers gathered to demand an end to the censorship of the theatre, and on the following day the September Laws were abolished. The new government eliminated newspaper taxes and security bonds, and soon hundreds of new journals appeared. *Robert Macaire* and other prohibited works soon returned to the stage. However, just as with the new July Monarchy, repressions soon returned (the first in August 1848), as security deposits were reintroduced and drama censorship returned.[5] Because of their broad public appeal, the Second Republic quickly saw the reinstallation of especially hard repression of caricatures and plays. Between 1848 and 1850, 185 republican periodicals faced 335 prosecutions and forty were forced to shutter their operations.[6] In July 1850 the Minister of the Interior, Pierre-Jules Baroche, asked the parliament to re-establish censorship on theatres, which they soon enacted, ending a period of liberalization and preceding Daumier's first *Don Quixote* painting. The French theatre censor who became a historian of theatre censorship, Victor Hallays-Dabot, said of this reversal, 'The raucous, aggressive, immoral theatre of 1848 must soon bend before the firm will of the government to bring order to the street and calm people's minds.'[7]

The Second Empire, as previous chapters have discussed, returned to authoritarian approaches to speech and increased surveillance and censorship of the press and theatres. Napoleon III's Article 22 from 17 February 1852 carried language over from the September Laws of 1835 and reinstated the prior authorization of prints.[8] Soon after, a law on 30 December 1852 acted to combat any plays that might antagonize class divisions or attack religion or authority.[9] In the mid-1860s, censors were given more discretion, and while Louis-Napoleon's government tried to appear to be more liberal and made an effort to stimulate the sales of books, journals, and plays through the loosening of some of these restrictions, certain topics were still carefully regulated, including subjects that might undermine state authority, religion and morals, or the social order.[10]

Like motifs from Molière and La Fontaine, *Don Quixote* was a revival from seventeenth-century literature that carried associations with opposition and censorship. Even though the text was two centuries old, comic performances of *Don Quixote* (vaudevilles, comedies, and comic operas) were censored throughout the nineteenth century. According to the French National Archives' record of performances submitted to the Minister of the Interior between 1802 and 1906, at least 105 small performances that were censored index the name Don Quixote.[11] At least five comic performances of Don Quixote were censored between 1835 and 1869.[12] The censorship of an 1864 play, *Don Quixote*, by Sardou at the Gymnase dramatique was written up in *Le Charivari* and was perhaps part of the context surrounding Daumier's adaptation of the series in the 1860s, especially given Daumier's longstanding attraction to the theatre.[13]

Plays that were censored during the Second Empire were not offered extensive notes or justifications in writing (some justifications would have been given orally, if requested).[14] And performances that were wholly rejected did not produce paperwork that was archived. However, some of the submitted scripts have suggestive notations from the censors. For example, the copy of Sardou's 1864 *Don Quixote* at the Gymnase submitted to the government shows the character first named 'The Emperor' was crossed out and changed to 'The King' in Act 3, Scene 1, indicating a resistance to the possibility of audiences drawing analogies with Napoleon III.[15] Similarly, in a performance of *Don Quixote and Sancho* performed at the Cirque Olympique in 1843, the character of 'Priest' was changed to 'Doctor'.[16] This modification was likely imposed to avoid any hint of anticlericalism, which was often the subject of subversive analogies in the theatre, as we saw in the previous chapter. Censors were clearly sensitive to the fact that *Don Quixote* could become a vehicle for speech about contemporary leaders and institutions.

An 1847 performance at the Théâtre Montmartre featuring a cast of just the two figures of Sancho and Don Quixote centres on leadership and the rule of the knight errant over a reluctant and critical Sancho. Like La Fontaine's *Fables*, this nineteenth-century interpretation of the book returns again and again to issues of good leadership and mismanagement: 'Oh! Let us serve a good master. Let us for him always be a good master.'[17] The *Don Quixote of husbands*, a vaudeville performed in 1869, is also about power. Here, a former actress is told by a husband whom she deems a 'tyrant' and 'master' that she could no longer take to the boards, a theme that could relate back to state control over theatres. These records suggest that in this mid-nineteenth century moment, *Don Quixote* was revived and reinterpreted by some playwrights to explore one person's responsibility for another, especially when one is in charge and one must obey, and this might offer a means of investigating the obligations and absurdity of power relations more broadly.

Don Quixote was also a bestselling book in France. In the nineteenth century, there were more re-editions in Paris than in Madrid, and its popularity surpassed other popular Spanish texts both in print and on stage (*Don Juan*, *El Cid*, *Carmen*).[18] Between 1821–25, six new editions were printed in Paris, and there was a global print run of somewhere between 19,000 and 21,000 copies. Six more editions were published in Paris between 1841–45 with a run of 11,000–20,000, according to the printers' declarations.[19]

Daumier likely read the popular 1836–37 French edition of *Don Quixote* translated by Louis Viardot.[20] Viardot's translation was illustrated with a whopping 800 engravings designed by Tony Johannot, who had also illustrated re-editions by Molière and La Fontaine.[21] Viardot's illustrated edition was the result of a game of one-upmanship between publishers as the technologies and ambitions of the illustrated book industry scaled up in the middle decades of the century.[22] *Le Charivari*, too, sharing a commitment to word–image relationships with these beautifully illustrated book volumes, enthusiastically informed the public about Viardot and Johannot's illustrated edition of *Don Quixote* in 1837.[23]

Viardot's translation was issued by Jacques-Julien Dubochet (1798–1868), an important publisher from the period who co-founded *Le National* (1830–51) and *L'Illustration* (1843–1944). *Le National* was a site of vitriol and criticism against King Louis-Philippe and its editor Alexandre Paulin was imprisoned on two occasions for sedition. *L'Illustration* was an illustrated journal expressing leftist dissent.[24] Dubochet was also the publisher of Rodolphe Töpffer, the first artist of comic strips, and both the publication of Johannot's illustrations of *Don Quixote* and Jean Gigoux's illustrations of Alain-René Lesage's novel *Gil Blas* demonstrate Dubochet's pioneering work in publishing comic and political material and integrating text and image.

In Dubochet's edition of *Don Quixote*, Viardot introduces his translation with a biographical essay on Cervantes, an essay that emphasizes Cervantes's imprisonment and embattled relationship with censorship.[25] Like Daumier, Cervantes's early reputation was shaped by a prison sentence, and Viardot frames his creation of *Don Quixote* as an act of vengeance for his mistreatment.[26] He cites three instances when Cervantes faced censorship of this work: from the religious adviser to the Duke of Béjar, after the latter extended his patronage not realizing the book was a satire, by the public through whisper campaigns and published pamphlets, and through censorship of the second volume by the archbishop of Toledo.[27] This was part of a broader framing of the author in nineteenth-century France, as we see performances of *Don Quixote* also making reference to the author's imprisonment. For example, in the second act of an 1864 marionette show *The little Don Quixote of La Mancha*, the proprietor of an inn tells Don Quixote and Sancho about a wounded soldier with Cervantes's name who was imprisoned.[28]

Similarly, an account by Émile Chasles titled *Miguel de Cervantes: his life, his times, his political and literary work* published in France in 1866 outlines the persistent frustration of the author with the pressures of excommunication and censorship. Chasles describes Cervantes as 'desperate, miserable, reduced to extremes' under these pressures, asking for absolution as a servant of the king and expressing the desire to leave Spain.[29] In Chasles's construction, Cervantes was an author for whom politics was paramount. His texts were expressions of rage; instead of being focused on stylistic innovations, he desired to influence politics, to appeal to the nation.[30] In ways that might have inspired sympathy from Daumier, this contemporary account characterizes Cervantes as being critical of his country and striving to change it through his art. Rather than blind patriotism, 'Cervantes offered a mirror to his country, like Molière and Aristophanes [the comic dramaturge] did to theirs. If telling the truth is a crime of high treason, he is a criminal. Cervantes's patriotism was a desperate patriotism: he judged because he loved.'[31]

For Viardot, Chasles, and other nineteenth century audiences, Cervantes navigated public denigration and religious opposition, emerging from prison to assail a popular literary genre through satire. It is easy to see Daumier sympathizing with an author who was both embattled and embedded political critique in his works out of love for his country. We should understand his exploration of the knight errant in the mid-nineteenth century as participating in a discourse that framed Cervantes as a figure struggling with his government and finding a language for political critique in his art.

Quixote's reception in France

The first translation of *Don Quixote* published in France was by Odin et de Rosset in 1614–18 and it was reissued eight times. The book met with immediate popularity, inspiring poetry, engravings, comedies, and literary derivations including sequels. In 1614, a fashionable dance was dubbed the *Don Quichot*. An even more popular translation by Filleau de Saint-Martin was first published in 1677 and was reissued an astonishing thirty-seven times under the *ancien régime*.[32] Pierre Perrault, author of the book *Don Quixote de la Mancha* (1679), found it strange that Cervantes's contemporaries, who usually had such delicate taste, would regard the book so highly, particularly because Quixote's adventures seemed to resist ordinary social behaviour.[33] Quixote departs from his community and lives in a world of chivalric delusion. Much of the humour is crass: the reader laughs at ugly women thought beautiful, urgent defecation, and barber's basins becoming helmets. Part of the book's popularity was perhaps anchored in a shared sense of confusion with shifting codes of manners and appearance in the seventeenth century.[34]

Cervantes's contemporaries recognized *Don Quixote* as a satire of the chivalric romance and as the parodic agent of the genre's destruction. In 1621, just six years after the second instalment of the book was published in Spain, Tirso de Molina wrote that Cervantes was 'the most speedy executioner of the expulsion of knight-errantly adventures'.[35] In his 1667 *Bibliothèque française*, Charles Sorel commented that, 'The Spanish are the first who created novels that are credible and entertaining. The *Ingenious Don Quixote de La Mancha*, a work by Cervantes, is an agreeable satire against chivalric novels.'[36] Later in the seventeenth century, French readers interpreted *Don Quixote* as a dangerous social satire because of its critique of the aristocracy. For instance, Father Rapin's 1674 *Reflections on the poetics of Aristotle and on the works of ancient and modern poets* claimed that Cervantes's resentment at being denied the patronage of the Duke of Lerma, Prime Minister of Philip III, motivated his ridicule of all the nobility of Spain ('toute la Noblesse d'Espagne') who were infatuated by chivalry ('s'était entêtée de Chevalerie'). This interpretation was repeated in Louis Moréri's *Grand dictionnaire historique* (1683).[37] Rapin and Moréri's works were soon translated into English in the United Kingdom and likely inspired Sir William Temple's (1690) judgement that *Don Quixote* 'had ruined the Spanish Monarchy'.[38]

The critical response to Cervantes's satire continued to develop in the eighteenth century, with analyses of *Don Quixote*'s exegesis, allusions, biographical studies, and intertextual connections. This period also saw extended interpretations of the novel's social critiques. And as the novel spread to England and France, Quixote's flight came to be seen as a rejection of the decadence and backwardness in Spanish society.[39]

In eighteenth-century France, *Don Quixote* lost some of its teeth in popular visual representations. Charles-Antoine Coypel (1694–1752) designed twenty-eight scenes from *Quixote* for decorative tapestries, a project spanning nearly four decades, from 1714–51.[40] It is one of the most influential and sustained responses to *Don Quixote* in France. However, there is no sense of anxiety about an individual's relationship to state power or mockery of the aristocratic classes. Coypel represents Don Quixote naturalized in a French aristocratic context, staging the novel as a piece of theatre and a comedy of manners. His narrative panels illustrate moments of the knight's contact with society, not his isolation, and do not satirize the aristocratic figures as Daumier might have been tempted to do. Instead, in the panel *Dorothy disguised as a shepherd* from 1752–53, Coypel relegates Don Quixote and Sancho to the background of a landscape that acts as a kind of theatre for aristocratic pleasure (Figure 4.2). A dead mule would spoil this party. The artist delights in the discovery and chaste deception of a beautiful young woman, Dorotea, who had been disguised as a man but was betrayed by her beautiful feet as she washed in a stream. Although Coypel avoids the novel's sharpest social critiques, this scene does acknowledge its humour. Quixote's fallen body closely echoes Dorotea's reclining position in the foreground. The knight is made to resemble a damsel in distress, hinting at Cervantes's ability to make chivalric romances ridiculous through parodic imitation. Daumier's paintings are spare and still in ways that are very different from Coypel's tapestry designs, but he may have taken some cues from Coypel's exploration of themes of

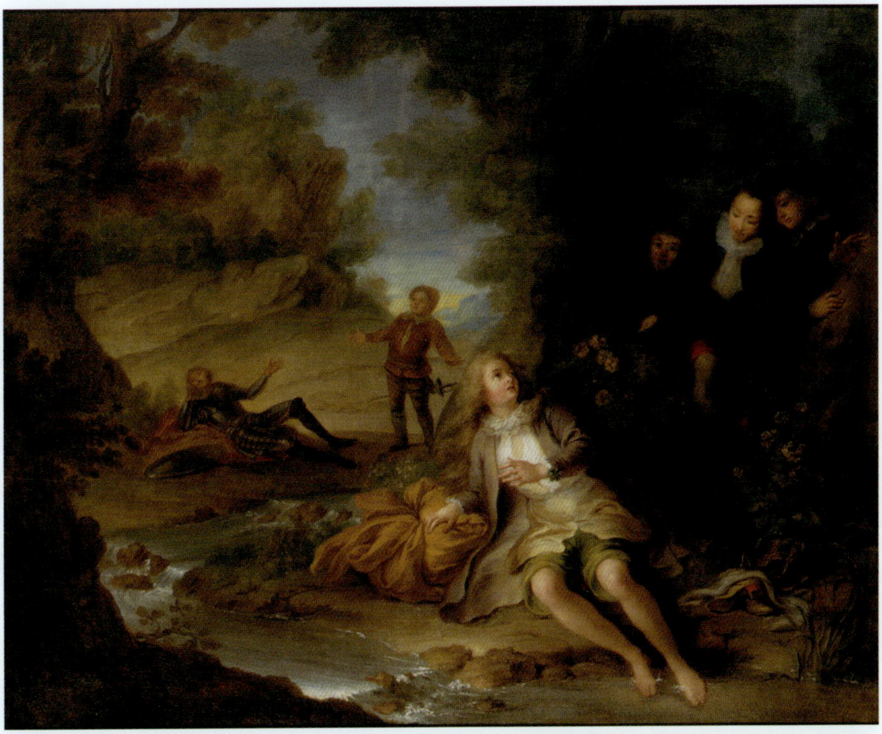

Figure 4.2 Charles-Antoine Coypel, '*Cardenio and the priest encounter Dorotea dressed as a shepherd*' from the story of *Don Quixote*, 1714–34

disguise and the performance of social roles. Coypel's works expand on the aspirational fantasies of men rising above their station and the discovery of high-born people masquerading as peasants, the same sort of play with identity and appearance that animated Molière's popular performances.

Coypel held the rights to the cartoons he made for the tapestries at Gobelins, printing engraved copies that earned him significant sums and popularized his iconography (a strategy he did not employ for his designs after Molière plays).[41] This entrepreneurial approach helped to make these images the most iconic representations of *Don Quixote* in the visual arts until the mid-nineteenth century. The tapestries were royal commissions and fit thematically into the spaces of court entertainment. Similarly, eighteenth-century commissions of *Don Quixote* scenes fulfilled by Charles-Joseph Natoire (1700–77) and François Boucher (1703–70) offered scenes of refined theatricality. Boucher was commissioned to supply a drawing in grisaille for an engraving by Pierre Aveline that would become part of a published series, *Principal adventures of the admirable Don Quixote*, marketed by Ravenet and Dupuis as engravings copied after paintings 'to follow those that have been engraved after the pictures of M. Coypel'.[42] Around 1735, the royal tax collector, Pierre Grimod Dufort, commissioned Natoire to create thirteen large paintings illustrating the story of *Don Quixote* for his billiard room at the Château d'Orsay. These pictures would serve as models for nine tapestries woven at Beauvais for the Hôtel Chamillart in Paris. Two of these scenes, *Sancho's departure for the island of Barataria* (c. 1735) and *Sancho's banquet on the island of Barataria* (1734–35), echo the pleasures of plenitude and diversion and the luxurious materials that would have surrounded Natoire's works in Grimod Dufort's billiard room (Figures 4.3 and 4.4).[43] There is no sense here that Don Quixote is at odds with his society.

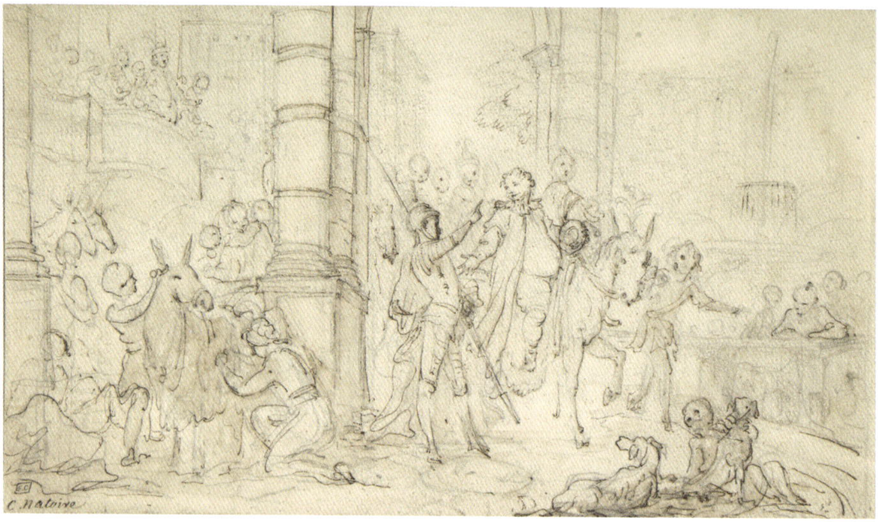

Figure 4.3 Charles-Joseph Natoire, *The departure of Sancho Panza for the island of Barataria*, 18th century

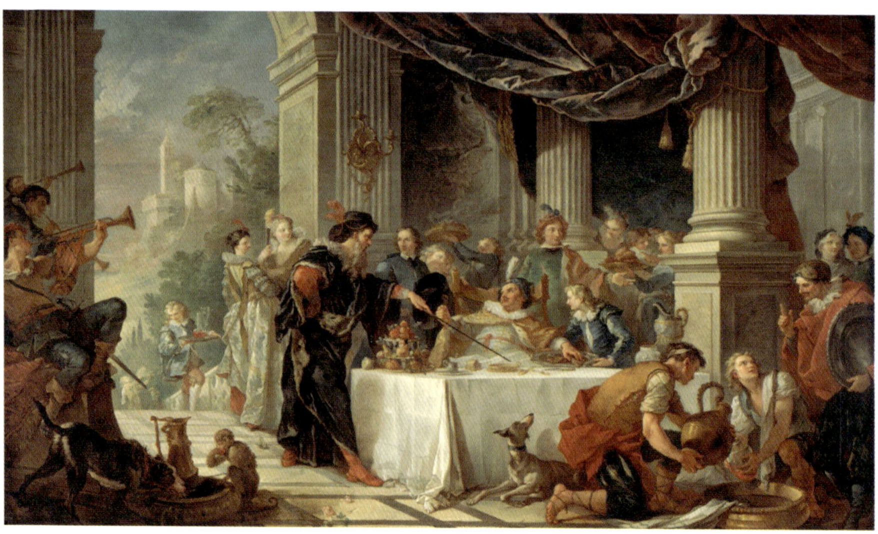

Figure 4.4 Charles-Joseph Natoire, *The feast of Sancho, governor of the island of Barataria*, 1735–44

Eighteenth-century interpretations of *Don Quixote* in French visual culture help to situate the strangeness, stillness, and formal self-reflexiveness of Daumier's paintings by contrast. Daumier's *Don Quixote and the dead mule* depicts Quixote and Sancho Panza's encounter with a half-devoured carcass and stages a confrontation between two artistic styles.[44] The pair stand arrested on the path of a vertiginous mountain pass. Daumier extends the spindly legs of Quixote's horse Rocinante to emphasize the length of the vertical canvas. Quixote's skyward lance rhymes with the sharp diagonal line of the mountain that cuts up towards the top left corner of the painting, and Daumier increases the verve of brushstrokes in sand, peach, grey, and lilac hues as the lance ascends. The artist lays down paint in a light, dry application that fails to cover the canvas's surface, concentrating pigment in a passage of the composition representing a dark bank of earth to the right of the pair, an effect that creates a sense of their enclosure in this wilderness. The mountain peaks give way – quite unusually – to blank canvas and the diagrammatic application of paint in the bottom half. Sancho's frame is markedly shorter and squatter than Quixote's, and his mule's head – a tangle of graphic lines more akin to Daumier's work with a lithographic crayon than the paint surrounding him – connects the painterly top half of the canvas with the mule carcass in the lower half. As does Quixote's armoured chest. A sharp, horizontal brown line and a strange scrabble of taupe paint divide the mule from the two figures it has stunned into stillness and separate two formal approaches.

Like Natoire's paintings, Daumier's *Don Quixote and the dead mule* takes into account the space for which it was commissioned, Charles-François Daubigny's country studio, reflecting his friend's interest in landscapes and collegial experimentation. Natoire's works were Italian in style (he and Boucher held successive Prix de Rome).[45] Like Veronese's *Wedding feast at Cana* (1562–63), *Sancho's banquet* fills a large composition with classical architecture and smaller vignettes of figures engaged in convivial activities. Natoire takes liberties in his translation of the text into pictorial form, loading the images with more figures and incident than Cervantes describes. He was not the only artist to embellish the text.

In the nineteenth century, *Don Quixote* motifs were represented by artists already admired by Daumier, such as Alexandre Decamps, who painted Don Quixote and Sancho Panza several times, Eugène Delacroix, and Théodore Rousseau, who produced a watercolour of the pair in 1847.[46] For Daumier's contemporary Gustave Doré (1832–83), the primary pleasure of the novel came from the rich fantasy life of the protagonist, the chimeras and illusions produced by his madness (Figure 4.5). The Librairie Hachette in Paris published Doré's illustrations in an edition of Viardot's translations from 1863.[47] They are populated by the chivalrous characters and fantastic landscapes from Quixote's imagination and organized by his mad logic. As one journalist noted in 1869: 'Doré's genius is his intuition; he recaptures lost worlds, incarnates himself in an era, rebuilds palaces carried away by storms, and his interpretation is the necessary complement to Don Quixote.'[48] In Doré's illustration 'Don Quixote reading and overrun by the characters from his chivalry books', Quixote raises his sword

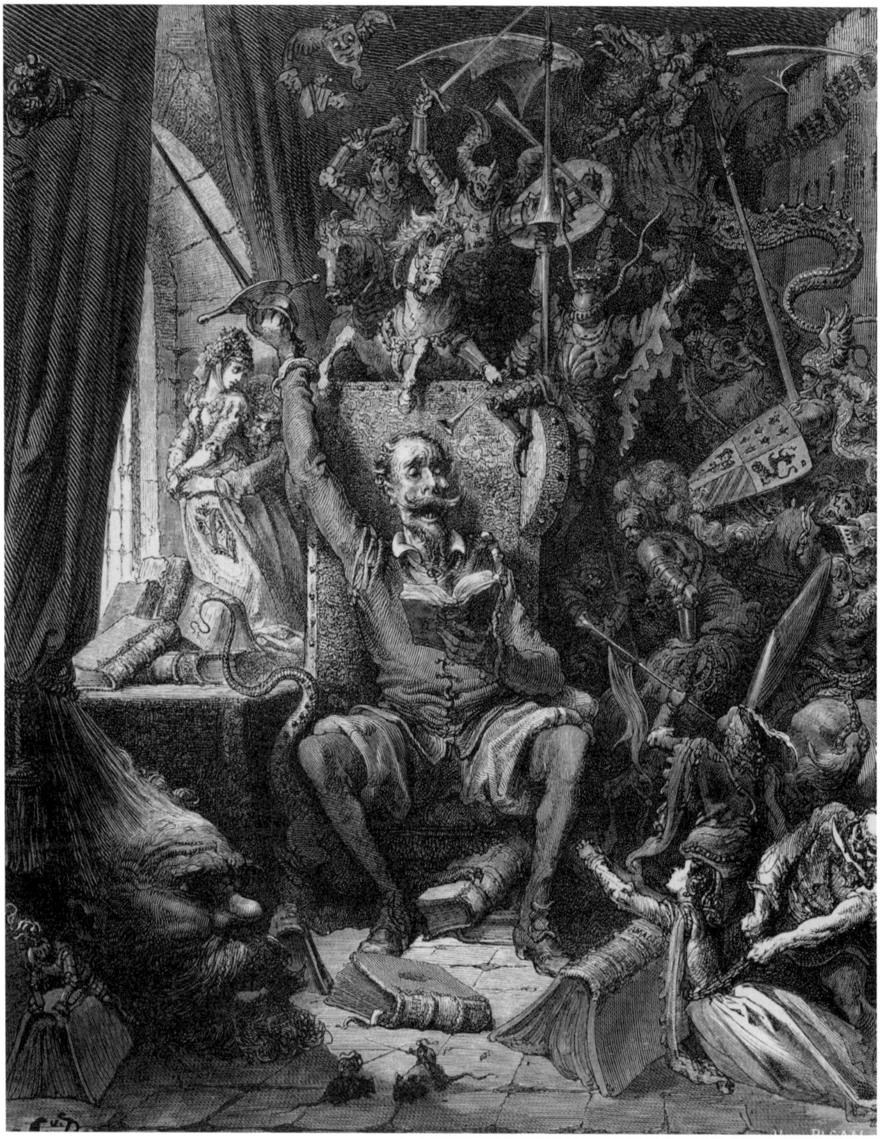

Figure 4.5 Gustave Doré, 'Don Quixote reading and overrun by the characters from his chivalry books'. Engraver Henri Pisan. Paris: Librairie Hachette, 1863

against the sunlight, battling the last anchoring vestiges of reality yet to be swallowed by his visions. The Baroque emotion and congested compositions of Doré's illustrations imitate the operations of chivalric romance.

The Romantic reinterpretation of *Don Quixote* dramatically departed from centuries of scholarship by disregarding or overlooking the novel's satirical mode.[49] Framed as men at odds with their times, both Cervantes and Quixote were aligned with the idea of the misunderstood genius in the Romantic imagination of the early nineteenth century, a persona taken up by many nineteenth-century artists. Alfred de Vigny conflated Cervantes and his protagonist in an article for *Journal d'un poète* in 1840: 'When Cervantes was dying, he was asked whom he had intended to depict in the person of Don Quixote. "Myself", he replied. "I wanted to express the misfortune of imagination and enthusiasm misplaced in a vulgar and materialistic society."'[50] By positioning Cervantes as an embattled and isolated artist at odds with his time, his advocates conferred upon themselves a sense of moral and political righteousness.[51]

For Romantics, Quixote became popular as a hero constantly disappointed by the disjuncture between his ideals and his circumstances. He was on a metaphysical or visionary crusade that repeatedly came into conflict with the mediocre reality of his life.[52] A review of Doré's illustrations and a performance of *Don Quixote* at the Théâtre-Lyrique in 1869 is helpful for situating the Romantic appeal of the novel in some interpretations in the visual and performing arts:

> This poor knight of La Mancha, this big heart, this loyal nature enamoured of beauty and justice, dreaming of battles against giants and monsters, enchanted palaces. This man who was so good, so brave, so eloquent, who was ridiculed by so-called reasonable people – unimaginative people– is one of the finest figures ever created in fictional literature. The great and heroic Cervantes, were he alive today, would contemplate with imagination the monument that Gustave Doré has raised nowadays next to his masterpiece.[53]

According to this critic, the conflict between Don Quixote's visionary spirit and the people who misunderstood him is evidence of both his prescient modernity and broader social dysfunction. He collapses Doré's appreciation for the author – stressing imagination as the key to both Quixote's and Doré's exceptionalism – and establishes a sympathetic alliance between the artist and the fictional outsider. It is useful to compare Doré's interpretation to Daumier's in this sense. Doré gives visual form to Quixote's rich interior life, whereas Daumier offers a different framework for understanding *Don Quixote*, one that interrogates authorial distance and constructions of genre in a similar way to Cervantes.

Doré's illustration 'Battle of the flock of sheep' makes vivid the conflict between the disappointments of Quixote's reality and the inaccessible ideal: Quixote sees a cloud of dust and believes he is charging into battle against an army, but instead sets upon the sheep whose bleating he mistook for military drumming (Figure 4.6). Doré obstructs Quixote's sight with his shield, signalling impaired vision and self-deception. He also presses the crush of animals towards the viewer, making the chaos of the flock running from Quixote's lance more dramatic and urgent. In Daumier's representation of Don Quixote charging sheep, titled *Don Quixote and Sancho Panza* (c. 1855, Figure 4.7), we neither join in the protagonist's delusion (we do not see an army) nor do we understand the dramatic irony of the narrator's position, where the viewer sees the sheep before

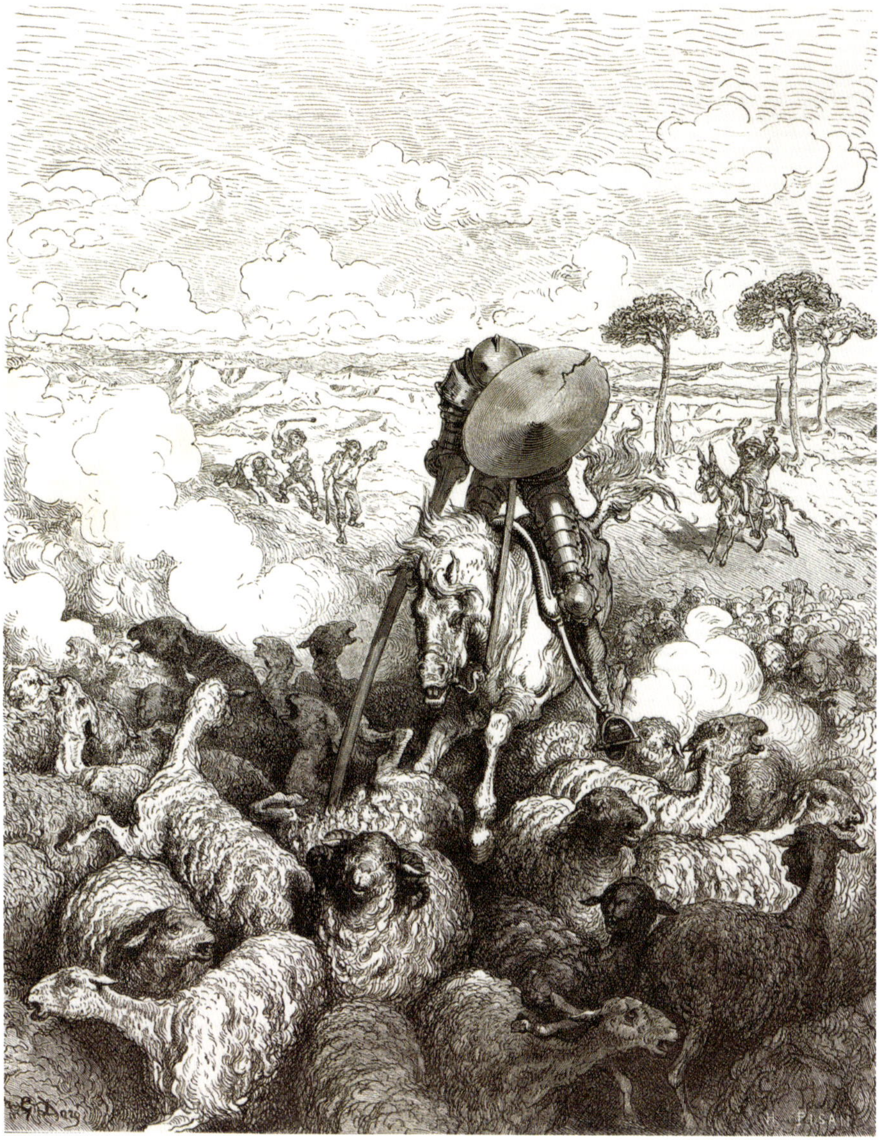

Figure 4.6 Gustave Doré, 'Illustration of Don Quixote (Battle of the flock of sheep)'. Engraver Henri Pisan. Paris: Librairie Hachette, 1863

Quixote. We may read Daumier's heavy tangle of white paint as a suggestion of a flock of sheep, though no sheep are pictured. Fundamentally, this passage of paint is a skein of matter that resists illusionism and remains open to interpretation.

Satire lends itself to visual expression. It is born from the awareness of the differences between appearance and discourse, and painting as a non-verbal medium offers the greatest variations of interpretive possibilities. The introduction to Charles Knight's analysis of literary satire begins with the description of a painting, a c. 1630 portrait by

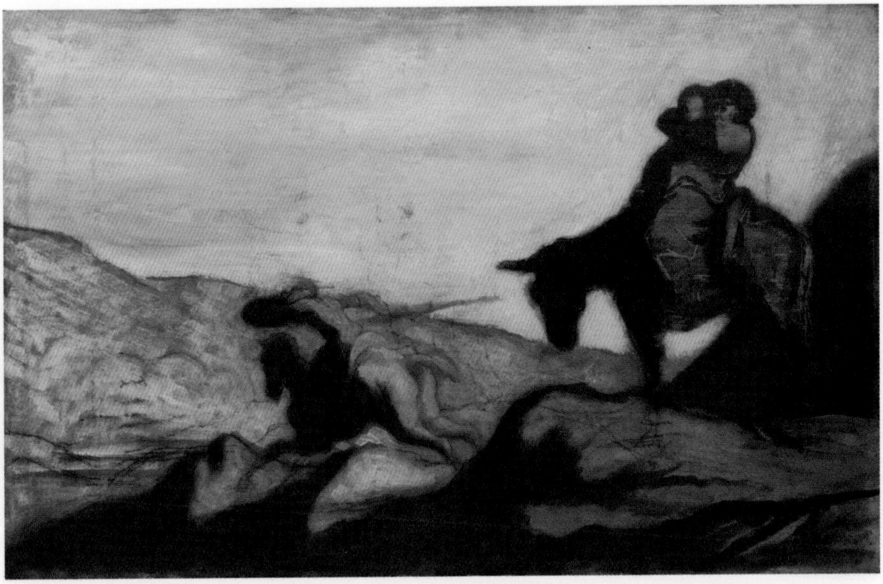

Figure 4.7 Honoré Daumier, *Don Quixote and Sancho Panza*, c. 1855

Diego Velázquez of the Greek philosopher Democritus, whose sitter may be the court jester. Knight tells us the painting best represents the properties of satire which are fundamentally imitative, modal, and open to interpretive play.[54] The passage of white and grey paint in Daumier's *Don Quixote and Sancho Panza* plays with the boundaries between imitation and recognition. In this section of canvas, the artist is representing neither sheep nor soldiers, but instead the space between perception and judgement. The visual world and its interpretive potential, the distances between the physical world and our own recognition of form, are constant themes throughout *Don Quixote*. Daumier repeatedly paints Quixote charging at the sheep because Don Quixote sees and interprets the physical world differently than his companion. Daumier's watercolour of this scene includes Quixote charging on horseback towards a hallucinatory line of figures on the horizon (Figure 4.8). When the artist squared off the painting in an oil sketch now in a private collection in Zurich, he abandoned the fantastical army. Finally, in the painting at the National Gallery in London, Daumier shifts the dramatic diagonal of the mountains downwards to make space for the confusion of the white paint. Though it is difficult to date works from this period with precision, this sequence suggests that Daumier moved to a version that played upon the interpretive openness of paint, matter that – like dust – can cover and obscure, merely suggesting what hand or foot might have stirred it. This would have been a compelling motif for an artist who so frequently had to negotiate the line between representation and obfuscation in response to censorship pressures in the illustrated press.

Frédéric Henriet's 1868 description of *Dead mule* (not titled in the article) in the *Gazette des beaux-arts* describes it in this way: 'Then Daumier, – a great artist also there

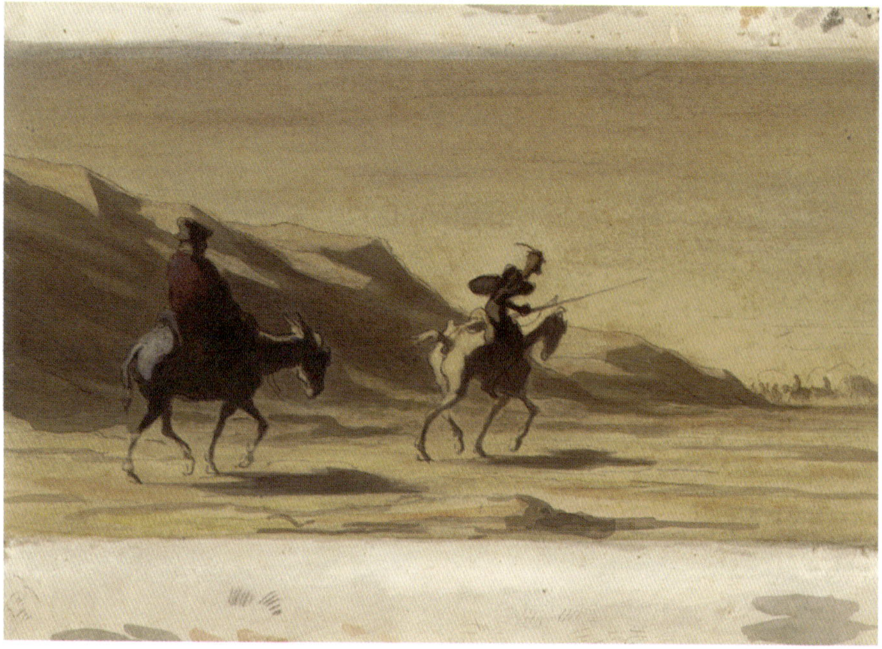

Figure 4.8 Honoré Daumier, *Don Quixote and Sancho Panza*, c. 1878

[Daubigny's studio] – has shown Don Quixote and his faithful squire in a deep gorge, moving towards conquest; in the foreground, the carcass of Rocinante is drawn with this science of osteology and the great draughtsmanship that makes Daumier a master.'[55] The writer incorrectly identifies which animal is in the foreground but captures the graphic quality of Daumier's energetic black-and-white vignette of the carcass, a style that does much to bring to mind a skeleton, the oscillating lines shadowing the mule's belly suggesting a ribcage revealed by a disintegrating corpse. The graphic lines describe desiccation and disintegration while avoiding more gruesome possibilities for representing decay.

Movement arrested by bones and death. A scrabble of painting encountering a passage of graphic line. Henriet captured these contrasts at the time, understanding that Daumier approached *Don Quixote* not as an exploration of aristocratic pleasure or folly but of process and stillness. It is also a reflection of contemporary values, just as prior interpretations of *Don Quixote* had been. There is some suggestion of this in the caricatural style of that great burst of skeletal lines capturing the dead mule. Daumier's first depiction of *Don Quixote* appeared in the 3 March 1839 issue of *Le Charivari* in a small vignette of the knight on horseback, lance in hand, illustrating an article written as a short play about 'Monsieur Bonsent' (Figure 4.9). The character Bonsent boasts about the popular sovereignty bestowed by the July Revolution and is taken away as a madman who is obviously delusional about the freedoms offered by the regime.[56] After he has been diagnosed several times as mentally deranged, he defends himself by declaring that his position

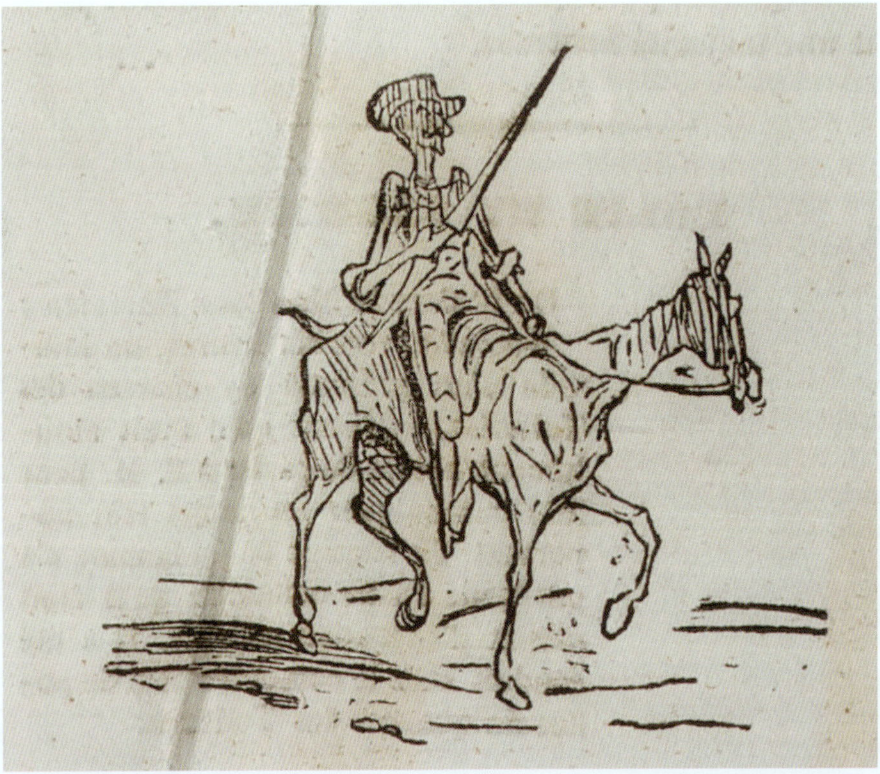

Figure 4.9 Honoré Daumier, illustration for F.-T. C. 'Folie et sagesse', *Le Charivari*, 3 March 1839

only touches on the madness of the 'monarchical Don Quixotes', before his arms and legs are tied together and he is carried away.[57] In its first manifestation in Daumier's visual oeuvre, *Don Quixote* is a metaphor for political madness, of being dangerously out-of-touch with reality. Like his engagement with La Fontaine's *Fables*, *Don Quixote* first emerged in Daumier's career in the 1830s as a means to express contemporary resentments with right-wing politics and then would later become the subject of a persistent painting practice that, I argue, carried some of the earlier associations with censorship and political critique.

Johannes Hartau has suggested that Daumier's Don Quixote was a proxy for the emperor Louis-Napoleon, a form initially emerging through his character of 'Ratapoil', a villainous cipher for republican resentments under Louis-Napoleon.[58] Ratapoil appeared in forty lithographs by Daumier between 1850–51, and he became a powerful typological condensation of the pessimism surrounding the rise of Louis-Napoleon during the Second Republic. Daumier is often given credit for Ratapoil, but he first appeared in the summer of 1850 in an article about Louis-Napoleon in *Le Charivari*, and Nadar and Cham drew Bonapartist agents in similar dress in the months preceding the election of 1848.[59] Ratapoil was an agent of the secret police, the Société du

Dix-Décembre, threatening, bribing, and agitating on behalf of Louis-Napoleon. He was depicted as a lanky and thin man who wore a weather-beaten hat (not unlike a tattered helmet) and a sharp beard and moustaches.[60] Daumier's print 'That good M. Ratapoil ... He has promised them ...' from June 1851 is emblematic of the character. It shows Ratapoil walking away after spreading propaganda in favour of Louis-Napoleon in the countryside (Figure 4.10). We can observe his silhouette, a tall angularity not unlike Quixote's, which is contrasted with a portly, gullible figure in the foreground. Like Robert Macaire, Ratapoil was a means to express resentment with the policies of a political movement by condensing its values into a typological character and avoiding a direct representation of a head of state when that representation was strictly censored.

Ratapoil disappeared from print in 1852 under strict Second Empire censorship of political speech in the press, and Daumier drew him only a few times again in 1871 after the Franco-Prussian War.[61] Hartau sees Ratapoil reemerge in the interim period in the tall angularity of Daumier's painted Don Quixotes. Though Ratapoil's likeness did share some basic physiognomic traits with Louis-Napoleon, this cannot be a direct transmogrification. Ratapoil is an agent of monarchist trouble, and in Daumier's hand Quixote does not seem to be a canny conspirator. He is stilted and tragic in a way that inspires a kind of sympathy absent from depictions of Ratapoil. Philip Kaenel maintains that we cannot identify Daumier's Don Quixotes directly with Louis-Napoleon because the figure would represent all the values the artist condemns.[62] Indeed, while Don Quixote might not simply be one thing for the artist, it is difficult to see the knight quietly arrested by the sight of death in *Don Quixote and the dead mule* as a proxy for the emperor.

In 1868, a year after Daumier painted *Don Quixote and the dead mule*, Don Quixote re-emerged in the illustrated press with leftist political messaging. The journalist and politician Henri Rochefort (1830–1913) appeared in the costume of the knight errant on the cover of *L'Éclipse* (1868–1919), a weekly satiric journal illustrated with André Gill's caricatures (Figure 4.11).[63] *L'Éclipse* was itself born from censorship battles. Its name suggests the shrouding of *La Lune* (1865–68), a journal edited by François Polo which was penalized for an unflattering *portrait-charge* of Napoleon III; Polo was also the editor of *L'Éclipse*.[64] Rochefort holds a lantern, a reference to his new leftist journal *La Lanterne* (1868–76) which was forthright in its opposition to Louis-Napoleon, so we presume he is staged as Don Quixote to suggest a mad quest on behalf of press freedom and liberal politics.[65] To Daumier's colleagues in the illustrated press in the 1860s, Don Quixote was a cipher for contemporary political expression; in Gill's case he represented the madness of charging forward in the republican opposition press in spite of serious legal constraints and consequences. In the period when Daumier would paint Quixote again and again, he was revived in both the press and the theatre to comment on the government and the status of free expression. Instead of seeing him as an agent of or proxy

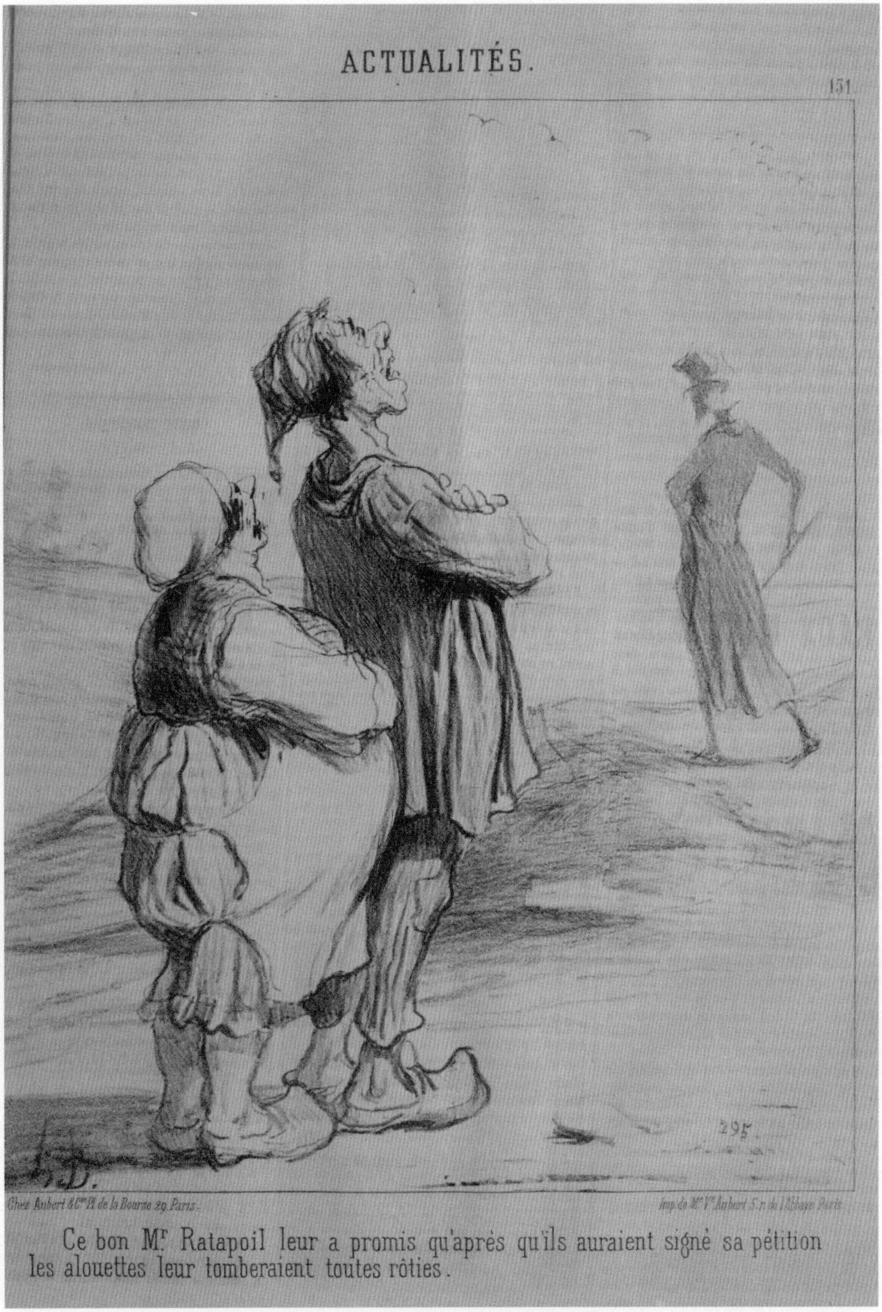

Figure 4.10 Honoré Daumier, 'That good M. Ratapoil … He has promised them …' ('Ce bon M. Ratapoil leur a promis'), *Le Charivari*, 20 June 1851

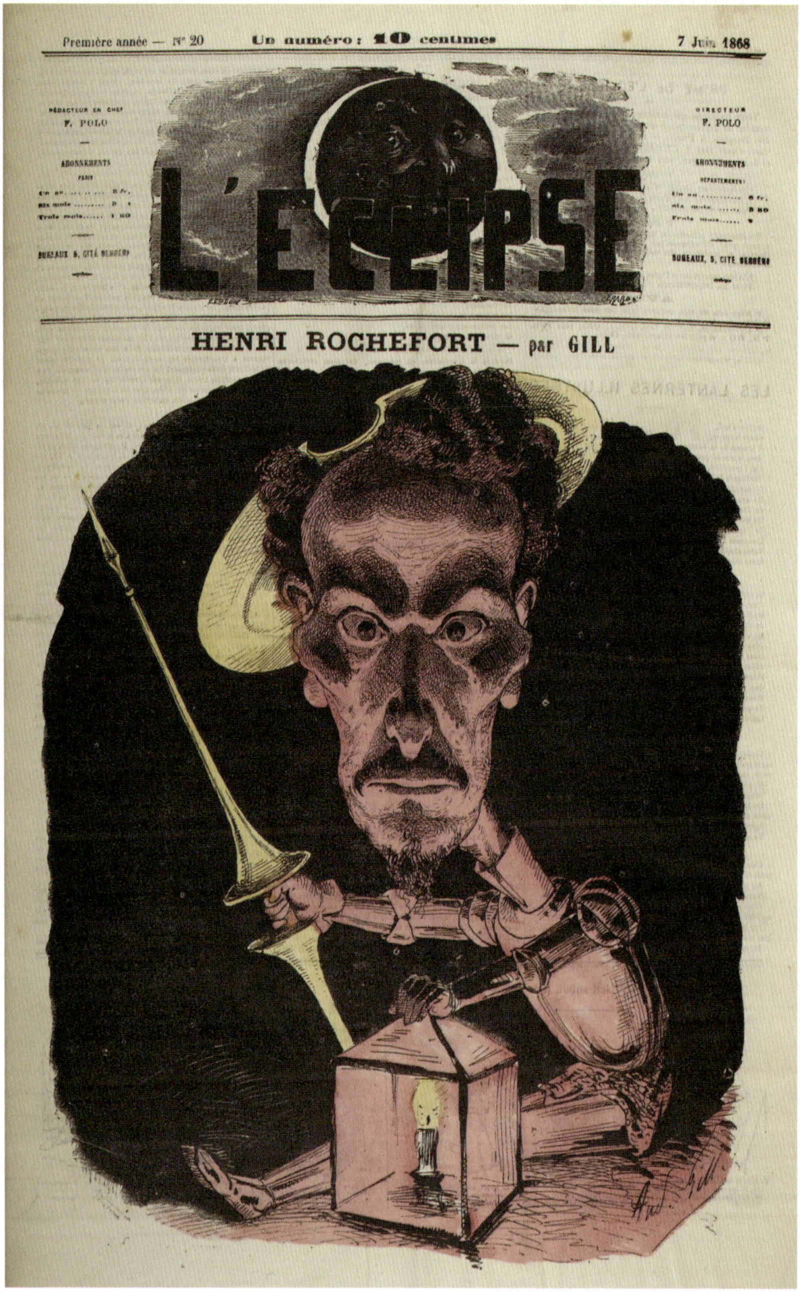

Figure 4.11 André Gill, 'Henri Rochefort [as Don Quixote]', *L'Éclipse* 20, 7 June 1868

for Louis-Napoleon, Daumier's Don Quixote is better understood as a condensation of disappointment, of censorship driving expression underground, of speech forced into abstraction. In Daumier's hand, we see the weight of disappointments and the pressures to obscure with paint the things that were not possible in print.

Self or satire

Until now, Daumier's exploration of Cervantes's novel has been interpreted biographically, as an allegorical self-portrait of a disaffected outsider.[66] Johannes Hartau made convincing arguments that Gustave Doré and Célestine Nanteuil drew Don Quixote as self-portraits and Alexandre Decamps represented himself as Sancho Panza.[67] Hartau was also the first to suggest that Daumier painted a portrait of himself as Don Quixote in *Don Quixote reading*.[68] In Rachel Schmidt's fine analysis of spatial imagery in representations of *Don Quixote*, she writes: 'Daumier, perhaps because of a deep personal identification with the idealistic madman after years of opposition to the politics of his government and the conventions of his society, represented a novelistically "romantic" Don Quixote.'[69]

A typical, if exceptionally eloquent, interpretation of Daumier's identification with the protagonist in *Don Quixote* comes from the twentieth-century journalist and writer Claude Roy. Roy writes that Daumier was a tragic figure, an outsider much like the errant knight, who suffered 'the painful and inescapable loneliness of an individual lost in a civilization that has no place for him. Daumier is the Stranger.'[70] He suggests a shared sensibility between the artist and the sad figure of Don Quixote, a shared disenchantment and illusion. In Daumier's obsessive repetitions, the artist and knight are doubled ('se dédoublait') or meant to identify with each other ('s'identifie'). Roy claims that Daumier's *Don Quixote and the dead mule* is a meditation on death and, specifically, a response to the deaths of his long-time friends, including Michelet, Corot, and Millet:

> The road is blocked and hope is dead: the carrion is put between the errant knight and us, between hope and the end. The old man redresses all the injustices, colliding with the final injustice. The travellers will arrive at the milestone, but it will be their last. It will be death.[71]

Daumier painted *Don Quixote and the dead mule* in 1867, one of the few of his paintings we can date with precision, and Millet and Corot did not die until 1875. This reading of Don Quixote as self-portrait needs to be revised: Daumier certainly struggled in the last decades of his life with finances, loss, imprisonment, ill health, and broad disillusionment, but the painting was likely part of a collaborative project with friends, not a product of a period of completely isolated labour. The artist was also, importantly, much less interested in self-representation than he was in issues relating to social patterns, politics, and the state of press freedoms.

The interpretation of Daumier's identification with Don Quixote adheres to the Romantic understanding of both the artist and of Cervantes's novel. Beginning in 1800, the reception of *Don Quixote* emphasized the idealization of the heroic individual, the novel's symbolic content – for instance, its representation of the spirit/flesh dichotomy or the social contradictions in Spanish history – and its anticipation of modern ideologies.[72] The early nineteenth century also saw the Romantic construction of the trope of the artist as misunderstood genius, where social isolation and underappreciation were evidence that the society surrounding the artist was too corrupted to recognize their talents.[73] In

Romantic constructions, being an outsider and failing to achieve fame or recognition in one's own lifetime gives an artist greater standing. Their difference is proof of their ability to think creatively, progressively, or beyond their time. This understanding of Daumier's *Don Quixote* series in particular has persisted throughout time and through many art historical accounts. However, the Romantic understanding of Daumier and his potential identification with Don Quixote neglects the novel's reception in the nineteenth-century illustrated press and fails to attend to the construction of the paintings themselves.

In the 1840s Daumier became part of a vibrant artistic community. In 1846, he moved to 9 Quai d'Anjou, close to Charles-François Daubigny (1817–78) at number 19, Auguste-Marie Boulard (1825–97) at number 13, and not far from Jean-Baptise-Camille Corot (1796–1875) at 15 Quai Voltaire.[74] It was a robust and industrious group of artists. Daumier, Daubigny, and Adolphe-Victor Geoffroy-Dechaume gathered at the nearby Hôtel Pimodan, formerly the Hôtel Lauzun, a '*hôtel particulier*' or private mansion, with other artists, writers, and poets including Charles Baudelaire. Boissard de Boisdenier organized the meetings, which often included Théophile Gautier, Théodore de Banville, Charles Baudelaire, and occasionally Eugène Delacroix.[75] A lavish eighteenth-century building, the Hôtel Pimodan had a series of paintings of scenes from the life of Don Quixote on the walls, likely establishing early associations between Quixote and social connectedness for Daumier.[76]

This social circle would extend into the countryside, where artists would find a productive and collaborative retreat from the capital. Charles Daubigny began to make trips back to his childhood home in Valmondois around 1834 or 1835. The railroad would not extend to this part of France until the 1840s, so he would make the trip either on foot or by stagecoach in the summer, and there he found a quiet painting retreat.[77] Beginning in 1854, he began visiting nearby Auvers-sur-Oise regularly with Corot, and in 1860 Corot advised him to purchase a piece of land covered in haricot beans where he would soon construct a country studio. In addition to Corot, Daubigny hosted many friends from the Paris social circle here, including Daumier, who also began spending his summers in Valmondois as early as 1853.[78]

Daubigny's studio was designed by Achille Oudinot and decorated by Daubigny, Oudinot, Corot, Daubigny's son Karl, and Daumier. In the dining room, Daubigny, his daughter Cécile, and Karl painted panels with flowers, fish, birds, rabbits, and vegetation. Daumier's *Don Quixote and the dead mule* was hung in the entryway which opened onto the artist's garden. According to accounts published before Daubigny's death, that room was filled with paintings of the countryside, including Karl Daubigny's seascapes of the coast of Normandy and a 'Virgilian' landscape by Corot.[79] Étienne Moreau-Nélaton's biography of Daubigny describes the circumstances:

> Other wall surfaces suited to soliciting the brush had been reserved by the master of the place for his friends. There Corot hatched the brilliant whims of his lush imagination. Daumier, whose friendship with Daubigny going back to their

> youth had established over time the most candid of intimacies, Daumier, I say, whom the banks of the Oise had captivated and who dedicated his very few hours of leisure to them, saw himself put to work on his own account and, summoned to comply, drew an epic Don Quixote in the stirrups of Rosinante.[80]

A book of etchings by Léonide Bourges records its presence in the entry hall (Figure 4.12).[81]

It is impossible to say whether Daumier considered the canvas to be finished, as it is difficult to determine whether the passages of graphic abstraction and bare canvas in *Don Quixote and the dead mule* were *informé* because the painting was constructed for a context conducive to formal experimentation or whether Daubigny simply bought an oil sketch in progress from his friend. Many of Daumier's paintings were privately reworked, often for years, and many were left unsigned and in uncertain states of finish. More alarmingly, some of Daumier's paintings were deemed so unconventional that collectors painted over the artist's brushstrokes (for example, *Man with a wheelbarrow*[82] and *Family on the barricades*[83]).

However, evidence suggests that the studio at Auvers was an important site for the exchange of ideas between Daumier and his friends, and its walls became a kind of canvas that recorded their shared work and playful experiments.

Don Quixote and the dead mule shares some compositional and thematic priorities with Daubigny's etchings published during this period of artistic retreat and collaboration. The

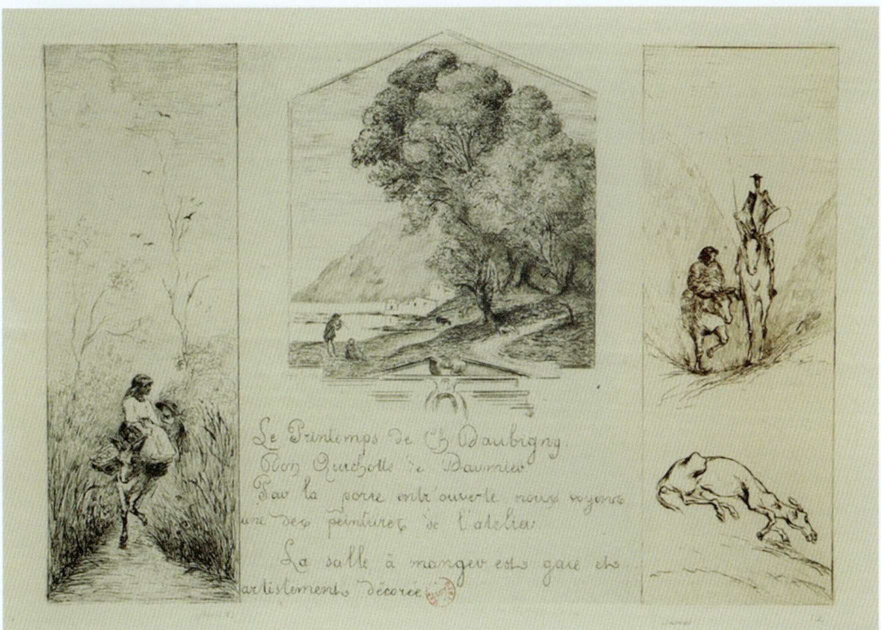

Figure 4.12 Léonide Bourges, *Daubigny. Souvenirs et croquis: [estampe] / eauxfortes par Léonide* Bourges, 1894

series, *Voyage en bateau* (1862), pictures life and artistic adventures at Auvers-sur-Oise. Published by Alfred Cadart, this collection features scenes of the artist at work in his floating studio, or *bateau atelier*.[84] Daubigny offers charming and often cartoonish images of amateur travel, drawn together by themes of discovery and pleasant sociability. The etching 'The search for an inn' (Figure 4.13) and Daumier's *Don Quixote and the dead mule* both include two figures traversing a mountain pass, conducting a quest (for meaning or shelter) outside conventional social spaces. Daubigny represents himself as the picture's protagonist, his lamp in the darkness acting as a kind of metaphor for the artist's vision. And *Don Quixote in the moonlight* (Figure 4.14), Daumier's drawing of Quixote keeping watch while Sancho sleeps on the earth, shares the reflective mood of Daubigny's nocturnal landscape and its emphasis on privileged vision. Although very different in tone and medium than Daumier's *Quixote* paintings, Daubigny's etchings offer some insights into the kinds of social and professional collaboration taking place at Auvers-sur-Oise, connections that should challenge current interpretations of the series as a straightforward expression of exclusion and loneliness.

The episode of Quixote's discovery of the dead mule is a very particular moment in the novel, in Part 1, Book 23, just after Don Quixote and Sancho first discover a discarded suitcase in the mountains, suggesting a person has thrown off their responsibilities and social costumes. They do not know it, but this is part of the eventual discovery of a man named Cardenio. Cardenio is a kind of proxy for Quixote, a poet who suffered romantic disappointment and who has also abandoned civilization.

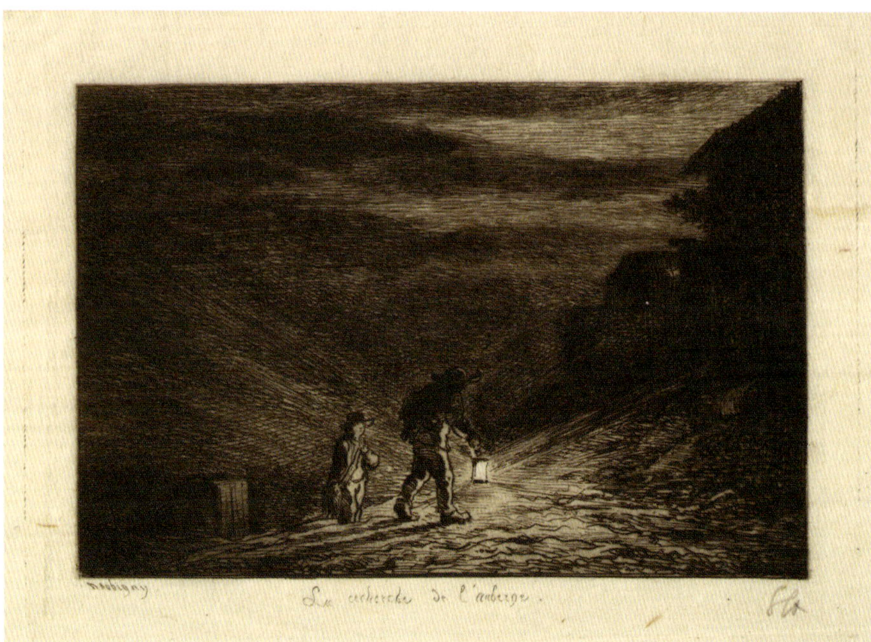

Figure 4.13 Charles-François Daubigny, 'The search for an inn' ('La recherche de l'auberge'), 1861

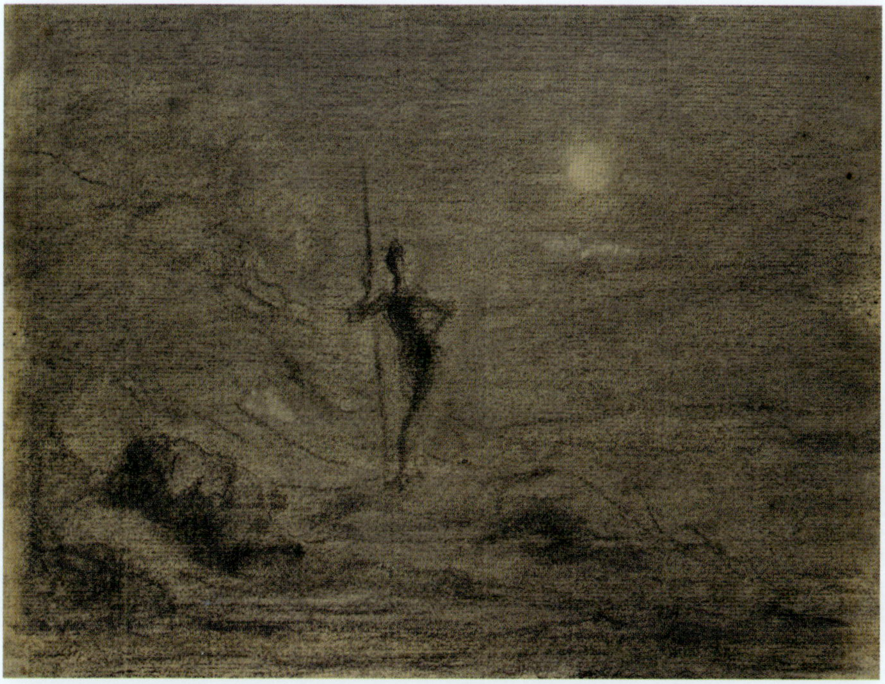

Figure 4.14 Honoré Daumier, *Don Quixote in the moonlight*, c. 1865–70

In the moment immediately preceding his encounter with the material remnants of Cardenio's presence, Cervantes describes a brief moment of mental diversion:

> As for [Don Quixote], as soon as he had entered the mountains that seemed to him just the place for the adventures he was seeking, he felt his heart leap with joy. He replayed in his memory the marvellous adventures that had befallen knights-errant in similar rough and solitary places, and he went along reflecting on these things, so absorbed and transported by them that he forgot everything else.[85]

Quixote's escape was a literary one: the landscape 'absorbed and transported' him because he was able to project remembered literary scenes onto its scrim. The dead mule would shock Quixote out of this dream-like interior state, its brute materiality shattering the illusion that objects in nature are indeterminate, fantastic, or equivocal. Daumier's choice to represent Quixote's encounter with the dead mule, when Quixote is startled out of his literary reverie, offers, in other words, a shocking contrast to the exploration of interior worlds.

It is a brutal encounter. Having already come upon an abandoned suitcase with some pages of poetry, they meet death and putrefaction:

> When they had almost completed the circuit of the mountain they found, at the edge of a stream, the corpse of a mule still wearing saddle and bridle, half devoured by wolves and crows.[86]

The death of Cardenio's mule made his escape absolute and irrevocable. Its decay marks the time of his delusion and isolation (six months, a goatherd tells us). The mule's death is also evidence of nature's rejection of man, a position at odds with Romantic philosophy and tendencies to see nature as a space of spiritual discovery and in mirrored correspondence with the human mind. If nature is filled with codes for understanding transcendental messages, the mule is a powerful sign for Cardenio. He set out into nature to seek a peaceful end to his life, but the mule's failed body lingers on the earth as evidence of his aborted plan.

A painting by Jean-Baptiste-Camille Corot confirms that Daumier was likely attending quite closely to the text of *Don Quixote* and the passage surrounding Cardenio's discovery. Moreau-Nélaton recounted that Corot painted his own interpretation of *Don Quixote* around 1865–68 for Daubigny's studio as a pendant to Daumier's work, and indeed their two scenes share a narrative thread (Figure 4.15).[87] Bruce Laughton calls Corot's composition a 'reversal' of Daumier's painting, but it is really a narrative extension.[88] Corot painted Don Quixote and Sancho as small figures silhouetted at left on a distant hill. Like Daumier's pair, Don Quixote and Sancho Panza stand midway up the painting, gazing down a vertiginous path at a figure between them and the viewer. The primary compositional differences in the vertical canvases are the proportion of the figures and the attention to landscape. Corot's figures are very small, and a tree dominates nearly two-thirds of the canvas. In Corot's painting, the intermediary figure is not Cardenio's mule, but Cardenio himself, naked and hauling himself out of a ravine. He pulls himself up on the branches of the enormous tree, a metaphor for his barbaric return to nature.

Daumier pictures a scene before Quixote meets Cardenio, when he was forced to confront a deeply unpleasant physical reality, a material obstruction that would end up leading to an unsettling replication of his own quest. Like Quixote, Cardenio banished himself from his home and society after a romantic disappointment and raved outdoors, drifting in and out of madness in the wilderness. But Sancho's presence is an anchor; a substantial, material hedge against the eruptions of solitary delusion that afflict Cardenio.

Solitude and its dangers are themes that run throughout Cervantes's novel, and Daumier expresses them in the contrast between the pair of figures at the top of his painting and the haunting skeleton below. For Cardenio, like another figure discovered hiding in the wild, Dorotea, nature is a space of banishment, the harsh landscape a fitting mirror for the inhospitable world.

> Is it possible that I have finally found a place that can serve as a secret burial for this body whose heavy burden I carry so strongly against my will? Yes, I think so unless the solitude these mountains promise deceives me. Woe is me! How many rocks and scrubs, who let me confide my misfortunes to Heaven through my moans, will keep more agreeable company than any person in the world.[89]

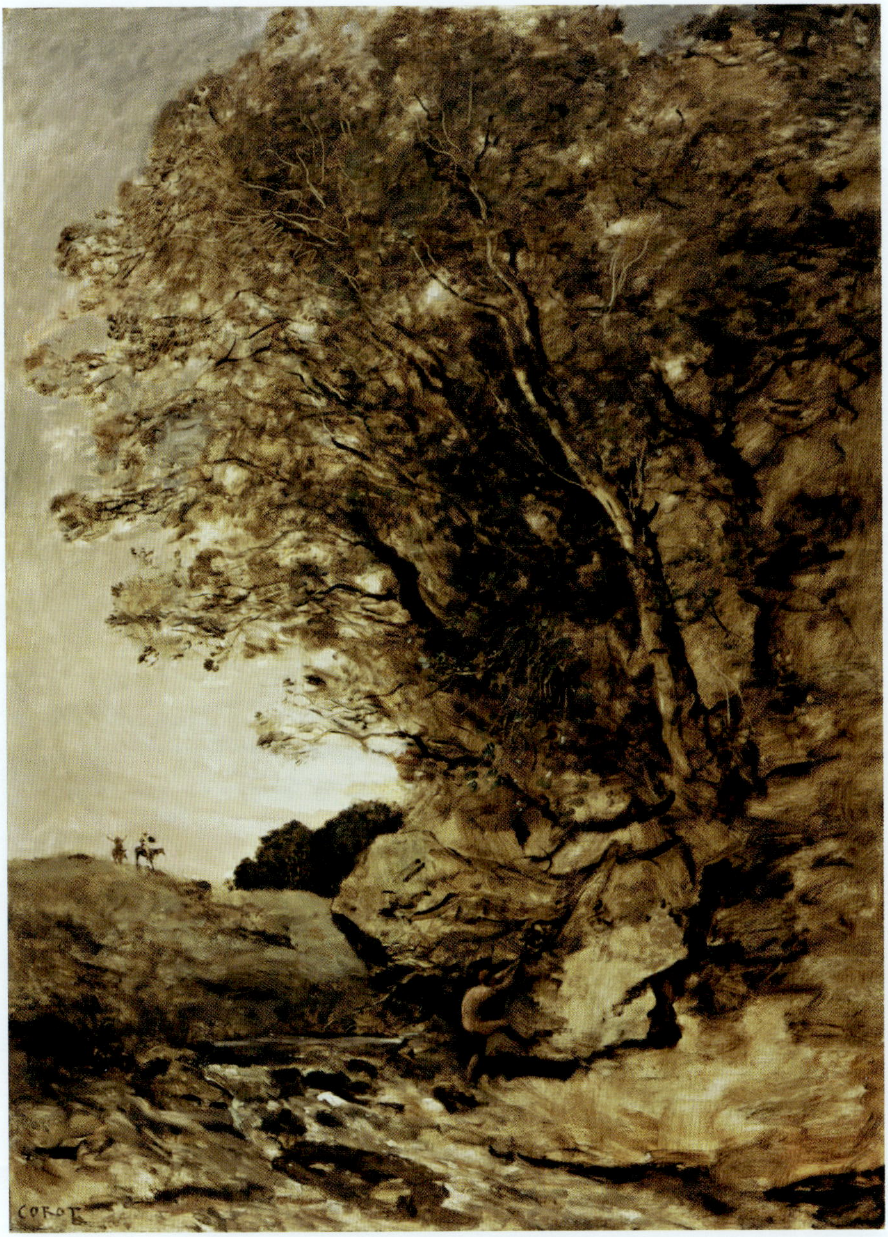

Figure 4.15 Jean-Baptiste-Camille Corot, *Don Quixote*, 1868

Solace is found in social connections and the understanding of new companions. It is only in their discovery that Cardenio and Dorotea avoid the fate of the mule. Corot's canvas pictures the encounter between a social party and an isolated madman. Don Quixote and Sancho, watching at a distance, become the positive terms in the contrast between the parties – paired/isolated, clothed/naked, resting/struggling, visual/tactile. Daumier's painting too sets up the top half of the painting – comradery, vision, volition – as a foil to the lonely skeleton in the foreground. His decisions to paint Cardenio's mule and to hang the painting in a space of collaborative art practice unsettle the common wisdom about Daumier's identification with Quixote as an outsider.

Conclusion

Although Don Quixote gives up his chivalric system of belief before his death, the conflict between reality and literary fantasy drives the novel. In Quixote's confrontation with a dead mule, Cervantes thematizes the struggle between imaginative distraction and material reality. This tension is, of course, a bigger theme in the *Don Quixote* books and is explored in Daumier's artworks of Don Quixote chasing sheep, but it is also a metaphor for the artistic process itself. Art is a record of the clash between the fantasies of the mind and the material properties of paint, crayon, and clay. It is the residue of a collision between two systems.

Daumier communicates this much better than Doré's illustration of Quixote's phantoms just a few years later. Perhaps this was because for an embattled political artist such as Daumier, giving form to the tension between imagination or intention and stinking, noxious reality was not just a creative puzzle to be solved but something that had the urgency and sustained interest of daily work. If Cervantes was framed in the French nineteenth century as an artist who wanted to hold a mirror up to his country in order to change its political system, then we might see his novel as a canny vehicle to explore the kinds of distance between reality and perception that were at the centre of nineteenth-century debates about art and political expression. This confrontation, the defining battle of Daumier's career, helps us understand why in the *Don Quixote* series we see his visual satire become darker, more stilted, and pessimistic.

It is well-documented that Cervantes dramatically upset narrative convention by staging himself as the editor of the text, which he claims was a found work authored by Cide Hamete Benegeli, destabilizing the reader's relationship with the narrator. The intertextual associations with sources outside the narrative and the hypertextual games within the novel suggest an interrogation of the act of writing itself.[90] Viardot's translation makes clear to nineteenth-century readers that this authorial distancing was a device used to imitate the chivalric romance, a parody so perceptive that Cervantes tricked seventeenth-century French academics.[91] This remarkably modern self-reflexivity was one of the reasons *Don Quixote* was so endlessly revived and reinterpreted. Daumier mirrors Cervantes's destructive use of parody in order to turn against the mechanisms of representation in painting. He exaggerates the interpretive possibilities of painting in *Don Quixote and Sancho Panza* to the point where a passage of paint fails to signify, and in *Don Quixote and the dead mule*, two representational systems come into contact, breaking any sense of absorptive illusionism, and making the viewer aware of formal operations being tested against each other.

Don Quixote and the dead mule stages a conflict between two systems of belief and therefore of representation. The absurd subjectivity and abstraction available in painting are pitted against the assertive representational claims of graphic art. *Don Quixote*'s multiple narrative styles, intertextual references, and fictional premise of a distant, foreign author translated by Cervantes all underscore and bring into question the nature of literary narration. *Don Quixote and the dead mule* references the schematic style of Daumier's own graphic art and is therefore similarly self-reflexive. It calls attention to the fact that the artist is imitating a set of references and filtering his expression through the contours of a style or movement. *Dead mule* is a scene of translation between literary fantasy – 'he went along reflecting on these things, so absorbed and transported by them that he had no thought for anything else' – and visual art and therefore between word and image, a dramatic allegory for Daumier's ambitions with the novel. In the striking transition from the thinly painted landscape to the graphic carcass of the mule, Daumier shows Quixote encountering both a dead animal and the dead matter of paint. But like Cervantes, he also includes a passage of pictorial satire. He injects the graphic arts into painting in the simplified lines of the mule carcass to make his work public, relevant, and political, bringing their immediacy and emotional impact into the rarefied space of the canvas.

Don Quixote and the dead mule was originally painted for the atelier of Charles-François Daubigny in Auvers-sur-Oise, a precious site of convivial sociability and escape in Daumier's life. The space provided a retreat from Second Empire politics and also offered opportunities for collaboration outside the academic tradition. The atelier is filled with landscapes by Daumier's intimates, artists who – like Don Quixote – believed that the retreat to imaginative wildernesses was an ethical response to a rapidly changing world. Daumier, however, offers *Quixote* and the unravelling of Cervantes's protagonist as a caution against nostalgia for a fictitious past or the promises of escape and isolation. The studio at Auvers offered, perhaps most importantly, a space for collaboration and formal experimentation, a place where Daumier could develop his translation of a book in order to pose questions about the ability of paint to signify.

Notes

1 Jerry Leath Mills, 'Equine gothic: The dead mule as generic signifier in southern literature of the twentieth century', *The Southern Literary Journal* 29, no. 1 (Fall 1996): 3.

2 Daumier showed *Don Quichotte et Sancho se rendant aux noces de Gamaches* at the Salon of 1850–51 along with *Femmes poursuivies par des satyres* and a drawing, *Silène*. Pierre Sanchez and Xavier Seydoux, *Les catalogues des Salons*, vol. 5 (Dijon: L'echelle de Jacob, 2001), 353. Maison claims I-33 is the painting displayed at the Salon 'by process of elimination'. K. E. Maison, *Honoré Daumier; Catalogue Raisonné of the Paintings, Watercolours, and Drawings*, vol. 2, 2 vols. (Greenwich, CT: New York Graphic Society, 1968), 70. However, while this painting is typically used as a stand-in for *Don Quichotte et Sancho se rendant aux noces de Gamaches*, its measurements do not match the Salon brochure (39 × 32 cm versus *Salon enregistrement des œvrages* which lists a size of 90 × 100 cm), and the canvas is believed to be lost. Bruce Laughton, *Honoré Daumier* (New

Haven: Yale University Press, 1996), 186; and Bruce Laughton, 'Daumier's drawings of Don Quixote', *Master Drawings* 34, no. 4 (Winter 1996): 404.

3 Jean Babelon, *Cervantes: Notice sur sa vie et son œuvre* (Paris: Bibliothèque nationale, 1947), 21.

4 Albert Boime, 'The Second Republic's contest for the figure of the Republic', *The Art Bulletin* 53, no. 1 (March 1971): 69–72.

5 Robert Justin Goldstein, ed., *The Frightful Stage: Political Censorship of the Theater in Nineteenth-Century Europe* (New York: Berghahn Books, 2009), 96–7.

6 Robert Justin Goldstein, 'Fighting French censorship, 1815–1881', *The French Review* 71, no. 5 (April 1998): 787.

7 'Le théâtre tapageur, agressif, immoral de 1848, doit bientôt plier devant la volonté bien arrêté du gouvernement de ramener l'ordre dans la rue et le calme dans les esprits.' Victor Hallays-Dabot, *Histoire de la censure théâtrale en France* (Paris, E. Dentu, 1862), 331–2.

8 'Décret organique sur la presse', *Le Moniteur universel: Journal officiel de la République Française* 49 (18 February 1852): 273.

9 Odile Krakovitch, *Censure des répertoires des grands théâtres parisiens (1835–1906)* (Paris: Centre historique des Archives nationales, 2003), 15; and *Le Moniteur universel: Journal officiel de la République Française* 366 (31 December 1852): 2231.

10 Judith Wechsler, 'Daumier and censorship. 1866–1872', *Yale French Studies*, no. 122, Out of Sight: Political Censorship of the Visual Arts in Nineteenth-Century France (2012): 56.

11 Luc Requier, Secrétaire de documentation, Archives nationales, Pierrefitte-sur-Seine, email message to author, 2 September 2022. The file referenced is under the Ministère de l'Intérieur, censure des répertoires des 'petits' théâtres parisiens, index des pièces (1802–1906) [finding aid] (Paris: Archives nationales, 2003).

12 Archives nationales, Pierrefitte-sur-Seine, France (hereafter AN) F/18/938 F/21/974, manuscript of play by Sauvage and Dupin, *Don Quichotte, ou les Noces de Gamache, ou Don Quichotte aux noces de Gamache* (1835); AN F/18/734, manuscript of play by Hervé (music Clapisson) *Don Quichotte et Sancho* (1847); AN F/18/709 F/21/967, manuscript of play by Coquatrix, *Un Hidalgo (du temps de Don Quichotte)* (1848); AN F/18/836, manuscript of play by Sardou, *Don Quichotte* (1864); AN F/18/738, manuscript of play by Barbier and Carré (musique Boulanger), *Don Quichotte de la Manche* (1869). These were all at large theatres. There are at least four more during this period in smaller theatres. See: Ministère de l'Intérieur, *Censure des répertoires des 'petits' théâtres parisiens: index des pièces (1802–1906)* [finding aid] (Paris: Archives nationales, 2003). Retrieved www.siv.archives-nationales.culture.gouv.fr/siv/IR/FRAN_IR_059966 (accessed 24 January 2024). AN AN F/18/1326, manuscript of play by unknown author, *Don Quichotte et Sancho Pança* (1843); AN F/18/1312, manuscript of play by unknown author, *Don Quichotte et Sancho* (1847); AN F/18/1330, manuscript of play by *Le Petit don Quichotte de la Manche* (1864); AN F/18/1202, manuscript of play by unknown author, *Le Don Quichotte de maris* (1869); AN F/18/1096/B, manuscript of play by unknown author, *Don Quichotte et Sancho Pança* (n.d.).

13 Louis Huart, 'Lettre de Sancho Pança à monseigneur l'évêque de Luçon', *Le Charivari* (12 October 1864): 1.

14 Wechsler, 'Daumier and censorship. 1866–1872', 54.

15 AN F/18/836, manuscript of play by Sardou, *Don Quichotte* (1864), [n.p].

16 AN F/18/1326, manuscript of play by unknown author, *Don Quichotte et Sancho Pansa* (1843), [n.p.]. All mentions of the 'curé' are struck out in the first act and substituted with 'docteur'.

17 AN F/18/1312A, manuscript of play by Hervé, *Don Quichotte et Sancho* (1847), 4.

18 Philippe Kaenel, "'Don Quichotte", Daumier et la légende de l'artiste'. *Artibus et Historiae* 23, no. 46 (2002): 166.

19 Roger Chartier, Henri-Jean Martin, and Jean-Pierre Vivet, *Histoire de l'édition française. du Romantisme à la Belle Époque*, vol. 3 (Paris: Promodis, 1985), 416–22.

20 Kaenel, '"Don Quichotte"', 166. Kaenel incorrectly lists the publication year as 1835.

21 Bruce Laughton, *The Drawings of Daumier and Millet* (New Haven: Yale University Press, 1991), 404.

22 Chartier et al., *Histoire de l'édition française*, 192, 338.

23 'Nous parlerons bientôt du *Don Quichotte*, illustré aussi par M. Tony Johannot, et qui possède un autre mérite non moins digne de nos éloges, celui d'être traduit par un homme qui possède également bien l'espagnol et sa propre langue, par M. Louis Viardot qui comptera parmi ses plus glorieux titres, l'honneur de nous avoir fait connaître enfin dans toute sa perfection l'inimitable chef-d'œuvre de la littérature espagnole et même de toutes les littératures.' 'Littérature: Molière illustré complet', *Le Charivari* (27 January 1837): 5–6.

24 Patricia Mainardi, *Another World: Nineteenth-Century Illustrated Print Culture* (New Haven: Yale University Press, 2017), 101–3.

25 Louis Viardot, introduction to '*L'ingénieux hidalgo Don Quichotte de la Manche*', by Miguel de Cervantes Saavedra, vol. 1, trans. and ed. Louis Viardot (Paris: J.-J. Dubochet, 1836–37), 1–48.

26 'C'est en mémoire de ces mauvais traitements qu'il commença le *Don Quichotte* par ces mots de bien douce vengeance: "Dans un endroit de la Manche, *dont je ne veux pas me rappeler le nom* ..."' Cervantes, *L'ingénieux hidalgo Don Quichotte*, trans. Viardot 1:25.

27 Cervantes, *L'ingénieux hidalgo Don Quichotte*, trans. Viardot 1:25, 31, 34.

28 AN F/18/1330, manuscript of play by unknown author, *Le Petit don Quichotte de la Manche* (1864). This was performed at the Marionnettes Lyriques, a theatre that opened in 1862 and held only puppet shows until 1866. After that it was called the Théâtre des Funambules. Fabien Palisse, 'Histoire des théâtres de marionnettes en France, en Europe et dans le monde. Volume 1: localisation, architecture et scénographie' (Master's thesis, École d'Architecture de Paris-Belleville, 1993), 29.

29 Émile Chasles, *Michel de Cervantes: sa vie, son temps, son œuvre politique et littéraire* (Paris: Didier, 1866), 210–11. Other French-language criticism of Cervantes from this period includes Charles Augustin Sainte-Beuve and Michel (Hermanos de) Lévy, *Nouveaux Lundis* (Paris: Michel Lévy frère, 1864–70); Prosper Mérimée, *Portraits historiques et litteraires* (Paris: Calmann Levy, 1894); A. Germond de Lavigne, *Les Deux Don Quichotte: Étude critique sur l'œuvre de Fernandès Avellaneda faisant suite à la 1re partie du Don Quichotte de Cervantès* (Paris: Didier, 1852); Ferdinand Loise, *Histoire de la poésie espagnole* (Belgium: M. Hayez, Imprimeur de l'Acadèmie Royale, 1868); Emile Gebhart, *Rabelais, la renaissance et la réforme* (France: Hachette Et Cie, 1877).

30 'Quand un pareil sentiment l'anime, gardons-nous de lui demander la perfection du style ou les grâces de Don Quichotte. Il laisse jaillir de son cerveau des improvisations qui soulagent sa colère et qui ne satisfont pas son goût d'artiste. Il oublie sa réputation d'écrivain pour la cause qu'il plaide, qui est l'urgence de sauver les captifs et de changer de politique ... ses œuvres sont des coups de hardiesse et des appels à la nation.' Chasles, *Michel de Cervantes*, 126.

31 'Cervantes a présenté le miroir à son pays, comme Molière et Aristophane ont fait chez eux. Si dire la vérité est un crime de haute trahison, il est criminel ... Le patriotisme de Cervantes est un patriotisme désespéré: Il a jugé ce qu'il aimait.' Chasles, *Michel de Cervantes*, 449.

32 Yves Giraud, 'Le "Don Qui Choque": Résistances du goût français due XVIIe siècle à l'œuvre de Cervantes', *Studi Di Letteratura Francese* 23 (1 January, 1998): 29.

33 Giraud, 'Le "Don Qui Choque"', 31–3.

34 Castillo, 'Don Quijote como prototipo de la novela europea moderna', in *Don Quijote por tierras extranjeras: Estudios sobre la recepción de la novela cervantina*, ed. Hans Christian Hagedorn (Cuenca: Ediciones de la Universidad de Castilla-La Mancha, 2007), 40.

35 'Ejecutor acérrimo de la expulsión de andantes aventuras.' Tirso de Molina, *Los cigarrales de Toledo*, quoted in Anthony Close, *The Romantic Approach to 'Don Quixote': A Critical History of the Romantic Tradition in 'Quixote' Criticism* (New York: Cambridge University Press, 1977), 9.

36 Giraud, 'Le "Don Qui Choque"', 33.

37 Louis Moréri, *Le Grand dictionnaire historique, ou Le Mélange curieux de l'histoire sacrée et profane 2e édition* (Lyon: J. Gyrin et B. Rivière, 1683).

38 A. P. Burton, 'Cervantes the man seen through English eyes in the seventeenth and eighteenth centuries', *BHS* 45 (1968): 2–3, quoted in Close, *The Romantic Approach to 'Don Quixote'*, 68–9.

39 Castillo, 'Don Quijote como prototipo de la novela europea moderna', 66–79.

40 Charlotte Vignon, Edith Grossman, and Charles-Antoine Coypel, *Coypel's Don Quixote Tapestries: Illustrating a Spanish Novel in Eighteenth-Century France* (New York: The Frick Collection, 2015).

41 Candace Clements, 'Noble liberality and speculative industry in early eighteenth-century Paris: Charles Coypel', *Eighteenth-Century Studies* 29, no. 2 (1995): 213–17.

42 Françoise Joulie, 'Natoire and Boucher: Two studies for a Don Quixote tapestry', *The Metropolitan Museum Journal* 39 (2004): 153–6.

43 Joulie, 'Natoire and Boucher', 153.

44 Daumier made three paintings (MD I-201, 202, and 209) and a drawing (MD 442–443) of this subject as catalogued by K. E. Maison. He perhaps made another sketch which was sold at the Hôtel Drouot, Paris in December 1998. The canvases at the Kröller-Müller Museum, Otterlo and The Metropolitan Museum of Art, New York have horizontal orientations, and Henri Loyrette suggests they are more reflective of Daumier's 1850s style in *Daumier 1808–1879*, 526–7.

45 Joulie, 'Natoire and Boucher', 153.

46 Johannes Hartau, *Don Quijote in der Kunst* (Berlin: Gebr. Mann, 1987), 201–2. See too H. S. Ashbee, *An Iconography of Don Quixote: 1605–1895* (London: The University Press, Aberdeen, 1895). A reproduction of Rousseau's work can be found in Ferdinand Lefman's etching, *Don Quixote and Sancho Panza*, in the journal *L'Artiste* 5 (15 November 1850): 193.

47 Miguel de Cervantes Saavedra, *L'ingénieux Hidalgo Don Quichotte de La Manche*, trans. Louis Viardot (Paris: Librairie de L. Hachette et cie, 1863). Engraver Henri Pisan.

48 'Le génie de Gustave Doré, c'est l'intuition; il retrouve les mondes disparus, il s'incarne dans une époque, il reconstruit les palais emportés par les tourmentes, et son interprétation est le complément obligé de Don Quichotte.' I. Lyon, 'Don Quichotte au théatre et Don Quichotte a la vitrine', *Le Journal Illustré* 6, no. 275 (16 May 1869): 160.

49 Castillo, 'Don Quijote como prototipo de la novela europea moderna', 68; and Close, *The Romantic Approach to 'Don Quixote'*, 57–8.

50 'Lorsque Cervantes mourut, on lui demanda qui il avait voulu peindre dans Don Quichotte: "Moi", dit-il. "C'est le Malheur de l'imagination et de l'enthousiasme déplacé dans une société vulgaire et matérielle"', *Journal d'un poète* (February/March 1840), 152, quoted in Close, *The Romantic Approach to 'Don Quixote'*, 55. The translation is Close's.

51 For a thorough historiography, see: Michel Melot and Neil McWilliam, 'Daumier and art history: Aesthetic judgement/political judgement', *Oxford Art Journal* 11, no. 1 (1988): 3–24.

52 Castillo, 'Don Quijote como prototipo de la novela europea moderna', 67–8.

53 'Ce pauvre chevalier de la manche, ce grand cœur, cette loyale nature éprise du beau et du juste, rêvant de combats contre des géants et de monstres, de palais enchantés; cet homme si bon, si brave, si éloquent, bafoué par les gens dits raisonnables, les esprits secs, est une des plus belles figures qu'ait créées la littérature d'imagination. Le grand et héroïque Cervantes, s'il

vivait aujourd'hui, contemplerait avec admiration le monument que Gustave Doré a élevé de nos jours à côté de son chef-d'œuvre.' I. Lyon, 'Don Quichotte au théâtre et Don Quichotte a la vitrine', *Le Journal Illustré* 6, no. 275 (16 May 1869): 159.

54 Charles Knight, *The Literature of Satire* (Cambridge: Cambridge University Press, 2004), 1–3.

55 'Puis Daumier, – un grand artiste aussi celui-là – a montré, dans une gorge profonde, Don Quichotte et son fidèle écuyer, avançant à la conquête; sur le premier plan, la carcasse d'une rossinante se dessine avec cette science d'ostéologie et ce grand jet de dessin qui font de Daumier un maître.' Frédéric Henriet, 'Les paysagistes contemporains: Daubigny', *Gazette des beaux-arts* 9, no. 2 (1 January 1874): 265.

56 Hartau, Don Quijote *in der Kunst*, 222–4. The unsigned illustration is embedded into the article: F.-T. C., 'Folie et sagesse', *Le Charivari* (3 March 1839): 2. Daumier did include his initials on the first illustration of three in the same style.

57 'Comme aussi, je ferais toucher au doigt la démence de ces Don Quichottes monarchiques qui poussent à mettre la lance en arrêt contre tout un peuple'. F.-T. C., 'Folie et sagesse', 2.

58 Hartau, *Don Quijote in der Kunst*, 222–41.

59 Laura O'Brien, *The Republican Line: Caricature and the French Republican Identity* (Manchester: Manchester University Press, 2015), 248–52.

60 Judith Wechsler, *A Human Comedy: Physiognomy and Caricature in 19th Century Paris* (Chicago: The University of Chicago Press, 1982), 91.

61 Wechsler, *A Human Comedy*, 91.

62 Kaenel, '"Don Quichotte"', 173.

63 Hartau, *Don Quijote in der Kunst*, 234; and André Gill, 'Rochefort comme Don Quichotte', *L'Éclipse* (7 June 1868): 1.

64 Armand Lods, *André Gill: sa vie: bibliographie de ses œuvres* (Paris: L. Vanier, 1887), 20–1. *L'Éclipse* continued to push the boundaries around political speech, and in 1868 Gill was prosecuted for obscenity in a trial which resulted both in the dismissal of charges and his creation of the pear-like icon, the 'melon of Gill'. Goldstein, *Censorship of Political Caricature*, 25.

65 As Judith Wechsler has described, beginning in 1866 Louis-Napoléon's government loosened some censorship standards to both seem more liberal and to encourage commerce in fields that included books and the press. In 1868, the government eliminated the requirement for preliminary authorization for new journals, thus the appearance of new journals like *L'Éclipse* and *La Lanterne* in this year. As Polo and Gill discovered, these tentative new freedoms did not extend to representations of Napoleon III. Wechsler, 'Daumier and censorship. 1866–1872', 56–60.

66 Kaenel, '"Don Quichotte"', 171. See, for example: Arsène Alexandre, *H. Daumier. L'Homme et l'œuvre* (Paris: H. Laurent, 1888), 200; Howard P. Vincent, *Daumier and His World* (Evanston: Northwestern University Press, 1968), 222; Werner Hofmann, *Daumier et ses amis républicains*, exh. cat. (Marseille: Musée Cantini, 1979), 7–14; Oliver W. Larkin, *Daumier, Man of His Time* (New York: McGraw-Hill, 1966), 194; Bruce Laughton, *The Drawings of Daumier and Millet* (New Haven: Yale University Press, 1991), 141; and Henri Loyrette, 'Don Quichotte', in Honoré Daumier, J. Douglas Campbell, Usher Caplan, National Gallery of Canada, Galeries nationales du Grand Palais (France), and Phillips Collection, *Daumier 1808–1879: National Gallery of Canada, Ottawa, 11 June–6 September 1999; Galeries nationales du Grand Palais, Paris, 5 October 1999–3 January 2000; Phillips Collection, Washington, 19 February–14 May* 2000, exh. cat. (Ottawa: National Gallery of Canada, 1999), 516–18.

67 Hartau, *Don Quijote in der Kunst*, 193–200.

68 Hartau, *Don Quijote in der Kunst*, 211–15; and Kaenel, '"Don Quichotte"', 171.

69 Rachel Schmidt, 'The romancing of Don Quixote: Spatial innovation and visual interpretation in the imagery of Johannot, Doré and Daumier', *Word and Image* 14, no. 4 (1998): 365.
70 'la solitude douloureuse et inéluctable de l'individu perdu dans un civilisation où il n'y a pas de place pour lui. Daumier est l'Etranger.' Claude Roy, *Daumier [Étude biographique et critique de Claude Roy]* (Genève: Skira, 1971), 107.
71 'La route est barrée et mortes les espérances: la charogne s'interpose entre le chevalier errant et nous, entre l'espoir et le terme. Le vieux redresser de tous le injustices se heurte à l'injustice finale. Les voyageurs arriveront à l'étape: mais ce sera la dernière. Ce sera la mort.' Roy, *Daumier*, 107.
72 Close, *The Romantic Approach to 'Don Quixote'*, 1–6.
73 Castillo, 'Don Quijote como prototipo de la novela europea moderna', 40–2; and Schmidt, 'The romancing of Don Quixote', 364.
74 Laughton, *Honoré Daumier*, 128, 176. Later in life, Boulard had a house in L'Isle-Adam, on the Oise River and close to Valmondois. *Daumier: 1808–1879* (Ottowa: Musée des Beaux-Arts du Canada, Ottawa, 1999), 564.
75 Maurice Gobin, *Daumier Sculpteur: Avec un catalogue raisonné et illustré de l'œuvre sculpté* (Geneva: Pierre Cailler, 1952), 16; and Roger Passeron, *Daumier* (New York: Rizzoli, 1979), 149. Both Boissard and Baudelaire lived in the *hôtel particulier* around this period.
76 Passeron, *Daumier*, 149.
77 'Bien avant les chemins de fer, vers 1834, il y a bien longtemps de cela nous allions avec mes jeunes amis, plusieurs fois chaque année, soit à pied, soit en diligence, au charmant pays de Valmondois, là où l'ami Daubigny avait été mis en nourrice chez Papa et Maman Bazot.' Étienne Moreau-Nélaton, *Daubigny raconté par lui-même* (Paris: Henri Laurens, 1925), 7.
78 Larkin, *Daumier: Man of His Time*, 160.
79 Frédéric Henriet, 'Les paysagistes contemporains: Daubigny', *Gazette des beaux-arts* 9, no. 2 (1 January 1874): 265.
80 'D'autres surfaces murales propres à solliciter le pinceau avaient été réservées par le maître du lieu à celui de ses amis. Corot y faisait éclore les étincelants caprices de sa luxuriante imagination. Daumier, dont les relations avec Daubigny, remontant à leurs années de jeunesse, avaient constitué avec le temps la plus franche des intimités, Daumier, dis-je, que les rives de l'Oise avaient le don de captiver et qui leur consacrait ses trop rares heures le loisir, se voyait mis à contribution pour son compte et, sommé de s'exécuter, dressait sur les étriers de Rossinante un épique Don Quichotte.' Moreau-Nélaton, *Daubigny raconté par lui-même*, 89.
81 Léonide Bourges, *Daubigny. Souvenirs et croquis: [estampe] / eauxfortes par Léonide Bourges* (1894), n.p.
82 Maison, *Honoré Daumier* 2:208.
83 Laughton, *Honoré Daumier*, 69.
84 Charles François Daubigny, *Voyage en bateau: Croquis à l'eau forte* (Paris: A. Cadart & F. Chevalier, 1862). Daubigny's series was at the forefront of the revival of etchings led by Cadart and Auguste Delatre (who worked with Daumier before his collaborations with Cadart). They would go on to found the Society of aquafortists soon after publishing Daubigny's collection of fifteen prints. Janine Bailly-Herzberg, 'French etching in the 1860's', *Art Journal* 31, no. 4 (Summer 1972): 382–3. Griselda Pollock discusses this revival, the 'black and white movement' of the 1860s in *Mary Cassatt: Painter of Modern Women* (London: Thames & Hudson, 1998), 24.
85 'Celui-ci, dès qu'il eut pénétré dans ces montagnes, qui lui semblaient des lieux tout-à-fait propres aux aventures qu'il cherchait, s'était senti le cœur bondir de joie. Il repassait en sa

mémoire ces merveilleux événements qui, dans de semblables lieux, âpres et solitaires, étaient arrivés à des chevaliers errants, et ces pensées l'absorbaient et le transportaient au point qu'il oubliait toute autre chose.' Cervantes, *L'ingénieux hidalgo Don Quichotte*, trans. Viardot 1:302.

86 'Quand ils eurent presque achevé le tour de la montagne, ils trouvèrent, au bord d'un ruisseau, le cadavre d'une mule portant encore la selle et la bride, à demi dévoré par les loups et les corbeaux', Cervantes, *L'ingénieux hidalgo Don Quichotte*, trans. Viardot 1:309.

87 Etienne Moreau-Nélaton and Alfred Robaut, *Histoire de Corot et de ses œuvres* (Paris: H. Floury, 1905), 265–6.

88 Laughton, *Honoré Daumier*, 145–6.

89 'Est-il possible qu'enfin j'aie trouvé un lieu qui puisse servir de sépulture cachée à ce corps dont je porte si fort contre mon gré la pesante charge? Oui, je le crois, à moins que la solitude que promettent ces montagnes ne vienne à me manquer aussi. Hélas! combien ces rochers et ces broussailles, qui me laissent confier par mes plaintes mes malheurs au Ciel, me tiendront une plus agréable compagnie que celle d'aucune homme de ce monde, car il n'en est aucun sur la terre de qui l'on puisse attendre un conseil dans les perplexités, un soulagement dans la tristesse, un remède dans les maux!' Cervantes, *L'ingénieux hidalgo Don Quichotte*, trans. Viardot 1:378.

90 Castillo, 'Don Quijote como prototipo de la novela europea moderna', 55.

91 Cervantes, *L'ingénieux hidalgo Don Quichotte*, trans. Viardot 1:139.

Conclusion

The real theatre is journalism.

(Anonymous, *Le Charivari*)

In the final autumn of writing this book in Norman, Oklahoma, Summer Boismier, a Norman High School English teacher, was put on leave for covering a bookshelf with butcher's paper with the label 'Books the state doesn't want you to read' and providing a QR code to the Brooklyn Public Library's Books Unbanned project, where students over the age of thirteen could sign up for digital access to books that had been censored by school districts across the United States. Not satisfied with her mere resignation, a candidate for state superintendent of schools then went after her teaching licence.[1] Boismier's actions in the classroom and punishment by the school leadership were both the result of Oklahoma's HB 1775, a law designed to prohibit teaching about race or gender in the classroom. HB 1775 states that 'Public schools in this state shall be prohibited from engaging in race or sex-based discriminatory acts by utilizing these methods, which result in treating individuals differently on the basis of race or sex or the creation of a hostile environment.'[2] The law's aim is the erasure of education about the diversity of embodied experience and the institutional structures that might impact those experiences.

This kind of law is not isolated to Oklahoma. The American Library Association has reported that from 1 January 2022 to 31 August 2022, there have been 681 documented attempts to ban or restrict 1,651 unique book titles in school libraries in the United States, and those numbers are likely quite low due to unreported bans.[3] In 2021, the most banned book in American public schools was a graphic novel, *Gender queer: A memoir* by Maia Kobabe (2019).[4] An image-heavy graphic memoir, *Gender queer* plays with panel and page structure to explore the author's journey to gender identity and self-understanding.[5] Well into the twenty-first century, images are still considered to be one of the most dangerous methods of speech because, like the theatre, they primarily rely on readers' understanding of the gesture and expression of bodies and faces, which are legible to populations considered particularly impressionable and dangerous to the long-term interests of the state.

Nearly two hundred years before American school districts were pulling Maia Kobabe's *Gender queer* and Art Spiegelman's *Maus* off the shelves, Honoré Daumier contended with legal restrictions on imagery in print, earning a fierce reputation in the political opposition for his six-month imprisonment for insulting the king with a literary analogy and his relentless testing of the boundaries of acceptable speech. Daumier came of age when the new technology of lithography made images widely accessible at a speed that matched the rapid changes to the political landscape, and early on he seized on the mask as a powerful metaphor for his caricatures of politicians. A new government brought to power by a popular movement that was partially driven by the press, the July Monarchy soon broke its early and fundamental promise to never re-establish censorship in France. This deception was shrewdly described by the mask. Philipon hollowed out Louis-Philippe's face into a mask, a visual device Daumier then extended to the parliamentarians upholding the king's government. Masks suggested duplicity and also provided an intermediary layer of denial in the face of laws that policed attacks on the king's reputation and parliamentary authority.

Daumier's sculpture series, *Celebrities of the juste milieu*, explored the same kind of intermediary step. A set of three-dimensional clay portraits that offered a narrative of democratic access to politicians and acted as a substitution referent, they protected the lithographic portraits published in *La Caricature* and *Le Charivari*. The mask-like visages of the *Celebrities of the juste milieu* prints communicate deception and repressed violence. In this series, produced during Daumier's formative professional years, the artist played complex games of subversion with censors, communicating his political opposition by sublimating direct speech with puns, physiognomic suggestions, and under the mask. Exploring the threshold between likeness and exaggeration, these caricatural portraits are shown to mediate between imitation and malformation, theorizing the mechanisms of satire in visual form.

Masks are also theatrical devices, a form of theatrical illusion that suggests the performance of social roles beyond the stage, and Molière was an important source of comic masking practice for Daumier. In the theatre, masks can allow actors to play ancient, familiar types. Molière engaged in this kind of masking, but he also used masks to reference contemporary figures on stage in ways that censors were not able to detect in the text prior to the performance. This kind of visual stunt created a productive tension between the abstraction of a well-known visual motif and the suggestion of speech that was current and critical. This was just the kind of balance Daumier would continue to explore with literary subjects in paint, drawing upon popular familiarity with Molière, La Fontaine, and Cervantes to make allusions to contemporary political issues.

The theatre became a symbol of political life not only because it was a space where disparate factions and classes gathered together, but also because parliament looked like a theatre, a connection Daumier seized upon in 'Lower the curtain. The farce is over'. Tensions were already made literal through the spatial separation of the pit, the loges, and other sections in the theatre, concretizing economic classes, but the theatre also reproduced left/right divisions in ways that mirrored the seating in the Chamber of Deputies. Theatres were sites of real agitation, where an audience could enact political conflict and assert speech through noise (applause, whistles, hisses, a well-timed cough) and also by throwing rocks, vegetables, and engaging in violence. Noise was much harder to censor than new plays, and audiences breaching the performances through shouts and applause collapsed the temporal distance between Molière, La Fontaine, and Cervantes and the nineteenth century, between dramatic action and political disputes.[6]

In another light, the theatre is also a sister art to the illustrated press. Both are popular art forms, which are democratic because they are able to speak to audiences without the (often) classed requirements of literacy. And their power was at times best theorized by the very censoring bodies that sought to regulate them. Caricatures and theatrical performances had much harsher restrictions imposed on them than the written word because of the danger that they were accessible and entertaining to broad swathes of the population, including the lower classes whose organizing potential the government feared.

The association between journalism and the theatre is articulated in a scathing 1849 article in *Le Charivari* that provoked the politician and journalist Louis-Désiré Véron to sue for both defamation and public injury.[7] It described journalism in this way:

> True journalism is also true comedy … from a combination of circumstances, from a product of the years, from a moral situation there is born a type, a character, a personage and the press seizes it, puts it on stage, immediately a crowd comes running to shout bravo at the journalist, pushing them until they have succeeded in formulating their comic type. Molière did not choose Tartuffe; his time imposed it on him. Today when the real theatre is journalism, was it possible that *Le Charivari* passed by your side without seeing you, you whom all the hands, all the voices showed it and cried 'Here is Fontanarose [Véron]!'?[8]

'The real theatre is journalism.' The journal saw itself as an evolution of popular performance, the best modern conduit for comic spectacle and political critique. The reference to *Tartuffe* is notable, too, as a frame for moral speech and contemporary values. In the mind of Daumier's colleagues, Molière was the most insightful mirror of his time. And like Molière's seventeenth-century plays, the nineteenth-century illustrated press would be the best reflection of its moment, producing a spectacle for the demanding crowd and placing the characters that defined the era 'on stage' for public assessment.

This reflection on comedy and journalism became a flashpoint for litigation. Véron was not named but was christened after the character of a charlatan doctor from an 1831 opera by Daniel-François-Esprit Aubert and Eugène Scribe, *Le Philtre*.[9] After Véron took *Le Charivari* to court in December 1849, *Le Charivari*'s editors promised that it would print the trial in a hundred thousand copies and have it illustrated by Daumier.[10] Indeed, Daumier would make a series of lithographs of Véron in *Le Charivari* in late 1849 and early 1850.

Daumier, who had learned stagecraft at the feet of his father, saw the theatre both as a metaphor for political performance and also subversive speech. The anonymous writer of the article 'Au seigneur Fontanarose' looked to the theatre for their title, using the stage as a screen to suggest an identity for a figure targeted in a political attack, a mask that referenced a character from the past even as it clued the reader into the political figure it was meant to represent. This construction explicitly named Molière and also mimicked the operations of the mask. Daumier's milieu used literature and the theatre as conduits for political speech, sharing a set of references with the audience of *Le Charivari* and testing the line of tolerance for press laws and those public figures whose identities were only thinly veiled.

Caricature shared the theatre's commitment to free, popular expression, a connection that helped drive Daumier's interest in the seventeenth-century literature of La Fontaine, Molière, and Cervantes, who were frequent subjects of theatrical revivals and reinterpretations and who had reputations that emphasized their own brave negotiations with censorship and state power. In 1820s France, Molière's plays became sites of impassioned public demonstrations against censorship and government overreach, and noise became an important thread through Daumier's subversive reinterpretation of the playwright. Noise may come from bloviating political and theatrical actors or it could be displaced onto audiences making vocalizations that were a discomfiting popular regulatory mechanism to those in power.

Power was the shared preoccupation of both Daumier and La Fontaine, the seventeenth-century author of *Fables* whose anti-authoritarian morals were obvious enough to keep him out of the highest echelons of academic favour for quite a long time, despite his broad popularity. Daumier's *The miller, his son, and the ass* of 1849 activated noise as a weapon of mockery and community self-management. Like the shouting women in Daumier's painting, the jests and clamour of the press were a powerful and healthy way to keep power in check.

Power was a theme that extended to subversive revivals of *Don Quixote* in the nineteenth century. Censors were sensitive to language in plays based on *Don Quixote* that might make connections to powerful figures (emperors and priests, for example), and the novel, like La Fontaine's *Fables*, explored ideas of leadership and power through humour.

In contrast to his representations of La Fontaine or Molière's plays, Daumier's paintings of *Don Quixote* were much darker and less tethered to the direct illustration of a narrative moment. In Daumier's hand we see a painful pessimism towards the end of a career witnessing numerous reversals to promised liberalizations to free speech in the press. The weight of those pressures condensed into abstraction and obfuscation, one end to a trajectory that began with the playful mask and ended with a confrontation between literary contemplation and the material challenge of making the fragile matter of paint signify when on the run.

Today, the battle lines of popular expression are still being determined in school board meetings in Oklahoma, in Pushkin Square, and elsewhere. Governments are so sensitive to critical speech that in September 2022 a UK barrister was detained and threatened with arrest for holding a blank piece of paper, for fear he would use it to protest the new king.[11] New COVID-19 restrictions in China are spurring a 'blank page revolution', where protesters are holding up blank sheets of paper to express anger over new policies while trying to evade crackdowns on dissent.[12] QR codes to the Brooklyn library have sprung up in yard signs in Norman, Oklahoma. Citizens continue to navigate restrictions with creative evasion, provoking state repression with the dangerous potentiality of a blank page.

In moments where political speech was restricted in the illustrated press in Daumier's lifetime, his investigation into the contours of satire and politics was not entirely suppressed but was instead embedded in his investigation of 'great men', first as parody and then more seriously through La Fontaine, Molière, and Cervantes, literary figures who were framed by nineteenth-century accounts as having manoeuvred through imprisonment, censorship, and official disfavour. Daumier brought painting into conversation with popular art forms beyond caricature – including fables and the performing arts – illuminating the rich relationships between image and text and creative avenues for political speech. His representations of theatrical and literary satire challenged the limits of political and artistic expression at moments when they faced redefinition by the repressive authority of government. Daumier was one of the sharpest theorists and canniest actors exploring the boundaries of speech, subversive revival, and creative disobedience – questions that remain open and urgent today.

Notes

1 Sean Murphy, 'Banned book lesson thrusts Oklahoma teacher into campaign', *AP News* (6 November 2022), https://apnews.com/article/2022-midterm-elections-entertainment-education-social-media-oklahoma-2a0efaa9fbd485df4e8657e2b95b901a (accessed 27 December 2022).

2 H.B. 1775, 'Prohibition of Race and Sex Discrimination', 2021 Reg. Sess. (Okla. 2021) (enacted as Okla Stat. tit.70, § 24–157 (2022)).

3 'American Library Association Releases Preliminary Data on 2022 Book Bans', American Library Association, 16 September 2022, www.ala.org/news/press-releases/2022/09/ala-releases-preliminary-data-2022-book-bans (accessed 27 December 2022).

4 'Top 10 Most Challenged Books Lists', American Library Association, 26 March 2013, www.ala.org/advocacy/bbooks/frequentlychallengedbooks/top10 (accessed 27 December 2022).

5 Kylee Carcione, 'Embodiment and identity construction: Liminal spaces in queer literature' (PhD diss., Indiana University of Pennsylvania, 2022), 23–7.

6 Alain Corbin, 'L'Agitation dans les thétres de province sous la Restauration', in *Popular Traditions and Learned Culture in France from the Sixteenth to the Twentieth Century*, ed. Marc Bertrand (Saratoga, CA: AMNA Libri, 1985), 110.

7 Véron sued in the sixth chamber of the correctional police. This suit was described on the front page of *Le Constitutionnel*, which Véron owned and directed, citing a 12 December article in *Le Charivari* specifically. *Le Constitutionnel* (23 December 1849): 1.

8 'Le vrai journalisme est comme la véritable comédie, il s'étoile dans les demi-teintes, dans les demi-caractères, dans les demi-ridicules. Quel métier que d'être la silhouette d'une silhouette, le couplet d'un couplet, l'ombre de Marivaux et de M. Scribe. Retire-toi de moi, mauvais plaisant, bel esprit, dit alors le public au journal. Mais que du concours des circonstances, du produit des années, d'une situation morale, il naisse un type, un caractère, un personnage et que la presse s'en empare, le mette en scène, aussitôt la foule d'accourir, de crier bravo au journaliste, de la pousser jusqu'à ce qu'il ait réussi à formuler son type comique. Molière n'a pas choisi Tartuffe; son époque le lui a imposé. Aujourd'hui que le vrai théâtre est dans le journalisme, était-il possible que le *Charivari* passât à votre côté sans vous voir, vous que toutes les mains, que toutes les voix lui désignaient en criant: "Voilà Fontanarose!"?' 'Au seigneur Fontanarose', *Le Charivari* (12 December 1849): 1.

9 Eugène Scribe and Daniel-François-Esprit Auber, *Le Philtre* (1831). Performance noted in: *Tables de la bibliographie de la France journal général de l'imprimerie et de la librairie*, 20, no. 27 (1831), 392n79.

10 'Encore au seigneur Fontanarose', *Le Charivari* (17 December 1849): 1.

11 Thomas Kingsley, 'UK compared to Russia after barrister threatened with arrest over blank piece of paper', *Independent* (14 September 2022), www.independent.co.uk/news/uk/home-news/anti-monarchy-protest-russia-police-b2166183.html (accessed 12 December 2022).

12 Billy Perrigo, 'Why a blank sheet of paper became a protest symbol in China', *Time* (1 December 2022), https://time.com/6238050/china-protests-censorship-urumqi-a4/ (accessed 12 December 2022).

Bibliography

Adhémar, Jean. *Honoré Daumier*. Paris: Tisné, 1954.

Alexander, Robert. *Rewriting the French Revolutionary Tradition: Liberal Opposition and the Fall of the Bourbon Monarchy*. New York: Cambridge University Press, 2003.

Alexandre, Arsène. *H. Daumier. L'Homme et l'œuvre*. Paris: H. Laurent, 1888.

Alhoy, Maurice Louis Huart and Charles Philipon. *Les cent et un Robert-Macaire, composés et dessinés par M. H. Daumier sur les idées et les légendes de M. Ch. Philippon; réduits et lithographiés par MM. ***; texte par MM. Maurice Alhoy et Louis Huart*. Paris: Chez Aubert et Cie, 1839.

Andrews, Naomi J. 'Selective empathy: Workers, colonial subjects, and the affective politics of French Romantic socialism'. *French Politics, Culture & Society* 36 (2018): 1–25.

Archives parlementaires de 1787 à 1860: recueil complet des débats législatifs & politiques des chambres françaises imprimé par ordre du Sénat et de la Chambre des Députés sous la direction de J. Mavidal et al., 2nd ser. Vol. 98 of 127. Paris: P. Dupont, 1898.

Armingeat, Jacqueline. *Lib Women: Bluestockings and Socialist Women*, translated by Howard Brabyn. Paris: L. Amiel, 1974.

Armstrong, Carol M. *Odd Man Out: Readings of the Work and Reputation of Edgar Degas*. Chicago: University of Chicago Press, 1991.

Ashbee, H. S. *An Iconography of Don Quixote: 1605–1895*. Aberdeen: The University Press, 1895.

Auerbach, Erich. *Mimesis: The Representation of Reality in Western Literature*, translated by Willard Trask. Garden City, NY: Doubleday Anchor Books, 1957.

Babelon, Jean. *Cervantes: Notice sur sa vie et son œuvre*. Paris: Bibliothèque nationale, 1947.

Bakhtin, Mikhail. *Rabelais and His World*, translated by Hélène Iswolsky. Bloomington: Indiana University Press, 1965.

Banville, Théodore de. *Petites études. Mes souvenir: Victor Hugo, Henri Heine, Théophile Gautier, Honoré de Balzac, Honoré Daumier, Alfred de Vigny ... etc.* Paris: G. Charpentier, 1882.

Barbier, Antoine-Alexandre. *Notice des principales éditions des Fables et des œuvres de Jean de La Fontaine*. Paris: Rignoux, n.d.

Barthes, Roland. *Le degré zero de l'ecriture*. Paris: Seuil, 1953.

Baudelaire, Charles. 'Quelques caracturistes français'. In *Curiosités esthétiques*. Paris: Michael Levy Brothers, 1868.

Beall, Karen F. 'The interdependence of printer and printmaker in early 19th-century lithography'. *Art Journal* 39, no. 3 (1980): 195–201.

Bechtel, Edwin de T. *Freedom of the Press and L'Association Mensuelle: Philipon Versus Louis-Philippe.* New York: The Grolier Club, 1952.

Bell, David Avrom. *The Cult of the Nation in France: Inventing Nationalism, 1680–1800.* Cambridge, MA: Harvard University Press, 2001.

Bénézit, Emmanuel. *Dictionnaire critique et documentaire des peintres, sculpteurs, dessinateurs et graveurs: de tous le temps ...*, Volume 4. Paris: Gründ, 1976.

Bergeron, Louis and François Théodore Claudon. *Fables démocratiques par Emile Pagès.* Paris: Aux bureaux du Charivari, 1839.

Bergman-Carton, Janis. 'Conduct unbecoming: Daumier and les bas-bleus'. In *Reclaiming Female Agency: Feminist Art History After Postmodernism*, edited by Norma Broude and Mary D. Garrard, 203–16. Berkeley, CA: University of California Press, 2005.

Blackburn, George M. 'Paris newspapers and the American Civil War'. *Illinois Historical Journal* 84, no. 3 (1991): 177–93.

Boime, Albert. *Art in the Age of Counterrevolution, 1815–1848.* Chicago: University of Chicago Press, 2004.

Boime, Albert. 'The Second Republic's contest for the figure of the Republic'. *The Art Bulletin* 53, no. 1 (March 1971): 68–83.

Bonnet, Jean-Claude. *Naissance du panthéon: Essai sur le culte des grandes hommes.* Paris: Fayard, 1998.

Borowitz, Helen O. 'Painted smiles: Sad clowns in French art and literature'. *The Bulletin of the Cleveland Museum of Art* 71, no. 1 (January 1984): 23–35.

Bourges, Léonide. *Daubigny. Souvenirs et croquis: [estampe] / eauxfortes par Léonide Bourges.* 1894.

Boutang, Pierre. *La Fontaine politique.* Paris: J.-E. Hallier/Albin Michel, 1981.

Bowyer, Emerson and Frick Collection. *David d'Angers: Making the Modern Monument.* New York: Frick Collection, 2013.

Bray, René. *Les Fables de La Fontaine.* Paris: Edgar Malgère, 1929.

Brown, Roy Howard. 'The formation of Delacroix's hero between 1822 and 1831'. *The Art Bulletin* 66, no. 2 (June 1984): 237–54.

Buraud, Georges. *Les Masques.* Paris: Encre Marine, 2015.

Butler, Ruth, Suzanne G. Lindsay, and Alison Luchs, eds. *European Sculpture of the Nineteenth Century.* Washington: National Gallery of Art; Oxford University Press, 2000.

Cain, Julien. *Honoré Daumier: Lawyers and Justice.* Boston: Boston Book and Art, 1971.

Calder, Andrew. *Molière: The Theory and Practice of Comedy.* London: The Athlone Press, 1993.

Calinescu, Matei. *Rereading.* New Haven: Yale University Press, 1993.

Cervantes Saavedra, Miguel de. *L'ingénieux hidalgo Don Quichotte de la Manche.* Vol. 1, translated and edited by Louis Viardot. Paris: J.- J. Dubochet, 1836–37.

Cervantes Saavedra, Miguel de. *L'ingénieux hidalgo Don Quichotte de la Manche.* Vol. 1, translated by Louis Viardot. Paris: Librairie de L. Hachette et cie, 1863.

Champfleury [Jules-François-Félix Husson]. *Exposition des peintures et dessins de H. Daumier.* Paris: Gauthier-Villars, 1878.

Champfleury. *Histoire de la caricature moderne*, 3rd ed. Paris: E. Dentu, 1885.

Champfleury. *Œuvres posthumes. Salons 1846–1851.* Paris, 1894.

Champier, Victor. *L'Année artistique. Année 1878(–1882).* Volume 1. Paris: A. Quantin, 1879.

Chartier, Roger, Henri-Jean Martin, and Jean-Pierre Vivet. *Histoire de l'édition française. Du Romantisme à la Belle Époque.* Vol. 3. Paris: Promodis, 1985.

Chasles, Émile. *Michel de Cervantes: sa vie, son temps, son œuvre politique et littéraire.* Paris: Didier, 1866.

Chaudonneret, Marie-Claude. *La figure de la République.* Paris: Éditions de la Réunion des musées nationaux, 1987.

Chazal, Gilles, Agathe Sanjuan, and Musée du Petit Palais, eds. *La Comédie-Française s'expose au Petit Palais [Paris 13.10.2011 – 15.01.2012]*, exh. cat. Paris: Paris-Musées [u.a.], 2011.

Cherpin, Jean. *Daumier et le théatre*. Aix-en-Provence: Edisud, 1978.

Childs, Elizabeth C. 'Big trouble: Daumier, Gargantua, and the censorship of political caricature'. *Art Journal* 51, no. 1 (1992): 26–37.

Cholakian, Rouben. 'Arsène Houssaye and the "Comédie-Française"'. *Romance Notes* 5, no. 2 (1964): 143–50.

Clark, T. J. *The Absolute Bourgeois: Art and Politics in France 1848–1851*. London: Thames & Hudson, 1973.

Clements, Candace. 'Noble liberality and speculative industry in early eighteenth-century Paris: Charles Coypel'. *Eighteenth-Century Studies* 29, no. 2 (1995): 213–18.

Close, Anthony. *The Romantic Approach to 'Don Quixote': A Critical History of the Romantic Tradition in 'Quixote' Criticism*. New York: Cambridge University Press, 1977.

Collingham, H. A. C. and R. S. Alexander. *The July Monarchy: A Political History of France 1830–1848*. New York: Longman, 1988.

Collins, Irene. *The Government and the Newspaper Press in France 1814–1881*. London: Oxford University Press, 1959.

Corbin, Alain. 'L'Agitation dans les théâtres de province sous la Restauration'. In *Popular Traditions and Learned Culture in France from the Sixteenth to the Twentieth Century*, edited by Marc Bertrand, 119–43. Saratoga, CA: AMNA Libri, 1985.

Couton, Georges. *La politique de La Fontaine*. Paris: Société d'édition 'les Belles lettres', 1959.

Cuno, James Bash. 'Charles Philipon and La Maison Aubert: The business, politics, and public of caricature in Paris, 1820–1840'. PhD diss., Harvard University, 1985.

Cuno, James. 'Obscene humor in French revolutionary caricature'. In *Representing the French Revolution: Literature, Historiography, and Art*, edited by James A. W. Heffernan, 192–212. Hanover, NH: University Press of New England, 1992.

Dantan, Jean-Pierre, Philippe Sorel, Musée Carnavalet, and Maison de Balzac. *Dantan Jeune: Caricatures et portraits de la société romantique: Maison de Balzac*. Paris: Direction des affaires culturelles de la Ville de Paris: Paris-Musées, 1989.

Daubigny, Charles François. *Voyage en bateau: Croquis à l'eau forte*. Paris: A. Cadart & F. Chevalier, 1862.

Daumier to Bocage (Pierre-Martinien Bocage-Tousez). April 1850. Private collection. Reproduced by The Daumier Register at www.daumier.org/biography/signatures-letters/ (accessed 26 January 2024).

Daumier, Honoré. *Hunting and Fishing: Twenty-Four Lithographs*. New York: Pantheon Books, 1945.

Daumier, Honoré and Lessing J. Rosenwald Collection (Library of Congress). *Law and Justice: Twenty-Four Lithographs*. New York: Pantheon Books, c. 1944.

Daumier, Honoré and Jacqueline Armingeat. *Lib Women: Bluestockings and Socialist Women*. Paris: L. Amiel, 1974.

Daumier, Honoré, J. Douglas Campbell, Usher Caplan, National Gallery of Canada, Galeries nationales du Grand Palais (France), and Phillips Collection. *Daumier: 1808–1879: National Gallery of Canada, Ottawa, 11 June–6 September 1999; Galeries nationales du Grand Palais, Paris, 5 October 1999–3 January 2000; Phillips Collection, Washington, 19 February–14 May* 2000, exh. cat. Ottowa: Musée des Beaux-Arts du Canada, Ottawa, 1999.

Delpech, François Séraphin, ed. *Iconographie Des Contemporains Depuis 1789 Jusqu'à 1829*. Paris: Delpech, 1832.

Delporte, Christian. '"Anastasie": L'imaginaire de la censure dans le dessin satirique (XIXe-XXe siècles)'. In *La censure en France à l'ère démocratique, 1848– …*, edited by Pascal Ory. Brussels: Éditions Complexe, 1997.

Desmares, Eugène. *Les Métamorphoses du jour, ou La Fontaine en 1831*. Paris: Delaunay, 1831.

Dillon, Emma. *The Sense of Sound: Musical Meaning in France, 1260–1330*. Oxford: Oxford University Press, 2012.

Djordjevic, Alex et al. 'New results for DR6'. Daumier Register. www.daumier.org/fileadmin/daumier_reference/DR6_E.htm (accessed 26 January 2024).

Drost, Wolfgang. *Jean de La Fontaine dans l'univers des arts*. Heidelberg: Carl Winter Universitätsverlag, 1991.

Duchartre, Pierre Louis. *The Italian Comedy: The Improvisation, Scenarios, Lives, Attributes, Portraits, and Masks of the Illustrious Characters of the Commedia dell'Arte*, translated by Randolph T. Weaver. New York: Dover Publications, 1966.

Duval, Edwin M. 'Chapter 4: Rabelais and French Renaissance satire'. In *A Companion to Satire*, edited by Ruben Quintero, 70–85. Malden, MA: Blackwell Publishing, 2007.

Duvert, Félix Auguste, Etienne-Vincent Arago, and Joseph Xavier Boniface. *Cagotisme et liberté, ou les Deux semestres, revue de l'année 1830*. Paris: J.-N. Barba, 1830.

E.-F. *Translations Into Verse From Comedies of Molière and Casimir Delavigne, Preceded by a Cursory View of French Dramatic Literature, to Which Are Added Original Poems, Imitations, School Exercises, and the Magic Lantern, a Satire*. Paris: A. and W. Galignani, 1829.

Erre, Fabrice. 'The "King-Jesuit" and the "King-Pear": The proliferation of seditious "mischief" against Charles X and Louis-Philippe (1826–1835)'. *Romanticism* 150, no. 4 (2010): 109–27.

Escholier, Raymond. *Daumier*. Paris: L. Michaud, 1913.

Explication des ouvrages de peinture, de sculpture, dessin, gravure etc. faisant partie de l'exposition de la Société des amis des arts de Lyon, en 1836. Lyon: Société des amis des arts de Lyon, 1836.

Explication des ouvrages de peinture, sculpture, architecture, gravure et lithographie des artistes vivants, exposés au Palais de Tuileries le 15 juin 1849. Paris: Vinchon, 1849.

Exposition des peintures et dessins de H. Daumier. Paris: Gauthier-Villars, 1878.

Fables choisies, mises en vers par M. de La Fontaine, avec la Vie d'Ésope, nouvelle édition, augmentée de petites notes pour en faciliter l'intelligence. Paris: David, 1715.

Fondation Maeght. *La sculpture des peintres: Honoré Daumier, Edgar Degas, Paul Gauguin, Pierre-Auguste Renoir … 2 juillet–19 octobre 1997*. Saint-Paul: Fondation Maeght, 1997.

Forestier, Georges. '"Portraits" de Molière'. In *Molière [Exposition organisée par la Bibliothèque nationale de France, Comédie-Française, Opéra national de Paris du 27 septembre 2022 au 15 janvier 2023]*, edited by Laurence Decobert, Joël Huthwohl, and Agathe Sanjuan, 26–43. Paris: Bibliothèque nationale de France, 2022.

Fournel, Victor. *Les artistes français contemporains*. Tours: Alfred Mame et Fils, 1884.

Fournier, Édouard. *Études sur la vie et les œuvres de Molière*. Paris: Laplace, Sanchez, et Cie, 1885.

Fried, Michael. *Manet's Modernism: Or, The Face of Painting in the 1860s*. Chicago: University of Chicago Press, 1998.

Fry, Roger. *Cézanne: A Study of His Development*. New York: Noonday Press, 1960.

Gebhart, Emile. *Rabelais, la renaissance et la réforme*. France: Hachette, 1877.

Geffroy, Gustave. 'Daumier sculpteur'. *Les Arts et les artistes* 1, no. 3 (June 1905): 101–8.

Ginguené, Pierre-Louis. *De l'autorité de Rabelais dans la révolution présente et dans la constitution civile du clergé*. Paris: Librairie des bibliophiles, 1879.

Ginisty, Paul. *Bocage*. Paris: Librairie Félix Alcan, 1926.

Gobin, Maurice. *Daumier sculpteur 1808–1879: avec un catalogue raisonné et illustré de l'œuvre sculpté*. Geneva: Pierre Cailler, 1952.

Goldsby, Robert W. *Molière on Stage: What's So Funny?* New York: Anthem Press, 2012.

Goldstein, Robert Justin. *Censorship of Political Caricature in Nineteenth-Century France*. Kent, OH: Kent State University Press, 1989.

Goldstein, Robert Justin. 'Fighting French censorship, 1815–1881'. *The French Review* 71, no. 5 (1998): 785–96.

Goldstein, Robert Justin. 'The debate over censorship of caricature in nineteenth-century France'. *Art Journal* 48, no. 1 (1989): 9–15.

Goldstein, Robert Justin, ed. *The Frightful Stage: Political Censorship of the Theater in Nineteenth-Century Europe*. New York: Berghahn Books, 2009.

Gombrich, E. H. *Art and Illusion: A Study in the Psychology of Pictorial Representation: The A. W. Mellon Lectures in the Fine Arts*. Washington: The National Gallery of Art, 1956.

Grunwald Center for the Graphic Arts, University of California Los Angeles, Bibliothèque nationale (France). *French Caricature and the French Revolution, 1789–1799*. Los Angeles: Grunwald Center for the Graphic Arts Wight Art Gallery, University of California: Distributed by the University of Chicago Press, 1988.

Guilhamet, Leon. *Satire and the Transformation of Genre*. Philadelphia: University of Pennsylvania Press, 1987.

Guillon, M. N. S. *La Fontaine et tous les fabulistes, ou La Fontaine comparé avec ses modèles et ses imitateurs, nouvelle édition avec des observations critiques, grammaticales, littéraires, et des notes d'histoire naturelle*. Paris: Veuve Nyon, 1803.

Hagedorn, Hans Christian, ed. *Don Quijote por tierras extranjeras: Estudios sobre la recepción de la novela cervantina*. Cuenca: Ediciones de la Universidad de Castilla-La Mancha, 2007.

Hallays-Dabot, Victor. *Histoire de la censure théâtrale en France*. Paris: E. Dentu, 1862.

Halm, Ben B. *Theatre and Ideology*. Selinsgrove, PA: Susquehanna University Press, 1995.

Harper, Paula. *Daumier's Clowns, Les Saltimbanques, et Les Parades: New Biographical and Political Functions for a Nineteenth Century Myth, Outstanding Dissertations in the Fine Arts*. New York: Garland, 1981.

Hartau, Johannes. *Don Quijote in der Kunst*. Berlin: Gebr. Mann, 1987.

Hemmings, F. W. J. *Theatre and State in France, 1760–1905*. New York: Cambridge University Press, 1994.

Henriet, Frédéric. 'Les paysagistes contemporains: Daubigny'. *Gazette des beaux-arts* 9, no. 2 (1 January 1874): 255–70.

Hofmann, Werner and Gaston Deferre. *Daumier et ses amis républicains: Musée Cantini 1 June–31 August 1979*, exh. cat. Marseille: Musée Cantini, 1979.

Honour, Hugh, David Bindman, and Henry Louis Gates. *The Image of the Black in Western* Art. Vol. 4, Part 1. Cambridge, MA: Belknap, 2012.

Ives, Colta Feller, Margret Stuffmann, Martin Sonnabend, Klaus Herding, and Judith Wechsler. *Daumier Drawings*. New York: Metropolitan Museum of Art, 1992.

Izambard, Henry. *La Presse parisienne: Statistique bibliographique et alphabétique de tous les journaux, revues et canards périodiques nés, morts, ressuscités ou métamorphosés à Paris depuis la 22 février 1848 jusqu'à l'Empire ... Précédé des lois actuelles qui régissent la presse, et suivi de la liste exacte de tous les journaux des départements*. Paris: P.-H. Krabbe, 1853.

James, Henry. *Daumier, Caricaturist*. London: Rodale Press, 1954.

James, Henry. *Daumier, Caricaturist*. Emmaus, PA: Rodale Press, 1954.

Johnson, James H. *Listening in Paris: A Cultural History*, Nachdr., Studies on the History of Society and Culture 21. Berkeley, CA: University of California Press, 2008.

Joulie, Françoise. 'Natoire and Boucher: Two studies for a Don Quixote tapestry'. *The Metropolitan Museum Journal* 39 (2004): 153–9.

Kaenel, Philippe. '"Don Quichotte", Daumier et la légende de l'artiste'. *Artibus et Historiae* 23, no. 46 (2002): 163–77.

Kelly, Mary Louise, Ashish Valentine, and Patrick Jarenwattananon. 'An anti-war protester in Moscow says the risk of arrest is worth it'. All Things Considered. NPR. www.npr.org/2022/03/04/1084627201/one-russian-anti-war-protester-on-why-shes-risking-arrest-to-speak-out (accessed 26 January 2024).

Kenny, Elise and John Merriman. *The Pear: French Graphic Arts and the Golden Age of Caricature*, exh. cat. South Hadley, MA: Mount Holyoke Art Museum, 1991.

Kerr, David S. *Caricature and French Political Culture 1830–1848: Charles Philipon and the Illustrated Press*. Oxford: Clarendon Press, 2000.

Knight, Charles A. *The Literature of Satire*. Cambridge: Cambridge University Press, 2004.

Krakovitch, Odile. *Censure des répertoires des grands théâtres parisiens (1835–1906). Inventaire des manuscrits des pièces F/18/669 à F/18/1016 et des procès-verbaux F/21/966 à F/21/995* [Finding aid]. Paris: Centre historique des Archives nationales, 2003.

Krakovitch, Odile. *Les pièces de théâtre soumises à la censure (1800–1830)*. Paris: Archives nationales: diffusé par la documentation française, 1982.

Krakovitch, Odile. 'Robert Macaire ou la grande peur des censeurs'. *Europe: Revue litteraire mensuelle* 65 (1987): 49–60.

Kroen, Sheryl. *Politics and Theater: The Crisis of Legitimacy in Restoration France, 1815–1830*. Berkeley, CA: University of California Press, 2000.

La Fontaine, Jean de. *Fables*, illustrated by J. J. Grandville. Paris: H. Fornier, 1838.

La Fontaine, Jean de. *Fables (Nouvelle éd. précédée d'une notice biographique et littéraire, accompagné de notes)*. Paris: Hachette, 1843.

La Fontaine, Jean de. *The Fables of La Fontaine*, translated by Elizur Wright. London: Bell, 1892.

La Fontaine Jean de. *La Fontaine's Fables*, translated by Walter Thornbury. New York: Cassell, Petter, and Galpin, 1886.

La Fontaine, Jean de. *La Morale en action des fables de La Fontaine: collection de vignettes dessinées par Henry Monnier et gravées par Thompson ...*, Vols. 1–2. Paris: Urbain Canel, 1828.

La Fontaine, Jean de. *La Morale en action des fables de La Fontaine: collection de vignettes dessinées par Henry Monnier et gravées par Thompson ...*, Vols. 3–4. Paris: Perrotin, 1830.

Lamennais, Félicité Robert de. *De l'esclavage moderne*. Paris: Pagnerre, 1839.

Larkin, Oliver W. *Daumier, Man of His Time*. New York: McGraw-Hill, 1966.

Laughton, Bruce. *The Drawings of Daumier and Millet*. New Haven: Yale University Press, 1991.

Laughton, Bruce. *Honoré Daumier*. New Haven: Yale University Press, 1996.

Laughton, Bruce. 'Some Daumier drawings for lithographs'. *Master Drawings* 22, no. 1 (1984): 56–133.

Lavigne, A. Germond de. *Les Deux Don Quichotte: Étude critique sur l'œuvre de Fernandès Avellaneda faisant suite à la 1re partie du Don Quichotte de Cervantès*. Paris: Didier, 1852.

Lemann, Bernard. 'Daumier and the Republic'. *Gazette des Beaux-Arts* 27 (February 1945): 104–20.

Lintilhac, Eugène. *Histoire générale du théâtre en France. La comédie: de la Révolution au Second Empire*. Vol. 5 of 5. Paris: E. Flammarion, [1904–10].

Lods, Armand. *André Gill: sa vie: bibliographie de ses œuvres*. Paris: L. Vanier, 1887.

Loise, Ferdinand. *Histoire de la poésie espagnole*. Belgium: M. Hayez, Imprimeur de l'Académie Royale, 1868.

Lyon, I. 'Don Quichotte au théâtre et Don Quichotte a la vitrine'. *Le Journal Illustré* 6, no. 275 (16 May 1869): 159–60.

Mainardi, Patricia. *Another World: Nineteenth-Century Illustrated Print Culture*. New Haven: Yale University Press, 2017.

Maison, K. E. *Honoré Daumier: Catalogue Raisoneé of the Paintings, Watercolors, and Drawings*. Vols. 1 and 2. Greenwich, CT: New York Graphic Society, 1968.

Mandel, Gabriele. 'Catalogue des œuvres'. In *Tout l'œuvre peint de Daumier*. Paris: Flammarion, 1972.

Marx, Karl. *The Class Struggles in France (1848–50)*, edited by C. P. (Clemens Palme) Dutt. London: Martin Lawrence, 1895.

McCallam, David. 'Waxing revolutionary: Reflections on a raid on a waxworks at the outbreak of the French Revolution'. *French History* 15, no. 2 (2002): 153–73.

McCauley, Anne. *A. A. E. Disderi and the Carte de Visite Portrait Photograph*. New Haven: Yale University Press, 1985.

McCormick, John. *Popular Theatres of Nineteenth Century France*. New York: Routledge, 1993.

Mellerio, A. & Louis de Nussac. 'La lithographie en France, Charles de Lasteyrie'. *Gazette des Beaux-Arts* 14 (1935): 106–19.

Melot, Michel and Neil McWilliam. 'Daumier and art history: Aesthetic judgement/political judgement'. *Oxford Art Journal* 11, no. 1 (1988): 3–24.

Mérimée, Prosper. *Portraits historiques et litteraires*. Paris: Calmann Levy, 1894.

Mills, Jerry Leath. 'Equine gothic: The dead mule as generic signifier in southern literature of the twentieth century'. *The Southern Literary Journal* 29, no. 1 (1996): 2–17.

Ministère de l'Intérieur. *Censure des répertoires des 'petits' théâtres parisiens, index des pièces (1802–1906) [Finding aid]*. Paris: Archives nationales, 2003.

Mirencourt, Eugène de. *Bocage*. Paris: Gustave Havard, 1856.

Moland, Louis. 'La Fontaine: Sa vie et ses ouvrages'. In *Œuvres complètes de La Fontaine*. Vol. 7. Paris: Garnier frères, 1872–76.

Moland, Louis. *Molière et la comédie italienne*. Paris: Didier, 1867.

Mongez, M. *Fables de La Fontaine avec notes grammaticales, mythologiques, etc.* Paris: Agasse, 1797.

Moreau-Nélaton, Étienne. *Daubigny raconté par lui-même*. Paris: Henri Laurens, 1925.

Moreau-Nélaton, Étienne and Alfred Robaut. *Histoire de Corot et de ses œuvres*. Paris: H. Floury, 1905.

Moréri, Louis. *Le Grand dictionnaire historique, ou Le Mélange curieux de l'histoire sacrée et profane 2e édition*. Lyon: J. Gyrin et B. Rivière, 1683.

Nerval, Gérard de. *The Salt Smugglers: History of the Abbé de Bucquoy*, translated by Richard Sieburth. Brooklyn, NY: Archipelago Books, 2009.

O'Brien, Laura. *The Republican Line: Caricature and the French Republican Identity*. Manchester: Manchester University Press, 2015.

Olmstead, William. *The Censorship Effect: Baudelaire, Flaubert, and the Formation of French Modernism*. New York: Oxford University Press, 2016.

Osiakovski, Stanislav. 'History of Robert Macaire and Daumier's place in it'. *The Burlington Magazine* 100, no. 668 (1958): 388–93.

Palisse, Fabien. 'Histoire des théâtres de marionnettes en France, en Europe et dans le monde. Vol. 1: localisation, architecture et scénographie'. Master's thesis, École d'Architecture de Paris-Belleville, 1993.

Papet, Édouard. 'Les Célébritiés du Juste Milieu (1832–1835)'. *Daumier: Les Célébrities du Juste Milieu (1832–1835): Étude et restauration*, 12–29. Paris: Réunion des musées nationaux, 2005.

Passeron, Roger. *Daumier*. New York: Rizzoli, 1979.

Petrey, Sandra. 'Pears in history'. *Representations* 35 (Summer 1991): 52–71.

Philipon, Charles. 'L'abdication de Daumier 1er'. *Le Journal amusant: journal illustré, journal d'images, journal comique, critique, satirique, etc.*, no. 297 (7 September 1861): 7.

Philipon, Charles. *Les Poires faites à la cour d'assises de Parie [sic] par le directeur de* la Caricature *vendues pour payer les 6,000 francs d'amende du journal*. Paris: Auffray, 1833.

Pichois, Claude. 'Les cabinets de lecture à Paris, durant la première moitié du XIX siècle'. *Annales. Economies, sociétés, civilisations* 3 (1959): 521–34.

Pinkney, David H. 'Conflict without compromise'. In *French Revolution of 1830*, 3–43. Princeton, NJ: Princeton University Press, 1972.

Pole, J. R. 'Representative institutions 1776–1876: Ideology, estates and interests'. *Parliaments, Estates and Representation* 27, no. 1 (2007): 19–35.

Pollock, Griselda. *Mary Cassatt: Painter of Modern Women*. London: Thames & Hudson, 1998.

Powell, Kirsten. *Fables in Frames: La Fontaine and Visual Culture in Nineteenth Century France*. New York: Peter Lang, 1997.

Powell, Kirsten. 'The press repressed: Themes of suppression of censorship of the press in caricatures of La Fontaine's fables'. In *Proceedings of the Western Society for French History*. Vol. 17, 347–59. Auburn, AL: Auburn University, 1990.

Powell, Kirsten, Elizabeth C. Childs, Christian A. Johnson Memorial Gallery, and Neuberger Museum. *Femmes d'esprit: Women in Daumier's Caricature*. Middlebury, VT: C. A. Johnson Memorial Gallery, Middlebury College, 1990.

Prest, Julia. *Controversies in French Drama: Molière's* Tartuffe *and the Struggle for Influence*. New York: Palgrave Macmillan, 2014.

Provost, Louis. *Honoré Daumier: A Thematic Guide to the Œuvre*, edited by Elizabeth C. Childs. New York: Garland, 1989.

Quideau, Florence. 'Origins of modernism in French Romantic sculpture: David d'Angers, Dantan-Jeune, Daumier and Préault'. PhD diss., Rutgers, The State University of New Jersey, 2011.

Rabelais, François and Pierre-Louis Ginguené. *Œuvres de Rabelais. Edition variorum augmentée de pièces inédites … avec des remarques de … Ginguené*. Paris: Dalibon, 1823.

Régent, Frédéric. *La France et ses esclaves: de la colonisation aux abolitions, 1620–1848*. Paris: Pluriel, 2012.

Requier, Luc. Secrétaire de documentation. Archives nationales, Pierrefitte-sur-Seine. Email message to author. 2 September 2022.

Revue universelle des arts. Vol. 4. Paris: Paul Lacroix, 1856.

Rey, Alain ed. *Le Robert. Dictionnaire historique de la langue française*. Vol. 1. Paris: Dictionnaires Le Robert, 1998.

Robert, Adolphe, Edgar Bourloton, and Gaston Cougny. *Dictionnaire des parlementaires français …: depuis le 1er mai 1789 jusqu'au 1er mai 1889*. Vol. 3. Paris: Bourloton, 1889.

Roger, F. *Excerpta, ou Fables choisies de La Fontaine, avec des notes nouvelles; édition prescrite et adoptée par la commission d'instruction publique pour les lycées et les écoles secondaires*. Paris: Delalain, 1805.

Rosanvallon, Pierre. *Le Moment Guizot*. Paris: Gallimard, 1985.

Rosenthal, Léon. *Daumier*. Paris: Librairie central des beaux-arts, 1912.

Roy, Claude. *Daumier [Étude biographique et critique de Claude Roy]*. Genève: Skira, 1971.

Rumelin, Christian and Cabinet d'art graphique. *Félix Vallotton: De la gravure à la peinture [Exposition organisée par Le Cabinet d'arts graphiques des musées d'art et d'histoire Genève du 7 octobre 2010 au 10 janvier 2011]*, exh. cat. Genève: Musées d'art et d'histoire de Genève, 2010.

Sainte-Beuve, Charles-Augustin and Michel (Hermanos de) Lévy. *Nouveaux Lundis*. Paris: Michel Lévy frère, 1864.

Sand, Maurice. *Masques et bouffons (comédie italienne)*. Paris: Michel Lévy frères, 1860.

Schmidt, Nelly. *Abolitionnistes de l'esclavage et réformateurs des colonies (1820–1851)*. Paris: Karthala, 2000.

Schmidt, Rachel. 'The romancing of Don Quixote: Spatial innovation and visual interpretation in the imagery of Johannot, Doré and Daumier'. *Word and Image* 14, no. 4 (1998): 354–70.

Seligman, Janet. *Figures of Fun: The Caricature-Statuettes of Jean-Pierre Dantan*. New York: Oxford University Press, 1957.

Sensier, Alfred. *Souvenirs sur Th. Rousseau*. Paris: Leon Techener, 1872.

Silvestre, Théophile. *Histoire des artistes vivants, français et étrangers, études d'après nature*. Paris: E. Blanchard, 1856.

Spingler, Michael. 'The king's play: Censorship and the politics of performance in Molière's "Tartuffe"'. *Comparative Drama* 19, no. 3 (1985): 240–57.

Starzinger, Victor E. *Middlingness:* Juste Milieu *Political Theory in France and England, 1815–48*. Charlottesville, VA: University Press of Virginia, 1965.

Taine, Hippolyte. *La Fontaine et ses fables*. Paris: Hachette, 1888.

Terdiman, Richard. *Discourse / Counter-Discourse: The Theory and Practice of Symbolic Resistance in Nineteenth-Century France*. Ithaca, NY: Cornell University Press, 1985.

Tiefenbrun, Susan. 'The art and artistry of teaching in the fables of La Fontaine'. *L'Esprit créateur* 21, no. 4 (1981): 50–65.

Tocqueville, Alexis de. *The Recollections of Alexis de Tocqueville*, edited by J. P. Mayer, translated by Alexander Teixeira de Mattos. New York: Meridian Books, 1959.

Touma, Josephine. 'From the playhouse to the page: Visual sources for Watteau's theatrical universe'. *Studies in Eighteenth-Century Culture* 40 (2011): 83–101.

Unger, Gérard. 'Daumier et Gizot: le choc inévitable'. *Cahiers Daumier: bulletin de l'Association des amis d'Honoré Daumier* 2 (spécial 2008): 61–3.

Unverfehrt, Gerd, Westfälisches Landesmuseum für Kunst und Kulturgeschichte Münster, Universität Göttingen, and Gutenberg-Museum Mainz. *La Caricature: Bildsatire in Frankreich 1830–1835 aus der Sammlung von Kritter: [Ausstellung] Westfälisches Landesmuseum für Kunst und Kulturgeschichte Münster 16 März–10 Mai 1980 Kunstsammlung Der Universität Göttingen 26 Oktober–7 Dezember 1980 Gutenberg-Museum Mainz 20 April–7 Juni 1981*, exh. cat. Göttingen: Kunstgeschichtliches Seminar der Universität, 1980.

Vaillant, Alain. 'Les sociétés d'auteurs et la censure au XIXe siècle'. In *La censure en France à l'ère démocratique, 1848*, 103–18. Bruxelles: Éditions Complexe, 1997.

Vignon, Charlotte, Edith Grossman, and Charles-Antoine Coypel. *Coypel's Don Quixote Tapestries: Illustrating a Spanish Novel in Eighteenth-Century France*. New York: The Frick Collection, 2015.

Vincent, Howard P. *Daumier and His World*. Evanston, IL: Northwestern University Press, 1968.

Walckenaer, Charles-Athanase. *La Fontaine en estampes, ou Nouvelle édition des Fables ... précédée de la vie de l'auteur, extrait du nouvel ouvrage de M. Walckenaer*. Paris: Nepveu, 1821.

Walckenaer, Charles-Athanase. *Histoire de la vie et des ouvrages de J. de La Fontaine*. Vol. 2. Paris: Nepveu, 1821.

Walton, Whitney. 'Writing the 1848 revolution: Politics, gender, and feminism in the works of French women of letters'. *French Historical Studies* 18, no. 4 (1994): 1001–24.

Wechsler, Judith. 'Daumier and censorship. 1866–1872'. *Yale French Studies*, no. 122, Out of Sight: Political Censorship of the Visual Arts in Nineteenth Century France (2012): 53–78.

Wechsler, Judith. *A Human Comedy: Physiognomy and Caricature in 19th Century Paris*. Chicago: University of Chicago Press, 1982.

Whitmore, Harry Earl. 'The "cabinet de lecture" in France, 1800–1850'. *The Library Quarterly: Information, Community, Policy* 48, no. 1 (1978): 20–35.

Wilson, Jeffrey R. *Shakespeare and Trump*. Philadelphia, PA: Temple University Press, 2020.

Wyndham Lewis, D. B. *Molière: The Comic Mask*. New York: Coward-McCann, 1959.

Zeldin, Theodore. *France 1848–1945*. Vol. 2. Oxford: Clarendon Press, 1977.

Index

Locators in *italics* refer to illustrations